SOVEREIGN LEGACY

Sovereign Legacy

AN HISTORICAL GUIDE TO THE BRITISH MONARCHY

William Seymour

SIDGWICK & JACKSON

LONDON

TO SARAH

First published in Great Britain in 1979
by
Sidgwick & Jackson Limited

Copyright © William Seymour 1979

ISBN 0 283 98554 2

Printed in Great Britain by
The Garden City Press,
Letchworth, Herts
for Sidgwick and Jackson Limited
1 Tavistock Chambers, Bloomsbury Way
London WC1A 2SG

Contents

List of Illustrations

PREFACE

In these short essays, which span fifteen hundred years of royal history, I have tried to give the reader who is interested in the story of majesty an accurate account of the salient points of each reign, and a brief character sketch of each sovereign.

Those who wish to study in depth the lives of those sovereigns must seek elsewhere than the pages of this book. Almost every ruler whose life is touched upon here has been the subject of numerous erudite works, and for that reason no bibliography has been given, for if justice were to be done and a comprehensive list produced, it would cover far too many pages.

As a people the British are rightly proud of their ancient heritage, and through visiting the many splendid palaces, castles and monuments open to the public a new light can be obtained upon vanished scenes. In recent years a new window has been opened on the past through the display of treasures that have been cherished and handed down from generation to generation by the families of the great houses of Britain, whose present owners welcome many thousands of visitors each year. At the end of every chapter there are brief descriptions and locations of the more important buildings, monuments, documents and objets d'art directly connected with the sovereigns of the dynasty discussed in that particular chapter, and which are readily accessible to the general public. The intention is to arouse the interest of the reader and guide him or her to the site, where, in almost every case, a full account of the place is available.

I am well aware that this has been done very expertly on more than one occasion in the past, but so great has been the interest shown by many people in the preparation of this book that I believe there is scope for a further study of this perennially fascinating subject in a fairly compendious form. It has been necessary to be selective in deciding what

11

to include in the gazetteer to each chapter, for there are so many places to visit and so many objects to be seen connected in some way or other with Britain's sovereigns, that to include everything would be imposs- ible. To the owners of those places or objects with a claim upon the recognition of posterity, and which may have been omitted from these pages, I owe an apology. No attempt has been made to give days and times of opening to the public, for these are apt to change and it is felt that no information is better than incorrect information.

I have been helped by many kind people in the preparation of the book, and it is not possible to mention all of them individually. But to some I owe a special debt of gratitude for their advice, encouragement and in some cases hard work. Foremost among these are William Armstrong, the managing director of my publishers, Sidgwick & Jackson, who master-minded the book in its infancy, and their manag- ing editor, Margaret Willes, who, besides spending long hours in amending and correcting the manuscript, has given me invaluable advice in the compilation of the gazetteer. Mrs Jane Stoddart, the late Mr Ivan Roe and Mr W. J. Emberton have read through various chapters and given me the benefit of their knowledge; Major-General W. D. M. Raeburn, C.B., D.S.O., M.B.E. was of great assistance in matters concerning H.M. Tower of London, I am grateful to the Marquess of Salisbury for allowing me to reproduce an entry from Lord Burghley's diary and also to Mr John Adams for his help over the colleges in Oxford.

I should also like to thank the staff of the London Library, Mrs Hudson (Assistant Archivist, Dorset County Council), Miss Kay Staniland of the Museum of London, Mrs Leslie Webster of the Department of Medieval and Later Antiquities, British Museum, Mr Christopher Munn of Belton House and Miss Barbara Tomlinson of the National Maritime Museum for assistance at various times. But the person to whom I am most indebted is my hard-working secretary, Miss Patricia Carter. She has not only typed and retyped the manuscript several times and put up with much grumbling and grousing, but her admirable personal library has saved me many journeys to London and elsewhere.

1
THE ANGLO-SAXON DYNASTY

Birth of a Nation

The Anglo-Saxon dynasty was the cradle of the British nation. The centuries that followed the withdrawal of the *Pax Romana* were in Britain, as elsewhere in Europe, mostly ones of turmoil and distress, known to history as the Dark Ages, in which war, murder, rapine and royal strife left their curse and vendetta behind. And yet these years, from the arrival of Hengist and Horsa in AD449 to the death of Alfred in 899, were the most formative in the emergence of the English race from youth to manhood.

As the great Roman Empire began to crumble, savage tribes from all over Europe moved in for the kill. In the British Isles the Picts from beyond the northern wall penetrated as far as Kent, and although driven back by the last of the legions, still standing guard amid the desolation of burnt-out villas, empty farmsteads and vanishing land-owners, other raiders from across the North Sea came to harass and burn the coasts directly the Roman soldiers had gone. Colonization followed closely on the heels of conquest.

Resistance to the invaders by the native Celts and Britons was spasmodic and of variable quality; but we know it existed, even if the details are vague. Legendary heroes, such as the Romano-British chiefs Ambrosius Aurelianus and Arturius*, certainly fought bravely and at times successfully, but others less valiant sought different measures. It seems quite possible that Hengist and Horsa were leaders of a mercenary band brought into Kent to assist the British chieftain Vortigern; but once there they soon discovered the weakness of their paymaster. If the manner of their arrival and the opposition they met with can no longer be certainly told, by the end of the sixth century – as much a century of

---

* These may have been one and the same person. Certainly Arthur, although never a king, is a historical figure.

13

storm and change as any in British history – these Teutonic tribes had most of the country in their grip.

Who were these men, so soon to give their name to the land, and from where did they come? They were a hard, cruel people, excellent seamen and fighters, who proved themselves to be good farmers. There were Jutes, who may have come from Denmark and given their name to Jutland,* Saxons from Frisia and north Germany, and the Angles who occupied the land called Angle between the Saxons and the Jutes. As they consolidated their position along the eastern coast and began to penetrate inland, so the three peoples gradually merged and even in some parts of the country married British women; thus a hybrid race soon developed. In the early days there were no kings or royal princes, but chieftains with long, blood-stained pedigrees tracing their descent back to such fierce gods as Woden, Thor and Tiu. They were pagans who had driven a Christian people before them into the fastnesses of Devon and Cornwall, the Welsh mountains and the wild lands of Cumbria and Strathclyde; they lived in dirty, squalid conditions with fear as their constant companion – fear of an enemy, of disease, of hunger and of superstition.

At first it seems that the physical barriers of the country kept the tribes somewhat apart, giving each a degree of independence; but gradually the numerous smaller family dynasties fell victim to a stronger hand, and amalgamation was achieved by consent or coercion. Before the end of the sixth century the more powerful chieftains had assumed the title of king, and there emerged what became known as the Heptarchy – separate kingdoms of Northumbria, Mercia, East Anglia, Essex, Kent, Sussex and Wessex. Northumbria, until the middle of the seventh century, was frequently split into the two kingdoms of Bernicia in the north up to the Forth, and Deira in what is now east Yorkshire.

Kings they were with kingdoms to rule, but they were still little better than rough warrior chiefs; not for them a palace, only a mud and wattle hut of slightly superior construction to those of their thanes – or war lords – which were grouped around the royal residence in a palisaded fortress. They were for ever quarrelling with their neighbours in an attempt to enrich themselves and enlarge their territories, and before long it became customary for one or other to obtain a position of ascendancy over his royal colleagues and hold what was called by Bede the *imperium*, but more usually known as Bretwalda. Thus one gets a loose confederation of kingdoms, but the extent to which the Bretwalda could control his sub-kings varied considerably and was always limited;

---

* It is possible that all these races came from the same part of north-west Europe – the country which lies between the lower Rhine and lower Elbe.

indeed, over distant Northumbria supremacy could have been little more than nominal.

One of the earliest of these kings to hold the Bretwalda was Ceawlin, the grandson of Cerdic the founder of the house of Wessex, who used his supremacy to enrol allies to overcome British resistance; in 577 he won a decisive battle against the Britons at Dyrham just north of Bath. Towards the end of the sixth century Ceawlin lost his overlordship to Ethelbert of Kent, and he in turn was succeeded by Redwald of East Anglia, who in 617 had defeated Ethelfrith the Northumbrian and conqueror of the northern Celts. And so on throughout the centuries this coveted but somewhat nebulous title passed from one king to another, by conquest or consensus, until the unity of all England was achieved. But long before that happened Christianity, whose flickering flame had been kept alight in the remote areas of the north and west by the greatness of St Columba and his monks, was relumed in the south of England.

The Britons had resolutely set their face against attempting to convert the savage, barbaric hordes that had swept them into the remote corners of their land, but Pope Gregory accepted the challenge with vigour, sympathy and understanding. In 597 a mission, headed by St Augustine, arrived in Kent and the first difficult and dangerous step that was to change the destinies of thousands had been taken. Kent was well chosen, for its king, Ethelbert, had married a Christian princess called Bertha, the daughter of Charibert, King of Paris, and although not a Christian himself he had restored the Roman church of St Martin for Bertha's use. Moreover, he held the Bretwalda at this time, and although his overlordship carried no powers of conversion by precept or example, he would have been a man whom the sub-kings looked up to.

For seven years, until their deaths in 604, Augustine, greatly encouraged and assisted by Gregory in Rome, made considerable progress. Ethelbert soon became a convert to the new faith, and although he lost the Bretwalda to King Redwald of East Anglia the latter accepted Christianity, albeit cautiously – he kept a foot in both camps by having two separate altars in his church, one dedicated to the worship of Christ, the other to a less merciful deity. But if the barbarians were beginning to see the light, the British prelates steadfastly refused to surrender their independence. A conference, organized by St Augustine and Ethelbert in the Severn valley to steer the British towards Rome, broke up in failure through the intransigence of the Christian Britons and the arrogance of St Augustine.

In the north the throne of all Northumbria had been restored, with the assistance of King Redwald, to the exiled Edwin, a man of authority whose reign of sixteen years was for the most part peaceful; and in 625 another great missionary, Paulinus, arrived at his court with a Christian princess from Kent as the King's bride. Thus the Christian faith came to the north, and for a time flourished mightily. But in 633 the peace and tranquillity so long enjoyed in these parts was shattered. Edwin was killed in battle near Doncaster and his victor, the British King Cadwallon, who had formed an unholy alliance with Penda, the savage and heathen King of Mercia, ruled the Northumbrians 'not like a victorious king, but ravaging them like a furious tyrant'. Paulinus and Edwin's queen wisely retired to Kent.

These were times of rapidly changing fortunes, and after only a year of agony some semblance of order returned to Northumbria when Oswald of Bernicia avenged Edwin and slew Cadwallon at the battle of Heavenfield near the Roman Wall. It was the last battle fought between Britons and Saxons and decisively established the latter. Oswald had spent years of exile in Iona and acquired a knowledge of the Celtic creed, and so, on coming to the throne, he looked to that quarter for help. Chief among those who responded was Aidan to whom he gave the island of Lindisfarne, from where a little later there originated the beautiful Lindisfarne Gospels. Thus we have two streams of the same faith flowing through the Northumbrian kingdom.

In Mercia Penda, still triumphant, covetous of gain and standing uncompromisingly for the worship of Thor and Woden, was not prepared to leave Oswald undisturbed as the standard-bearer of a proselytizing creed. In 642 at the battle of Maserfield he defeated the northern King, whom he slew, decapitated and dismembered. For thirteen years darkness covered much of the midlands, but in 655 Oswy. the younger brother of King Oswald, settled the account at Winwaed in Yorkshire, in which battle Penda, to the regrets of few, was killed. Now all-powerful on both sides of the Humber, Oswy 'converted the Mercians to the grace of the Christian faith'. Thus throughout the island, excepting a few individuals whose private worship was ignored, the grim war-gods from a distant past had been superseded by the God of justice, peace and love.

There remained, however, a damaging difference between the Roman and Celtic persuasions; those in the north and midlands strongly favouring the monastic orders that had established their Church, those in the south and west adhering to the more liberal communion of Rome. The conflict was almost as great as between Christian and heathen; both kinds of Christianity could not exist side by side. An attempt, which was mainly successful, to resolve these grievous differences was made at the Synod of Whitby in 664. It was a cross-roads in the history of the British race; here after long and serious discussion the supporters of Rome, led by Wilfrid, then Abbot of Ripon, gained most of what they sought, the Celtic leader, Colman, withdrawing in high dudgeon to Iona. Henceforth Northumbria would form a part of the Church of Rome, Mercia soon conformed, and almost the whole country was united in one faith.

There followed nearly two centuries of contention and rivalry, with supremacy going first to one king and then another. It is not necessary to tread the labyrinth of these dynastic and military intrigues and antagonisms. But two men in their very different ways stand out above the crowd. In Northumbria, during the twilight of her supremacy, there lived in the great monastery of Jarrow – founded and wonderfully equipped with learned works by Benedict Biscop – the Venerably Bede (673–735). He had come there at the age of seven, and he lived there all his life learning and teaching. His literary output was staggering; he wrote history, theology, poetry and natural science and his *Ecclesiastical History* is a work of rare distinction which tells the story of the conversion with lucidity, learning and accuracy. Most of his thirty-six works still survive. He was a craftsman for England, for posterity and for his faith.

The other outstanding man of these turbulent years was Offa, King of the Mercians from 757 to 796, and in his own words *rex Anglorum*. If this was a pardonable hyperbole – for he had no authority north of the Humber and not always in Wessex – he certainly through war, diplomacy and marriage obtained the regal primacy of most of England, and his self-styled title set a target for others to aim at and eventually achieve. We know all too little about this King, but it is clear from the heavy hand he laid upon the under kings that he was a masterful man, and from the fact that he was the Emperor Charlemagne's 'dearest brother', with whom he exchanged marriage contracts, that England under him was a power to be reckoned with. His excursion into foreign affairs – and he was the first English king with sufficient authority to warrant this – extended to Rome, where his relations with the Pope were at first uncertain but eventually cordial.

The scholar Alcuin had high words of praise for Offa: 'You are a glory to Britain and a sword against its enemies.' But he is best remembered for the monumental earthwork that he erected as a barrier between Saxon England and the still largely untamed Britons. This great obstacle known as Offa's Dyke, ran continuously, except where forests made it unnecessary, from the Dee to the Wye. It was an engineering work of exceptional skill, and its construction in the reign of one man is a marvel of the times. For much of its course it followed a boundary largely recognized, and there is evidence that in places its construction was to British advantage, which seems to suggest that the dyke was built as a permanent boundary rather than a military fortification.

On Offa's death his empire fell to pieces, and the same fate at the

same time befell the northern kingdom of Northumbria. There was at
present no stability within the various kingdoms, even Christianity was
still only skin deep; remove the strong arm and the society it controlled
was apt to disintegrate. A few years before Offa's death the first tremors
of a catastrophe that was to tear asunder the whole island had been felt
along its southern shores. The Norsemen in their long-ships were about
to make their contribution to the cold-blooded ferocity of those times.

These colourful, flamboyant men, more savage and daring than any
that had invaded the island in the past, had not been driven from their
homeland by external pressure as had the Anglo-Saxons, but because
the land they cultivated could no longer support a growing population
and, more particularly, because they were excellent seamen and
accomplished sea-robbers. The Vikings – so called from the viks and
cracks of the Scandinavian fiords that they loved to inhabit and from
where they launched their raids – were to erupt across the continent of
Europe, across the northern seas and into the Mediterranean, looting
and pillaging right up to the gates of Constantinople. But their early
raids on England were hit-and-run affairs. Later they were to spread
across the country in iconoclastic fury.

Buccaneering became a profitable business and the rich monastic
houses were a prime target. In 793 the settlement of Lindisfarne was
raided and left in ruins, its great treasures pillaged or destroyed. The
same fate awaited Iona in 802, but in the year after Lindisfarne, when
making a similar attempt on Jarrow, the pirates received a bloody nose
and were not seen off the English coast again for forty years. Not until
835 did fleets of two and three hundred vessels crowd the rivers and
waterways of the island, and a further thirty years were to elapse before
the Great Army, as it was called, over-wintered in England and began to
put down its roots.

How did the English kings stand up to the very treatment that their
forebears had meted out to the Britons? Once the dyke had broken and
the bitter waters of destruction had overflowed much of the land, was
there a man strong enough to cry halt? The kingdom of Wessex found
the men, ready and able to defy the Danes and in so doing established
the supremacy of their house over all England. Egbert was elected King
of Wessex in 802, when the Mercians held the Bretwalda, but in 825 at a
battle near Malmesbury he defeated a Mercian invasion, and followed
this up by sending his son, Ethelwulf, into Kent, where first the men of
Kent and then the East Saxons in Essex submitted to Egbert's overlordship; by 829 he had gained the paramountcy of all the English kingdoms
including that of Northumbria. Five years later the Vikings were upon
him, but he held them at Charmouth, and in 838, by now an old man, he
smote them with great slaughter at Hingston Down close to Plymouth.

Egbert died in 839 and his son, who had been sub-king in Kent, succeeded him. Ethelwulf was not cast in the same mould as his father or that of his great son, but he maintained the supremacy of Wessex and had his successes against the Danes, notably at a battle near Basingstoke in 851, where he 'inflicted the greatest slaughter upon the heathen host that ever we have heard tell of up to the present day'. He died in 858 and his four surviving sons then occupied his throne in fairly rapid succession. During these years – 858 to 871 – the Danes established themselves with every sign of permanency in the north and east of the country; Wessex still held riches and prizes that they were determined to plunder.

In the next two years, and in the course of eight battles, the Danes hammered at Wessex, the most important of the engagements being fought at Ashdown. Most probably the site was the high ground of the eastern Berkshire downs some fifteen miles north-west of Reading. The opposing armies formed up in two columns on the morning of 8 January 871, with the Danes holding a hillside position; King Ethelred (Ethelwulf's third son and Alfred's brother) retired to his tent to hear mass just before the Danes began to make their move, but Alfred, wisely deciding that prayer alone would not defeat the pagans, gave orders to attack. There was little finesse about fighting in those days, it was a noisy affair of battle cries, sword, spear and axe play; Alfred, we are told, led his men up the hill 'like a wild boar', and in due course being joined by their king and his household troops, the Saxon army utterly routed the Danes and pursued them with much slaughter to the safety of their Reading defences. It was not a decisive victory, for the Danish army took the field again after a fortnight; but had it been lost total darkness would have spread across the land. Hitherto the Danes seemed invincible; Ashdown was a victory for confidence and Christianity.

King Ethelred died in 871 – possibly from wounds incurred in the last battle of this campaign – and was buried at Wimborne. The Witan had no hesitation in electing Alfred as his successor in preference to Ethelred's infant son, for these were harsh times and the need was dire. If it was the obvious choice it was certainly a wise one, for Alfred belonged to the small and select band of truly great English kings.

His immediate task was to clear his kingdom of Danes. He saw the need for time and had the courage and wisdom to buy the enemy off and reorganize his troops – for Alfred was the first English King who really understood how to make the best use of limited resources. Like all successful commanders he had his share of luck, and occasionally his usually sure-footed judgement would go astray and the enemy would steal a march on him. In 878, when disaster struck his army, Alfred was forced with a few followers to take refuge on the island swamp of Athelney; here he remained for a few months, not in despair, still less in fear, but because it was close to his allies of the west and a good hideout from which to operate guerrilla raids.

From here, at Easter time, he emerged to lead the assembled *fyrd* to their greatest victory at Ethandun – modern Eddington. As with most of the Saxon kings' battles the precise site is not known, but probably Alfred found the Danes entrenched on the Imber ridge three miles north-east of Warminster. All Bishop Asser (who wrote at some length about Ashdown) tells us of this battle is that, 'The next morning he [Alfred] removed to Ethandun, and there fought long and fiercely in close order against all the armies of the pagans, whom with divine help he defeated with great slaughter, and pursued them flying to their fortification' – which was at Chippenham. This victory gained Alfred fourteen years of comparative peace.

His third and last campaign began in 892, when the Great Army, fresh from ravishing France and supported by Danes living in that part of eastern and north-eastern England by now known as the Danelaw, sailed up the Thames and spread south and west in a vast three-pronged attack. Alfred, who had never been entirely fit, was now too infirm to play the leading role, but in Edward, his son, and Ethelred of Mercia, his son-in-law, he had two young lieutenants of great merit. In four years of bitter fighting the Danes made little headway, and eventually every thrust was beaten back, until in 896 they cried enough. The Great Army broke up; some went to France, while others exchanged the sword for the plough in the Danelaw.

Alfred is sometimes only remembered as a slayer of Danes, a burner of cakes and a player of the harp. His greatest work, however, was in the fields of education and administration. He had a passion for learning, and a determination that his people should have educational opportunities. He had, also, an inventive turn of mind, producing a candle clock and a reading light. Besides compiling his *Book of Laws,* Alfred spent very many hours translating into the vernacular learned books on Christianity and the sciences; well ahead of his time, he never claimed scholarship for himself, but in his humble way he laboured to bring the fruits of others within reach of all.

In military matters he reorganized the *fyrd.* In future there were to be two classes of call-up, and at any one time fifty per cent of those eligible for service would be at home tending their land. A further contribution to the defence of the country was Alfred's system of *burhs,* by which a chain of strong earthworks was constructed round every place of importance. These fortresses, which varied widely in design, were manned and maintained by men from the surrounding countryside. Thirty-one such strategic posts are mentioned in the *Burghal Hidage,* and they brought order and design to the defence of Wessex. Not content with strengthening the land defences of his country Alfred, who was a man of wide horizons, saw the value of sea power to an island race. He ordered long-ships to be built of superior dimensions to those of the Danes, and, although it was not until his son's reign that his fleet became truly effective, Alfred was probably the founder of the British navy.*

Alfred died in 899, a gentle, peace-loving man born into a fiery, lawless age. He nevertheless faced up to his task with courage and determination; no toil was too hard, no dangers too great. Christianity, which he saved for England, was his beacon; it inspired him every day of his life and through it he showed friend and foe alike that its great principles of love and forgiveness could triumph over brute force.

The ruthless destruction of everything Christian by the Vikings has not left much to see from England's Saxon heritage. Although during this period there were no palaces as we came to know them, and military fortifications were constructed of materials that for the most part have left little trace, the churches that have survived from the seventh and eighth centuries show that the Saxons could build for posterity. Similarly the items of gold, silver and jewellery that have been found present a very high standard of craftsmanship for a comparatively primitive people.

Brixworth, Northants.
All Saints Church is the largest and finest surviving Saxon church in the country, probably dating from 675, and is one of the few churches to survive Danish vandalism. It is not possible to associate the church with a Mercian king with any degree of certainty, but King Ethelbald may have built it in honour of St Boniface. Brixworth is six miles north of Northampton.

Cambridge, Corpus Christi College
The Anglo-Saxon Chronicle is a series of historical records written in Saxon-English and giving an outline history from Julius Caesar's invasion of Britain. Originally compiled on instructions from King Alfred, it is the work of many authors and was continued up to the year 1140. The authors and editors were probably able to incorporate Latin material of a much earlier date than Alfred, nevertheless large parts of their early and some of their later history is inaccurate. The oldest extant copy, known as the Parker Ms and designated by

---

* This is not to say that his immediate predecessors had no ships. Certainly Egbert and Ethelwulf possessed some, and Alfred's eldest brother, Athelstan, successfully engaged some Viking ships off Sandwich in 851.

the letter A, is in Corpus Christi College, Cambridge, and dates from the tenth century. Another copy is in the Department of Manuscripts at the British Library.

Canterbury, Kent

St Martin's Church. Queen Bertha came from a Christian family, and when she married King Ethelbert of Kent, he built a church for her, in which – in 597 – he was himself baptized by St Augustine. St Martin's, which stands a little to the east of St Augustine's Abbey at Canterbury, and is the oldest parish church in the country, quite possibly incorporates a part of Queen Bertha's church, and is most impressive in its simplicity and antiquity.

London, The British Museum

Sutton Hoo ship-burial. This superb collection of funeral ornaments was excavated from a ship burial at Sutton Hoo in Suffolk in 1939. They probably adorned the grave of the East Anglian King Redwald (593–625?). They are of great interest in showing the high standard of craftsmanship available at that time to a Saxon court. Ship burial was a Swedish, not a Saxon, custom, and some of the relics that were found – the helmet for example – are of Swedish design. This strengthens the belief that the East Anglian royal house – the Wuffingas – were of Swedish origin. Among the many treasures the sceptre, helmet and silver bowls are outstanding.

The Lindisfarne Gospels were written in about AD 690 for Eadrith, who had succeeded St Cuthbert as Bishop of Lindisfarne. Eadrith's successor, Etholwold, had the gospels encased in a binding of gold, set with precious stones. They show that a very high standard of calligraphy and illumination had been reached as early as the eighth century. The book is on display in one of the rooms of the Department of Manuscripts at the British Library.

The Burghal Hidage was compiled at the end of Alfred's reign, or perhaps a little later, and records the thirty-one forts, known as *burhs*, with which Alfred encircled Wessex – Kent is omitted, the list starting in the east with Sussex. In the British Library can be seen two manuscripts (the earliest written *c.* 1025) which are early copies of the Burghal Hidage.

Queen Ethelswith's rings. Ethelswith was Alfred's sister and she was married to Burhred, King of Mercia from 852 to 874. Two of her rings, again of high craftsmanship, can be seen in the Medieval and Later Antiquities Department of the British Museum.

Offa's Dyke. Offa was King of Mercia from 757 to 796. He was the most powerful Saxon King of his time, and the great dyke that he constructed from the estuary of the Dee near Prestatyn to the estuary of the Severn near Chepstow (about one hundred and twenty miles) was intended almost certainly as a boundary to mark the western extremity of his realm with the Celts in Wales. As a means of defence it would have been difficult to hold throughout its great length. Parts of the dyke are clearly visible through the counties of Wales down to Chepstow, although the northern sections have mostly disappeared.

Oxford, Ashmolean Museum

The Alfred Jewel dates from the ninth century, and is yet another example of the high standard of Saxon craftsmanship. Furthermore, it tells us that Alfred and his court were not entirely absorbed in waging war against the Danes, but had the time and inclination to enjoy the creative arts. The jewel is pear-shaped and just under $2\frac{1}{2}$ inches long and $1\frac{1}{4}$ inches at its greatest width; the design is in cloisonné enamel on a gold plate, and the frame terminates in the head of an animal made of sheet gold; the hollow of the mouth is crossed by a gold pin. It would seem, therefore, that it was originally attached to a wood or ivory stem, and may have been a form of sceptre or part of a staff. The band of gold filigree is inscribed AELFRED MEC HEHT GEWYRCAN – 'Alfred ordered me to be made'.

St Cleer, Cornwall

King Doniert's Stone is a cross-shaft of granite which, although bearing Saxon ornamentations, is itself in the Celtic tradition of memorial stones, and may commemorate the drowning of Durgarth, the Celtic King of Cornwall, in the River Fowey somewhere around 870. It is an interesting reminder of the virtual independence of Cornwall, which lasted into the eleventh century, despite the strenuous efforts of Kings Egbert and Athelstan.

Wareham, Dorset

Alfred's 'burh'. One of the fortifications, created by King Alfred to protect the kingdom of Wessex from Danish invasions, can be clearly seen and explored by visitors to this attractive Dorset town.

Whitby Abbey (North Yorks).

The most famous event that took place at Whitby was the synod summoned by King Oswy of Northumbria in 664 to decide the differences that existed between the Roman and Celtic Churches. Oswy had founded the first Abbey of Whitby in 657 with St Hilda as the first Abbess and in this Abbey King Oswy and his Queen were buried, as were King Edwin and St Hilda herself. It is impossible to tell who lies buried in the graves still to be seen, for the Danes destroyed the Abbey in 867, and it is thought that King Edmund I removed St Hilda's bones from here to Glastonbury. Recent excavations, however, have revealed traces of seventh and eighth century origins, including the foundations of cells, in which Saxon inmates lived. The magnificent ruins still to be seen standing above the bay date from the first half of the thirteenth century, but there is nothing left of the extensive monastic buildings.

Winchester Cathedral (Hants.). This magnificent church, which succeeded the Saxon Minster, was begun in 1079 and has fine early Norman work in the transepts. It contains the bones of Saxon kings (starting with King Cynegils 611–43, the first Christian King of Wessex) in the six mortuary chests in the presbytery.

2

THE ANGLO-SAXON DYNASTY

United Kingdom

Alfred's son, known as Edward the Elder, had already distinguished himself under his father, and there was little doubt that the Witan would elect him to be king. The succession, however, was disputed in a very feeble way by that son of Ethelred who as an infant had been passed over in favour of his uncle, Alfred. When he failed to make any headway towards the throne in Wessex, this man, now in middle age and called Ethelwald, took himself north to the Danes in Northumbria, who promptly made him their king. There followed two years of bitter internecine strife between Edward and the kingdoms of Northumbria and East Anglia, until in a most destructive battle, called the Holme, both Ethelwald and Eric, King of East Anglia, were slain.

No king in England at this time could expect to reign in peace for very long, and much of Edward's twenty-four years on the Wessex throne were spent in fighting. His most notable victory occurred in 910 at Tettenhall in Staffordshire, when three Danish kings and four earls were slain and their northern army was most savagely mauled. In his exacting work of pacification and unification, Edward was greatly assisted by his courageous and energetic sister, Ethelflaed. On the death of her husband, the Ealdorman of Mercia, Ethelflaed took full charge of the province and assumed the title of Lady of the Mercians. Brother and sister marched and counter-marched across half England, taking and fortifying towns, defeating armies, making covenants and accepting homage, and when the Lady of the Mercians, perhaps worn out by martial exertions, died in 917, Edward, who had already taken London and Oxford into his own hands on the death of his brother-in-law, got himself acknowledged as ruler of Mercia.

When Edward died in 924 his authority south of the Humber was supreme, and if his overlordship of Northumbria and recognition by King Constantine in Scotland was more nominal than actual, it was a suzerainty with a better foundation than any previous southern king had yet achieved. He had prepared the way for the complete subjugation of the Danelaw, and his son – the third distinguished member of a most talented family – was to proceed further with this ever broadening tale of glory.

Athelstan, when a boy of about four, had been presented with the mantle and insignia of a Saxon warrior by his grandfather, Alfred; and later he was sent to learn the duties of an atheling at his aunt's court in Mercia. At the time the Lady of the Mercians was blazing across England, like a shooting star across the firmament, Athelstan would have been a youth of about eighteen. He grew up as a Mercian and this would have been a considerable advantage to him later on.

Athelstan saw quite clearly where his duty lay; it was to complete his father's work and make England one kingdom under the house of Egbert. He practised diplomacy with some skill, and only resorted to the sword when it was necessary to bring to heel the more recalcitrant Danish leaders in Northumbria and the ever aggressive King Constantine in Scotland. By 937, when Athelstan was called upon to face the most serious crisis of his reign, he was the acknowledged overlord of the northern kings and Welsh princes, and the Britons in Cornwall had accepted the Tamar as their boundary.

But the northern warriors did not lie easily under the English yoke. They maundered sullenly amid their austere hills and misty marshes, and came to the belated realization that only through strength could they hope to triumph. Olaf from Dublin and Constantine had scores to settle with Athelstan, and they rallied to their banners a large number of discontented Celts and Danes from north Britain, and were joined by Viking pirates ever eager for the spoils of war. A huge armada of some six hundred ships sailed up the Ouse, and, disembarking near Tadcaster, the polyglot army struck south. Athelstan and his brother, Edmund, met them at a place called Brunanburh, which was probably close to Rotherham, and the battle that followed, and which lasted for most of the day, must have been one of the fiercest fought on English soil. Eventually the northerners bent and then broke before the storm of sword and spear, and Athelstan had set the seal on his father's and grandfather's work. It was above all a great victory for the southern kingdoms; henceforth theirs would be the controlling power in England.

Athelstan survived Brunanburh by a little over two years. He now styled himself *Rex totius Britanniae*, a title recognized in England and in much of Europe, where he was the brother-in-law of three of the most influential princes. These family connections and his position in England gave Athelstan a greater degree of influence in Continental affairs than any English king had enjoyed since Offa, or would enjoy again until Canute. He died in October 939 and was succeeded by his half-brother Edmund.

Edmund's reign of rather less than six years followed much the same pattern as his immediate predecessor's. Danish troubles in the north claimed his attention for most of two years, and by striking hard and swiftly he lost none of the ground that his brother had gained. A promising reign was brought to a tragic and unnecessary end when Edmund was fatally stabbed while going to the assistance of one of his thanes who had been attacked at a banquet. It was 946, and the King was only twenty-four.

His eldest son was just seven, and the Witan, as was their custom, passed him over in favour of Edmund's youngest brother, Edred, who was himself only twenty-two and said to have been something of an invalid. If this were so, a courageous and resolute spirit dwelt within a weak body, for during the eleven years that he reigned he quenched the Danish fires that had so often and so cruelly set all Northumbria alight. The great task to which Edward, Athelstan and Edmund had set their hand had now been almost completed. Edred left his successor a large, prosperous, but peaceful Danish settlement covering half England and enjoying its own customs, but owing allegiance to an English king. His nephew Edgar was to build upon the fruits of his work.

Edgar became King of Wessex in 959 (although in 957 he had been elected King of Mercia and Northumbria in preference to his elder brother, Edwig). Edwig had been only fifteen when he came to the throne, and during a short reign of three years – largely dominated by two ambitious women – he fell foul of the clergy, banished the great Dunstan from the realm, and had he not died in time might well have wrecked the work of three generations. Edgar was seventeen when he succeeded his brother in Wessex, but he was a lad of much stronger metal. He dealt firmly and wisely with brief outbreaks of revolt in the northern Danish areas, Wales and Thanet; but for the most part his reign was one of unprecedented peace in which opportunity was taken for considerable reconstruction of both secular and ecclesiastical institutions.

Edgar was a gifted King possessed of patience, energy and unfailing sagacity, who by 973 had succeeded in uniting his English and Danish subjects into one peaceful nation. He had reigned for fourteen years without being crowned; we do not know why, but perhaps he wished to wait until he had accomplished the task of pacification and unification. Whatever the reason, in 973 at Bath, Dunstan, whose exile had lasted only two years and who was now Archbishop of Canterbury, crowned Edgar in a new and most impressive service that was largely of the

Archbishop's devising. The Coronation Oath predates Edgar by some two hundred years. But the mystic ritual now used to crown English kings and queens in the service of coronation and anointing, with its beautiful anthem 'Zadok the Priest' (a nexus between the old and new faiths), the investiture with sword and sceptre, and the acclamations of the peers, is in a tradition that originated a thousand years ago when Archbishop Dunstan placed the crown on Edgar's head. Two years later he buried this good King at Glastonbury Abbey.

The expectation of life under the hard conditions of Saxon England cannot have been long, but the house of Egbert that had now ruled Wessex for 175 years had a particularly bad record in this respect. Kings frequently died very young, leaving minors as their heirs. This was all right if they had brothers, for the Witan would prefer an uncle to a boy, but occasionally – as in the case of Edred in 946 – there was no other choice. Edgar died at the age of thirty-two in 975 and not only was the country left with another minority, but he had left two boys by different wives, the elder of whom had to contend with a scheming and most unpleasant stepmother.

This lady, Elfthryth by name, had powerful connections and had it not been for Archbishop Dunstan and the clergy, who came down firmly in favour of Edward, the rightful heir, her son, Ethelred, might have got the throne. Queen Elfthryth was deeply annoyed; she retired to Corfe Castle, where she bided her time in sullen obscurity.

The three years of Edward's reign were free from war, although there was a serious confrontation within the Church between Dunstan's monastic party and the cathedral clergy of Mercia, but Edward was not seriously involved in this. Apart from some signs of having a tyrannical disposition, there was no reason to believe that he would not have made a good king – he could scarcely have made a worse one than his half-brother.

On the afternoon of 18 March 978, after a day's hunting, the King rode up the hill to Corfe Castle, the majestic ruins of which still stand like some old warrior proud and silent amid the timeless antiquity of the Purbeck hills, to call upon his brother and stepmother. At the great gateway he was met by the Queen Mother's thanes, and as he drank the wine offered to him in the saddle they suddenly stabbed him; his horse carried him some yards before he fell dead, and his murderers then pitched his body into a mean hovel for the night. Edward's youth and the circumstances of his death, 'was never a worse deed done among Anglekin', won for him a martyr's crown.

The egregious Elfthryth at once offered her eleven-year-old son for election and the Witan had little choice but to comply. Brought to the throne through the malice of a triumphant faction, Ethelred the

Redeless* was to rule for thirty-eight of some of the most bitter and shameful years of English history. That the fruits of the long struggle for unity should be wantonly cast away by this cruel, dishonest and perfidious King, whose talent for choosing wrong counsellors and capacity for misgovernment were unequalled in the annals of his dynasty, enraged the whole nation and greatly encouraged its enemies. In recent years England had become a rich land and accumulated great treasures; with her defences down she was once more a land fit and ready to be plundered.

History was about to repeat itself. The Vikings in Europe were becoming restless and they looked greedily towards a weakened England. As on the occasion of their first appearance, almost two hundred years before, they were at first content to probe and plunder before landing in strength. Once more the southern coast was ravished and the people of Cornwall, Devon, Hampshire and Kent felt the heavy hand of the Norsemen. One glimmer of brightness illuminates the darkness of these days. At Maldon in 991 the Ealdorman of Essex, Byrhtnoth, faced a Danish army encamped on the isle of Northey in the Blackwater estuary. Not for this nobleman a tame surrender to Danegeld, but a defiant challenge hurled across the narrow strip of water to the Danish heralds. 'Not so lightly shall ye come by the treasure: point and edge shall first make atonement, grim war-play, before we pay tribute.' It was boldly done, but to no avail; the Danes had the better of 'point and edge', and slew the brave Byrhtnoth.

As fresh hordes of Danes swept into the country in the last decade of the century, all Ethelred would do was to bleed his treasury of thousands of pounds of silver; the enemy took the money and as was their wont soon returned for more. Then in 1002 this foolish, despicable King issued a decree that was both a crime and a colossal blunder. Persuaded, almost certainly without foundation, that numerous Danes living quite peaceably in the Danelaw, and some even in his service, were plotting his destruction, Ethelred sent out secret orders that on St Brice's Day (11 November) all these people, both male and female, should be slaughtered. One of the victims of this massacre was Gunhild, a sister of Sweyn Forkbeard, the ruling King of Denmark and for the last eight years the principal scourge of England. His revenge was as terrible as it was predictable. In two separate invasions, in 1004 and 1006, he tore the entrails out of the country and pillaged its treasury.

Ethelred muddled on, misruling in the south and marauding in the north. The catalogue of miseries that befell the country is too long for repetition; some idea of the shame and degredation experienced by the

* Meaning ill-counselled; although the more realistic interpretation of Unready has made this King the butt of history.

ealdormen and thanes can be found in the contemporary pages of the
Anglo-Saxon Chronicle. After 1006 Sweyn, although ably represented
by blood-thirsty jarls such as Thorkil the Tall, did not himself raid
England again until 1013, when he returned not only to plunder but to
possess. He thought in terms of a Scandinavian Empire, and with him
this time he brought his young son, Canute. Once more a Danish army
tramped south from the midlands with a flail of steel, but now towns and
shires were more ready to submit; London resisted for a while and
Wessex too, but by the end of the year, with Ethelred having fled to
Normandy, the whole country did homage to Sweyn.

But the Norseman, now advanced in years, had not long to live;
within a month of Ethelred's flight he was dead. His soldiers proclaimed
his son king, but the Witan turned again to the rightful ruler, 'For they
said that no lord dearer than their born lord could be, if he would hold
them rightlier than he ere did.' Fortunately 'their born lord' had less
than two years in which to abuse his countrymen's newly placed trust,
for he died on 23 April 1016. Ethelred the Redeless had found the
country united and prosperous; he left it divided and impoverished.

Like his father before him, Ethelred sowed seeds of trouble through
having two families by two wives. In his eldest son, Edmund, soon to be
known as Ironside, England had a warrior prince with a dauntless heart,
from whom great things could have been expected had destiny not
decided otherwise. Married, against his father's wishes, to the widow of
a Danish earl, he had sizeable possessions in the Danelaw, where he was
extremely popular and from where he recruited a considerable army of
men who had suffered from the ferocious incursions of his father.

Canute had left the country on Ethelred's return from Normandy,
but not for long, and in 1015 he was back at the head of an army to claim
the throne. Edmund's valiant efforts on behalf of his father were met by
the latter's hostility, and both now and later he had to contend with the
base treachery of his brother-in-law Eadric Streona, who turned his coat
at least three times. Nevertheless, when Ethelred at last died much of the
country, including Mercia and London, acknowledged Edmund as
king, but unfortunately a more powerful faction in the south had turned
to Canute. Thus the country was once more sorely divided.

Edmund, faced with grave difficulties that only swift action could
overcome, marched into Wessex, where many of the thanes returned to
their allegiance, and with their help he won two much needed victories
against the invader at Penselwood near Shaftesbury and Sherston in
Wiltshire. These were followed by two others near London and a fifth at
Otford in Kent. Canute tholed his mauling as best he could and took
ship round the Kent coast to Essex, where, before Edmund – who
pursued by land – had caught up with him, he carried out plundering

raids into Mercia. But Edmund now had the larger army and he brought Canute to bay before he could get his army and his plunder back to his ships.

There followed the great battle of Ashingdon. Edmund, on the tide of victory and justifiably full of confidence, attacked the Danes on their hillside in a pattern strikingly similar to that adopted by his forebear, Alfred, at Ashdown. Victory would most probably have gone to the Saxons had not Eadric Streona first allowed the Danes to get between his contingent and Edmund's, and then left the field without striking a blow. In the words of the Chronicle, 'Ealdorman Eadric did as he had often done before . . . and thus betrayed his liege lord and all the people of England.'

When darkness enveloped the Essex promontory that October evening the English army was in defeat, but not in rout; there was no pursuit and Edmund made his way to Gloucestershire. In so much awe did Canute hold him that he agreed to split the kingdom; Edmund was given Wessex and perhaps – although it is not certain – East Anglia and East Mercia. It was an arrangement that boded ill for the future, and must surely have led to further bloodshed, had Edmund not died suddenly three weeks later, on 30 November 1016.

The Witan offered the crown to the young Canute; they probably realized that he would have taken it anyway, and it must have been obvious to them that he alone could re-unite the country. Canute, born a pagan but baptized a Christian, became a devout churchman; but his Christianity was in many ways a thin veneer which covered a harsh, cruel and ruthless nature. He quickly banished Edmund Ironside's two boys and it was not his fault that they escaped death and finally found sanctuary with the King of Hungary; Ethelred's eldest surviving son he murdered. Nor did he stop at princes of the blood; the heads of all those likely to cause this stern, ambitious man trouble rested lightly on their shoulders. The net swept deep and wide and among its catches was that treacherous ealdorman, Eadric Streona.

Under Canute the concept of a Scandinavian Empire became a reality; he was absolute King of Denmark, and St Olaf of Norway ruled, until being expelled in 1028, by his favour. But England had conquered him as much as he had conquered her, and most of his time was spent in his adopted country. He paid off the Great Army (admittedly with huge sums of Danegeld) and sent the troops home, and he determined that Danes and Englishmen should henceforth live 'under the laws of King Edgar'. He posed as a pious King – although at times it must have been a bit of a strain – and held the English saints in deep veneration. In particular he spent much thought and money on the restoration of the Abbey of St Edmundsbury, built in memory of Edmund, King of East

Anglia, who in 870 had been put to death by Canute's forebears for refusing to become their vassal. And many other churches enjoyed his munificence.

The administration of the country was broad-based; Danes and Englishmen had parity in posts of responsibility, and indeed at the end of Canute's reign every important post was held by an Englishman. His own bodyguard, consisting of the famous house-carls, was an exception, probably being formed from what was left of the Great Army. The greatest concentration of power under the King was to be found in the four earldoms of Northumbria, Mercia, East Anglia and Wessex. This delegation of authority worked well enough while Canute lived, but under the weak rule of Edward the Confessor, England became dominated by the jealous emulation of these great nobles.

Canute died at Shaftesbury on 12 November 1035, and was buried alongside English kings in the very English city of Winchester. At his death the great Nordic confederation that he had built up collapsed amid his squabbling, half-barbaric sons, and the English throne formed a large part of the squabble. Canute had married secondly Ethelred's widow, Emma of Normandy, who must have been a coldly calculating lady. The bargain she struck was that her sons by Canute should take precedence over those by his first wife, and in return she would banish to her brother of Normandy her two boys by Ethelred. This had all the ingredients for the making of a really messy pottage. And so it turned out.

Earl Godwin, who had married into Canute's family and who was the most powerful of the magnates, at first aligned himself with the Queen Mother and supported the claim of her son, Hardicanute. But the Witan wanted his half-brother, Harold, who had the advantage of being in the country, while Hardicanute was in Denmark with problems of his own. The danger of an unsatisfactory compromise in the shape of a shared kingdom, with the prospects of civil war, was averted by a rapid succession of events. Hardicanute found it difficult to leave Denmark, but Alfred – Ethelred's eldest son by Emma – suddenly appeared in Kent at the head of six hundred men, ostensibly to visit his mother. But even if you know your mother dislikes you, it is unusual to visit her with six hundred soldiers, and Godwin felt it his duty as Earl of Wessex to bar his passage. But he proceeded to go well beyond the bounds of duty. He offered Alfred the hand of friendship and hospitality and then allowed him and his men to be taken in the night by a band of ruffians acting on orders from Harold, who killed the soldiers and blinded Alfred.

Godwin and Harold having thus been reconciled through the blood of Alfred (he died from the effects of his brutal treatment) it was a short step to banish Queen Emma and declare Harold King of all England.

For three years he reigned undisturbed, dying in 1040 just in time to avoid the avenging hand of Hardicanute, who, having at last settled matters in Denmark, was preparing an invasion to claim his own.

With the exception of Godwin, who had a certain amount of explaining to do before the Witan, and a costly present to give the new King in expiation of his treatment of Alfred and defection to Harold, the English people welcomed the arrival of Hardicanute. However, their pleasure was short lived. Hardicanute was unscrupulous, cruel and vicious. He had inherited all of his father's savage ruthlessness unalloyed by any of Canute's undoubted gifts. Two utterly insensate acts committed in the first year of his reign were hardly likely to endear him to his new subjects. They may not have been unduly worried by the barbaric treatment he accorded his brother's corpse, which he had exhumed and flung into the Thames; but the heavy tax levied to pay for the King's foreign ships and the terrible vengeance he wreaked on Worcester and the surrounding countryside, when two of his house-carls had been murdered there, cast aside all veils and presented him to them as a grasping, vindictive tyrant.

Fortunately the reign was a short one. Hardicanute collapsed while proposing the toast at the wedding of a thane's daughter, and died a few days later on 8 June 1042. Earl Godwin, who knew his man and was reaching for power, at once pressed for the return of the old Saxon line in the person of Edward, Ethelred's second son by Emma. The Witan and most of the country were almost certainly in agreement, but Canute's nephew, Sweyn, was in England at the time and it is reasonable to suppose that the young Danish dynasty did not give in without some sort of struggle, for Edward – whose deep piety would not have allowed him to recognize kingship without holy anointing – had to wait almost a year for his coronation.

The character of King Edward, whose subjects first called him the Confessor and who was later canonized, is something of an enigma. Usually he is stamped as a weak King, largely because he was content to allow the great earls – particularly Earls Godwin and Leofric, and latterly Godwin's son, Harold – to acquire enormous power and for much of the reign to organize the affairs of the kingdom. But this quiet, unassuming man who, having been brought over from his beloved Normandy, would have been more content to dwell in a monastery than a palace, was capable of occasional flashes of will-power; and a man who retains his throne for twenty-four years, often friendless and very much alone, amid the usual turmoil and strife of these times, cannot possess a character entirely overlaid with weakness. Out of place, and sometimes out of patience, among the rough, ambitious Saxon earls, he was the exemplar of many of the virtues that more widely practised were, in the course of time, to make Britain a civilized nation.

Apart from border clashes in Scotland and Wales, Edward's reign was free from external wars, but the stress laid upon the country through the influence of the King's Norman courtiers and his insistence on giving important benefices to Norman prelates nearly provoked civil war. Early in the reign the house of Godwin – into which the King married – gained the ascendancy, and although in 1051 Godwin and his sons were exiled, within a year they were back again at the head of an army and dictating terms which the unfortunate Edward found it prudent to accept. Thereafter the family – especially after the death of Mercia's Earl Leofric – had the country much to themselves.

In the closing years of the reign the pious Edward devoted himself increasingly to religious study and in particular to rebuilding the Benedictine Abbey of St Peter, situated two miles west of London amid the marshes of Thorney. This church, the West Minster (of which no trace now remains above ground), he intended should become a private dependency on him and his successors. In these years of meditation and contemplation in matters spiritual and architectural, the King became more than ever remote from the mundane affairs of government, which inevitably passed to the great provincial rulers, of whom Harold Godwinson had become the most influential.

Edward's marriage to Godwin's daughter was no love match, and although with one notable lapse he seems to have shown her kindness, he was either unwilling or unable to perform one of the more natural functions of a husband and he left no children. Therefore when in 1057 Edmund Ironside's son, called to England after an inexplicable delay, died before he could even see his uncle, Harold must have realized that the throne was within his grasp. The lustre of his victories against Gruffydd ap Llywelyn increased his prestige and stamped him as the foremost commander in the country, but the manner in which he sacrificed his brother, Tostig, a great favourite with the King, in order to pacify the north was perhaps better for the country than his own immediate prospects.

Nevertheless, when on 5 January 1066 the saintly Confessor died in the new palace he had built (later to become the hub of an empire) within sight of his recently consecrated West Minster in which he was buried, Harold had established himself so firmly in the inner councils of the Witan that they immediately elected him king.

The country needed a strong man at once, for although no one seriously considered the boy Edgar*, there were two other candidates

---

* Edgar Atheling was the grandson of Edmund Ironside, and had come to England with his father from Hungary. The Norman Conquest extinguished any hope this heir of

for the throne ready to press their claim by force of arms. Duke William of Normandy was the Confessor's cousin, and he had some reason to believe that Edward wished him to succeed, and every reason to be angered at Harold's *coup d'état*, for he had extracted an oath from the Earl that he would not oppose William's accession to the English throne. King Harald Hardrada's claim was flimsy in the extreme, being based upon some vague agreement between Hardicanute and Magnus, King of Norway, made more than twenty-five years before, but it served as an excuse for the Norwegian giant, reckoned the greatest captain of his day, to open the floodgates of one more Viking invasion.

Harold might have made a great King had the wheel of fortune not spun against him; of his ability to rule we can only guess, but he had courage, vigour and native shrewdness in good measure, and he was an outstanding leader. Unlike his predecessor, religion did not smother him, but he possessed a spark of that divine fire which through the ages has inspired men to create buildings *ad majorem Dei gloriam*. On 3 May 1060 Harold's foundation of the Holy Rood of Waltham was consecrated. Originally designed as a religious college with a dean and twelve secular canons to work among the people of the nearby forest, it became in due course the beautiful abbey that we see today.

Most of the nine months during which Harold occupied the throne were spent in preparing for an invasion on two fronts. Throughout the summer he concentrated on the nearest of his foes and kept the *fyrd* in readiness in the south; but by the first week of September their rations and pay were running out and being mostly subsistence farmers they were sorely needed on their own farms. There was nothing for it but to disband the levies. And then it was that the enemy struck; not in the south, but in the north. Harald Hardrada, joined by King Harold's outlawed brother, Tostig, had sailed up the Ouse and disembarked at Ricall.

Harold wasted no time; left with only his house-carls, not long out of his sick bed, and with 180 miles to cover, he set off for York. As he went, the men of England, responding to their King's valour and vigour, rallied to his standard. He covered the distance in the space of four days; it was one of the great marches of history. But before he arrived at Stamford Bridge, where his troops utterly routed the Norsemen, slaying their king and Harold's brother, the northern earls of Northumbria and Mercia had given battle at Fulford and lost. It was understandable, but unfortunate, that they should have engaged the enemy, for the mauling they received prevented them from taking part in the next great fight. It

the Saxon royal line might have had of succeeding, although he would not admit to that and was for some time a trouble and anxiety to William I, William II and Henry I, before going on his travels and joining a crusade.

is at least arguable that Fulford lost Harold the battle of Hastings.

William, who had waited many days for a favourable wind, got it on 27 September and the next day disembarked his troops (some eight thousand men and two thousand horses) at Pevensey, while Harold was still in the north. Hastening down Ermine Street ahead of his army, the English King paused just long enough to visit his abbey at Waltham and gather up fresh levies, before marching to the aid of his own West Saxons, whose lands Duke William was ravishing. In fact, it might have been better had he dallied a little longer than the six days he spent in London, for his army would have been in better shape and William was unhappy and undecided; he dared not move too far from his base, and the longer Harold delayed, the greater became his anxiety.

But on the morning of 14 October Harold, with an army by now almost equal in numbers to that of the Normans, took up a strong defensive position on the Senlac ridge to await the advancing Norman host. The great battle of Hastings, at which the destiny of a dynasty was decided, lasted for most of the day. For many hours no one could tell which way the fight would go, first one army and then the other held the advantage. But in the late afternoon the crisis came; William attempted a death-blow with the concerted attack of his three arms – cavalry, infantry and archers. The house-carls fought valiantly under an avalanche of iron and steel, but the solid phalanx of Saxon soldiers, who until that time had stood rock-like upon the ridge, at last began to crack.

The Normans gained the plateau and started driving wedges into the gaps; Harold's brothers had already fallen, and a little after sunset the English King was seen to stagger and clutch an arrow that had pierced his eye. As Harold leant upon his shield in fearful agony, a body of four Norman knights stormed their way to the last ring of house-carls. These brave men closed their ranks and died with their King under the Golden Dragon of Wessex and the banner of the Fighting Man. The Normans had triumphed; but there was great glory for England that day.

As in the period described in Chapter 1, little remains physically to remind us of the years from 900 to 1066. Time and the Danes – not to mention the Parliamentarians in the Civil War – have proved great levellers. These were years of gradual consolidation and unification for England, and inevitably to achieve this many battles had to be fought. The exact site of two of the most important battles of this period are known to us, but some doubt surrounds others, such as Maldon and Ashingdon, fought against the Danes.

Bayeux Tapestry (Bayeux, Calvados, France). This is a length of embroidery worked on linen with a woollen thread, measuring 230 feet 10½ inches by 19¾ inches. It is the story of the Conquest from the time of Harold's arrival in France on a visit to Duke William, until the time of his death at Hastings. It is the most informative account of these great events that exists, and is very accurate in detail. The tapestry was not, as is sometimes stated, the work of William's Queen, Matilda, and her ladies, but was most probably commissioned shortly after the battle of Hastings, by William's half-brother Odo of Conteville, Bishop of Bayeux. Originally in Bishop Odo's cathedral at Bayeux, the tapestry escaped fire in 1077 and 1159, and was again nearly destroyed at the time of the French Revolution. It is now to be seen on the first floor of a permanent exhibition gallery in the former Bishop's Palace in Bayeux.

Cheddar (Somerset) was an important centre in the later Saxon period. It was a meeting place of the Witan in the tenth century; King Edmund (939-46) occupied a hunting lodge there and other Saxon kings (including Alfred) were associated with this small town. The site of the royal house was excavated in 1961 and the earliest buildings date from the ninth century. Cheddar is on the A371 between Axbridge and Wells.

Corfe Castle (Dorset). This great Saxon castle standing guard in the gap (Corfe was the Saxon word for gap) in the range of the Purbeck Hills, which run east to west in what is called the Isle of Purbeck in south Dorset, was the principal residence of King Edgar (959-75). It was at Corfe that Edgar's son, Edward the Martyr, was done to death, almost certainly at the instigation of his stepmother – recent attempts to whitewash the Queen based on certain passages in the Anglo-Saxon Chronicle are unconvincing. The castle was destroyed in 1646 by order of Parliament, but the ruin is most impressive, for much of the original building – the King's Tower, the Queen's Tower, the Martyr's Gate, parts of the Chapel, etc – still stands, and the whole is traceable from the existing ground plan. As Corfe is approached along the A351 from Wareham, the castle glowers down from its lofty eyrie and its strategic importance is readily discernible. It could not have been easily taken except through treachery or starvation.

Durham Cathedral (Co. Durham). In the Cathedral can be seen the stole, maniple and girdle which were made at the command of Queen Elflaed at the beginning of the tenth century for the Bishop of Winchester, and presented to the shrine of St Cuthbert by King Athelstan on his visit to Chester-le-Street in 934. These remarkable relics of Cuthbert, who was Bishop of Lindisfarne from 685 to his death in 687, and who together with the Venerable Bede (whose remains were also brought to Durham), is the most revered saint in the north country, were found in 1827 well preserved in a series of three coffers, the innermost one being the original coffin for the Saint's body. The shrine had been removed from Lindisfarne at the time of the Danish raids at the end of the ninth century, and when Athelstan – who was in the north on a punitive expedition against the Scottish King Constantine – presented his gifts, the monks had not yet found the final resting place for their Saint. They came to Durham in 995, and in 998 'the White Church' was dedicated. This church was destroyed in 1091 to make way for the building of the present magnificent cathedral, and in 1104 the body of St Cuthbert was laid behind the high altar.

Greensted-juxta-Ongar, Essex. St Andrew's Church is the only survival of a Saxon log church in England. The walls of the nave are composed of the half-trunks of oak trees, split vertically, with the curved portion of each tree facing outwards. The exact age of the church is not known, but it certainly dates from before 1013, when it was used as a resting place for the body of St Edmund, the English King martyred by the Danes in 870, on its return from London to Bury St Edmunds in Suffolk.

Battle of Hastings (Sussex), 14 October 1066. Some of the fiercest fighting took place in the present grounds of Battle Abbey and Battle Abbey Park, which lie just to the south of the town of Battle on the A2100 road to Hastings. This is the best vantage point from which to view the battlefield. The Abbey ruins are impressive: William, to commemorate his victory, founded a monastery which was built by the monks of the Benedictine Abbey of St Martin, Marmoutier. The memorial church of St Martin was dedicated in February 1094 in the presence of William II.

Kingston-upon-Thames, Surrey. Near the Guildhall is a large sandstone slab on which seven – possibly eight – Saxon kings were crowned during the tenth century. It seems likely that as early as the seventh century, Saxon kings resided at Kingston, but King Alfred's son, Edward the Elder, was the first sovereign to be crowned on the stone, and that was in the year 900. In 978 Ethelred, the Redeless, was the last king to be crowned at Kingston, but the town – described in the Domesday Book as a royal manor – continued to be closely connected with the sovereign, and King John gave it its first charter.

Battle of Stamford Bridge (North Yorks), 25 September 1066. This battle, together with that of Fulford, which immediately preceded it, were two of the most decisive in English history, for they made possible William the Conqueror's success at Hastings. King Harold II's great march from London to Yorkshire and his subsequent defeat of King Harald Hardrada was a magnificent feat, but it temporarily weakened his fighting strength. Even so, had the two northern earls, Morcar and Edwin, not engaged the Norseman at Fulford, where they suffered total defeat five days before Stamford Bridge, their army might yet have tipped the scale in Harold's favour at Hastings. There is little now to be seen of the battlefield of Fulford; but a good idea of the fight at Stamford Bridge can be obtained from the Danes Well garage area of the town, which is eight miles east of York on the A166. The actual field, where the main battle took place, is now private property, but the line of Harold's advance from York and the site of the bridge across the Derwent held by an unknown Viking hero can be viewed without difficulty or trespass.

Waltham Abbey (Essex). Earl Harold brought masons over from Normandy to build his great church on the site of a smaller one, which had contained a crucifix whose remarkable healing powers are said to have cured Harold of paralysis. The church was consecrated on 3 May 1060 (Holy Cross Day), and was originally very much larger than the present building; the reputed site of Harold's grave beyond the present east wall is where the high altar would have been. Waltham became an abbey in 1184, being subject only to the King and the Pope. At the Dissolution it was despoiled, only Harold's nave being saved from destruction and the seven Norman bays became the nucleus of the beautiful parish church. Waltham Abbey is in Epping Forest, about six miles south-west of Epping on the A121 Waltham Cross–Epping road.

3

THE NORMAN DYNASTY

England had been conquered by one of the great men of history, and from the Norman Conquest there flowed many blessings. William could so easily have destroyed everything he found, and in wiping the slate clean imposed alien laws and customs on a people who, after centuries of struggle, were beginning to emerge from the dark forests of uncertainty into the broad, sunlit uplands of confidence and opportunity. Changes were inevitable – although many of them had already begun – and the native tongue was sadly mauled; but much of the constitution and the laws of Alfred and his successors were preserved and, most importantly, enforced. For harsh, and at times ruthless, though the Conqueror was, he gave order and discipline to the land; and if he continued and built upon much that he found he kept the large landowners in leash as much as the commonalty.

William cautiously felt his way round London, and it was not long before his calculated acts of intimidation made the magnates realize that resistance would be futile. They met him at Berkhamsted, and there offered their personal submission and, on behalf of the Witan, the crown. William would not, however, trust himself within their city until a detachment had been sent to raise some temporary fortifications. These were thrown up in the south-east corner of the city, where a little more than ten years later William ordered Bishop Gundulf to build the White Tower.

The King was crowned in Edward's West Minster on Christmas Day 1066, and three months later he returned to Normandy, where he was reunited with his wife, Matilda, to whom he was entirely devoted and who was perhaps the only person to enjoy his complete confidence. At Whitsun 1068, when William considered the country sufficiently settled, Matilda crossed the Channel to receive her queenly crown, but until her death in 1083 much of her time – alternately helped and hindered by her eldest son Robert – was spent in administering Normandy in William's absence. Apart from having to take up arms in 1077 against the weak and at times troublesome Robert, William, unlike his successors, ruled Normandy in peace, although the people of Maine, where Robert ruled by virtue of his marriage to the heiress of the last hereditary Count, were twice called upon to pay the price of revolt.

It was not to be expected that the islanders would accept Norman domination without a struggle, more especially as in William's absences in Normandy his lieutenants were both arrogant and oppressive. Wherever a leader or a faction could stir the neighbourhood the disaffected, and they were many, rallied to the cause. The west country, now the refuge of Harold's family and hitherto largely undisturbed, harboured foolish ideas of independence; the Welsh Marches were quickly alight; the men of Kent went so far as to enrol the help of Count Eustace of Boulogne (the man who had caused the breach between Earl Godwin and King Edward); in the north Earls Morcar and Edwin formed a league against the Conqueror; Malcolm, King of the Scots, harried Northumberland, while his brother-in-law Edgar Atheling joined hands with the Danes and sailed up the Ouse; and in East Anglia, Hereward the Wake held out among the Fens.

William, in the course of three years, crushed these rebellions with the utmost severity. The Chronicler tells us that 'He was a very stern and violent man, so that no one dared do anything contrary to his will.' His passage through the northern counties was like a roaring flame through a cornfield; whole tracts of country were left devastated with not a house standing, and families were forced to find what refuge they could among the hills and dales. York was sacked and the Minster burnt; thanes lost their lands to Norman barons, while lesser men, although mostly left in possession of their holdings, were quite liable to be subjected to the tyranny of the forest laws. William 'loved the stags as dearly as though he had been their father', and early in his reign he imposed extremely harsh penalties for those breaking the forest laws. To be caught 'bloodyhand' (as the term was) slaying a stag could involve death and certainly blinding.

But all this was the worst side of the Conquest, brought about by the Englishman's natural dislike of foreigners – particularly at this time Normans – and the inability to understand, until it was too late, that this strong and self-disciplined man was utterly ruthless towards those who attempted to thwart his will. A conquered country always has to pay a heavy price and in the process many must suffer. However, the Normans preserved much of what they found; the Witan – or Great Council – and the system of local government survived with the additional blessing that for the first time since Canute supreme authority rested at the centre. The day of the big earldoms was over, and by breaking up provinces into small estates, William effectively abolished regional autocracy.

By 1071 the English had learnt the hard way, and when in 1075 some of his French earls, whom the Conqueror had loaded with lands and titles, broke out in revolt, they were quickly suppressed, for by then the people understood that the strong hand of the King was infinitely preferable to the injustices of many petty tyrants. For William's new feudal superstructure, based on military and state service through land tenure, was already being seen as an effective instrument of royal power. Here was a statesman of high administrative competence, and a man well able to control the new ruling class of earls, bishops and abbots that he had built up, and who in return for what they had been given had sworn to support the King in Council, and to serve him in battle with their knights and vassals.

For the purpose of maintaining order, and for assessing the wealth of the land and the landowners, William employed two widely differing but equally effective measures. He built numerous castles, and he ordered commissioners in every shire and hundred to carry out a great survey of the holdings large and small in their area. They were instructed to record the state of the land (arable, pasture, swamp, woodland), the number of domestic beasts, the number of fishponds and mills - indeed information of every kind that had a bearing on what could be taxed, and on who owned land under the crown from which military service was due. Started in 1086 and completed within the incredibly short time of a year, this tremendous piece of descriptive information was originally drawn up in long parchment rolls, but later copied into two volumes - and called by the English 'Domesday'. Because the survey predated the Conquest in its records, we can see how little the basic structure of Saxon polity was changed by the Normans, but on the other hand how great was the confiscation of land.

The castle was the emblem of Norman superiority. It was the hated symbol of oppression and cruelty, for through it - to a greater or lesser degree, depending upon the relationship between the king and his barons - the peasant was kept under strict surveillance either in the service of his lord, or in his dungeons, and from it that same lord might sally forth to do battle for or against his sovereign, taking with him his unwilling serfs. Often built upon the site of Saxon earthworks, the keep in William's reign was likely to have been made of wooden logs, to be transformed in a generation or less into massive stone buildings. Many of these great fortresses built in the eleventh and twelfth centuries still survive in part, but there are places - such as Old Sarum - where simple Saxon earthworks have long outlived Norman stone. But whether of wood or of stone, until a more civilized era some centuries later rendered the castle and its inmate comparatively harmless, it was an innovation viewed by the majority with considerable repugnance.

In the summer of 1087 a Normandy border dispute instigated by the French King, Philip I, flared up and once more William led his troops out of Rouen on a punitive expedition. Philip had raised a laugh at his court with a rude jest about William's corpulence, and the Conqueror had certainly put on weight with age. But always of a strong, stocky physique he had, at sixty, lost none of his old fire, as the men of Mantes were soon to discover. However, while he was riding through their blackened town his horse stumbled and William received an injury – probably from the pommel of the saddle – that proved fatal. They took him back to Rouen, where for six weeks he languished in considerable pain, but with his faculties completely clear to the end, which came on 9 September.

In his time William was sometimes called the Great; it was an epithet richly deserved. He was a great captain; a wise and patient administrator; and if he was at times cruel, he was seldom vindictive and stern measures were often necessary to bind together into one disciplined whole the two peoples he came to rule. In this he was successful; the castles he built may have been regarded as the badge of an oppressor, but under William's strong hand they served a good purpose. It was said that a man 'with his bosom full of gold' could cross the land unharmed. He gave the country security, because he bound the powerful magnates in loyalty to the Crown.

William had always shown a marked preference for his second son and namesake, and as he lay dying he took steps to ensure that William and not the weak, easy-going Robert should succeed him on the English throne. This second son, whom men called Rufus from the colour of his hair, and perhaps also from his fiery temperament, was broad-shouldered and thickset like his father, whom he greatly admired and who was probably the only man he ever feared. He wasted little time in hurrying to England and presenting his credentials to his father's archbishop, Lanfranc, who being satisfied that he was the late King's choice, crowned Rufus at Westminster on 26 September 1087.

William Rufus was a thoroughly bad man; he had inherited the cunning and courage of his father, but beyond that little. He was cruel, vindictive, blasphemous and completely unscrupulous; a man with a great capacity for causing human woe. Nevertheless, his English subjects were prepared to tolerate him in the interests of peace, for he was a strong King who dealt with his troublesome Norman barons (who, owing allegiance to two men, were apt to play one off against the other and favour the weaker) sternly. They rallied to his cause when in 1088 certain barons rose in favour of Duke Robert, and they fought for him in his successful campaigns in south Wales and northern England, where Rufus took Cumberland from the Scots. But their participation in the Normandy battles, which raged fiercely throughout this reign and for most of the next, was not always popular, although at Tinchebrai the English felt that they had at last avenged Hastings.

Rufus always hoped to wrest Normandy from Robert and reunite it with the English Crown. At times the contest was a three-cornered one, for Henry – the Conqueror's youngest son – had obtained large estates in Normandy and would be found first on one side and then on the other. Furthermore, these strange, ill-assorted brothers would occasionally patch up their quarrels and act in concert against a common foe. It was while about to embark his army from Hastings on a foray against the French that Rufus, most uncharacteristically, had summoned certain bishops to bless the enterprise, and the occasion was turned to a more pleasing purpose when the assembled bishops dedicated the Conqueror's memorial church of St Martin's, Battle, with its high altar on the spot where Harold fell.

Apart from ambitions in Normandy and risings in England, which occupied much of Rufus's time and energy, the reign was notable for the King's contempt for the Church and Churchmen. Archbishop Lanfranc, who died in 1089, might conceivably have exercised some control over the King, although Rufus had already become displeased with the Italian, who was one of the greatest primates in the long history of Canterbury; but with his death the way was left open for the evil advocacy of the current favourite Ralph Flambard. Rufus did not need much prompting from this man to see how advantageous it would be to bring the Church into line with the feudal system, whereby duties were performed in return for land revenues and emoluments, and conversely, when these duties lapsed, the benefices reverted to the Crown. Canterbury made an excellent starting point.

After this system of appropriation had been working for four years, to the disquiet of all leading Churchmen, William Rufus fell seriously ill. Whether he thought himself dying and feared God – which is contrary to the general belief – or whether he thought he could bargain with the Lord for his life, he made many concessions and granted several amnesties (none of which he kept on his recovery) and agreed to appoint Anselm, then Abbot of Bec, to the vacant see of Canterbury. In so doing he laid up further trouble for himself and the English Church, for Anselm (like Lanfranc from north Italy, and also like him a great archbishop) was not the man to indulge in obsequious grovelling to royalty.

The trouble between the King and his Archbishop chiefly concerned two matters – although it was a perpetual conflict between good and bad – the question of Church revenues, and in particular those of Canterbury, and the recognition of Pope Urban II at the time of the schism. Both men were strong-willed; neither was prepared to give ground. The quarrel smouldered and flared throughout the reign with altercation usually followed by conciliation, until in 1097 Anselm was allowed to leave the country and did not return until after Rufus's death.

William II is now best remembered for two things: the magnificent banqueting hall he added to Edward the Confessor's Palace of Westminster, and his mysterious death in the New Forest. It was in about 1097 – or perhaps a little earlier – that Rufus ordered the construction of Westminster Hall; much of his building still stands today, although it was buttressed and re-roofed in the reign of Richard II, and certain structural alterations have been made over the centuries. For many years the interior of this fine piece of Norman architecture was, when not setting the scene for the great State trials, cluttered up with the various courts of law and even stalls and booths selling all manner of wares from spectacles to sweetmeats; but since the end of the last century, visitors have had an unimpeded view of its spacious grandeur. Nevertheless, when the building was finished in 1099, its founder complained that it was 'too big for a chamber and not big enough for a hall'.

On the first night of August 1100, William II, his brother Henry, William de Breteuil, Robert FitzHamon and Walter Tyrell slept in a hunting lodge in the New Forest. The next afternoon they set off for the chase, and it was towards evening that William was killed. Much has been written about the King's death; nothing is certain, and it cannot be enlarged upon here. But from the tangled maze of available evidence, three points seem to emerge. It was premeditated murder, almost certainly with the connivance of the Church; Walter Tyrell did not aim the fatal arrow, but because of his subsequent flight to Normandy has been under suspicion ever since; Henry was in the plot and may even have killed his brother, although the finger of guilt points more clearly to FitzHamon as the man who actually drew the bow.

No sooner was William dead than the hunting party left the forest. The body of the King was found by a charcoal burner called Purkis and taken to Winchester, where Henry – who had made straight for the capital to get himself acknowledged as king – had it interred with indecent haste. William de Breteuil arrived at Winchester not long after Henry and immediately raised his voice in favour of Duke Robert, but Henry would have none of it and if de Breteuil had any supporters (it may be assumed that there were some barons who still disliked the severance of England from Normandy) they were quickly overruled, and a makeshift Witan duly elected him king. The coronation took place in London and here again Henry would brook no delay; Anselm was still out of the country, York was too far away, and so the ceremony was performed by the Bishop of London.

Henry was the best of the three brothers. He was a much wiser man than Rufus; he had the sense to build upon his father's work and he gave England, through the royal servants, a permanent officialdom. The great officers of State, such as the Chamberlain, Treasurer, Marshal, Constable, Steward and above all the Justiciar, who presided over the Curia Regis and deputised for the King in his absence, were the creation of this hard-working man who loved a tidy and orderly administration. He was not nearly as cruel as Rufus, nor as weak as Robert; but in frequently displaying leniency towards his enemies, he stored up unnecessary trouble for himself.

Henry played himself in carefully and cleverly. Almost at once he issued an important charter whereby he sought to appease both the Church and the baronage by pledging himself to respect their rights, privileges and liberties, most of which had been taken from them in the reign of his brother. He was well aware that trouble would come from Normandy – Duke Robert was on a crusade, but would soon be back and many barons would surely rally to his cause – and so in order to curry favour with the English, upon whom he must rely for much of his fighting strength, he let it be known that he would restore the laws of Edward the Confessor. Furthermore, he chose for a wife, Eadgyth, the daughter of Malcolm of Scotland and Margaret; Margaret was the sister of Edgar Atheling and so Eadgyth – or Matilda as she was called to please his Norman subjects – was of the Saxon royal blood, the great-granddaughter of Edmund Ironside and in descent from Egbert, the founder of Britain's royal line.

As a major part of his reconciliation with the Church, Henry sent an urgent message begging Anselm to return to his post, and in earnest of his good intentions, he clapped the egregious Ralph Flambard into the Tower. But this early example of Henry's leniency led to the first occasion of a spectacular escape from the great fortress. Henry had allowed the Bishop to have every comfort, and one day his resourceful friends concealed a rope within a large flagon of wine. The Bishop, a heavy man who had not before been called upon to leave his lodging by rope, made a hash of the steep descent and arrived at the bottom of the tower in poor shape; but his friends quickly got him away to Normandy, where he immediately started stirring up trouble with Duke Robert and his followers.

Robert also found encouragement from many of the Norman barons in England, who saw better prospects for gain under a weak sovereign. Chief among these was Robert of Bellême, head of the house of Montgomery and Earl of Shrewsbury. Duke Robert of Normandy landed at Portsmouth with a considerable force and marched towards London. The two brothers met near Alton, but no blood was shed and a treaty followed the reconciliation by which Robert agreed to surrender his claim to England. However, proceedings were taken against the rebel earls and many were banished. But the Earl of Shrewsbury tricked his way into an escape and immediately took up arms against the King.

The house of Montgomery, particularly in the Welsh Marches, was very powerful; Robert of Bellême and his two brothers occupied numerous castles, chief among them being Arundel, Tickhill, Shrewsbury, Caroghova and Bridgenorth. Henry's policy at home was the simple one of never allowing the old baronage to become too strong; he preferred men around him who owed everything they had to his munificence. Accordingly he set out at Easter 1102 to defeat Robert by systematically reducing his castles until, some three months later, by then before the castle of Shrewsbury, he found him deprived of allies, bereft of hope and with no choice but to surrender.

The Earl and his brothers, to the delight of almost everyone, were stripped of their possessions and abjured the realm. 'For three and thirty years from that time he [Henry] ruled England in peace . . . nor in all these years durst any man hold a castle against him.' This was as well, for in France it was a very different matter. Nor did the quality of mercy receive its just reward; Robert of Bellême was to prove as contumacious in France as in England, and not until 1113 was he once more captured and this time confined to Wareham Castle for the remainder of his days.

It took Henry a further three years to achieve what his brother, William, had failed to do – the reunification of Normandy and England. Duke Robert, always a weak and by now an embittered man, had with the arrival of Robert of Bellême in Normandy finally met his hour of disaster. The exiled Earl soon became the virtual ruler of Normandy; and although Henry attempted to dislodge him through skirmish and negotiation the conclusive battle – so far as Normandy was concerned – had to wait until 1106, when at Tinchebrai Henry, greatly aided by his English soldiers, won a decisive victory. As a result of this battle Duke Robert suffered perpetual imprisonment in England; but once more Henry pardoned Bellême. Admittedly he was still immensely powerful; but this would seem all the more reason for extinguishing him. Alive he could – and indeed did – cause more trouble.

Henry was now virtually unchallenged; Normandy was ruled not from Rouen but from London, and although the King of France would prove difficult, causing Henry to become the first, but by no means the last, English King to fight the French with German allies, at home he had time to set about the strengthening of internal government. In his reorganization of the country's fiscal and legal systems he was greatly helped by Bishop Roger of Salisbury; between them they laid the foundations upon which Henry's grandson was to build.

There was at this time no difference between the King's public and private purse; all the revenues from the vast royal estates were accounted for and disposed of by the King through the barons of the Exchequer – so called from the chequered cloths used for ease in calculations. Twice a year, in Westminster Hall, the county sheriffs – often men connected with the Curia – rendered to the Exchequer the returns from their county taxes, fines and other incomes, Every penny was carefully checked and accounted for; it was a meticulous system well ahead of its time.

Henry's English subjects liked him for his use of their own language, and all his subjects admired his administration and revered his justice. It was stern, but it was fair, and only occasionally (as with the savage forest laws, and when he permitted his own granddaughters by an illegitimate son to be blinded) was it cruel and vindictive. They called him 'the Lion of Justice', and it was a soubriquet that was well deserved, for he overhauled the powers and duties of the county and hundred courts, making it obligatory for the major cases to be sent to the Curia Regis, where Henry himself often sat in judgement. On the other hand the King's officers, or Justices as they became, were sent from the Curia to assist sheriffs in the county courts. The barons might hold sway in their manorial courts, but the King's officers could be seen to administer sound justice throughout the land.

In 1120 Henry, who had just concluded a successful four years in Normandy, sailed home from the port of Barfleur. His only legitimate son, William, a natural son and daughter, the Earl of Chester and several other important people preferred to travel in the new fifty-oar vessel called *The White Ship*. It was towards the end of November and the night was dark, but the sea was not particularly rough; however, the sailors were – having been liberally supplied with wine by the young Atheling and his friends. In an attempt to show off their boat's speed they ploughed her into some rocks, and all on board – save a butcher from Rouen – perished. It was a tragedy from which Henry never fully recovered, and from which England was to derive nearly twenty years of misery.

Queen Matilda had died two years before *The White Ship* went down, and in 1121 the King took as his second wife, Adelaide, the young and beautiful daughter of the Count of Louvain. But when after five years she was still childless, the question of the succession loomed large in

Henry's mind. It was not as yet hereditary, but there was little doubt that had William lived there would have been no dispute; however, until he died in 1128 another William – Duke Robert's son – posed an unpleasant possibility for Henry, and he determined upon the unprecedented step of getting the throne of England and Normandy settled upon his daughter Matilda.

Matilda had been widowed a year previously by the death of the Emperor Henry V. She was now commanded to leave her German subjects, with whom she was very popular, and return to England, there to be acknowledged (with some reluctance) on oath by the lords spiritual and temporal as Henry's rightful successor. It was January 1127, and before the year was out Henry had married her to Geoffrey of Anjou; a match as politically expedient to Henry as it was socially undesirable to Matilda – a lady who had become accustomed to the rank of Empress.

Henry died on 1 December 1135, having given England thirty years of almost uninterrupted peace, during which he did much to merge the Saxon and Norman occupants of the country into one composite nation. But his hopes for a peaceful succession, if indeed he really had them, soon proved illusory. With his nephew Stephen, Count of Mortain and Boulogne, a weak, good-natured but ineffective man, gaining the throne England clattered into anarchy. It happened this way.

Matilda and Geoffrey Plantagenet (so called from the sprig of broom – *Planta genista* – he invariably wore in his helmet) were in Anjou when Henry died. Stephen was also at his home, but the Boulonnais was closer, and with that promptitude that frequently – although at times unwisely – manifested itself throughout his reign, he crossed the Channel to stake his claim, while the magnates were still considering how best to abjure their oath to the unpopular Matilda. Stephen, who had large estates in England, was well known there and liked; he was the son of the Conqueror's daughter, Adela, and through his marriage to Matilda (one wonders whether the Normans knew another girl's name!), the daughter of Mary of Scotland and Count Eustace of Boulogne, his children were descended from the Saxon kings. He was Henry's favourite nephew, and next to his daughter would probably have been his choice as successor; the fact that he was the youngest of Adela's three sons would not necessarily debar him, for the elective system, although not used on this occasion, had not completely disappeared.

In selecting his legitimate daughter to be his successor in preference to his natural son, Earl Robert of Gloucester, who had many suitable qualifications of character and ability, Henry seemed to indicate that the Normans now put more stress on respectability than was the case in the Conqueror's time. Earl Robert showed no inclination to press what claim he might have, but from the very first loyally supported his half-sister until his death in 1147. Thus it was that Stephen found the gates of Dover and Canterbury shut against him by Earl Robert's men. Nevertheless, in London and Winchester (where his brother, Henry, was Bishop) matters went well for him and by promising liberal concessions to the Church he gained the Treasury and the Crown. It rested heavily upon his head, for he had gained it neither by inheritance nor election, and almost at once dire troubles beset him both at home and abroad.

Geoffrey of Anjou lost no time in sending his wife into Normandy to stir up trouble there, while at home the Welsh and Scots soon saw that the strong central government that Henry had built up was being torn apart by the rapacious barons. Struggle and strife in England suited them admirably. The Welsh created great devastation around the lands bordering the Dee and Wye, while King David of Scotland led an army in support of his niece that consisted mainly of savage marauders, who seemed to rejoice in the delirium of death and killing as they marched south.

Only the courage and resolution of Thurstan, the aged Archbishop of York, who called out the Yorkshire *fyrd*, saved the north. Preaching a holy war he and his deputy, the Bishop of Orkney, rallied the mixed army they had assembled under a sacred standard. Too old to march himself, Thurstan sent his troops from York to Thirsk and thence to Northallerton, where three miles beyond the town, at a place called Cutton Moor, on 22 August 1138, they utterly defeated the Scots. This fierce fight, in which the slaughter was immense, became known from the great mast the English had erected on a wagon, with a pyx at its head containing a consecrated wafer and three sacred banners hanging from a cross-piece, as the battle of the Standard.

Shortly after the battle the Earl of Gloucester, who had somewhat deceitfully done homage to Stephen for his lands, issued a declaration of war upon the King, and in September 1138 Matilda landed in Sussex. She came with a modest force of 140 men-at-arms and Stephen, who was already busy quelling revolts in the south, could have easily taken her; but with a chivalrous gesture that may have been honourable to his name, although certainly of no help to his cause, he gave her a safe conduct to her brother's stronghold of Bristol. There followed fifteen years of bitter strife, baronial brigandage, famine and pestilence, before some sort of order and design was eventually extracted from chaos and confusion.

The long list of clamant disasters that befell both sides as battles and sieges, often fought with imported mercenaries, followed one another cannot be fully recorded, but there were some important landmarks that pick out the course of this deadly conflict between the Conqueror's two grandchildren. Such a one was the battle of Lincoln, fought on 2 February 1141. The people of Lincoln appealed to Stephen against the Earl of Chester, who had occupied Lincoln Castle and was making unwarrantable demands upon the local population. Stephen responded with his usual promptitude, but by the time he arrived Chester had left the castle in the hands of his wife and had sought help from his father-in-law, Robert of Gloucester. The two Earls joined forces and approaching Lincoln from the south marched to the broad plateau immediately north of the city. Here Stephen met them, and the two armies – with Gloucester's to the north – faced each other in three divisions. The battle seems to have been a poor affair, with Stephen's troops very ready to desert. But the King himself fought bravely at the head of his infantry, wielding first the sword, and when that broke, an axe that someone thrust into his hands. But eventually he was felled by an enemy slinger, and although not badly hurt he was forced to surrender. Most of his men had fled, the city was given over to sack, and Stephen was sent prisoner to Matilda at Gloucester, and from there to Bristol for safe keeping.

This left the stage clear for Matilda, if she could come to terms with the all-powerful Church. Stephen's brother, Henry, Bishop of Winchester, struck a hard bargain with her, but she accepted (for later in strength one can always repudiate what was done in weakness) and went through a form of anointing that appeared sufficiently authentic to enable her to style herself Lady and Queen of England. The Londoners received her cautiously; but soon, when she showed the arrogant and intransigent side of her character, they rose and drove her from their city, infinitely preferring the kindly, if incompetent Stephen, whose release they repeatedly demanded.

Year after year the country, especially the southern half, was called upon to endure fresh agonies. In a desperate and muddled struggle for Winchester much of the city, including the Conqueror's palace, was destroyed. Earl Robert was captured, but in 1141 exchanged for Stephen, who a year later had successes at Wareham and Cirencester before laying siege to Oxford, where Matilda had her headquarters. This time there was to be no chivalrous conduct towards a woman adversary; but Matilda made a romantic escape from the castle across the frozen fields, accompanied by four attendants all splendidly camouflaged in white.

Matilda repeatedly urged her husband to cross the Channel with reinforcements, but he was too busy winning Normandy; however, their young son, Henry, came over for the first time in 1142. Aged only ten, he was yet old enough to understand the horrors of a civil war that left a barren land with fields untilled, crops ungathered, cattle straying, towns unoccupied, and the great barons little better than savages plundering at will. He would not forget the tribulations that could befall a weak government.

On 31 October 1147 Matilda's faithful half-brother, the Earl of Gloucester, died; his death heralded the end of her personal chances. In February 1148 she left England for ever; a sad, frustrated woman. But her departure made little difference to Stephen's authority, which was no greater than before. In January 1153 Prince Henry made his fourth visit to England, and this time he came at the head of a sizeable army. He had recently shown in Normandy and Anjou that although still young he was not without military skill, and in an England tired from years of fruitless butchery his presence raised men's spirits like sparkling wine, for it bade fair to end an epoch of cruelty, turbulence and divided loyalties.

Nor did he disappoint his well-wishers. Malmesbury was gained through a convenient sleet storm and the faint-heartedness of Stephen; and then from Wallingford, where a short truce came to nothing, Henry marched his men to Bristol, Winchcombe, Warwick, Leicester, Stamford and Nottingham, gaining strongholds and castles from a now irresolute baronage. While Henry was at Nottingham the King's eldest son, Eustace, a brutal and unpleasant man with none of his father's engaging qualities, fortunately died. Two years previously Stephen had attempted, unsuccessfully, to get him recognized as his heir; now, with his wise and charming Queen recently dead, he seemed to have had no further ambitions for his family. The moment was opportune to put an end to this senseless blood-letting.

The Church, through the person of the Bishop of Winchester, took the initiative; no doubt he was anxious to rectify, in so far as it was possible, what he had started eighteen years before when he had accepted his brother as king. A compromise was agreed upon whereby Stephen was to rule all England until he died; Henry was recognized as his heir and Stephen promised 'to cherish him as a son' and agreed that 'in the business of the kingdom I will work by the counsel of the Duke'. William, Stephen's second son, was allowed to retain his personal possessions in England, and, of course, Boulogne.

On 25 October 1154, less than a year after Henry had done homage and sworn allegiance to him, Stephen died. During the 'nineteen long winters', as the Chronicle styled them, much harm had been done. Control by the King had gone, the royal revenues had been dissipated, baronial castles had sprung up housing little Caesars who preyed upon the countryside. Nothing positive was achieved from this reign, save the building of St Stephen's Chapel at Westminster – and that was pulled down in 1292. Men yearned for the strong, efficient government of Henry I: in his grandson they were to get it.

Throughout Britain traces of Norman architecture can still be seen to a greater or lesser degree. Norman castles retained their military value for many years after the dynasty had disappeared, and they have therefore been much altered. Churches, too, have undergone considerable restoration over the centuries, but a great many still stand that owed their origin to the times discussed in this chapter. The list is far too great to be included in its entirety, and there is space only for the more important buildings and works of art that can be easily seen and which have some fairly obvious connection with the monarchs who have been described and their servants.

Bamburgh Castle (Northumberland) stands on the brink of England, sheer with the cliff on the Northumbrian coast. First the Romans and then the kings and later the earls of Northumbria had fortifications at Bamburgh; but William II besieged and took the place from Robert Mowbray, Earl of Northumberland, and thereafter – save for a short break in the reign of Stephen, when the King of the Scots' son had it – the castle remained a royal possession until the reign of James I. The keep is twelfth century, but the rest of the castle has been restored. This impressive, solitary ruin stands some sixteen miles north of Alnwick on the B1341, or B1342 out of Belford.

Battle Abbey (Sussex). Very little remains of the Conqueror's church of St Martin, which is supposed to have had its high altar on the site where Harold fell at Hastings; but the ruins of the abbey are both extensive and impressive.

Berkhamsted Castle (Herts.). Very little remains to be seen of the masonry, but the earthworks are most impressive. It was at Berkhamsted that Edgar the Atheling, together with Earls Edwin and Morcar, met Duke William and submitted, thus ending the campaign that had begun at Hastings. Hitherto there had almost certainly been no fortification of any kind at Berkhamsted, and it is probable that the nucleus of the fine motte (45 ft high and a top diameter of 60 ft) dates from the time of the Conqueror's half-brother, Robert, Count of Mortain, who was given possession of Berkhamsted by William.

Falaise Castle (Calvados, France). In 1027 William the Conqueror was born in the château de Falaise. The castle is now a ruin, although the original keep is still well preserved, and the chapel dates from the Conqueror's time. The castle dominates the town, which lies thirty kilometres south of Caen on the N158.

Gloucester Cathedral (Glos.). In 1072 William the Conqueror made his friend, Serlo, the first abbot of the new foundation of an abbey which, with a monastery, had been founded in honour of St Peter as long ago as 681. Serlo destroyed the old church, and commenced a new one on the same site, much of which is still standing. The monastery (one of the great Benedictine houses) suffered severely from fires during the twelfth and thirteenth centuries, but repair and restoration work was continuous, and Serlo's church remained the monastery's place of worship until the Dissolution, which for this monastery took place in 1540. Henry VIII then created the diocese of Gloucester, from what was a part of the large Worcester diocese.

This magnificent cathedral, with its breathtakingly beautiful Great Cloister, which was begun in 1373, is the repository of much English history. It was on the site of the present chapter house, leading off the cloister, that William, on Christmas Day 1085, ordered the preparation of the Domesday Book. Apart from the crypt, and Norman nave, there is an interesting legacy of the Conqueror's time in the memorial to his eldest son, Robert Duke of Normandy. This unsatisfactory ruler of Normandy had been defeated and captured by his younger brother, Henry I, at Tinchbrai, and spent the last twenty-eight years of his life a prisoner in Cardiff Castle, where he died in 1134. He was buried in the abbey, and a wooden sarcophagus surmounted by a painted wooden effigy can be seen in the middle of the presbytery. The effigy belongs to the thirteenth century, but the sarcophagus is of a much later date.

London, Westminster

St Stephen's Hall. This hall, which was the Chamber of the House of Commons between 1547 and 1834 (the Commons had no single regular meeting place before 1547), stands on the site of the chapel built by King Stephen. The chapel was pulled down in 1292 by Edward I to make way for a much grander two-storeyed building, the under storey of which is the present Chapel of St Mary Undercroft – the crypt chapel of the House of Commons.

The Tower of London. In the south-east corner of the Roman city, William I erected a strongpoint to overawe the populace. It was originally probably constructed in wood, but the Conqueror instructed Bishop Gundulf of Rochester (a renowned military architect) at some point after 1077 to build a stone keep. Twenty years later his keep was completed: a massive building, combining, inside a strong defensive position, living quarters, offices, store rooms and a small, beautifully simple chapel dedicated to St John. This keep, later to be known as the White Tower (Henry III had it whitewashed inside and out), was of a size and spaciousness that had not been seen before in England, and its grandeur was enhanced by the severity of the Caen stone.

Westminster Hall. This is the only survivor of three great halls built by the first two Norman kings principally for accommodating the large number of magnates who were present when the court celebrated any of the principal feasts – the other two were at Winchester and Gloucester.

William Rufus had Westminster Hall built during the 1090s, and is said to have held his court there for the first time in 1099. It was 240 feet long by $67\frac{1}{2}$ feet wide, and was the biggest hall in England. Nevertheless, at its completion Rufus was said to have complained that it was 'too big for a chamber and not big enough for a hall'. Although it has undergone considerable alteration and repair, it has never been enlarged and the walls below the level of the string-course are substantially unaltered.

The New Forest (Hants.). The alleged site of the tree near which William Rufus was killed stands about a quarter of a mile to the north of the A31 road from Ringwood to Cadnam, some three miles south-west of Cadnam. The site is marked by a memorial stone conveniently laying the blame for an *accident* on history's scapegoat, Sir Walter Tyrell.

Rochester Castle (Kent). The first castle at this strategically important place, where the Dover road crosses the Medway, was built soon after the Conquest, but the present fortress dates from William Rufus's time and was the work of Bishop Gundulf of Rochester. Around 1127, in the reign of Henry I, the Great Keep was added. Gundulf's walled enclosure was surrounded on the landward side by a moat, and the remains of this can still be seen, but the most impressive ruin is the keep, now maintained by the Department of the Environment.

Winchester, Hants.
Hospital of St Cross. Henry of Blois, brother of King Stephen, founded the hospital in 1136 for the maintenance of thirteen poor men. Three hundred years later, Cardinal Beaufort made an endowment to support eight impoverished noblemen. These almshouses are thought to be the oldest in Britain, and their full complement is twenty-five brothers – seventeen black brothers, who wear a black gown and cap denoting the earliest foundation, and eight red brothers, who represent Cardinal Beaufort's endowment. St Cross is on the A333 road a mile to the south of Winchester.

Windsor Castle (Berks.). William I quickly realized the strategic importance of the chalk eminence in the Thames Valley, which was the only natural strongpoint for a fortification between Wallingford and London. Here he built Windsor Castle. No building stone is to be found at Windsor, and, as William was in a hurry, his castle was a wooden construction with an inner line of defence and a deep ditch which spanned the castle from the northern escarpment to the southern palisade. Rather naturally, nothing remains above ground of William's fortress; Henry II replaced with stone his great-grandfather's wooden stockades.

4

THE PLANTAGENET DYNASTY

The Angevins

On ascending the throne, Henry II wasted no time in setting about the task of putting right the damage that had been done during the long and dark years of civil strife. The new King was a short, thick-set man completely careless of appearance, capable of considerable charm and courtesy, but possessing a violent temper, which for the most part he kept under control. Cunning, yet cultivated, Henry had a boundless energy that was a constant source of anxiety to both friend and foe. Equally proficient on the battlefield and in the council chamber; he made friends with Churchmen, but not with the Church.

In March 1152 Louis VII of France and his queen, Eleanor of Aquitaine, obtained a divorce on the rather spurious grounds of consanguinity, and the exceedingly wealthy and attractive heiress was snapped up by Henry – then in his twentieth year – with an opportunism that outstripped the aspiring Count of Blois. Already Duke of Normandy, Henry by this marriage became (under the nominal suzerainty of the French King) the master of south-western France, which with Anjou and Maine gave him a kingdom that stretched from the Cheviots to the Pyrenees.

His reign divides itself fairly naturally into three parts. The early years of consolidation, during which Henry dismantled many of the castles that had been illegally constructed during the previous reign, brought the barons into obedience, restored the overlordship of Wales, recalled the grant of the northern counties from the Scottish king and with the help of his most able and devoted Chancellor, Thomas Becket, pointed the country once more towards peace and security. Then came the long quarrel with this same Chancellor by then (1162) Archbishop of Canterbury, which culminated with Becket's murder in 1170. Lastly came the years of sorrow when his ungrateful and scheming sons were at the centre of rebellions both in England and in France. Superimposed on these three main channels were lengthy preoccupations with his vast Continental domains, his involvement in Irish and Welsh affairs and, above all, his enduring work on law reform.

Henry is best remembered for the unfortunate affair with his archbishop, whereas his true memorial should lie in those institutions he created that long outlived him, the most important of which – in slightly altered form – are with us to this day. Throughout his reign, and in particular during the last ten years when he had the help of his great Justiciar, Rannulf de Glanville, Henry was busy reviving and adding to the work of his grandfather, Henry I. Itinerant judges were again assigned to regular circuits of the counties, and although trial by ordeal still survived, trial by jury as a definite legal instrument was one of his innovations. The various assizes and constitutions that proclaimed Henry's laws had one principal object, which was to unite the nation under the King's law. To see the fair administration of this law in the shire and hundred courts, or in Westminster Hall, by the King's judges was the great ambition of his life. In making the system of freehold tenure subject, in the case of dispute, to the royal and not the baronial courts he turned a feudal state into a nation; but his attempt to extend the powers of the temporal courts over those of the spiritual, when a crime had been committed against the law of the land, brought about the conflict with the Church and Thomas Becket.

Thomas Becket had a complex character with an adaptability that reflected genius. He combined astute political insight with a grandeur at first of person and latterly of spirit. He believed passionately in whatever cause he embraced; as Chancellor he was able to identify himself with Henry's views, however extreme, but as Archbishop he became the uncompromising champion of the Church and obdurately resisted every attempt by Henry to reform the ecclesiastical law. As Chancellor he was always resplendent in the most gorgeous clothes; when he died as Archbishop he was found to be wearing a horse-hair shirt that was crawling with lice

Persuaded, against his better judgement, to become Archbishop in 1162 he immediately, to Henry's chagrin, resigned the chancellorship. There were to be no more hours of shared work and sport that had cemented the close friendship of King and Chancellor; instead, there soon began a momentous struggle lasting over eight years and terminating in the tragic mistake of murder. The disputes between the two men were varied, but could be summarized in Becket's contention that the Church was the giver, and not the receiver, of laws and above the King's jurisdiction.

In 1164 the Archbishop was worsted by what became known as the Constitutions of Clarendon, and having reluctantly signed the document soon, to the King's fury, reneged. That year he fled the kingdom and for the next six years remained in France, while both parties stood rigidly upon their rights and resisted all attempts at mediation. A formula for his return, which Becket knew very well was no more than an armed truce, was worked out at the end of 1170, and in December of that year the Archbishop returned to his see.

He found his lands despoiled and his barns pillaged, and while the common folk greeted him in their thousands with tears of joy, there were others more important who hounded and insulted him. Not long before his return, Henry had taken the unprecedented step for England of having his eldest son, also called Henry, crowned and, in defiance of tradition, the ceremony had been performed by Becket's great enemy the Archbishop of York. Becket had replied by getting the Pope to excommunicate York and the bishops who assisted him, and on Christmas Day he thundered out a sermon in Canterbury Cathedral denouncing those responsible for his present misfortunes and pronouncing sentence of excommunication on a number of them. It was on hearing of this that Henry, who was then near Bayeux, in a fit of fury bellowed, 'What idle and coward knaves have I nourished as vassals, that faithless to their oaths, they suffer their lord to be mocked by a low-born priest!'

The result of these hasty words is well known; four knights slipped quietly away to the coast and taking boat to Kent committed on 29 December the crime that was to cause Henry so much trouble and genuine remorse, and which was to preserve for a further four hundred years the liberties of the Church.

It is a measure of Henry's greatness that he overcame the national and international obloquy poured upon him for the terrible consequences of a momentary loss of temper. For a short time his throne was in the balance, but the Pope, who might well have excommunicated him, was impressed by his deep-felt grief at the deed and in any case had need of him in his struggle with the Holy Roman Emperor. Henry, for his part, no longer perplexed by the furious fulminations of his Archbishop, quickly reasserted himself and undiscouraged by the malice of his enemies turned his indefatigable mind to the problem of Ireland.

Looking at the whole Irish question with hindsight we need not be unduly surprised to learn that the first attempts to subjugate the wild men in their primitive bogs was a story of bloodshed, disappointment and partial failure. Before this time the English had made no attempt to disturb the rule of the sword – or more accurately the axe – through which the Irish kinglets rose and fell, and although in 1155 the English Pope Adrian IV had tried to persuade Henry to undertake the reform of the Irish Church, an opportunity for intervention in Irish affairs did not present itself for more than ten years. But when in 1167 Dermot MacMurrogh, King of Leinster – a particularly brutish man – found himself in difficulties he appealed to Henry for help.

Henry was too preoccupied and Dermot got help first from King Rhys of south Wales and then from Richard, Earl of Pembroke (Strongbow). In January 1171 Dermot died and by the summer of that year, after a certain amount of treachery and a series of bloody fights and sieges, the Earl of Pembroke was able to present Henry with the keys of Dublin, Waterford and Wexford. The King himself was in Ireland from October 1171 until April 1172, and established the English settlement which, until 1185, under a series of competent administrators, continued to grow in strength. But in April of that year Henry sent his pampered youngest son John – then a boy of eighteen – to become King of Ireland. Within six months John and his courtiers had completely antagonized all the Irish chieftains, and had he not abandoned his mission, all earlier achievements would have been undone. When Henry died his work in Ireland was incomplete; law and order existed within the confines of a fairly narrow English pale, but in the bogs and mountains beyond, personal and tribal vendettas were as bitter as ever.

As Henry moved towards the dusk of his life, family troubles and disloyalties made the closing years ones of sorrow. Throughout most of the last nineteen years he was plagued by border raids and tiresome rebellions – more especially in his Continental dominions. But there were moments of triumph; those of the barons who thought they had grievances against the King, and therefore supported in England the rebellion of his eldest son, were completely subdued in the course of a year; the Welsh princes were brought back to their allegiance; and, best of all, in 1174 William the Lion of Scotland, who had also marched on behalf of the young Henry, was captured. But on the Continent affairs continued to be far from happy.

The vivacious and hot-blooded Eleanor of Aquitaine was not the type of Queen to submit tamely to the royal libido. And besides the famous 'fair Rosamond' Clifford there were other ladies to cause her concern – including, perhaps, her intended daughter-in-law, Alice of France. When, therefore, she was not in prison at the command of her husband, Eleanor spent her time promoting the cause of her sons with her former husband the King of France, and inciting them to rebellion.

Louis needed little prompting to take up the cause of the brothers, the three eldest of whom had been given by their father too much land and power too soon for the health and happiness of everyone. In 1173 Henry, known as the Young King, his brothers Richard and Geoffrey (John was only six then), pledged themselves never to forsake the King of France nor make peace with their father save through him, and Louis for his part agreed to assist the Young King to gain the throne of England. For the next sixteen years, with only the briefest of breaks, Henry was fighting against his sons, sometimes against all of them, at other times with one against the others.

Richard clung to Aquitaine with ruthless determination; neither King Henry (who wanted it for his youngest son, John Lackland) nor the rebellious barons (who wanted it for themselves) could overthrow him, and, although only eighteen, he already had the makings of a fine commander. In 1175 he patched up his quarrel with his father, and in 1183 was found in arms with the King against his brothers Henry and Geoffrey. The Young King died in 1183 and his brother Geoffrey three years later; both of them steeped in rebellion against their father and deeply involved with Philip Augustus, the new King of France. But Henry's agony was not over for a further three years. The end came in 1189, with Richard again in revolt, Henry's beloved Le Mans destroyed by his enemies, and, cruellest blow of all, the ungrateful John vitiated, like his brothers, by selfishness and greed, turned against him. Sunk in misery, weighed down by treachery, Henry gave up the struggle on 6 July. He was buried at Fontevrault, where his body still lies.

Richard was in no hurrry to return to the country of which he was now King. He left it to his mother to prepare the way for his triumphant homecoming. Entering London in September, the new King was greeted on all sides with overwhelming enthusiasm. His subjects were not to know that in the course of a ten-year reign he would spend less than that number of months in England, and pillage the country's treasures and Treasury for the purposes of conducting an almost continual Continental war, to launch him on a crusade and to rescue him from the clutches of the Holy Roman Emperor.

One should not judge Richard as a King, for he was scarcely more than a chivalrous knight with a touch of the troubadour, called by birth to rule and by inclination to fight. Tough, masterful and at times ruthless and vindictive – characteristics in common with other princes of that time – he was, unlike many of them, colourful and capable of occasional flashes of charm. If he did not perform the duties of a King, he certainly contrived to look like one. A tall man with long reddish-gold hair, well proportioned and of great physical strength, he displayed enormous energy when not suffering from bouts of recurring fever. Although he had the outward appearance of a warrior, and was indeed a commander in the field of rare distinction and unquestioned courage, there was another side to the man which showed a well-developed aesthetic sense. Brought up in France by an adored and adoring mother,

Richard acquired a love of fine clothes and beautiful things. He was a self-confessed homosexual and inclined to make love and drink to excess.

The King's coronation on 3 September 1189 was the most splendid spectacle the Londoners had yet seen; but after it came the reckoning. Richard's one over-riding desire was to quit England as soon as possible and join the Third Crusade to retake Jerusalem, which had fallen to the Saracens, under their great leader Saladin, two years before. But first money had to be raised by all and every means. The King virtually put his kingdom up to auction; counties and castles came under the hammer; the regents were required to pay huge sums for their privilege; scutage (a tax payable in lieu of military service) was levied; sheriffs were dismissed and forced to buy back their offices; and William the Lion, King of the Scots, was enabled to regain his English estates on payment of a large sum. In this way the money 'rolled like nuts in the Exchequer', and on 12 December 1189 the King sailed from Dover for Normandy.

Affairs in Normandy and Anjou occupied much of 1190, but in the late summer Richard set off overland to Naples and from there he took ship to Sicily, where he joined his army and the French King who had preceded him. The winter months were spent in skirmishing and bickering with Tancred, the last Norman King of Sicily, and in trying to pacify Philip of France, much incensed at Richard's refusal to marry Alice, who had undergone a most humiliating courtship. She was well out of the marriage, for Richard was not destined to make a good husband; while in Sicily his mother produced Berengaria of Navarre as a bride, whom he married a little later in Limassol. It is doubtful if he ever loved her better than he did his mother, and she certainly played little part in his life.

He left Sicily in April 1191, Cyprus was captured in quick time by means of a brilliantly successful military operation and at last, in July, the English King arrived before the walls of Acre to join the other crusaders, some of whom had been there for a very long time. Indeed, the siege of Acre had been in progress for two years and more than 100,000 crusaders had been killed or had died during its investment.

The fifteen months that Richard spent in the Holy Land were ones of audacity and excitement; he was by far the greatest warrior-prince to oppose Saladin, whose open admiration he evoked. He put new heart into the besiegers and with the example of his personal valour before them they took the city before a relieving Saracen host could arrive. There followed the great victory at Arsuf, which opened the road from Jaffa to Jerusalem, and although he failed to lead his men in triumph against Jerusalem, before he left – on receipt of disturbing news concerning his brother John from England – Richard had concluded a treaty with Saladin that secured the pilgrims' way for a further fifty years.

The journey home was a strange adventure and no one knows what prompted Richard to choose the long and dangerous overland route through Austria, whose Duke Leopold he had antagonized in the Holy Land. It ended with thirteen months spent in the Emperor's dungeons and a ransom of 150,000 silver marks, which was twice the annual revenue of England. It was a measure of their need for him that his subjects, in order to purchase his return, were willing to sacrifice the immense treasure that had built up in church and city coffers.

During Richard's long absence abroad affairs in England had kept a steady course. At no time was there a return to the anarchy of Stephen's reign, although for a while serious anti-Jewish rioting cast its shadow over the country. But occasional dangers and difficulties arose, chiefly through the oppressive antics of William de Longchamp, Richard's Chancellor and Justiciar, and the ambitions of Prince John. The former made himself so unpopular that he had to flee the country disguised as a woman, while John's behaviour was much as might be expected from a medieval prince who had learnt that he had not been nominated to succeed his brother. He intrigued with the enemies of the State and did his best to usurp the throne, before eventually agreeing to assist in the collection of the King's ransom. When Richard reached England on 13 March 1194, John had prudently removed himself to Normandy in the shadow of King Philip, but some of his supporters still held out in various castles.

Richard, having reduced one of the last of these – Nottingham – proceeded to levy yet more money through auctions, scutage and land taxes. Possibly some of this went towards paying for his second coronation, because immediately after that curious event another great auction of public offices was held and then, after only six weeks in England, the King joined his fleet at Portsmouth and sailed for Normandy for the last time.

Much of the remaining five years of Richard's life were spent alternately in fighting and parleying with King Philip, building his almost impregnable fortress, Château Gaillard, and, when occasion demanded, in carrying fire and sword through his own rebellious territories. The end came – appropriately enough – when he was in pursuit of treasure trove found near Limoges, which had not been entirely surrendered. A simple siege, a solitary archer, a crossbow bolt from the blue, and Richard Coeur de Lion was mortally wounded. He died on 6 April 1199 and was buried beside his father at Fontevrault. Summoned to his death-bed the archer was forgiven, and even rewarded, by the King; but his sister, Joan, was not impressed with such magnanimity. She had the man blinded, flayed and ripped apart by horses.

Richard I spoke no English and spent only ten months of his reign in England, but through his courage on the battlefield he greatly enhanced the reputation of his country abroad, and through his long absences he proved that the institutions which his father had built up were strong enough in themselves to ensure justice and stave off anarchy.

In the last years of his reign, King Richard had forgiven his brother for his wayward behaviour during his absence, and John had fought in Richard's army during the King's final campaign in France. When Richard died, John was staying with his nephew, Arthur (his brother Geoffrey's son), in Brittany, but he wasted no time in claiming his inheritance. It is said (without any certainty) that as he lay dying Richard, who had formerly favoured Arthur, did in fact nominate John to succeed him. In any event the Archbishop of Canterbury, the Chief Justiciar and William the Marshal – the principal statesmen of the time – decided that John was preferable to Arthur and on 27 May 1199 John was crowned in Westminster Abbey.

John's reputation has suffered at the hands of two chroniclers, Roger of Wendover and Matthew Paris. Both were deeply influenced by that period when he dared to take issue with Holy Church; both displayed a vivid imagination and wrote a picturesque but biased account that was often wildly inaccurate. John certainly possessed most of the vices of the Devil's Brood (as the Angevins were sometimes called), but also some of their virtues. He was by no means totally bad; indeed much that he did was good.

John was nearly thirty-two when he came to the throne. Like most of his forebears he was thickly built, but at five feet five inches he was small even for those days, and therein may lie the key to at least one facet of his character, for it is not unknown for small men in positions of authority to attempt to assert themselves by pompous posturing. He had inherited his father's violent temper; he was capable of capricious and tyrannical acts, but he was not noticeably more cruel or ruthless than many rulers of that time. He possessed considerable patience and understanding, was intelligent, and had a keen interest in learned books. John was a cunning man and (with some reason) deeply suspicious. He was a kindly and considerate husband – which was more than could be said for his father or brother – and he loved the good life. In military matters, the fact that he had only two real victories (Mirebeau and Rochester) is no reflection on his prowess as a soldier. He was a good commander, but lacked the luck to be a successful one.

In a far from trouble-free reign, three principal events stand out –

John's continuing enmity with the King of France that was to cost him Normandy and a fair slice of his Angevin Empire; his quarrel with the Pope over Stephen Langton; and the long struggle with some of his more recalcitrant barons. Meanwhile, his administration of home affairs – particularly his interest and concern with the process of law – and his Irish, Scottish and Welsh problems were dealt with skilfully and firmly.

In England and Normandy John had been elected King in preference to Arthur, but this was not so in Maine, Anjou and Touraine, where the barons chose the twelve-year-old Prince. Nevertheless, by 1200 John was recognized as the lawful master of the Angevin Empire. But two years later war broke out with Philip through John's failure to attend the French King's court in Paris to resolve problems over his marriage with Isabelle of Angoulême. At first all went well for John; Arthur's attempt to capture his grandmother (that truly remarkable old lady, Queen Eleanor) on her way to assist her son, resulted in a rapid and perfectly executed manoeuvre by John that not only saved the Queen, but ensnared Arthur and a number of rebel leaders.

After his capture at Mirebeau Arthur was sent to Falaise and was heard of no more. That John had him killed can hardly be doubted, but how and where will never be known. There was nothing unusual in this; murder was an occupational hazard for claimants to the throne, especially if they indulged in rebellion. The rest of the campaign was not distinguished; although John narrowly failed to bring off a masterpiece of tactics. An ambitious combined land and water operation to relieve the threatened Château Gaillard foundered on the essential requirement of synchronization – the river-borne force being late onto their objective. Depressed with this failure, and the growing disloyalty of his Norman barons, John returned to England at the end of 1203 to raise money for further operations, leaving his castellans to hold out until his return.

The end of Normandy became certain when Château Gaillard fell in March 1204. Caen, Bayeux, and Coutances soon surrendered, and on 24 June, with no relief in view, the commander of Rouen admitted the French King to the capital. To Englishmen at that time the loss of Empire was a great blow, and for the rest of his reign John's thoughts and energies were constantly turned towards the regaining of his lost possessions. But with hindsight we can see that in due course that loss was inevitable, and even at the time it had advantages, for it enabled England to become for the first time since the Conquest more inward looking, and to concentrate on developing its own rather than an alien culture.

The long drawn out quarrel with Pope Innocent III followed a deadlock over the successor to Hubert Walter in the see of Canterbury.

John, who incidentally had a flair for choosing good men for positions of importance, wanted John Gray, Bishop of Norwich, but the monks of Christ Church Priory, Canterbury, whose prerogative it was to elect the archbishop, had their own candidate. The Pope, on being appealed to, attempted to resolve the problem with a nominee of his own, Stephen Langton, one of the most distinguished scholars and Churchmen of the day. John was adamant that he would not have Langton; tempers became frayed, reason flew out of the window and in March 1208 the Pope placed a sentence of interdict* upon England, and eighteen months later excommunicated John.

It has been said that the withdrawal of Church services at a time when people were deeply religious was a terrible deprivation, but it does not seem to have had much outward effect other than to enable John to greatly enrich his treasury through the sequestration of Church property. The personal excommunication, on the other hand, bit deep because it offered Philip a splendid opportunity, backed by papal authority, to invade the kingdom of a man whose barons were thinking in terms of deposition (and even murder) and some of whose subjects, especially those in Scotland, Ireland and Wales, were rumbling into opposition. Clearly something had to be done, and John in his cunning adroitly turned the tables on his opponents.

In May 1213 he drew up a document granting to the Pope and his successors the entire realm, and agreeing to become his vassal. At the same time, he seems to have been considering an even more startling measure. It is known that he sent emissaries to Mohámed el-Nassir the Moorish Emir, and if we are to believe Matthew Paris's story (which is probably greatly embellished), he offered to place his kingdom under the Emir's suzerainty and adopt Mohammedanism. In any event, by putting himself and his country under the protection of Rome, John check-mated Philip's well-advanced invasion plans, and, having got the French King at a disadvantage, inflicted a severe defeat on his ships with his own navy. Archbishop Langton, at last established on the throne of St Augustine, absolved John from his excommunication, but soon showed his disapproval at the King's *volte-face*, which put the English Church too much in the power of Rome, and with one of those quirks of fate was shortly to find himself suspended from his functions by the Pope who had pressed upon him the primateship.

By the beginning of 1214 John was ready to launch a major offensive against Philip in the hope of regaining his lost French territory. He had for some months past been building up an alliance with his nephew Otto of Germany and, among others, the counts of Holland, Flanders and

* An interdict meant that all Church services ceased.

Boulogne. The grand design was a pincer movement to crush Philip somewhere in the region north of Paris. John would approach from the south and his allies come in from Flanders in the north.

The King landed at La Rochelle in February 1214 at the head of a formidable army – mostly mercenaries, for a great many of his barons had refused his summons for overseas service. After executing a series of marches and countermarches across Poitou, Anjou and Touraine, avoiding battle but consolidating his position and confusing his adversary, John found his way north barred by a large army commanded by Philip's son, Prince Louis. At this point his Poitou barons decided to desert him and John, always fearful of treachery and its results, abandoned much of his equipment and hastily recrossed the Loire.

Louis did not pursue, but the bloodless victory enabled him to send a part of his force to aid his father for the decisive action in the north. At Bouvines in Flanders Philip utterly defeated John's allies. This, the only pitched battle of the campaign, firmly established the French monarchy; destroyed John's hopes of regaining the lost parts of his former Empire; and pointed the way down the miry road that led to Runnymede.

John arrived back in England on 13 October 1214 to face the cupidity, ambitions and grievances of a discontented baronage. An outward calm had only thinly veiled a seething discontent for some years past; the northern barons in particular resented the royal interference and but for John's successful campaign against the Scottish King in 1209, they might have made trouble earlier. When it came to actual rebellion in May 1215 not all of the barons, not even most of them, but enough to be effective were in revolt. The trouble originated with Henry II's reforms, and although John had made some concessions, these did not noticeably relax the royal control, and he had recently levied a heavy scutage on those knights who had broken their contract by refusing military service. This, heaped upon taxes and curtailment of privileges, real and imagined, was remorselessly used to make a case for rebellion against a recently defeated and humiliated King.

John might have made a pre-emptive strike and nipped rebellion in the bud, but he hesitated for fear of antagonizing the neutrals – who formed the larger part of the baronage – and he knew that his case was not so strong as in 1212, when the leaders of the dissident group were contemplating much more drastic action. Now the cry was back to the Charter of Henry I, a useful platform which some say Langton had suggested. And so John took what precautions he could. He had the Pope squarely on his side as soon as he had promised to take the Cross; he procured the use of Rochester Castle from Stephen Langton, and he brought over Poitevin and Flemish mercenaries. Nevertheless, he always hoped to avoid war and, after a bad beginning, when London fell to the rebels and outbreaks of violence flared up throughout the country, he asked Langton, who was respected by both sides, to arrange a truce. The result was the celebrated meeting on 15 June in Runnymede meadow.

Magna Carta was a long reactionary document of some sixty-three articles that were chiefly concerned to clarify the rights and privileges of the upper classes. It set out to loosen the stranglehold of central government, and to curtail the power of the crown. That government was not above the law was one of its fundamentals; another was the right of justice and fair trial for all. But it ignored many important matters, and it offered no hope of immediate peace, for it sought too much from the King. One clause alone (61) set up a council of twenty-five barons who were given the job of ensuring baronial rights with the power of enforcement if the articles of peace were broken – in fact a licence to rebel, which no king could countenance. The importance of this rather hastily prepared document was that it formed the basis of the Great Charter issued in the next reign.

Neither party was content with what had been done at Runnymede, and the feeble peace soon collapsed. The closing year of King John's life was perhaps his greatest. He found himself at bay with many of the towns ranged against him, his capital city in the hands of the rebels, the Welsh and Scots on the side of his foes, and Louis the son of his lifelong enemy, King Philip of France, in England at the head of a French army. But he had the valuable support of the Pope, some of the most distinguished barons remained loyal, and he commanded a tough mercenary force to whom war and bloodshed were a profession. With this armament he did battle on the whole successfully, showing considerable energy, military skill, and at the end an amazing capacity to overcome and endure the exhaustion of an ailing body.

The King was at Dover when the peace was broken and his first engagement, and signal success, was the taking of Rochester Castle*, which opened the way for other rebel strongholds to follow suit and surrender. There was to be no close season for fighting during the winter of 1215–1216, and John, in a lightning campaign through the midlands and north, delivered a series of hammer-blows that struck a chill in the heart of all rebels – and incidentally devastated the homes of many poor people who had no part or interest in this quarrel. By the spring of 1216 it seemed that the King must have triumphed, had not the call to France

* This virtually inexpugnable fortress was eventually taken through mining below the south-east corner of the keep. Visitors to the castle can easily appreciate the magnitude of such a task.

from the rebel leaders in London been answered, and Louis landed at Thanet on 22 May.

John, probably fearful that his mercenaries might not fight fellow Frenchmen, refused an open fight with Louis, and that summer the Prince did much as he pleased in the south until the garrison at Winchester checked him. But elsewhere John's castles held firm and he spent the late summer strengthening his hand along the Welsh marches. By September the King was ready to undertake another rapid foray north, and he hoped to catch the Scottish King on his way home from doing homage to Louis in London. In this he failed, but his campaign in the fen country and Lincolnshire was everywhere successful.

By the middle of October John was a very sick man, but he refused to deviate from the grilling regime of endless riding, fighting and – probably the worst of all for him – feasting. The loss of his regalia at the mouth of the Welland must have been a crushing blow, for John loved his jewels, but he struggled on, to die in the Bishop of Lincoln's castle at Newark on 19 October 1216. Before he died he made those present swear fealty to his son, Henry, and expressed a wish to be buried in Worcester Cathedral, where his splendid tomb, topped by his effigy carved in Purbeck marble, can still be seen.

John left a divided kingdom; Louis held London and much of the south-east, and in the north there were still a number of rebellious barons. But by his death John had preserved his dynasty, for almost all the barons would prefer a boy king of their own royal line to a usurping Frenchman. Moreover, Henry – hastily crowned in Gloucester Cathedral on 28 October, with a gold circlet doing duty for the lost crown – was in capable hands. That venerable royal servant, William the Marshal, agreed to become Regent; and although the somewhat dangerous Bishop of Winchester, Peter des Roches, insisted on being the King's guardian, the strong arm of the Justiciar, Hubert de Burgh, was only temporarily employed in the defence of Dover Castle and would soon become available.

Two decisive victories, one on land at Lincoln and the other at sea off Dover, destroyed Louis' hopes, and under generous terms of surrender he sailed away in September 1217, leaving Henry the undisputed King of England. The difficult and dangerous times at the beginning of the reign were responsible for the reissuing of the Charter, which Pope Innocent had somewhat foolishly quashed in 1215, and to which his successor, Honorius III, and that champion of liberty, Stephen Langton, now gave their blessing and encouragement. The new Charter did indeed modify some of the more obnoxious clauses to the royal prerogative, and there was a separate Forest Charter. A further reissue took place in 1219, and in 1225 under the guidance of de Burgh it was renewed in virtually its final form. Hubert de Burgh was a great statesman and soldier, and while his firm hand was on the helm the country gained strength. In 1232, however, five years after Henry had officially declared himself of an age to rule the kingdom, he hounded de Burgh out of office in particularly shabby circumstances, and the affairs of State began to go downhill.

Henry was a man of medium height and strong build with a handsome head enhanced by a prominent nose; his otherwise fine features were spoilt by a drooping eyelid. He was capable of great charm (although his affection was chiefly reserved for those who flattered him) and his piety was absolutely genuine. But there was much to dislike about him. He was weak, and like so many weak men he was obstinate; he was quick-tempered, vainglorious and a decided sybarite. At a time when the country needed a strong hand and dominant personality, he was too easily influenced by bad advice and inclined to surround himself with the Savoyard and Provençal relations of Queen Eleanor and his disagreeable half-brothers. Frequently forced to bow to the passions of the hour, he was incapable of honouring any pledge.

With de Burgh gone and des Roches once more at his side, the King slid from one crisis to another: conflicts with his prelates and some of his barons, who were determined that he should rule without the help of his foreign friends; a disastrous campaign in France trying to regain the French possessions that his father had lost; punitive expeditions against the Welsh princes; and in 1254, worst of all follies, an entanglement with the Pope over an offer (with exorbitant financial liabilities attached) of the Sicilian crown for his second son, Edmund.

By 1258 it had become clear to almost everyone that Henry III was a failure as a King. The actual crisis of this year was a financial one, brought about by the absolute refusal of the Great Council to advance any money for the ridiculous Sicilian adventure. The King had always maintained the closest relationship with Rome, much to the annoyance of his own clergy, who greatly resented the papal place-men and extortions. He must therefore have been deeply distressed when his ally the Pope, weary of his weakness and vacillation, threatened to excommunicate him and bring the whole land under an interdict unless the money for the expedition was quickly forthcoming. Clearly something had to be done; but the barons had had enough of foreign interlopers and illusory empires and demanded certain safeguards as the price for rescuing their King from his stubborn ineptitude. About the end of April, a small cabal of the more powerful of their number headed a party of knights who arrived armed at the Palace of Westminster, and so frightened the King that he agreed that a committee of twenty-four should meet at Oxford on 11 June to draw up terms for what was to become a constitutional revolution.

The foreigners would have to go, but there would also have to be total administrative reform. Government in future could not be conducted by the king alone, but by the king in council. The Provisions of Oxford provided for conciliar government that was cumbersome and complex, but in that summer of 1258 England took an important step forward along the road to constitutional monarchy; and through the Provisions of Westminster, which came into force a year later, important changes were effected in land tenure and a much needed curb was put on ecclesiastical and baronial jurisdiction. The Provisions of Oxford were a form of written constitution which laid down the method whereby the clergy and the barons were to play their part in the running of the country. The magnates, as well as the king, were called upon to fulfil certain obligations towards their tenants, and all took the oath in 1258 to uphold the terms of the Provisions. Henry took the oath and bided his time; but his son, the Lord Edward, reacted strongly against the new arrangements and was with difficulty persuaded to swear, perhaps by his father, who never could understand why anyone regarded an oath as binding.

The man who now began to come to the fore was Simon de Montfort, the younger son of a French count. He had married the King's sister, Eleanor, in 1228 and three years later came to England to claim his rather doubtful inheritance of the earldom of Leicester and stewardship of England. His relationship with the King was a love-hate one, with hate eventually predominating. In 1258 Simon was certainly not the leader of the barons, but when they began to weaken and Henry set about undermining the Provisions, he stood out as the most steadfast and determined of them all. In 1260, by which time Simon was their acknowledged leader, there was a cleavage in the baronial ranks, the powerful Earl of Gloucester had quarrelled with Simon and Henry was quick to make capital out of this split. Simon went into voluntary exile and Henry then felt strong enough to revoke the Provisions and to revert to personal government with the aid of his foreign friends.

In April 1263, with the country crumbling into civil war, Simon returned from France and resumed the leadership of the diminishing band of magnates who were still prepared to honour their pledge. Fighting flared up, a truce was arranged and as a last resort Simon agreed that both parties should put their cases for arbitration by King Louis (who happened to have married a sister of Henry's Queen). Simon may have imagined that this saintly man would be scrupulously fair, but he must have known that kings stood for absolute monarchy. The Mise of Amiens, as Louis' award of January 1264 was called, was completely predictable: the total overthrow of the Provisions of Oxford and a reversion to the status quo of 1258. With the barons (or at least many of them) not prepared to surrender the fruits of their long, wearisome struggle, civil war became inevitable.

At the battle of Lewes, which was fought on 14 May 1264 over the downland running between Offham Hill and the present gaol, fortune, which had hitherto remained insensible to Simon's struggle, now favoured the barons. With an army half the size of the King's, they gained a surprising victory. The King, his son and his brother, Richard, Earl of Cornwall (the latter in somewhat ignominious circumstances) were all made prisoner, and Simon de Montfort became for a year the virtual dictator of England.

Simon's power was massive, but so were his problems. His only authority to rule was through the captive King, and for this purpose he set up a council of nine to advise the King, but with the real power residing in a triumvirate consisting of himself, the young Earl of Gloucester and Stephen Berksted, Bishop of Chichester. His autocratic and illegal position was never popular among a people who were staunchly monarchical: his firm hand smoothed out much of the chaos, but with the Lord Edward escaping from confinement and the barons falling out among themselves another armed contest became inevitable.

But before all hope of peace was lost there occurred in January 1265 a most important Parliament – important not for its deliberations, but for its composition. On this occasion, besides 120 clergy and 23 barons, the writ was broadened to include two burgesses from every city and town as well as two knights from every shire. Maybe the Commons were called because Simon needed their support, but the very fact that they were necessary shows a growing awareness that representatives of shires and boroughs had an integral part to play in the management of the country's affairs. The seed had been sown which King Edward was to nurture, and from which the modern polity of England would eventually emerge.

A campaign, which began in June 1265, ended with the battle of Evesham on 4 August. This time, squeezed between the arms of the River Severn, there was little room for manoeuvre, and with the barons again outnumbered by almost two to one the result was not just their defeat, but a two-hour massacre. Simon was hacked down fighting fiercely to the end, and later his body was dismembered. The King, brought along by Simon and unrecognizable in full armour, only saved himself by repeatedly calling out, 'I am Henry of Winchester, your King. Do not harm me.'

The Earl of Leicester was dead, but such was the plight of the Disinherited Barons, as they were called, that his war lingered on until, by 1267, the last of his followers had been winkled out of such formidable and inaccessible refuges as Kenilworth Castle and the Isle of Ely. For the next three years, until he went on a crusade in 1270, the Lord Edward was increasingly in charge of the country's affairs. Already a fine commander, he was soon to become a great King, who understood and espoused the more important causes for which his uncle had fought and died.

Henry III died on 16 November 1272. He had reigned for fifty-six years, and if he had not been a very wise and effective ruler, later generations are indebted to him for his love of art and architecture. In the early days of his reign, from the nearby Palace of Clarendon, Henry could watch the progress of Bishop Richard Poore's magnificent new cathedral as it stretched to the heavens amid the pastoral peace of Salisbury's water meadows. Perhaps this inspired him to his greatest contribution to posterity, the rebuilding of Westminster Abbey to the memory of its founder, Edward the Confessor. Besides these two major works the reign also witnessed the building of many abbeys, churches and chapels, which for centuries have enshrined the life and faith of our people.

The Plantagenets were enthusiastic builders; the larger part of most of the great castles surviving today date from the twelfth, thirteenth and fourteenth centuries. Westminster Abbey and Hall were virtually rebuilt by Plantagenet kings; many of their beautiful tombs, noble statues and monuments and other magnificent works of art, are still with us. There are also documents of considerable interest, relating to events of importance that occurred during these times, and which are either on view to the public or can be seen on application.

In the 120 years that span the reigns of the four kings discussed in this chapter there was a tremendous amount of building carried out on the orders or the inspiration of the various monarchs, both in England and in Normandy. Space will not permit a discussion of all the kings' works during this period, but the most important of those that can be readily visited are described below.

Beaulieu Abbey (Hants.). In 1200 King John was in contention with monks of the Cistercian Order in regard to the taxation of the large income that the Cistercians obtained from land. At some point King John, on learning that the Cistercians had rejected his tax demand, threatened – and possibly even carried out – certain reprisals. But in the course of time he repented of his action and not only withdrew his tax demands, but agreed to found a new Cistercian Abbey.

The site chosen in the New Forest, five miles south-east of Lyndhurst, was known as *Bellus Locus Regis*, which in the French became *Beau Lieu*, and later the place adopted the name of Beaulieu. At the time of its foundation, John expressed a wish to be buried at Beaulieu, but later in his will he opted for Worcester Cathedral, where he now lies.

In 1204 thirty monks and lay brothers from Cîteaux came to Beaulieu to found the new abbey, which was visited on three occasions by King John. During its time as an abbey, Beaulieu was a celebrated place of sanctuary, and gave refuge, among others, to Perkin Warbeck in 1497. In 1538 the abbey was largely destroyed after the Dissolution of the Monasteries, but fortunately certain parts – the gatehouse, cloister, and the monks' frater – were not entirely wrecked and these parts of the abbey can still be visited.

Bury St Edmunds Abbey (Suffolk). This great abbey, the dimensions of which can be easily traced amid the present impressive ruins, was begun about 1090. In 1095 the remains of St Edmund, the Christian King of East Anglia martyred by the Danes in 870, were translated from the old abbey church. The abbey was visited by Henry II and his two sons, Richard and John, and it was here on 20 November 1214 that Archbishop Langton read out to a number of assembled barons Henry I's charter, and the barons swore on either the high altar or the choir altar that unless King John adhered to the liberties granted in this charter, they would resort to arms against him. This meeting led inexorably, as the King's obstinacy and obscurantism continued, to Runnymede and Magna Carta. The names of the barons, near to the spot where they swore their oath, are listed for visitors to see. Apart from the ruins of the church, there is little left of the vast complex of buildings, which stood as a foremost Benedictine house until its dissolution in 1539; instead, in what was the great court, there is now a pleasant and colourful public garden.

Canterbury Cathedral (Kent). In December 1170 four knights, thinking to do their Lord and Sovereign's bidding, murdered Thomas Becket at the foot of the steps leading to the choir – the site of his martyrdom is now commemorated by a plaque. Henry II suffered genuine grief at the brutal killing of his Archbishop and former friend, and the aftermath of this unfortunate affair brought out the full greatness of the King.

The building of Canterbury Cathedral had been begun exactly a hundred years before Becket's murder, when Lanfranc became Archbishop of Canterbury. He built the cathedral along the lines of his abbey church at Caen, and the work was completed in the remarkably short time of seven years. Lanfranc's building was somewhat altered by his successor, Anselm, and four years after Becket's death it was largely destroyed by fire. Rebuilding went ahead throughout the last quarter of the twelfth century and the cathedral continued to be enlarged and beautified at various times during the fourteenth and fifteenth centuries.

Eure, France
Château Gaillard. Richard I built this great fortress 'the saucy castle', which

dominates the Seine at Les Andelys, and the work was completed in the incredibly short space of one year. Now it is only a ruin – but a very imposing one – and its principal interest lies in the magnificent feat of its construction, and the fact that, although fully provisioned, it was actually taken by the troops of the French King, Philip Augustus, in 1204.

The approach to the castle is along a one-way circular road from Grand Andely, and back via Petit Andely. Les Andelys is thirty-nine kilometres south-east of Rouen.

At **Chinon (Indre et Loire, France),** which lies on the north bank of the River Vienne, a tributary of the Loire, can be seen the ruins of the great Angevin fortress, which was the favourite residence in France of Henry II, and where both he and his son, Richard I, died. The château dominates the town from its high eminence overlooking the river. Here Joan of Arc begged Charles VII to allow her to lead an army against the English at Orléans, although the great hall, where the interview took place, and much else of the castle has long since disappeared.

Corfe Castle (Dorset). (See also Chapter 2.) This castle was used by King John as a safe retreat for Queen Isabelle and Prince Henry during the rebellion of 1215.

Dover Castle (Kent), of all the many medieval castles was, perhaps, the most important strategically, for it guarded the coast of England at its closest point to what was once an English possession, and later the land of the hereditary enemy. The present massive stone complex began with the erection of the rectangular keep by Henry II in the 1180s, but the modern castle stands on Roman ruins. Henry II also built the eastern side of the outer curtain with flanking towers, which indicate the beginnings of the concentric principle. More work on the castle was carried out in King John's time, when the castle featured prominently, withstanding, under the command of Hubert de Burgh, the assaults of the French troops led by Prince Louis. Henry III spent more than £7,000 on strengthening and improving the castle, principally completing the outer curtain, which, when finished, enclosed as much as thirty-five acres. His son, the Lord Edward, was confined for a time in the castle's dungeons after Henry's defeat at Lewes.

Battle of Evesham (Worcs.), 4 August 1265. It is difficult for visitors to see the site of this battlefield, much of which has been built over. The battle probably took place around Battle Well, now an overgrown tangle of grass and rubbish which lies off a rough track running due west, one hundred yards south of Twyford House, which stands about a mile north of Evesham on the road to Stratford. Here Prince Edward had his battle line, which Simon de Montfort, advancing from Evesham, strove to break, but he was enveloped by Edward's two flanking divisions, which virtually annihilated Simon's force. For a full account of this battle, and that of Lewes (page 77), see *Battles in Britain* (Sidgwick & Jackson, new edition 1979).

Fontevrault Abbey (Maine et Loire, France). In the abbey, which is situated in a beautiful, sequestered valley between Saumur and Chinon, just a few kilometres off the D947 road that runs parallel to the south bank of the Loire, lie buried King Henry II and his wife Eleanor of Aquitaine, King Richard I and King John's wife, Isabelle of Angoulême. The colouring on the effigies is in a state of remarkable preservation. Apart from the historical interest, the lovely abbey buildings and the cloisters are very well worth visiting. In the nearby St Michael's Church can be seen the altar that once stood in the abbey, and certain other adornments, including the abbey bell.

Gloucester Cathedral (Glos.). (See also Chapter 3.) On 28 October 1216, when the cathedral was the Benedictine Abbey of St Peter, it was the scene of Henry III's crowning when he was only nine years old.

Hailes Abbey (Glos.). This Cistercian Abbey was founded by Richard, Earl of Cornwall, Henry III's brother, and dedicated in 1251. No part of the medieval church remains above ground, but the walls of the cloister and of the chapter house are impressive, and the extensive excavations have revealed much of the abbey foundations and enable the visitor to follow the whole ground plan. There is a very good museum in the grounds with maps and documents portraying the history of the abbey. Earl Richard, like his brother, was a keen builder; he was responsible for large-scale works at both Wallingford and Launceston Castles and he also founded a nunnery for Augustinian canonesses at Burnham in Buckinghamshire. The Abbey lies two miles north-east of Winchcomb.

Opposite the abbey ruins is a delightful little parish church dating from the twelfth century, with some fascinating, partly restored, medieval wall paintings.

Kenilworth Castle (Warwicks.). Henry II took over Kenilworth from the de Clinton family, and from then until the time of the Civil War the castle played an important part in English history. It was at this time a very imposing and exceptionally strong lake-fortress. Henry II did not in fact occupy the castle, for de Clinton remained in possession, but it was surrendered to King John in 1199, and he visited it on several occasions between 1204 and 1215. He spent a considerable sum of money building the outer wall and strengthening the twelfth century keep, both of which can still be seen. Henry III foolishly gave the castle to Simon de Montfort, and although Henry's son, the Lord Edward, gained a decisive tactical victory over the younger de Montfort's army in 1265, he did not capture the castle. After Simon de Montfort's death at Evesham that same year, the castle was held by his son, also Simon, against all assaults by the royal troops, and was only surrendered through lack of food. Henry III then gave it to his second son Edmund, Earl of Lancaster.

Le Mans (Sarthe, France). On the south-eastern outskirts of this town, which lies to the north of the Angers-Orléans axis, the Abbey of Our Lady of Epau is situated in quiet surroundings, still unspoilt by the sprawl of Le Mans. It was founded in the thirteenth century (building took from 1229 until the dedication by the Bishop of Le Mans in 1234), by Berengaria, Richard I's Queen, and her tomb with its pleasant effigy can be seen in the south transept of the large church. It is the only monument or tomb in the whole church and is impressive for its simplicity. The chapter house and other parts of the monastery, as well as the church, are open to the public, but the abbey is not easy to find; the approach from the centre of the town is by a turning off the Paris–Orléans road through a new housing estate, at the end of which it is signposted.

Battle of Lewes (Sussex), 14 May 1264. It is still perfectly possible to examine the ground over which this battle was fought, just to the north of Lewes. There are tracks and footpaths leading to a very good vantage point at the top of Offham Hill. Simon de Montfort drew up the Barons' army in four divisions on the downs above Offham, while Henry III's troops occupied the area immediately to the north of the gaol. The main fighting probably took place in the vicinity of the Offham chalk pits, and towards the end of the two spurs, which run south-east from the plateau towards the castle and the prison respectively.

London

The Tower of London. (See also Chapter 3.) During the reign of Henry III large sums of money were spent almost every year on some part of the Tower. He was not the first king to make use of the place as a royal residence, but he was the first to make it worthy of one. Much of what he built has either disappeared or undergone complete change – for example the Wakefield, Lanthorn and Bloody Towers were all his creation – but through his work on the palace, his whitewashing, embellishing and gardening, he did his best to soften the grimly grey battlements and frowning machicolated turrets.

Westminster Abbey. Henry III had a passion for building, which was perhaps the most admirable side of his character. His principal purpose in the Abbey, which he virtually rebuilt, was to provide a shrine to house the jewelled casket containing Edward the Confessor's remains. He brought over to England Italian craftsmen, skilled in the art of mosaic, to work on the shrine, which was started in 1245, and was under construction for more than twenty years.

Orford Castle (Suffolk). Only the keep of this great castle, which was built by Henry II between 1165 and 1173, remains. It stands in elemental solitude on the Suffolk coast some five miles south of Aldeburgh, looking across to the North Sea and the old sea port that gave it its name. The great polygonal tower shows that Orford was once one of the finest and most modern castles in the country. Its design, which had broken away from the more usual rectangular pattern, enabled it to have greater fire power and therefore a more effective defence. It was also well equipped inside with three main floors on which were two halls, spacious chambers, garderobes, storerooms and two kitchens. The curtain wall that surrounded the keep had rectangular flanking towers.

Originally built for internal security as well as coastal defence, Orford quickly proved its worth when Hugh Bigod, Earl of Norfolk, supported Henry II's troublesome eldest son in one of his insurrections. Later King John made successful use of the castle during his baronial troubles of 1215–16. Orford remained a royal castle for most of the thirteenth century, but in the fourteenth century it was leased privately and its royal connection ceased.

Rochester Castle (Kent). (See also Chapter 3.) The castle underwent sieges in the reigns of John and Henry III. The custody of Rochester Castle was granted by Henry I to William de Corbeil and his successors at Canterbury in perpetuity, but in 1215 John asked Archbishop Langton for it to be placed in the hands of a royal custodian. Some agreement was reached, but it is not clear whether Langton actually did hand it over; at any rate, in September 1215 it was seized by a party of rebel barons, besieged in October by John and eventually taken when the south-east angle of the keep collapsed as a result of mining. In the following year the castle was captured by Prince Louis of France, when he was fighting for the rebel barons, but returned to royal hands in 1217. During the Barons' War the castle was again besieged when in 1264 it was held for King Henry by Roger de Leybourne. Simon de Montfort and the Earl of Gloucester invested it and captured the bailey, but, as in 1215, the garrison withdrew to the keep. Once again the massive walls withstood the missiles of siege engines, and this time no mine was sprung and the insurgents withdrew after a siege of only ten days.

Runnymede, Berks.
Magna Carta was signed in June 1215 in the meadow that lies between Windsor and Staines. The place is called Runnymede and there is a monument in the meadow denoting the site where it is thought King John's tent was pitched. There are four copies of the Charter still extant – two in the British Museum, one at Lincoln Cathedral and one at Salisbury Cathedral.

Salisbury Cathedral (Wilts.). The new cathedral was another of Henry III's great architectural works. He could watch the progress of the building from his nearby palace of Clarendon (of which nothing is left above ground). The cathedral was started by Bishop le Poore, and consecrated in 1258 in the presence of Henry and his Queen Eleanor.

Worcester Cathedral (Worcs.). In this cathedral are buried King John and Henry VII's elder son, Prince Arthur. King John had expressed a wish in his will to be buried in the cathedral between the shrines of Saints Oswald and Wulfstan, and his splendid tomb, with its effigy (the oldest royal effigy in England) lying upon a slab of Purbeck marble, is to be seen in the choir. Nearby is Prince Arthur's chantry chapel, built on the orders of Henry VII by the skilled workmen who were engaged on the building of his own fine chapel in Westminster Abbey.

The oldest part of this lovely cathedral is the Norman crypt, which dates from the time of St Wulfstan who became bishop in 1062. There is an exhibition in the crypt each summer from May until October depicting the history of the cathedral. The chapter house, which lies just to the east of the very attractive cloisters, is also Norman, but much of the present building dates from after a fire which broke out at the beginning of the thirteenth century. The Lady Chapel was begun in 1224, and Bishop Wakefield (1375–95) completed the magnificent nave.

Windsor Castle (Berks.). (See also Chapter 3.) Henry II replaced much of his great-grandfather's wooden stockades with stone. On the Conqueror's earthwork, which over the years had settled into an uneven circle, what is now known as the Round Tower was erected, and Henry also walled that part of the castle lying to the east of St George's Chapel, and built Winchester Tower – later reconstructed by William of Wykeham. On the site of the original Upper Ward, Henry built a range of private apartments, and a great hall on the north flank of the Lower Ward. The material for the walls was local, known as heath stone and coming from the beds of Bagshot Sands, but the stone for the royal apartments was brought from Bedfordshire quarries, and the lead for the roofs came from as far afield as Cumberland.

Henry III used the castle as one of his principal residences, and built the Tower, which bears his name, at the southern end of the cross-wall along the Deanery Ditch.

5

THE PLANTAGENET DYNASTY

A New Dawn

The reign of Edward I is a great landmark in English history. The thirty-five years of his kingship were certainly not ones of tranquillity, indeed there were many years of turmoil and strife, but they marked a surging forward of constitutional progress, and if we accept that a united kingdom was, and still is, an ideal to be aimed at, the reign was also one of national progress. Continental affairs receded; England became more English under a King who did more than any of his predecessors since Alfred to shape the life and character and promote the fame of his people.

Edward had a magnificent presence. Well above the average height he had powerful arms and long legs (hence the nickname Longshanks), a good crop of hair that turned snow white in old age and fine features – save for an inherited drooping eyelid. He combined many of the qualities, and the better ones at that, of his great uncle, Richard I, and of his great grandfather, Henry II. He had all the love of panache that so distinguished Richard; he was a great warrior and in days of peace he gloried in the tournament and joust, and was never so happy as when mounted on a good horse with hounds at his heels and a hawk upon his wrist. And yet he was a conscientious administrator, a clever diplomat and a lawgiver and reformer of exceptional merit.

There was, of course, another side; he had an imperious will, which he did not like to have obstructed, and although there were flashes of that fierce Plantagenet temper and occasional cruelty, the quality of mercy was high. Many·of his laws were aimed at strengthening the monarchy, but his extortionate tax demands were made more for the welfare of the country than for the purpose of self-aggrandizement. He could control his contemporaries because he was tough and usually uncompromising, but unlike his father and grandfather he had the good sense to give way on the few occasions when he saw it was necessary.

The new King, who had been abroad since 1270, was in no hurry to assume the reins of government; travelling via Sicily, the papal court and France - much of the time accompanied by his Queen, Eleanor, whom he loved dearly - he eventually landed in England on 2 August 1274 and was crowned in Westminster Abbey seventeen days later. The first part of the reign saw a flood of legislation; and one statute followed closely upon another as the King, together with his Chancellor, Robert Burnell, laboured to codify and strictly define the rights and duties of the magnates, to enquire into and stamp out abuses, define the jurisdiction of the courts and completely overhaul the tenurial land law. Much of this legislation, which got under way in 1275 with the first Statute of Westminster, was not new, and in so far as it affected the royal prerogative was conservative and aimed to uphold the supremacy of the King in legal matters. But the importance of the many statutes was that they surveyed, arranged and codified a whole field of legislation, and that the laws were enacted by the King in Parliament.

Certainly Edward's constant need to raise money for his military ventures had a direct bearing on the number of parliaments called; but he treasured Justinian's dictum that 'that which touches all should be approved by all', and it is his fully representative Westminster Parliament of 1295 - later to be known as the Model Parliament - rather than his uncle's (Simon de Montfort's) illegal one of thirty years earlier, that can be truly called the first great English Parliament. Edward transformed what had been a temporary expedient, necessary under duress, into a fully representative assembly of the three estates. From the chrysalis of these early parliaments there was to emerge, after many vicissitudes, the doctrine of no law without Parliament's assent.

Edward held the Church in great respect and was a devout and sincere Christian; but this did not prevent him from being unrelenting when he considered that Churchmen had stepped beyond the bounds of lawful ecclesiastical authority. He was at times in conflict with two of his primates and the Roman Curia. The quarrel with Archbishop Peckham, whom Edward had been forced to accept against his will, covered much the same ground as Henry II's dispute with Becket - clerical immunity from secular jurisdiction - but the moderation, tact and skill of both parties, particularly that of the King, kept the struggle from erupting into a dangerous crisis.

It was in this reign that the Jews were expelled from the realm. Through their virtual monopoly of the banking business they had become extremely rich and as usurers were very unpopular outside royal circles, where their wealth had its uses. But Edward disliked them on economic and social grounds, and for the twelve years prior to their expulsion they had been subjected to grievous restrictions, maltreatment and punishments. Their melancholy wanderings, which started, so far as England was concerned, in 1290 were to last for almost four hundred years.

The Welsh problem had been with successive English kings since Saxon times; recently it had been the policy to keep these Celtic men in check through the great Marcher lords, who tended to become virtually independent of the Crown. Edward had had an unsatisfactory apprenticeship with Marcher lords and Marcher problems, and apart from an overwhelming desire to bring English laws and justice to this wild country and unite the two peoples under one peaceful government, he was anxious to put a curb on the ever-feuding, over-powerful robber barons of the March.

An opportunity to interfere in Welsh affairs was not long in coming. The most powerful prince in what at that time was not a united people was Llewelyn ap Gruffydd of Snowdonia. This man had, by a treaty of 1267, got himself acknowledged as Prince of Gwynedd and acquired an inflated opinion of his own importance. He refused to attend Edward's coronation, and made continuing and feeble excuses to avoid doing homage. He had been Simon de Montfort's man in the Barons' War, and had recently married Simon's daughter, Eleanor.

By 1276 Edward's patience with Llewelyn's defiance was exhausted and an army was raised to invade the principality in the summer of 1277. The whole business was over in three months. By seizing Anglesey, the Welsh granary, Edward got behind Llewelyn and cut his supplies, while his brother, Edmund of Lancaster, advanced from the south to close the pincers. Llewelyn sought peace, and by a treaty signed on 9 November 1277 he was made to surrender land in the north-east and certain fortresses, two of which were given to his brother, David, who had been Edward's ally.

Edward immediately took military precautions, which included building a number of new castles, such as those at Rhuddlan and Flint, and strengthening existing fortifications. But it was an uneasy peace, and in March 1282 David, who was discontented with his share of the victory against his brother, suddenly swooped upon Hawarden Castle and a much more serious and difficult campaign had begun. The whole of north Wales rose against the English. Llewelyn joined his brother, and soon there was fighting in south Wales as well. In June Edward took command in person, and gradually David and his Welshmen were driven back from their base in Denbigh; but a similar operation to that of 1277, involving a sea-borne invasion of Anglesey and an advance to the mainland across a bridge of boats, ended in disaster. David retired on Snowdonia, and the English faced a winter viewing a snow-covered panorama of forbidding mountain peaks. Archbishop Peckham was sent to negotiate, but the terms were unacceptable to the Welsh, now in a strong position.

However, before the end of the year the tide turned; aided by a deserting Welshman, who showed them a ford, the English won a great victory at Orewin Bridge. Llewelyn was ambushed and slain, and in the new year Edward received fresh levies of Gascon mercenaries. By the summer the war had dwindled to a hunt for David; at the end of June he was caught, and in October hanged, drawn and quartered. There was no further resistance, and Edward proceeded with annexation. Castles were built from which to maintain the peace. Conway and Caernarvon were new, and in magnificence were to match Caerphilly (begun in the last reign) in the south; older fortresses, such as those at Bere and Harlech, were strengthened – indeed the latter was virtually rebuilt. In March 1284 came the Statute of Wales defining the new form of government, and a month later Prince Edward (the first English Prince of Wales) was born in the old timber-built castle at Caernarvon.

In Scotland Edward was not so fortunate. He had to deal with a people whose spirit was as stern and resolute as any on earth, and moreover they found two leaders who combined a rugged determination with a fire and zeal that drew forth wonderful exertions from their troops. All might have been well had Alexander III's grand-daughter, known to history as the Maid of Norway, to whom Prince Edward was betrothed, not died on her way to ascend the throne. The regents, or guardians as they were called, asked Edward to arbitrate between the Competitors, and after prolonged confabulations he gave judgement for John Balliol against Robert Bruce. The decision was indubitably the correct one, but Edward quickly showed the Scottish King and people that he regarded King John as no better than his vassal, and humiliated him to such an extent that war became inevitable.

In 1294 Edward was already in contention with Philip IV of France over Gascony. Not only did King John refuse to help Edward, but he reaffirmed the 'Auld Alliance' with Philip. Leaving his brother to deal with the French, Edward gave his full attention to what he considered was an act of rebellion. Berwick was sacked with a savagery reminiscent of a more barbarous age, and the Earl of Surrey utterly defeated the Scots at Dunbar. Edward made a leisurely progress through Scotland, demonstrating his puissance by such acts as the removal to England of the Stone of Destiny from Scone. In June Balliol sued for peace, and together with other important prisoners he was sent to England.

Scotland was occupied and the outlook was black indeed, but from adversity painful efforts were extorted. In William Wallace the Scots found a strong man possessed with abundant courage and energy, capable of inspiring them in the cause of ridding Scotland of the English.

He raised the standard of revolt in June 1297, and this was a most propitious time for Scotland, because Edward was at loggerheads with the clergy and in almost open conflict with two powerful nobles, the Earls of Hereford and Norfolk. Together with Sir Andrew de Moray, Wallace and his men met with some local success, and with Edward out of the kingdom the job of repelling them fell upon Surrey, by now an old man. Indeed at Stirling Bridge on 11 September he was to prove himself far too old for responsible command. Crimes such as failing to take sound advice, oversleeping and allowing half his force to be cut off on the wrong side of the River Forth, resulted in total defeat.

This disaster had important consequences many miles from Stirling. The disaffected barons saw their opportunity to press forward inexorably for a reaffirmation of the Great Charter, for many of them had grown apprehensive at the increasing authority of the Crown. Important concessions were made concerning the right of taxation and military service abroad – this latter concession heralded the replacement of feudal armies by men enlisted for pay. No doubt Edward would have had to submit to such demands anyway – and he was soon to repudiate most of them – but defeat at Stirling Bridge left his government very vulnerable to prowling barons so long as he and a large army remained in France.

But Edward was not the man to be worsted for long by a rebellious knight. Affairs in France were going badly; Edmund of Lancaster had been duped by King Philip, and Gascony was lost in 1294 (returned by treaty in 1303) and since then nothing positive had been achieved. But Edward realized that he could not fight on two fronts, and with the aid of the Pope a series of truces were made with Philip, strengthened by marriage contracts between Philip's sister, Margaret, and Edward,* and Philip's daughter Isabella and Prince Edward. Thus relieved from pressure in France, Edward arrived in England in March 1298, and immediately ordered military levies to assemble at York in May. This army, which numbered around 2,500 cavalry and 12,500 infantry (most of the latter were Welshmen) crossed the Border in July and finally met Wallace's army – inferior in numbers, but strongly positioned on the southern slope of Callendar Wood – on the 22nd of the month. The battle of Falkirk was won for Edward through a combined pincer movement of his cavalry, and the excellence of his archers, who shot down the Scottish schiltrons, isolated once their cavalry had left the field.

Falkirk was a resounding victory, although Wallace escaped into the forest behind; for seven years this luckless and hunted outlaw avoided

* Eleanor of Castile had died on 28 November 1290.

capture, until in July 1305 he was betrayed and suffered a traitor's death at Smithfield. But the torch that Wallace had lit was soon to be carried by another, with equal courage and tenacity of purpose. Robert Bruce, grandson of the Competitor who had lost Edward's award in 1292, held land in England and Scotland, and had actually fought on the English side in the nationalist rising of 1302. This reflected no love for England, but merely that it best suited his personal views on who should be King of Scotland. These he put into action in February 1306, when having murdered a possible rival in John Comyn, the Younger of Badenoch, he had himself crowned on 27 March.

Edward, whose health was now in steep decline, was enraged at the news of this *coup d'état* and determined once more to take the long road north. He was so weak that he could travel only by litter, and he was not present at the battle of Methven and Dalry, where Bruce was defeated. Bruce himself was not taken, but a little later many of his family fell into English hands and were treated infamously by Edward. The winter of 1306-7 was spent by the King and Queen at Lanercost Priory; but with the reappearance of Bruce in 1307 and his initial successes that summer, Edward decided that he must again mount his war-horse and take the field in person. The effort was, however, too much for his exhausted body; he died on 7 July 1307 at Burgh-on-the-Sands.

The last years of this great King had not been happy ones; his second wife, Margaret, although by all accounts charming, could never take the place of his beloved Eleanor, and the big disparity in their ages proved at times a disadvantage. Edward became a lonely, cantankerous old man whom few dared to oppose; indeed by the accident of death and the skilful alliances he made for his numerous children, there were few outside the family circle left to oppose, for he had brought almost the entire nobility under his personal control.

For thirty-five years England had been well governed by a King who can be numbered among her greatest. But he left behind him a son who had not been given much of an apprenticeship in kingly duties and a situation that was quite beyond the paltry abilities of this weak, pleasure-loving young man of twenty-three. Bruce was on the rampage in Scotland, and at home the barons, no longer restrained by the old King's terrifying person, soon began to reassert themselves.

Edward II had all the physical attributes of his Plantagenet forebears, his height, strength of body and distinctive features made it very obvious that he was not the changeling an unwise impostor declared him to be. But he was totally unfitted to be a medieval king in the days when abdication, which would have allowed him a way out, was only resorted to under extreme pressure. And a constitutional monarchy, which might have allowed him to indulge, without giving too much offence, in his rural (and rustic) pursuits, was still a long way off. He chose his friends and acquaintances unwisely, he was pleasingly loyal to them, but either would not or could not control them. He was cultured and by no means unintelligent, but he was a lotus-eater and incapable of subordinating his personal preferences to his royal duties.

Trouble was not long in coming, and it centred round his great favourite Piers Gaveston. This arrogant but accomplished Gascon had been Edward's friend since boyhood. Whether or not there was a homosexual relationship, Edward I obviously thought there was, and he banished Gaveston from the kingdom, but he was back directly the new reign began. Gaveston was anathema to the barons, for apart from the fact that the King had eyes and ears only for him, his mordant sense of humour was usually exercised at their expense, and he could defeat most of them with a lance. Edward created him Earl of Cornwall and with incredible folly made him regent when he left for France to marry Isabella. By 1308 Gaveston had become impossible and the King was forced to send him away, but he was back the next year.

In 1310 the magnates imposed upon Edward an elected council of twenty-one to draw up a series of ordinances for the better running of the kingdom. Among the reforms these Lords Ordainers, as they were called, tried to force upon the King was the permanent expulsion of Gaveston. After much bullying the King submitted to this ordinance, and once more the hated favourite departed. When he again returned and flaunted his authority the barons, nominally under Edward's first cousin and principal opponent, Thomas of Lancaster, took matters into their own hands and butchered him in June 1312.

Any small esteem in which the barons held the King was extinguished after his débâcle in Scotland against Bruce. Edward had made a pathetic attempt in 1310 to carry out his father's dying command to chastise the Scots, and had achieved nothing. Now, in 1314, challenged to relieve Stirling Castle and hoping to impress his authority on his barons by a resounding victory, he marched a huge army – from which Lancaster and some of the Ordainers were conspicuously absent – to its doom. Outnumbered by more than three to one the Scots, under their great commander, won a resounding victory between the Bannock and Pelstream burns on St John's Day, 24 June. The disaster of Bannockburn meant that until the truces of 1319 and 1323 (confirmed in 1328 by the Treaty of Northampton) the northern counties were never safe from savage Border raids, while in 1316 the Great Famine cast its terrifying shadow over the whole country.

The defeat in Scotland also removed from Edward for the next four years the last vestiges of personal control. The Earl of Lancaster, of whom very little good can be said, now headed the council that kept the King tightly trammelled. But in 1318 Edward's personal prospects took on a new slant; the ascendancy of the so-called Middle Party under the Earls of Pembroke and Hereford did not greatly alter his position, but the rise to power of the two Despensers (father and son, both called Hugh) kindled a brief spark of energy and success, before collapse and extinction engulfed him.

The Despenser family was of some importance on the Welsh March, and the two Hughs were inordinately ambitious and greedy. The son had married one of the Gloucester heiresses, and, not content with his share of the estate, attempted to take over the rest, and also some castles that had recently been given by the King to Roger Mortimer. This provoked almost open rebellion on the part of the Marcher lords and the King was forced to exile the Despensers. But this time Edward was not prepared to sit quiet under such treatment; this attack on his new friends galvanized him into his one piece of confident aggression.

Success came quickly and almost painlessly on the March, because Lancaster had withdrawn his powerful support from the barons on learning that his treasurer, Robert Holland, had defected to the King. But before marching north after Lancaster, who had retired on to his castle at Pontefract, Edward seized the Bishop of Hereford's lands and committed Roger Mortimer to the Tower. Both men were to get their revenge. Meanwhile Lancaster was foolish enough to seek the help of Robert Bruce, which cost him the support of the northerners and ensured his defeat at Boroughbridge on 16 March 1322. He was captured the next day, and Edward speedily avenged the loss of his 'brother' Piers Gaveston.

The Despensers were recalled and remained at the King's side for the final five years of this melancholy reign. In 1324 Charles IV of France seized most of Gascony, leaving only a narrow coastal strip, and when the Queen suggested that she might go to France to mediate with her brother, the Despensers (for whom, with every reason, she bore a bitter hatred) unwisely agreed. Once there she refused to return unless the Despensers were removed; as her mediation had proved fruitless Edward contemplated invasion, but was advised instead to send his young son, from whom it was said Charles would accept homage for the duchy. But nothing came of it, and soon the Queen was joined by her lover, Roger Mortimer, who escaped from the Tower.

In September 1326 the pair of them, with troops loaned by the Count of Hainault in return for a promise of marriage between his daughter, Philippa, and Prince Edward, landed in Suffolk and met virtually no resistance from a people who had had enough of the Despensers and their kind. Hugh Despenser was captured at Bristol in October and his son at Llantrissant on 16 November. Edward was also taken there on the same day and sent to winter in Kenilworth, where he was deposed. The Despensers presented no problem; they were done to death by traditional methods; but a king's person was still considered too sacrosanct for judicial murder, and Edward was too strong to die from natural causes unnaturally imparted. He was conveyed from castle to castle, always incarcerated under appalling insanitary conditions and given very little food. Finally, on 21 September 1327, he suffered a subtle but most brutal death at Berkeley Castle.

The reign of Edward II was in many ways an unhappy interlude between two great epochs; but it was not an unmitigated disaster. The first Edward by the end of his reign had acquired the power to suppress any attempt to override his imperious will. The weakness of his son let the bubble burst. During the interregnum of centralized authority there was much to deplore, but through the many parliaments that were called the steel bands of autocracy were swept away and the road left clear for a more liberal progression. Edward III was to pursue a dynastic policy very similar to that of his grandfather, and by marrying his sons into the great landed families would present his successor with some of the troubles suffered by his father. But before that occurred there was to be a reign of fifty years in which England, through social, political and economic change, would gain strength and become, as it were, a new nation.

For the first three years of his reign Edward III was merely the puppet of Mortimer and his lover, Edward's mother; but he was old enough and intelligent enough to realize the magnitude of their crime and to understand the shame to which they had put the country – and incidentally his signature – by the Treaty of Northampton that gave Scotland independence. In 1328 Edward had married Philippa of Hainault, who was to prove a wonderfully loyal, wise and kindly Queen, and in 1330 the first of their seven sons was born. It was time for the King to claim his rightful place. With the help of Henry of Lancaster (whose father, Thomas, had caused Edward II so much trouble) and a handful of others, he gained access to Nottingham Castle and surprised Mortimer in his bedroom. From there he was sent to the Tower and the gallows; but Edward treated the dictator's followers with commendable generosity, and his mother he sent to Castle Rising in Norfolk, where, on an allowance of £3,000 a year, she spent the greater part of her later years.

At the age of eighteen Edward III had assumed his duties in fact as well as in name. England, although she did not know it then, had another great King. His soldiers were the most powerfully armed in

Europe; his ambitions were at times megalomaniac; he was to achieve much by conquest, but sadly live to see it all vanish in the mists of incompetence and greed. Edward was the personification of a medieval king; tall and of fine physique, he gloried in warfare, the tournament and the chase, and in the great halls of his many residences he could be affable, generous and a splendid host. But with these knightly accomplishments there went a determination to rule and not be ruled, and to achieve this he recognized the need for conciliation. His principal fault was to involve the nation in too many wars for his own glory and to pacify the barons.

In home affairs Edward successfully steered a middle path. There was no question about who held the chief executive and administrative power; but the importance of Parliament greatly increased, and the establishment of the Commons as a permanent and integral part of government dates from this reign, as indeed does the separation of the two Houses. It is true that the stress of war required the King to seek constantly fresh supplies of money from his Parliament; however, Parliament was not content to act merely as the King's treasurer, but demanded a consultative role, and the Commons were determined that their periodic petitions for the redress of grievances should be embodied in parliamentary statutes and precede supply. Moreover, when they considered that the limit of absolute monarchy had been reached – as happened in 1341 and 1376 – they now had the collective power to force the King to agree to reasonable reforms.

But Edward did not try to play the despot, and on the rare occasions that he went beyond the acceptable bounds of sovereignty he could usually claim State necessity. He encouraged manufacturers, and in particular he took considerable interest in the wool trade with the Low Countries. His naval victories enabled English commerce to thrive and find new markets as far afield as the Mediterranean. He gave encouragement to education, which is reflected in the new colleges established in his reign, and besides his own building work – most of which has not survived – we owe to his reign the beautiful Crécy window in Gloucester Cathedral and Salisbury's magnificent spire. But Edward is best remembered for his military prowess and that of his knights, and the remarkable achievements of his archers.

The Treaty of Northampton had to be erased; Scotland must come back into the fold; but Edward was bound by the Pope to preserve the peace. However, history came near to repeating itself. Edward Balliol, son of John Balliol, was willing to pay homage to Edward for Scotland, and Edward did nothing to stop him from marching across the Border at the head of English troops in an attempt to wrest the kingdom from the boy King, David Bruce, who as it happened was Edward III's brother-in-law. The regent, the Earl of Mar, was a most incompetent soldier and Balliol gained the throne; King David was sent by his followers to France to await happier times.

By the Treaty of Roxburgh, signed in November 1332, Balliol agreed to become Edward's liegeman, which gave the English King the opportunity he wanted to interfere actively in Scottish affairs, when at the end of the year Scottish patriots drove Balliol out of the country and ravished the Border. Edward laid siege to Berwick and by so doing lured the Scots into open warfare in order to save the town. Throughout his military career Edward's strategy had the ultimate aim of inducing his opponents to give battle. Once this was achieved, his tactics were to take up a strong defensive position to be held by his men-at-arms fighting on foot and flanked by his incomparable archers, whose long-bows out-ranged anything the enemy could bring against them. And so it turned out at Halidon Hill, just north-west of Berwick, where on 19 July 1333, the Scots attempted to attack a strong position over marshy ground and were mown down by the English arrows that sped 'as thick as motes in the sunbeam'. It was a victory to avenge Bannockburn, and, more importantly, to give confidence at home in a new captain and fear abroad in a superb weapon.

Balliol was back, for a time, but there was a price to be paid, which included the ceding of much of south-east Scotland. This drove the Scots once again into the Auld Alliance, and although Edward continued to campaign in Scotland for more than three years, in 1337 he had to leave her ravaged, but unconquered, in order to turn his attention to her by now active ally, Philip VI.

At the death of Charles IV in 1328 the direct line of the House of Capet became extinct. Edward, through his mother, a daughter of Philip IV and sister to Charles, might have had a viable claim to the throne had not France adopted the Salic Law; as it was, Edward did homage to the new Valois King for his French lands. However, when the French fleet moved into the Channel and started raiding, thereby aggravating an already serious dispute concerning the wool trade, and Philip VI in 1337 confiscated Gascony, Edward assumed the royal arms of France and used his claim to the French throne (a claim that was not finally repudiated until 1802) as a signal for war. The Bishop of Lincoln was sent to build up a coalition from among the numerous states of the Holy Roman Empire, and after considerable delays, procrastinations and financial problems the first serious assault of what became known as the Hundred Years War was opened against Cambrai in autumn 1339.

In contrast to Edward's great naval victory at Sluys in 1340, which gave England command of the seas for a generation, the first years of the war on land were most unsatisfactory for him, involving a lot of marching, appalling difficulties and expense with his allies, and a complete inability to draw Philip's army into open battle. Nor would the French King accept Edward's chivalrous offer to decide the issue by personal combat. Between 1340 and 1345 little went right for Edward's campaign; expenses mounted alarmingly, the German alliance collapsed, and although he overran Brittany in support of John de Montfort, claimant for the duchy, it was a hollow victory. Meanwhile in 1341 David went back to Scotland and Border raids soon followed.

But the campaign of 1345–6 was more encouraging. Earl Henry of Derby and Sir Walter Manny, two of Edward's best commanders, had met with considerable success in Gascony at the end of 1345, although by April of the following year they were in difficulties. Edward had probably first thought of going to their aid, but was persuaded to alter his landing and subsequent campaign to Normandy. Landing at La Hogue on 12 July 1346 he accepted the risk of marching north-east to join up with his Flemish allies. It was a brave move, for Philip was amassing an army many times the size of his small force of some nine thousand men, and the very fact that Edward burned and pillaged such important towns as Caen as he marched made it essential for Philip to come into the open to destroy the menace.

Indeed it is difficult to understand just what Edward was trying to do, for in a very short time he had got his army into difficulties and in attempting to fall back on the coast – where incidentally his seamen had mutinied and returned home – he was nearly trapped by Philip's large army of thirty thousand men in unfavourable ground south of the Somme. After he had made several vain attempts to cross, a peasant directed him to the ford at Blanchtaque. The French army in close pursuit crossed the river at Abbeville, and found the English drawn up for battle in three 'divisions' on the forward slope of a ridge just north-east of Crécy. It was late in the afternoon of 26 August, and foolishly the French could not resist an immediate onslaught led by their Genoese cross-bowmen. Nothing could prevail against the English arrows; and as the Genoese crumpled and recoiled, the men-at-arms advanced over their dead bodies in all the majesty of war. Between 6 and 10 pm, in a dozen or more attacks, an avalanche of unflinching Frenchmen rode to death or captivity.

It was a total victory; the long-bow was established queen of the battlefield, and offensive defence the tactics of the day. But there were no positive gains until Calais was eventually taken after a year-long siege. Edward was to labour on in France for a further thirteen years, until in 1360 the Treaty of Bretigny produced an uneasy peace that lasted for nine years. In the meantime his eldest son, the Black Prince, who at the age of sixteen had won his spurs at Crécy, showed that he had inherited his father's flair for war. At Poitiers in 1356, using much the same tactics as those employed at Crécy – with minor alterations required to meet the French dismounted attack – he completely defeated a larger army commanded by John, the new King of France, whom he took prisoner. This victory with its important prize marked the zenith of Edward's military triumphs, for he already held the King of Scots prisoner.

After Crécy Philip in despair had turned to King David to take the pressure off him by a full-scale invasion of England. David needed no encouragement to cross the Border; but it would seem that he had been misinformed about the English strength in the north, which Edward had been careful to husband. His mistake was shown when, after devastating much of Cumbria he camped in a leisurely fashion just outside Durham, with an English army, under the Archbishop of York, which was not much smaller than his own, only eight miles away. On 17 October 1346 the Scots were brought to battle at Neville's Cross, just west of Durham, and after three hours hard fighting defeated. Their King, who was wounded and captured, was to remain in captivity for twelve years, during which time his subjects alternately bargained for his release and indulged in bitter guerrilla fighting against Edward's troops. Eventually, for the huge sum of £100,000 which this spineless man was not worth, they got him back.

Edward's dynamic energy drove him forward with bewildering rapidity from battlefield to battlefield and council chamber to tilt-yard. Until the last sad years, when his active mind was prematurely arrested, it was always questing into fresh and exciting fields, especially those where chivalry played a part. A close-knit brotherhood of knights needed something tangible to bind them to the spirit of the Paladin Arthur, and in 1344 at Windsor, Edward instituted his Round Table; four years later he created twenty-four founder knights, besides himself and the Black Prince, of the 'Fraternity of St George'. The Order of the Garter – a name perhaps inspired by the Fair Maid of Kent's mishap at the Calais ball – was to be Christian as well as illustrious, and included a college of twenty-five canons under a dean and twenty-six Poor Knights, elderly men whose principal duty was to pray for the souls of departed knights.

But very soon all the feasting, the tournaments and chivalrous romanticism inspired by the new Order were to be swept into the corner by a scourge far more terrible than war, which, spreading rapidly from Asia Minor, cast a grim shadow over Europe claiming, it is estimated, one third of the population. The Black Death, so called from the colour of the haemorrhages and boils that preceded delirium, agony and death, was by January 1349 rampaging through England. During the reign there were three visitations of the plague 1348–9, 1361–2 and 1369.

Through it the King lost two members of his family – his daughter Joan at Bordeaux in 1348, and his wife in 1369. This terrible affliction, added to all the other problems that beset Englishmen at this time, drove society to the limits of endurance, but – although we must suppose the manpower situation was affected – did not abate the fighting.

The Treaty of Bretigny lasted from 1360 to 1369, although the Black Prince, who held court at Bordeaux, had become involved in the conflict for the throne of Castile, and in 1367 won his greatest victory at Najera, close to Pampeluna. But in doing so he contracted dysentery, which so weakened him that by 1371 he was home and unfit for further service. The next round in France was mainly conducted by his younger brother, John of Gaunt, who was not an inspired commander and the French, now under Charles V, refused to give battle but gained all they needed in a war of attrition. A disastrous campaign ended in a truce agreed at Bruges in June 1375, which was to last until the end of the reign. It left England with only Calais and a coastal strip from Bordeaux to Bayonne.

The last years of the reign were a sad anticlimax to the triumphs and tragedies, the glory and renown that had been Edward's and England's. The old King, now in his dotage, was at the mercy of his magnates, his powerful family – seemingly jockeying for position, for it was known that the Black Prince was dying – and above all of an unscrupulous mistress. There was no lack of fuel for discontent; the recent military reverses made people realize how much they had suffered in taxation and hard service for a cause that had produced precisely nothing in the end.

In 1376 the Commons, in what was called the Good Parliament, were able to use powerful and capacious arguments, through their forceful Speaker, Peter de la Mare, to enforce their demands that the King's expenditure should be checked, his mistress, Alice Perrers, should be dismissed the court, and two fraudulent ministers should be punished. Admittedly, in the following year Lancaster (John of Gaunt), imprisoned de la Mare, brought back Alice, and in a Parliament packed with subservient members undid much of the work of the Good Parliament; but that was only a temporary reverse from the growing principle that whoever controlled the purse-strings virtually controlled the country.

On 21 June 1377 in his palace at Sheen, almost alone – deserted at the end by his family and even his mistress – Edward III died. A fortnight later he was buried beside his Queen in Westminster Abbey. His eldest son had preceded him to the grave exactly a year before. His grandson and heir, Richard of Bordeaux, was only ten years of age.

Richard II was crowned on 16 July 1377; it was the first recorded occasion on which the King's champion made his challenge at the coronation banquet in Westminster Hall.* The reign of twenty-two years can be divided into four parts – the years of tutelage and early manhood, which lasted until 1387; the two years of ignominy and suppression; the seven comparatively quiet years of personal rule, and the final years of storm and disaster. Two of his uncles overshadowed much of his life; John of Gaunt, 'time-honour'd Lancaster', whom he first mistrusted and then came to appreciate as his staunchest supporter and a most honest servant to the State; and Thomas of Woodstock, Duke of Gloucester, who would go to all lengths of malice, cruelty and mendacity.

Judgements of Richard range from that of the most splendid of men and wisest of monarchs, to a dangerous tyrant whose deposition was essential, with many gradations of opinion in between. He had the temperament, ability and courage to make a great king, but the handicaps were too many to be overcome. Son of a much loved and revered father; thrust upon the throne at the age of ten; for twelve years trussed, threatened, bullied and deprived of friends, it is scarcely to be wondered at that when at last he came into his own his innate and overdeveloped sense of kingship gradually took charge.

Like most of his breed his appearance was regal and his temper was foul; but even his bitterest enemies cannot deny that his physical and moral courage were unassailable. He preferred peace to war, beauty and the gentler things of life to the rough and tumble of the tilt-yard. His adoration for his wife, his loyalty to his friends and his many human qualities were endearing. Unfortunately one cannot overlook the last two years when he seemed to be both·mad and bad – and, in the end, sad.

The first four years of the reign, when Richard was under the tutelage of a council of regency, might appear on the surface to have been uneventful. But there was a deep stirring of discontent at the failure of Lancaster and others to make any headway in the war with France; at the hopelessly wasteful fiscal policy of the council and in particular with three increasingly vicious and unfair poll-taxes that were levied. Throughout the spring of 1381 there was general unrest, and the first outbreak of open revolt occurred in Essex; this was quickly followed by

---

* Sir John Dymoke, had inherited the right to act as King's champion through his wife, Margaret, a descendant of Philip Marmion, who may have performed the duty at the coronation of Edward I in 1274. At the beginning of the banquet the champion rode into the hall and flung down his gauntlet in challenge to any who disputed the Sovereign's title. Henry Dymoke, at the coronation of George IV (19 July 1821), was the last champion to perform the duty.

another in Kent. Leaders were found in Wat Tyler, Jack Straw and a priest, John Ball, whose eloquent and fiery sermons gained him the reputation of a prophet. A large number of angry peasants converged upon London, and Richard was hurried from Windsor Castle to what was thought would be the safety of the Tower.

The mob was let into the City through treachery and for three days there was looting and burning; all about the King seemed paralysed with fear, but this boy of fourteen remained perfectly calm throughout. On 14 June he agreed to meet the rebels at Mile End; in his absence at this confrontation, the Tower was broken into, his Chancellor and Treasurer summarily executed and his mother molested. The promises made at Mile End being insufficient to disperse the mob, another meeting was arranged for the following day at Smithfield. Here Tyler, half drunk with alcohol and totally with power, behaved in a most insulting manner towards the King. A dangerous fracas developed in which Tyler was mortally wounded by the Mayor, and his infuriated supporters were about to rush the King's party. Only Richard had the manhood to dare; even at this early age his sense of kingship urged him to an almost desperate throw; putting spurs to his horse he rode towards the excited crowd and shouted 'Let me be your leader. You shall have from me all that you seek', and his courage won the day as he rode off the field at their head.

The social revolt of 1381 had been a failure; the impact of its terrifying explosion and initial success could never be maintained. The peasants' demands were swept aside, but the landed aristocracy had had a bad fright, and at least there were no further poll-taxes for more than a century. There followed five years which, judged by what had gone before and was to follow, were comparatively quiet, although the court was riddled with cabals of favourites and Richard committed several indiscretions in their interests. In January 1382 the King married Princess Anne, sister of King Wenceslas IV of Bohemia. This was an arranged marriage, which quickly became a love match, and it was everyone's misfortune that it lasted for only twelve years.

During those years when the King was coming to manhood, but still under the tutelage of the able and much-liked Simon Burley, powerful factions were developing. Soldiers back from the French war were good material for private armies. The very seeds of strife, in the form of 'Livery and Maintenance', were sown during this reign. We find a royal party, a Lancastrian party and an anti-Lancastrian party, with the bishops mostly aligned with the barons against the court. With John of Gaunt out of the country, chasing a Castilian Crown, it needed only a major indiscretion by Richard, such as creating his pleasant but not very competent favourite, Robert de Vere, Marquis of Dublin (the first title of its kind) and later Duke of Ireland, to unleash upon him the wrath of his youngest uncle, Gloucester, and the powerful clique of unscrupulous and self-seeking myrmidons that adhered to him.

In October 1386, in the misnamed Wonderful Parliament, Gloucester and his henchman the Earl of Arundel dismissed and impeached the King's very distinguished Chancellor, the Earl of Suffolk, and substituted Arundel's brother. Other important posts were given to Gloucester's nominees, and a Commission of Government was formed, consisting of Gloucester, the two Arundels and eleven others, who took complete control of affairs for a stated period of one year. Richard was reduced to a mere figurehead; but he had his deposed friends around him that Christmas at Windsor, and although outwardly he bore adversity with composure, inwardly his mind was formulating plans. He built up what military might he could – and it was very little – and secretly he took legal opinion of his judges, who in answer to his questions pronounced the Commmissioners traitors and their actions illegal and invalid.

But the secret was not well kept, and Gloucester determined on forceful action. The situation deteriorated rapidly. De Vere, who had been sent by Richard to be Justiciar of Chester, was in the autumn of 1387 busily recruiting troops from that loyal county, and when the opposing nobles assembled at Waltham Cross the scene appeared set for civil war. But de Vere was no match for Henry Bolinbroke, Earl of Derby (Lancaster's son), who commanded the opposition troops, and he led his four thousand Cheshire men into a well-laid trap at Radcot Bridge in Oxfordshire. There was little fighting and de Vere escaped in the December fog and got to France, but Richard was now completely at the mercy of Gloucester. He and Lords Arundel, Derby, Nottingham and Warwick had constituted themselves Lords Appellant, and in what was rightly called the Merciless Parliament they accused the King's party, which included such able men as Suffolk, Tresilian (the Chief Justice) and Simon Burley – of treason, and exiled or executed almost every one of the King's closest friends.

The Commission of Government's powers had long since lapsed, but the Lords Appellant continued to rule in an illegal and incompetent way. They took care to enrich themselves for their pains on behalf of a King whom they had reduced to a cipher, but their attempts to renew a profitable war in France proved futile, while against the Scots their army under Northumberland's son, Henry Hotspur, suffered the worst defeat of the reign at Otterburn in June 1388. But the caprice and ambition of the King was to bring their skulduggery to an unexpected conclusion.

Bereft of friends and advisers, alone with his wife and his sadly tarnished but never abandoned regality, he quite suddenly, in May 1389, determined to claim his own. Maybe the knowledge that Lancaster was about to return from Spain strengthened his resolve to meet malice with guile. Be that as it may, he astounded the Great Council by pointing out to them that he was of an age to rule; and then declaring that for twelve years his people had been sadly misgoverned, he demanded of the Chancellor the Great Seal. The Lords Appellant and other magnates were cornered; they had no choice but to obey. Richard at last had the reins of government in his own hands; cautiously but firmly he began to rule.

Inevitably new appointments to the great offices of State were made, but Richard did not recall his exiled friends and eventually most of his former enemies were reinstated in the council, with the welcome addition of Lancaster. During the next seven years he made mistakes, but on the whole he governed through his chosen council wisely, and his first expedition to Ireland in 1394 was an inspired and intelligent break with tradition, which met with great satisfaction. Had he not been recalled after eight months to deal with problems connected with the Lollards, he might conceivably have achieved a settlement that would have avoided much subsequent frustration and bitterness.

A few months before he left for Ireland, Richard lost his Queen. His grief, understandably, was for some time inconsolable, for they had become twin souls; she was the rock he clung to amid the shifting quicksands of kingship. It is possible that her loss affected his later behaviour, but this is unlikely; it is more probable that for some years he had been coldly calculating the moment to revenge himself on those who had persecuted him. The couple were childless, and his second wife, Isabelle of France, could in no way replace Anne, for she was a child of only eight. Their marriage was the binding truce signed with the French King in March 1396.

Whether or not Richard's revenge was planned, he certainly took care to see that he did not strike before he was absolutely ready. He waited until he had built up a private army of his own, and he made sure that the majority of the aristocracy were now on his side. By 1397 he had reached the climax of his personal power and in June of that year there occurred the flashpoint with Gloucester. At a banquet held in connection with the handing over of the fortress of Brest to the French, Gloucester insulted the King in front of the assembled company. Both men now realized that a showdown was inevitable. Gloucester sought to forestall any action by Richard by getting the five Appellant lords to agree that the King must be imprisoned for life. But one of their number, Nottingham, betrayed the plot and Richard acted at once. He ordered the immediate arrest of Warwick and Arundel, and himself rode with an escort to apprehend his uncle at his castle in Essex, from where he was taken to Calais to be imprisoned under Nottingham, who was Captain of Calais.

In September 1397, Richard, escorted by his bodyguard of Cheshire archers, attended a Parliament in which eight new Lords Appellant were given the task of appealing against their predecessors. Nottingham had turned King's evidence, and Derby being the son of Lancaster was for the moment safe, but Warwick and Arundel were found guilty. The former, because he had made a full and useful confession, was exiled, but Arundel was executed. Richard now created five new dukes - among them Derby to be Duke of Hereford and Nottingham Duke of Norfolk - and by the end of the year, with his acts of vengeance so far commendably restrained, his position was secure.

But the dream of autocracy had probably long occupied the foremost place in Richard's mind, and the desire to exercise power became an obsession. He now launched out on a series of desperate and most misguided courses. He was determined that the two remaining 1388 Appellants, Hereford and Norfolk, should be punished (Gloucester had died, or more likely been killed, in Calais) and they played into his hands by a private quarrel, which a parliamentary committee ruled should be decided in the lists - the deadly and spectacular trial by battle. The scene was set at Coventry in September 1398; a huge crowd from all sectors of the population had come to watch the two great lords fight to the death. Imagine their fury and disappointment when the King, to the amazement of all, stopped the fight and decreed that Norfolk should be banished from the realm for life and Hereford for ten years.

There was some sense in this decision from Richard's point of view, for at a stroke he rid himself of both men instead of one. But in the following year he blundered. The great John of Gaunt, Duke of Lancaster, now honoured and revered by all, died on 3 February 1399. His estates were enormous and, through the palatinate granted by Edward III, almost independent of the Crown. Richard had promised Henry (now Duke of Lancaster) at the time of his banishment, that on his father's death he should receive the whole estate. Now he confiscated it and extended Henry's banishment to life. Maybe no one baron should have held so vast a domain, but a promise had been broken and every magnate now felt himself insecure.

In July 1398 the Earl of March, Richard's viceroy in Ireland, had been killed and this made a second expedition to Ireland necessary. The King and his army landed at Waterford on 1 June 1399. He had left the kingdom wide open to attack, with his subjects becoming increasingly exasperated at his incompetent and unpopular government. While he was struggling through the Irish bogs trying to come to terms with the

King of Leinster, Henry of Lancaster seized his opportunity. Landing at Ravenspur on the Humber in July he quickly gathered a large force to his standard – including the Percies, whom he is said to have promised that he had no designs on the throne, but had come only to claim his own. He made for Bristol, where he found and hanged the Speaker of the Commons and two of Richard's ministers. The King's last surviving uncle, Edmund of York, had been left as regent. He was a weak, ineffective man who quickly made terms with the usurper; and Henry, freed from any internal trouble, marched north through Wales to intercept the King on his return.

Richard eventually reached the safety of Conway Castle, from where he could quite easily have made his escape by boat, but by deeds of basest treachery he was made to surrender on false terms, and sent prisoner to the Tower. Soon his signature was obtained to a deed of abdication, which was ratified on 30 September 1399, and the next month he was taken – disguised as a forester – first to Leeds Castle and then to Henry's castle at Pontefract. Early in January 1400 a plot to destroy Henry and his sons at Windsor was discovered, and this sealed Richard's fate. He was certainly dead by 14 February, very probably starved to death. He was buried first in humble circumstances at King's Langley, and it was not until 1416 that Henry V (who had received much kindness from Richard) gave permission for his remains to be removed to Westminster Abbey to be beside his beloved Queen Anne.

In the reigns of the four Plantagenet kings described in this chapter, building went on at an even greater pace than during the earlier part of the dynasty. This was largely due to the many castles built in Wales by Edward I, some of which are mentioned below. But the work of these kings was by no means confined to the military sphere, for during this period England's heritage was enriched by many alterations and additions to existing ecclesiastical and secular buildings, and indeed by the construction of many new buildings and educational establishments such as New College, Oxford, the design of which was to have considerable influence on later buildings in that lovely city.

Battle of Bannockburn (Central Region, Scotland). The battle was fought on 23/24 June 1314 near Stirling, between the English army commanded by Edward II, and the Scots under Robert Bruce. It ended in total victory for the Scots. The greater part of the battle area is now built over, and it is not easy to get a clear idea from walking the ground. However, from the higher ground around Foot o' Green, which lies one mile south-west of Bannockburn, one can visualize the Scots position on 23 June and the English attack across the

Bannock burn. And, by going down the side road in Bannockburn that leads north from the A9 towards the A905 (Ordnance Survey one-inch map, Sheet 54), the visitor comes to a track running parallel to the railway line which leads almost to the burn. It was somewhere near here that the English army must have crossed on the night of 23/24 June. But walking the ground is not essential, because the National Trust for Scotland have an excellent exhibition at the Monument, which is just off the Glasgow road (A80) at Bannockburn, where there is a good model of the field of battle, and an audio-visual account of the lead-up to Bannockburn and of the battle itself.

Berkeley Castle (Glos.), was the scene of the murder of Edward II. The King was done to death in a small cell in the keep, which can still be seen much as it was in his time. The castle, which has had no substantial alterations made to the existing structure since the reign of Edward III, was built as the condition on which Henry II, then Duke of Normandy, took the grant of the manor and honor of Berkeley from Roger de Berkeley, a supporter of King Stephen, and gave them to Robert Fitzharding, his own loyal supporter. This was in 1153 and Fitzharding built the keep. Later Henry arranged a marriage between Fitzharding's eldest son, Maurice, and Roger de Berkeley's daughter, Alice. Maurice proved a more enthusiastic builder than his father, and under him the castle began to take shape. Berkeley Castle is twenty miles north of Bristol and can be reached by leaving the M5 at Junction 14.

Berkhamsted Castle (Herts.). (See also Chapter 3.) This castle, which stands some six miles west of Hemel Hempstead, was a favourite residence of both Henry III and Richard II. In 1336 it was granted to the Black Prince, and he used it as a prison for King John of France after he was captured at the battle Poitiers.

Canterbury Cathedral (Kent). (See also Chapter 4.) Behind the high altar, near the site of St Thomas Becket's shrine, is the tomb of the Black Prince, Edward III's eldest son, who was buried there in 1376. The tomb is surmounted by a magnificent effigy of the Prince, while above it hang the Prince's surcoat, helmet, shield and gauntlets.

Castle Rising (Norfolk). This castle is now chiefly associated with Queen Isabella, the wife of Edward II, who, after the murder of her husband, spent much of her time at Castle Rising, until her death in 1358. It would not be correct to say that she was kept in any sort of captivity there as a result of her notorious collaboration with Roger Mortimer, which ended in the murder of Edward, but certainly a close watch was kept on her. She was granted the use of other castles, including Leeds in Kent, and Edward III always treated her with proper filial respect.

The castle was built c 1150 in the reign of Stephen by William d'Albini, who had married Henry I's widow. In 1544 it was granted by Henry VIII to the third Duke of Norfolk. The two-storeyed keep is one of the largest and most ornate in England, but of the outer walls only a part of the gatehouse still remains. Castle Rising is four miles north of King's Lynn, off the A149 road.

Chirk Castle (Clwyd), was built on orders of Edward I as one of the Welsh border castles (of which it is probably the finest example) that had the task of keeping the Welsh within their territory. It was not, however, completed until 1310 in the reign of Edward II. It stands magnificently on the high ground above the River Ceiriog, commanding the lovely Ceiriog Valley. It must have been a formidable fortress, but it has undergone many alterations, notably by Pugin in the last century, for more peaceful purposes. It is a rectangular building with an inner courtyard, and the massive corner towers are a reminder of its former puissance; but there is a Tudor section and some of the state rooms date from the second half of the eighteenth century. The village of Chirk is on the A5 road, a few miles south-west of Llangollen, and the castle stands about a mile to the west of the village.

Conisbrough Castle (South Yorks.). This castle, whose great keep, with its six massive buttresses (of which four were functional), is one of the finest examples of medieval architecture and one of the best preserved keeps of all British castles, has royal connections with Edward II and Edward III. It was built by Hamelin Plantagenet, the bastard brother of Henry II, but came into Edward II's possession in 1322 after the execution of Earl Thomas of Lancaster – who had seized the castle from a Hamelin descendant. Edward kept it for six years before handing it back to the Hamelins, but Edward III got possession of it when the Hamelin male heirs failed. The castle was occupied by members of the reigning families for some two hundred years until Henry VIII granted it to the Carey family.

Conisbrough Castle stands two miles off the A1(M) on the Doncaster-Rotherham road, and the visitor can, by climbing to the upper floors, readily appreciate its dominating position and near-impregnability.

Edinburgh Castle dominates the city from the great basalt rock that it crowns, and of which it seems to be a living part. Some sort of fortress has sat upon this rock since the seventh century, and probably earlier. Much of Scottish history is centred round the castle, for until the Abbey of Holyrood was built, it was the only place of royal residence in Edinburgh. Four English kings – Edward I and Edward III, Richard II and Henry IV – have marched into Edinburgh and laid siege to the castle, but only the Edwards gained entry, and Edward III might not have done so had not Robert Bruce ordered his lieutenant, Thomas Randolph, to dismantle the fortifications after he had won back the castle in 1313. The oldest building to survive is St Margaret's Chapel (she was Malcolm III's Queen), which dates from the end of the eleventh century, and it was in this chapel that Edward I received the oaths of fealty, after he had taken the castle in 1296.

Edward I's Castles. In order to keep the peace in Wales, Edward I built a series of castles which virtually hemmed in north Wales on three sides, and all of which could be supplied by sea if the need arose. These castles were mostly constructed under the direction of Master James of St George and his deputy, Master Giles of St George, but Edward himself planned their strategy and carefully approved their designs. The first, Flint, was begun in 1277, and during the next ten years there were to be a further five new castles built in north Wales, together with improvements to at least two of older date. In addition, Caernarvon and Conway are examples of walled towns built to protect the colony of loyal citizens. At Rhuddlan, Harlech and Beaumaris, Master James adopted what later became known as a concentric plan, which was designed to ensure defence in depth, and in its simplest form consisted of an inner curtain wall encompassed by an outer curtain wall, which in its turn was surrounded by a moat, and quite often the moat was protected by a timber palisade.

Beaumaris Castle (Gwynedd). Here is a castle that cannot compete in grandeur with Caernarvon, Conway or Harlech, but it is probably the most perfectly patterned of all Edward's castles, having the most complete (although not the first) concentric design. It was built to protect the valuable corn granary of Anglesey and the passage of the Menai Strait, and although made ready for use in the short space of three years in 1298, building continued until well into the fourteenth century (and indeed the castle was never fully completed), by which time military tactics had changed and castle besieging was no longer popular. Beaumaris is in Anglesey, five miles along the A545 after crossing the Menai Strait.

Caernarvon Castle (Gwynedd). This is the largest of Edward I's north Wales castles, and vies with Conway in strength and magnificence. It was clearly built to be a palace as well as a fortress. It was begun in 1283, but in 1294 the Welsh under Prince Madog overran Caernarvon, doing a lot of damage and necessitating the second building stage, which lasted from 1296 to 1301. The castle was besieged a hundred years later in 1402 by Owen Glendower, but it proved far too strong for his men.

Conway Castle (Gwynedd). One of the most impressive of Edward I's castles, with its commanding view across the estuary of the Conway River. It was, moreover, built in the incredibly short space of five years; begun in 1283, it was first garrisoned two years later. The garrisons of these castles were never large – perhaps sixty men or less.

Flint Castle (Clwyd). The first of the great fortresses built by Edward I, begun in 1277 and not completed until 1285. In 1399 Richard II came to the castle as a prisoner of Henry Bolingbroke, and from within its walls made known his agreement to abdicate.

Harlech Castle (Gwynedd). Perched high on its eagle's eyrie, backed by mountains, Harlech has the most commanding position of the eight built by Edward I in Wales. The castle was constructed between 1285 and 1290, and played no significant historical role until 1401 when it was besieged by Owen Glendower, but not taken (the garrison was beset by plague and forced to surrender) until 1404. Glendower then made Harlech his capital and lodged his family there; they were still in residence when in 1408–9 the castle was retaken by Gilbert Talbot, and Glendower's wife and family were made prisoner. During the Wars of the Roses the castle was for long a Lancastrian stronghold, and after Henry VI's capture in 1460 gave refuge to Margaret of Anjou. It was besieged and taken in 1468 for the Yorkists by Lord Herbert.

Rhuddlan Castle (Clwyd). This castle was begun, like Flint, in 1277 and finished in 1280 (five years before Flint); much more of it survives than is the case with Flint, and although the lower outer wall has mostly gone, the concentric design is easily recognizable – but not so perfect as at Beaumaris. An interesting feature of this castle is the deep stonefaced, dry moat, which protected the castle on three sides – the River Clwyd forming the other barrier – and to which there was access by steps (still there) leading down to sallyports.

Eleanor Crosses. Queen Eleanor died at Harby in Nottinghamshire on 28 November 1290. Her body was removed to Westminster in twelve stages and, at each of the twelve places where the bier rested for the night, Edward ordered a memorial cross to be erected. These places were Lincoln, Grantham, Stamford, Geddington, Northampton, Stoney Stratford, Woburn, Dunstable, St Albans, Waltham and in London, West Cheap and the King's Mews at Charing. Only three of these crosses still remain and they are at Geddington, Northampton and Waltham – the finest being the one at Geddington.

Gloucester Cathedral (Glos.). (See also Chapters 3 and 4.) Founded in 1289 and several times damaged by fire, Gloucester Cathedral gained prominence through the death of Edward II, because it was chosen for his burial place. Shortly afterwards, Gloucester received large numbers of pilgrims who came to venerate the murdered King as a martyr; their considerable offerings were put to good effect and greatly enhanced the beauty of the cathedral. Edward III built a splendid tomb for his murdered father, and, as a result of that King's victory at Crécy, a magnificent window was commissioned as a monument two years after the battle.

Kenilworth Castle (Warwicks.). (See also Chapter 4.) The castle had been in possession of the house of Lancaster for over fifty years when Henry, the third Earl, brought Edward II to it as a prisoner. At this castle Edward signed his abdication before being moved to Berkeley Castle in 1327, where he was murdered. The daughter of the fourth Earl married John of Gaunt, Edward III's third (surviving) son. It was John of Gaunt, a man of great character and breadth of vision, who converted Kenilworth from a formidable and uncomfortable stronghold into a pleasant fortified palace. Much of his very fine great hall, which was on the first floor and measured 90 feet by 45, is still standing.

Lanercost Priory (Cumbria). The priory was built in the twelfth century and here Edward I spent his last winter before his death in 1307. The priory is two miles north-east of Brampton, off the A69.

Leeds Castle (Kent). This flawless jewel of medieval architecture, perched upon an island in a lake, was for two and a half centuries closely associated with England's sovereigns, and in particular with their queens. Royal ownership began when William de Leyburn gave the castle to Edward I, and Edward, in 1278, gave it to his beloved Queen, Eleanor of Castile. Here they spent many happy days in what was virtually their country home. Edward greatly strengthened the castle's defences, so that it became not only a home, but a formidable fortress. The chapel, which was rehallowed in 1978, is the second oldest (that of St John in the White Tower being the oldest) Chapel Royal that survives – albeit no longer acting as a Chapel Royal.

The queens of Edward II, Richard II, Henry IV and Henry V all in their turn owned this beautiful palace. Henry VIII, who carried out much repair work – particularly to the Gloriette, perhaps the finest part of the present castle – and built the Maidens' Tower to house the maids of honour, eventually gave the castle to Sir Anthony St Leger, and it passed out of royal hands. Leeds is five miles south-east of Maidstone just off the A20 road.

London
The Jewel Tower (Westminster). The fourteenth-century Jewel Tower stands apart from the other buildings at Westminster Palace and marks the south-west limit of the medieval palace. Work began on the tower in 1365 under the supervision of the Master of the King's Works, Henry Yevele, and it was used to house Edward III's personal valuables, which had previously been the responsibility of the wardrobe at the Tower of London.

The Wilton Diptych (The National Gallery). The Wilton Diptych is a wooden panel painting dating from c. 1400. One side of the panels shows Richard II being presented to the Virgin and Child by his three patron saints: Edmund, the Saxon King martyred by the Danes in 870; Edward the Confessor; and John the Baptist. On the reverse is the white hart, the personal symbol of Richard II, and the King's arms quartered with martlets, by tradition the arms of Edward the Confessor.

St Stephen's Chapel (Westminster). (See also Chapter 3.) The original chapel was pulled down in 1292 by Edward I, who began rebuilding it under the direction of Master Michael of Canterbury. The work continued during the reigns of Edward II and Edward III and was completed in 1348, when Edward III established a college of canons to serve the chapel. The under storey of this chapel is now the Crypt Chapel of the House of Commons.

The Tower of London. (See also Chapters 3 and 4.) Throughout its first seven hundred years this formidable fortress played a grim part in the story of England's sovereigns. Only once, however, has it been overrun by the mob and turned over to sack, pillage and murder. This occurred at the beginning of Richard II's reign. At the time of the rebellion of 1381 the young King was moved to what was considered the safety of the Tower, but, while he was acting heroically at Mile End and Smithfield, the mob was treacherously allowed to enter the Tower. Savage terror ensued: the Archbishop of Canterbury, the Chancellor, Simon of Sudbury, and the King's Treasurer, Sir Robert Hales, were seized in St John's Chapel and butchered on nearby Tower Hill.

The Beauchamp Tower was built at the beginning of the fourteenth century.

It took its name from Thomas Beauchamp, that Earl of Warwick who was one of the Lords Appellant in Richard II's reign, and who was imprisoned there in 1397. The Byward Tower, the gatehouse of the outer ward, was built by Edward I, but received considerable additions at the time of Richard II.

Westminster Abbey. (See also Chapter 4.) The **Coronation Chair,** and in a shelf beneath it the **Stone of Destiny**, both came to the abbey in the time of Edward I. Edward had removed the stone from Scone in Perthshire, where it had stood for at least three hundred years and possibly as much as eight hundred, during the summer of 1296 when he was on a punitive expedition against Balliol. He ordered the chair to be made when the stone was brought to England, and since that time every British sovereign, with the exception of Mary I, has sat over the stone during the coronation ceremony. The origin of the stone is unknown, it may well reach back to Neolithic times, and before it found its way to Scotland, may have served in Eastern countries as an inauguration stone. It is thought to be of meteoritic origin.

In the Chapel of Edward the Confessor, the most sacred part of the abbey, stands the tomb of Edward III, with a fine effigy of the King in gilt-bronze by John Orchard. Around the sides of the tomb are little effigies of Edward's many children, including the Black Prince and John of Gaunt. Nearby stands the beautifully decorated tomb of Richard II with his beloved first Queen, Anne of Bohemia. In the abbey's undercroft, on the east side of the cloisters, can be seen the wooden effigy of Edward III, which was carried at his funeral. In the abbey hangs a portrait of Richard II, painted during his lifetime, and showing the King full face, enthroned in his coronation robes.

Westminster Hall. (See also Chapter 3.) Built by William II, the Hall remained substantially unaltered until the reign of Richard II, but in 1393 it was decided to rebuild. The architect responsible was the Master of the King's Works, Henry Yevele, but the superb hammer-beam roof went up under the direction of Hugh Herland, whose father had designed the roof of Windsor's great hall, and his carpenters. The old walls of the Hall were retained, but strengthened and heightened and the Romanesque windows were replaced by ones in the new Perpendicular style. As a part of the rebuilding, Richard ordered that thirteen stone statues of the kings from Edward the Confessor to himself should be placed in the niches in the hall, and a further two (of unknown subjects) were to be placed in niches outside over the main north doorway. Of these statues, nine still stand inside the hall. The work was incomplete at the time of Richard's deposition, but Henry IV ordered it to be continued, and it was completed in 1401.

Stirling Castle (Central Region, Scotland), perched on its high rock above the town, was one of the strongest places in Scotland. It was in attempting to relieve the castle in 1314 that Edward II fought, and lost, the battle of Bannockburn. The present buildings date from the fifteenth century, but the historical importance of its position in medieval times can readily be appreciated by the visitor today.

Windsor Castle (Berks.). (See also Chapters 3 and 4.) This was the birthplace of Edward III in 1312, and, when he was not campaigning, he spent much time there. With the help of the Bishop of Winchester, William of Wykeham, who for five years was in charge of the King's Works, he rebuilt a great part of the castle – and much of his building can still be seen. Edward III also spent considerable sums of money repairing and embellishing the chapel that was to be the spiritual home for his new Order of chivalry – the Garter. Henry III had built a chapel on the site of the present Albert Memorial Chapel in 1240, and Edward refounded it in honour of the Virgin Mary, St George and St Edward. For 135 years this chapel was the shrine of the Order of the Garter.

York Minster (North Yorks.), as we see it today – the fifth building on the site – was begun about 1220 and completed only after 250 years' work. It has connections with many English sovereigns, notably Edward III, who married Philippa of Hainault in the choir of the Norman church in 1328. Thanks to the discipline imposed upon his troops by Sir Thomas Fairfax in 1644, the Minster did not suffer the usual vandalism of Parliament's soldiers, and in consequence it retains the finest collection of English glass in its 109 medieval windows. In St Stephen's Chapel is buried Richard le Scrope, the Archbishop of York who was beheaded in 1405 for conspiring against Henry IV. The western side of the choir screen is enriched by the statues of English kings from William I to Henry VI.

6

THE HOUSE OF
LANCASTER

Henry IV dated the commencement of his reign from 30 September 1399, on which day a great assembly (which could not ·legally be constituted a Parliament, for the throne was unoccupied) dutifully declared King Richard deposed. A full Parliament was summoned for 6 October to give formal approval to this act of usurpation. It is a measure of their distaste for Richard's recent actions and the state of bewilderment that Henry's whirlwind campaign had thrown them into, that only one voice was raised in opposition. The brave Bishop of Carlisle, Thomas Merke, suffered imprisonment and loss of his see for his temerity. Nor did Henry want Parliament to think it was to their goodness he owed the throne (although before long they made it look that way), for while he was careful to carry them with him, he based his claim to kingship first on the totally spurious grounds of hereditary title,* and secondly by right of conquest.

The coronation took place on 13 October. There was an awkward moment when Richard from his cell in the Tower declared that the mystique of kingship, having been conferred upon him by his holy anointing, could not now be taken away; but this was overcome by the miraculous discovery, after a disappearance of many years, of the only authentic sacred oil of Edward the Confessor. However, it needed more holy oil than could be contained in that small ampulla to remove the terrible burden of guilt that was to be Henry's constant companion down the narrow road that led from the throne to an early grave.

A reign that began with such authority, so many high hopes and such

---

* Henry hoped to gain general acceptance of an absurd legend that Edward of Lancaster, and not Edward I, was the eldest son of Henry III. Therefore the last four rulers were not legitimate kings and he was the rightful heir to the throne through his mother Blanche of Lancaster.

apparent promise, was shaken by revolt almost before it had started, and had gone sour before it had reached the third of its thirteen years. As a young man Henry seemed possessed of all that fortune could bestow; intelligent, of fine physique, a formidable fighter in the lists, who had built up a great reputation in England and France, twice a crusader in Lithuania, a considerable linguist, and a traveller who had made the pilgrimage to Jerusalem. And yet the rigours and problems of kingship – especially for one who had usurped the throne – and a nagging conscience that probably contributed to extreme ill health, made him an old man at forty and a dead one at forty-seven.

The reign was to contain no great disasters, and only one positive achievement – the foundation of a new dynasty. It was for the King an almost uninterrupted struggle against his Parliament for money and his Welsh subjects for authority, and at varying times against some of his principal magnates. The rebellion of the Twelfth Night in 1400 failed through betrayal and the fact that the earls who instigated it had misjudged the temper of the country. Richard, whom they hoped to reinstate, died as a result of it, and so did the leading magnates involved and twenty-seven of their followers. But although it was alarming, it was never dangerous, which might well have been the case had not Henry acted with speed and determination against the next revolt of his English subjects.

The Percy family, under their head the Earl of Northumberland, ruled the north of England almost as independent princes. Moreover, their tentacles reached into north Wales, where the impetuous and ambitious Henry Hotspur was for a time Justiciar. More importantly there was a vague family connection with the Welsh nationalist rebel, Owen Glendower.* It was not long before the Percies became dissatisfied with the King, who they reckoned (with some justification) owed his position largely to them, and by whom they thought (without any justification) they had been hardly treated.

In the summer of 1402, while the King's troops were fumbling against Glendower in Wales, the Percies had won a resounding victory at Homildon Hill, in the Till Valley, against the Scots. In this battle the important Earl of Douglas, among many others, had been captured. The King, quite legitimately, demanded his ransom, but Hotspur refused to hand the Earl over. Further alleged grievances concerned lack of support while Hotspur was Justiciar of North Wales and the fact that Henry had broken his promise to them that he would not ursurp the throne.

* Edmund Mortimer, who married Glendower's daughter, was Henry Hotspur's brother-in-law.

In 1403 they posed a real threat to Henry, for they intended joining with Glendower to overthrow the King, and – it was alleged – place the young Earl of March, Richard's rightful heir, upon the throne. Henry was at Nottingham on 12 July, with an army that was marching to join Northumberland against the Scots. Hearing of Hotspur's revolt, he marched at once to meet him before he could make a junction with Glendower or be joined by his father. The armies met on 21 July about two miles north-east of Shrewsbury, where, after Henry's offer to discuss the rebel grievances had been refused, battle was joined. The fight lasted until nightfall and was fiercely contested (it was the first fought on which both sides used the long-bow); the King lost the Earl of Stafford and some nine knights, and the Prince of Wales was wounded in the face, but as soon as Hotspur was seen to fall his men gave up. Northumberland's brother, Thomas, Earl of Worcester, was captured and executed, and Northumberland himself surrendered on 11 August. Henry deprived him of his office of Constable, which went to Prince John (later Duke of Bedford), but six months later he was set at liberty and restored to his estates.

However, it was not long before the Earl was concerned with a further and even more serious revolt, which involved the partitioning of the kingdom. By 1405 Glendower had reached the apogee of his power, and it is possible that it was in this year that he, Northumberland and Edmund Mortimer agreed, in what was called the Tripartite Indenture, to split England between Northumberland and Mortimer (with Northumberland getting far the greater portion) and give an enlarged Wales to Glendower. Also prominently involved in this plot was the Earl Marshal (Thomas Mowbray), Lord Bardolf and Richard Le Scrope, Archbishop of York.

Glendower played no active part in the rebellion, and indeed the Earl of Westmorland nipped it in the bud before Northumberland could participate. He and Bardolf escaped first to Scotland, then to Wales and finally to France; but in 1408 they were back again and in arms against their King, and this time both were killed in a skirmish at Bramham Moor. The tragic mistake of 1405 was the execution of the Archbishop of York, who had been persuaded by Westmorland at Shipton Moor to disband his army, and was made prisoner somewhat treacherously. In spite of the Archbishop of Canterbury's urgent plea for clemency, Henry had had enough of rebellions and was determined to make an example. Scrope became a martyr, Henry suffered agonies of conscience and people ascribed the serious turn that his illness took at this time to his wicked act. In fact he probably suffered from either a series of strokes or **epileptic fits, and the 'leprosy' that later greatly disfigured him was perhaps an extremely violent form of eczema.**

The principal domestic problem of the reign was lack of money, but another was Lollardy. Henry was pious and his religion was orthodox; he stood stoutly behind Parliament and Archbishop Arundel on this question, even though he may have been tempted by the Lollard suggestion that the Church's enormous wealth could be put to better use in his own treasury. Parliament in 1401 passed the statute known as *de Heritico Comburendo*, and men began to burn in this reign for the denial of a word – transubstantiaton – and the fires were to intensify over the next 150 years. The Lollards in England, the Hussites in Bohemia, perhaps spawned by the Great Schism, were certainly the roots of reformation.

During the reign there were nine parliaments. The very act of usurpation made the King's position, vis-à-vis his Parliament, a delicate one. Henry may not have liked the thought that he ruled by the grace of his magnates assembled in Parliament, but it cannot be denied that he depended greatly on public opinion and constitutional authority. At the beginning of the reign he declared his intention of not pressing for numerous grants and subsidies, and Parliament was continually pressing him to 'live of his own', but it was an impossibility. Since the first Parliament no other king had been so hard pressed for so long, and on the whole he bore such treatment with great patience. He submitted to outrageous interference with his household, his choice of councillors was attacked and limited, and even his treatment of rebel prisoners was criticized. But he needed money, and only Parliament could give it to him – and that they did very grudgingly. The fact that he had ten treasurers in thirteen years clearly indicates the impossibility of satisfying the King's many financial needs.

There were numerous incidental expenses connected with the reign – as, of course, with all reigns. A State visit by the Byzantine Emperor Manuel II; the return to France of Richard's Queen Isabelle; Henry's daughter's dowry and his own, not very popular, second marriage to Joan of Navarre; household expenses; Calais, Guienne (Aquitaine), Scotland and Ireland, and internal revolt.

Henry was the last English King to lead an army into Scotland, and the expedition achieved nothing; but shortly after Homildon Hill he had a slice of luck when the boy King James I was taken captive on his way to France. The Scottish regent, Albany, had no wish to see him back, and in fact James remained in England for eighteen years, and Henry had little further trouble from Scotland. Apart from becoming mildly, and somewhat humiliatingly, involved in the Burgundian-Armagnac rivalry he also managed (with the help of a spirited military effort by the citizens of Bordeaux) to keep clear of any major trouble in France.

But in Wales the situation was very different. After being completely unable to cope with Glendower's successful guerrilla tactics on no fewer than five occasions, Henry eventually entrusted the subjugation of that country to the Prince of Wales. The Prince in a long stretch of campaigning between 1404 and 1409, in difficult country and against a fleeting target, did as well as could be expected, for he was kept very short of funds and occasionally had to finance his troops from his own resources. Furthermore he was pitted against a most able opponent.

One can have a lot of sympathy for Owen Glendower; he was a well-liked and well-educated landowner, who fell foul of the heavy hand of Lord Grey of Ruthven, who provoked him into action from which there was no going back. Until 1405 he posed a threat that Henry could never ignore and his skilful guerrilla tactics won him castles and prestige. But in that year the tide turned against him; French assistance proved ineffective, and inch by inch Prince Henry drove him back through his mountain strongholds. When Northumberland died in 1408 and Harlech Castle fell (with most of Glendower's family inside it) in 1409, his hopes of success had gone. In 1410 he launched his last, unsuccessful, offensive, and from that time he literally disappeared from the scene.

For the last three years of his life Henry's health became an increasingly heavy burden that kept him from travelling far, but in no way diminished his determination to hang on to the reins of power. Inevitably much of the day-to-day government passed to the Prince of Wales, whose relations with his father were sometimes stormy. There is no reason to believe exaggerated reports of his continual wild behaviour, although the natural exuberance of youth may occasionally have caused some misgivings. There was only one rupture between father and son that looked as though it could be serious, when in 1411 there was a movement afoot to depose the King and put Prince Henry on the throne. But the Prince was able to convince his father of his loyalty, and their relationship continued on a fairly smooth course until Henry's death on 21 March 1413.

Henry had striven hard to rule well and in great measure he had succeeded. He had brought the Welsh back into the fold and had avoided serious trouble with both France and Scotland. At the end his seizure of the throne may have caused him remorse and regret, but he was able to hand it on intact to a son who had no such feelings. Henry has sometimes been accused of breaking a solemn promise not to usurp the throne, and in so doing founding a dynasty that caused the Wars of the Roses. Having once landed in England he had to go forward to the throne or die, and the Wars of the Roses need never have been fought if Henry VI had proved capable of ruling.

However much anxiety the flamboyant gusto of his youth may have caused the Prince of Wales's councillors, they had to admit that when he ascended the throne the hallmarks of his career henceforth were dedication to duty and a seriousness of purpose. He inherited a title that was by no means secure; but during his reign of nine years (more than half of them spent out of the country) Henry V, largely through the brilliance of his military leadership and his fearless justice, compelled widespread admiration and affection, for he seemed to his subjects to be all that a king should be. By the time of his death he had consolidated his dynasty, but through his early demise he left its future wide open to destruction.

Henry was crowned on 9 April 1413 when he was twenty-five years old, but already a very complete man with much military and administrative experience. From what little we know of his physical appearance, he would seem to have been of slight build, but strong and athletic; his thin, cadaverous face with its high cheekbones and long nose was set alight by the eyes – gentle and smiling when at ease, but flashing fire when the King was provoked. The severe lines of the face could indicate a ghazi, and indeed Henry's religion bordered upon the fanatic. His great courage, high administrative competence and ruthless determination are readily apparent in every milestone of his reign.

At the beginning of 1414 Henry had to suppress a Lollard rising, which centred round his former friend Sir John Oldcastle, who had recently escaped from the Tower. The plot aimed at Henry's death, and although considerable numbers of the sect moved upon London the whole operation was ill-conceived and ineptly executed. Henry had no difficulty in rounding up the rebels and about one hundred paid for their temerity with their lives, but Oldcastle escaped and was not brought to the stake for a further four years. Henry's religion was strictly orthodox, and his attitude and actions towards Lollardy are entirely understandable and do not amount to persecution. He was the founder of three religious houses, and he was just as determined to suppress any laxity on the part of monks in orthodox establishments as he was to root out those whom he considered to be dangerous deviationists.

Perhaps because he was out of the country for so long, Henry had very little trouble with his parliaments, who on the whole responded generously to his frequent calls for money with which to conduct his campaigns. But even with the taxes they gave him and the fact that his second offensive in Normandy was partly self-supporting, he never had enough, and the crown jewels and much else besides were constantly in pawn.

Henry's overriding desire was to break the twenty-year truce made by Richard II in 1396, and once more plunge the country into a devastating dynastic war with France. Apart from a natural wish for the pursuit of glory, this most English of kings undoubtedly convinced himself of the validity of his great-grandfather's claim to the throne of France – and therefore his, in spite of his father's usurpation, by right of succession. But there were other, and more practical, reasons for renewing hostilities. There were signs of restlessness – the recent Lollard plot was one – among some of the magnates, and there was lawlessness throughout the country with vagabonds committing acts of brigandage. A little blood-letting, and the opportunities for loot that a hopelessly divided France offered, could take care of some pressing domestic problems.

Both the Armagnacs and the Burgundians desired Henry's assistance in their damaging feud, and here was the chance for diplomacy, the necessary cover of respectability that cloaked a determination to invade. Early in 1415 the King's uncle, the Earl of Dorset (later. Duke of Exeter) was sent to the French court to make outrageous demands, which included the Crown of France, or – failing that – that part of the country that had been possessed by Henry II as well as the land ceded under the Treaty of Bretigny, plus King John's ransom (still unpaid since Poitiers) and the hand of Princess Catherine with a dowry of two million crowns. The Armagnac negotiators, headed by the Duke of Berry, made very reasonable counter-proposals, but Henry had no intention of finding these acceptable, and preparations for a large-scale invasion went ahead.

The embarkation of some ten thousand troops and much stores and equipment was getting underway in Henry's armada of fifteen hundred ships, when what became known as the Southampton Plot was betrayed. The King was at Porchester Castle on the last day of July 1415 when the Earl of March, whom the conspirators planned to proclaim king after Henry's assassination, exposed the whole shabby affair. Henry reacted to the danger in a characteristically calm way; summoning the magnates to a council meeting he asked their advice on what he should do, whereupon the guilty men, headed by his own cousin the Earl of Cambridge and one of his most intimate friends, Lord Scrope of Masham, confessed. Justice was swift and exemplary – the leaders were executed; it was the last treason trouble of Henry's reign, but it showed that the memory of 1399 lingered on.

On Sunday 11 August the fleet sailed for the mouth of the Seine. Harfleur on its north bank was besieged, but it proved most stubborn. In spite of his preponderance of numbers and heavy siege equipment, which included guns, it took Henry five weeks of assault and battery before the small garrison sought terms. It was a victory, but gained at appalling cost, for a third of his men were casualties from fever and dysentery. Paris was now unattainable; but to accept the advice of his council to return home almost empty-handed was unthinkable to Henry. He would tempt Providence and the French army by marching to Calais across 150 miles of hostile country; with a force reduced to about nine hundred men-at-arms and five thousand archers, it was a grave and desperate venture.

The crossing of the Somme was fraught with as much danger and difficulty as Edward III had found before Crécy; eventually Henry's little army shook off the shadowing French vanguard and crossed at Béthencourt. On 24 October – the eve of the Feasts of Saints Crispin and Crispinian – Calais was still seventy miles away and the English found the road barred by a vast French army. Henry encamped in the hamlet of Maisoncelles; it was a very wet night. On the morrow, before dawn, he led his desperately tired, damp and hungry men to the edge of a recently sown, large and soggy corn field. The French army of between twenty and thirty thousand men were drawn up for battle about a thousand yards away in a very confined space between the Tramecourt woods on the one side and those that surrounded the castle of Agincourt on the other.

Only the ground was in Henry's favour, and the odds were so appalling that, although more than ready to fight, he had offered to return his prisoners and even Harfleur in exchange for an unhindered passage to Calais. But the French were not prepared to forgo the victory and ransom money they felt sure was theirs. They relied upon weight of numbers; the English, once more, upon the long-bow, and the daring leadership of their King. For almost four hours the two armies stood motionless, glaring at each other. Then at about 11 am Henry gave the command 'Banners advance! In the name of Jesus, Mary and St George!' The English army, no more than six thousand men, advanced to within three hundred yards of the French host, and there the archers drove in their stakes and made ready their bows.

The story of this heroic battle is well known: how, stung by the flight of arrows, the great French army was galvanized into action, and subsequent slaughter. Cramped for space, the mounted men-at-arms, the pride of the French nobility with their golden banners bearing the royal emblem, advanced across the mud in crowded array, only to be shot down in huge struggling heaps, or pierced by stakes and later clubbed to death. Over their prostrate bodies came unmounted men determined to kill; but unsupported by their guns or cross-bowmen they, too, were destroyed. Within an hour the slaughter was so great that the heaps of dead came up to the shoulders of the living. Henry himself had fought like a lion throughout, his helmet dented, his sword arm seldom still save when he went to the assistance of his wounded brother of Gloucester. His cousin, the Duke of York, lay dead on the field, but the English casualties were negligible – probably no more than five hundred – while the French may have lost as many as eight thousand men, and the roll call included some of the most distinguished names in France. Others, such as the Dukes of Orléans and Bourbon, survived Henry's unfortunate order to massacre all save the most valuable prisoners, when in the afternoon a potentially dangerous situation arose. Against odds of at least four to one the English had gained a magnificent victory; it was a victory the fruits of which were not plentiful, but it gained for Henry fame immortal.

Back to a hero's welcome, and a Parliament whose generosity was almost unbounded, Henry spent much of the next two years in diplomacy. At a considerable cost in entertainment he achieved, through the Treaty of Canterbury (signed 15 August 1416), an offensive/defensive alliance with Sigismund, the Holy Roman Emperor. Sigismund had two dominant wishes, to end the Schism and to unite Europe in a crusade against the Turk. Henry, through a strong representation at the Council of Constance, assisted him in bringing the Schism to an end, but he felt that his contribution to the unification of Europe should be his conquest of France. So long as France remained divided – and the rift between the rival factions remained as great as ever – this was perhaps just possible. Henry's strenuous diplomacy ended at Calais in October 1416, where he obtained a free hand from the tricky Duke of Burgundy for his forthcoming campaign in France, and the full support of the Emperor.

The second invasion of France was on a grander scale. The seas had been swept clear of enemy by the Earl of Huntingdon, who gained a victory against a combined French and Genoese fleet in June; and on 30 July 1417 the army, numbering some ten thousand combatants and many supporting echelons, set sail from Southampton. They disembarked on the west side of the Seine at Touque. During the Agincourt campaign Henry had shown faith in his destiny, unbounded courage and superb leadership; during the next three years he was to combine these virtues with sound strategic planning and a logistical flare unsurpassed by any of his predecessors.

France was in a state of chaos. King Charles VI was insane more often than not. His Bavarian Queen, Isabelle, was banished from Paris by the Armagnacs for her profligacy and became the pawn of the Duke of Burgundy. Together they entered Paris after the murder of the Count of Armagnac, but the Dauphin escaped to assume the leadership of the Armagnacs. Nevertheless, in spite of this internal turmoil, Henry had set himself a most formidable task, for almost every town on the way to Paris was fortified and there were many that could not be by-passed.

The siege of Caen lasted a fortnight, and its successful conclusion in so short a time was due principally to the skill and courage of the King's brother the Duke of Clarence, and the efficacy of Henry's new arm – artillery. Reinforced by troops under the Earl of March, Henry now turned south, before commencing the siege of Falaise on 1 December. This town, and its almost impregnable castle, were well defended, but no relief was forthcoming and the threat of starvation forced the garrison to capitulate on 16 February 1418.

The next major objective was Rouen, the capital of Normandy. Rouen was much better prepared to withstand a siege than either Caen or Falaise; the suburbs had been razed and the land around laid waste; the garrison was well provided with food and cannon shot, and for five months – from August 1418 to January 1419 – it was a war of attrition, with the defenders daily expecting relief from Paris, and Henry unable to penetrate the walls. But without relief no siege can last for ever, and on 19 January Henry rode through the sadly battered streets of his duchy capital. There was no sack, but during the siege twelve thousand non-combatants had been turned out of the city to perish from hunger beneath its ramparts.

Rouen had been held by Burgundians, who had patched up their differences with the Armagnacs – now Dauphinists. But not for long, because on 10 September 1419, on the bridge of Montereau, the Duke of Burgundy was treacherously murdered by the Dauphinists. His young successor made haste to seek an alliance with Henry, and for the price of revenge was prepared to sell his country. Henry's terms were harsh and humiliating – the hand of the King's daughter, Princess Catherine, with a large dowry, the Crown of France for him and his heirs on the death of Charles, and the regency until that time. These terms were incorporated in the Treaty of Troyes on 30 May 1420.

There was to be one more serious siege before Henry and his bride returned home. Montereau was carried by assault fairly quickly, but the strong fortress of Melun held out for four and a half months of bitter fighting, much of it underground during mining and counter-mining operations. Henry took his full share of this subterranean hand-to-hand combat together with his brother and the Duke of Burgundy, but his behaviour towards the vanquished, especially the Scots mercenaries, when the fortress eventually capitulated in November 1420, showed signs of cruelty and petulance – characteristics hitherto not much in evidence.

Triumphant Christmas festivities in Paris, where Henry was welcomed as regent of France and heir to the throne, could not conceal the fact that the whole of France south of the Loire – save for Guienne – was held by the Dauphinists. It was not surprising, therefore, that after three months in England, spent partly showing his Queen to the people,

Henry sailed for France once more on 10 June 1421. Matters had not gone well in his absence; in March Clarence had been killed and his army routed by the Dauphinists at Baugé; as a result the Duke of Brittany decided to go over to the Dauphin, and the Burgundian alliance was shaken, but re-established when Henry met the Duke at Montreuil.

The strategic situation was perilous at this time; the Dauphin held a chain of fortresses that penetrated like a knife into northern France, and Henry was forced upon the defensive. Had the Dauphin been more adventurous matters could have gone badly for the English, but he consistently refused open battle and gradually Henry made headway, capturing Dreux, Beaugency and Rougemont. The last important siege of his career, that of Meaux, was his most brilliant. His tactics, improvisation and administration in the face of incredible difficulties, disease, hunger and loss of morale were of the very highest order. It was seven long months before the defenders asked and received terms that were merciful. Meaux had restored the balance in Henry's favour in the north, although much of France was still unconquered, and by now his health had begun to deteriorate.

On 6 December 1421, while the siege of Meaux was at its height, Queen Catherine gave birth to a son – a son that Henry was never to see, for he died in the castle of Vincennes on 31 August 1422. The long journey home was an impressive affair, and eventually his body reached Westminster Abbey on 7 November. The lovely chantry chapel housing the tomb was completed in 1441, and the richly embellished effigy was the gift of his young Queen.

When he knew he was dying Henry V, with characteristic thoroughness, made careful arrangements for the future of his realm and the regency of his infant son. John Duke of Bedford was to be regent of France, and his younger brother, Humphrey of Gloucester, regent of England, but subordinate to Bedford. Besides his uncle of Bedford the boy's two great-uncles, Henry and Thomas Beaufort, together with Richard Beauchamp, Earl of Warwick, were to be his tutors and governors, and it was perhaps to the wisdom of Warwick that Henry owed the most. His mother, Queen Catherine, was entirely disregarded; three years later she married the master of her wardrobe, Owen Tudor, and became the grandmother of the future Henry VII.

The minority lasted for fifteen years and was largely concerned with the struggle in France, where first one side and then the other gained the advantage. Although Bedford was a fine soldier, the discipline imposed by Henry V on his troops was lacking, with dire results. When in 1435 England refused the offer of generous peace terms, Burgundy made

THE HOUSES OF YORK AND LANCASTER

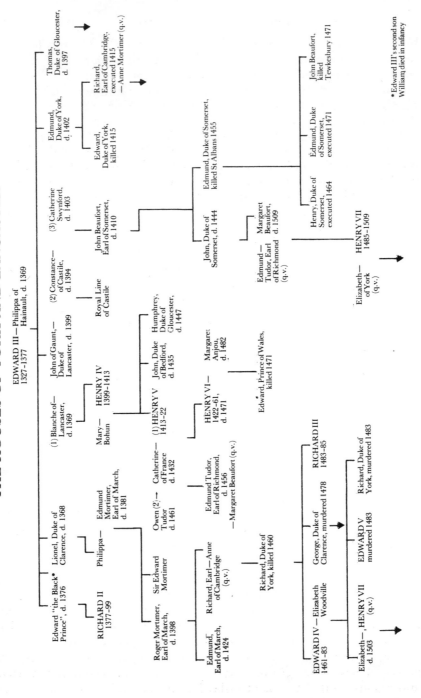

peace at last with France and Bedford died, the end was in sight. The small English army became no match for the resurgent French, fighting for national independence.

In 1437 Henry began to assume personal control. He proved over the years to be a kindly, very simple and pious man, who was easily led; but he was not unintelligent, and at brief intervals showed that he had a will of his own. His misfortune was that in this age of rule by kings he was mistakenly loyal to a faction who constantly mismanaged affairs of State. He stands condemned as the man chiefly responsible for the Wars of the Roses, which dominated his reign, because he headed an administration that was incompetent and untrustworthy, while he himself was too weak to cope with the passions and artifices of those fierce and dangerous times.

Henry tried to please everybody, which was an impossibility for a medieval king; moreover, he was easily imposed upon, and very soon the executive power became invested in a small clique in which members of the Beaufort family, and William de la Pole, Earl (later Duke) of Suffolk, were prominent. By 1445 the King was twenty-three, and it was very obvious that his weak character was likely to be dominated by any wife with a will of her own. The Beauforts were therefore anxious to find a queen who would be bound to them by ties of gratitude. In Margaret of Anjou, the daughter of René, Duke of Bar and Lorraine and titular King of Sicily, whose sister was Queen of France, they certainly found a girl with a will of her own. The couple were married at Titchfield Abbey on 22 April 1445; the subsequent surrender of Maine, for which she was – perhaps not unfairly – blamed, got her married life off to a bad start. Her fiery, tempestuous nature was in utter contrast to Henry's meekness, and any thoughts in the years to come that the King might save his throne through negotiation with the Yorkists was to find no support from this determined lady.

During the next five years the men who had previously led the nation – the Duke of Gloucester, Cardinal Henry Beaufort, John Beaufort, Duke of Somerset, and the Duke of Suffolk – disappeared by fair means or foul, until in 1450 the King's principal counsellor was Edmund Beaufort, second Duke of Somerset, who for the past few years had been busy losing every important town and province in France that Henry's father had so gloriously conquered. In August 1450 all Normandy had gone and only Guienne remained. In a year's time that too would be lost, and by 1453 the English were left with just a precarious foothold in Calais.

The country was full of bewildered, discontented ex-soldiers, who had been driven out of France and disbanded; robbers roamed the roads and woods, and the evils of unlawful Livery and Maintenance were weakening traditional loyalty to the Crown and binding the lesser nobles and their tenants to their more powerful neighbours, who thus formed independent armies. The King ruled not so much through Parliament as through his chosen council – dominated largely by the Beauforts. Queen Margaret, who was already exhibiting signs of that courage, determination and masterful spirit which were the essence of her character, greatly favoured Somerset, and was said to have been responsible for the Duke of York's removal from France and banishment to the lieutenancy of Ireland.

Political agitators and military adventurers found ready material to hand in these dark days. One such man, calling himself Jack Cade, marched on London at the head of a large band of Kentish men in the summer of 1450. His army was eventually dispersed and he himself killed, but it was a typical example of the lawlessness of the times. Possibly Cade had Yorkist backing; certainly his articles of complaint included a demand for the expulsion of the ruling clique and the recall of the Duke of York. Anyway, with the present Government discredited both at home and abroad, the Duke felt strongly the need for action.

Richard, Duke of York, was the son of that Earl of Cambridge who had been executed after the Southampton Plot. He was descended on his father's side from Edward III's fourth son, Edmund, Duke of York, and through his mother, Anne Mortimer, from Lionel, Duke of Clarence, Edward III's second surviving son. After the death of the fifth Earl of March, the Mortimer claim to the throne had descended to him. York left Ireland in August 1450 and landed in Wales. Henry recalled the Duke of Somerset from Calais and made half-hearted attempts to intercept York, but on these failing he weakly submitted to receiving him and listening to his complaints and demands – without, however, acceding to them. Although York's open enmity for Somerset could have sparked off civil war at any moment, it seems almost certain that neither then, nor when fifteen months later he had led a more threatening march on London, did he seek the kingdom. At this time he probably only wished to dispute the way in which the excesses of royal power had fallen into the hands of a clique or faction.

His mistrust and dislike for Somerset was founded upon an Act of Henry IV. In 1407 that King had carefully regulated the descent of the Crown in an Act of Parliament which had never been repealed, and while recognizing the legitimacy of his Beaufort half-brothers he had specifically debarred their line from any claim to the throne. Save for the childless Henry, the Lancaster line was extinct, and Richard of York was unquestionably his heir. But Somerset was in direct male descent, through the Duke of Lancaster, from Edward III, and all that was needed was for the favourite to slip an Act through Parliament repealing Henry IV's prohibitory clause.

York had been excluded from the King's council, although his talents as an administrator and soldier were probably superior to Somerset's. He saw clearly what was wrong with the country, and he believed himself capable of righting those wrongs. For a little while he took no overt action, but having failed to move the King by constant supplication, he determined to rid the country of Somerset and purge the government, if need be by force. Early in 1452 he marched south from his castle at Ludlow at the head of a large army. London closed its gates against him, so he camped at Dartford. The King, with a much bigger army, moved to Blackheath. Civil war seemed imminent, but neither side wanted it and York realized that he was in no position to fight. He had committed high treason, but he was far too strong to be punished. On taking a solemn pledge not to disturb the peace again, he was given his freedom.

In 1453 the King was dramatically released from his troubles. A sudden start plunged his feeble mind into oblivion, and for fifteen months he remained in this state of suspended animation, declaring on his recovery that he remembered nothing. Parliament was faced with having to appoint a regent. The court favourite, Somerset, had been successfully impeached by the Duke of Norfolk for the French catastrophes and was in the Tower, but Queen Margaret felt that her claim was paramount. She was, however, somewhat preoccupied, for on 13 October 1453 - after eight barren years - she produced a son. Parliament hesitated, but eventually the Yorkists won the day and in March 1454 the Duke of York was appointed Protector of the Realm. He was also given the captaincy of Calais, recently held by Somerset.

The country remained comparatively quiet until, at Christmas 1454, the King recovered his senses. He wasted little time in reversing most of what York had done and in restoring Somerset to freedom and responsibility. York retired to his castle of Sandal, near Wakefield, where he and the Yorkist lords brooded sullenly upon the scene. Not only all that he stood for, but his very life, was now only prey to time and occasion. He determined upon a resort to arms. In the middle of May 1455, at the head of three thousand men, he marched south.

The first battle of St Albans on 22 May was little more than a street scuffle lasting only half an hour, but it brought to the fore on the Yorkist side Richard Neville, whose aunt was married to York, and who through his own marriage to the heiress, Anne Beauchamp, became the fifteenth Earl of Warwick. The Yorkist victory was largely due to Warwick, and although the total casualties were less than 150, Edmund Beaufort, second Duke of Somerset, and one or two other important Lancastrians lay dead, and the King - who had received a flesh wound - was taken back to London with every mark of respect. First blood in the

Wars of the Roses had been shed, but the time of bitter hatreds and
savage reprisals was still five years away; now the victors behaved with
moderation.

The next four years saw an uneasy truce in the land; Margaret and
the court party once more gained the ascendancy at the end of 1456, and
York was sent back to Ireland. The Lancastrian power was, for the
moment, formidable, for, apart from a short period when Henry was
again incapacitated by illness, they had the magic of the Crown on their
side. By 1459 Margaret felt herself strong enough to take military action,
and although her troops were defeated at Blore Heath that September, a
few days later a large army led personally by Henry – displaying on this
occasion unwonted determination and vigour – was sufficient to frighten
the Yorkists off the field without battle. York fled to Ireland and
Warwick to Calais. But the latter was back by June 1460 to win a
decisive victory at Northampton.

At the time of this battle Margaret was in the north, but Henry was
present and once again was ignominiously conducted to London. York
now came there too and claimed the Crown, but he had acted
prematurely, for neither the lords temporal nor spiritual wished to
change the dynasty at this time. A compromise was reached whereby
Henry should rule for his lifetime, and should be succeeded by York. It
seemed an admirable expedient, but it failed to take into account one
important factor. Henry might agree to disinherit his son, but Margaret
certainly would not.

The indefatigable Queen, helped by Henry Beaufort, third Duke of
Somerset, and the northern earls, immediately set to work organizing
another army and at the battle of Wakefield (30 December 1460) her
troops defeated York, whose head ended up on his city walls adorned by
a paper crown. He was succeeded by his eldest son, Edward Earl of
March, who was only eighteen. On 2 February 1461 he won the battle of
Mortimer's Cross, but on the 17th of that month Warwick was defeated
at St Albans, although the Lancastrians were kept out of London.
Warwick now determined that he would palter no longer with a puppet
king; the Yorkists had crossed the Rubicon, and a fortnight after their
defeat at St Albans the young man whose badge the losing army had
worn was proclaimed Edward IV at Westminster.

The rest of the struggle, which had now become far more bitter, really
belongs to the reign of Edward IV. After St Albans Henry was reunited
with Margaret, and the next three years belong in a special way to the
Queen. We can only condone her behaviour if we remember that she
was French, and a queen without a throne; her interests centred round

her husband and her son, for England she cared not a straw. Nevertheless, we can have nothing but praise for her indomitable courage in the face of defeat, anxiety and extreme hardships, for her perseverance and her skill.

The royal fugitives hovered between Scotland and northern England. Their peregrinations cannot be gone into here; sufficient to say that for Scottish aid Margaret gave away Berwick, and for French she mortgaged Calais. She became a supplicant at the French and Burgundian courts, and with the aid of the devoted Pierre de Brézé, and a slice of English treachery, she gained the important northern castles of Alnwick, Bamburgh and Dunstanburgh. But it helped her little, for further defeats in the north soon followed. Margaret retired to France, and eventually Henry's hiding place in the Lake District was betrayed and he arrived as a prisoner at the Tower on 24 July 1465.

In 1468 Warwick quarrelled with Edward over the French alliance and changed sides. A wide and bloodstained gulf separated him from Margaret, but eventually she accepted his plea for forgiveness and as a pledge of his new alliance his daughter and co-heiress, Anne, married Edward, Prince of Wales. Thus at Michaelmas 1470 Henry VI was restored to the throne by the man who five years before had escorted him to the Tower crying "Treason, treason and behold the traitor'. But Edward returned from exile in March 1471 and won the battles of Barnet and Tewkesbury. Warwick was killed at Barnet and the Prince of Wales at Tewkesbury, and on 21 May King Edward entered London in state with Queen Margaret his prisoner. That very day Henry VI was reported to have died in the Tower 'of pure displeasure and melancholy'; Edward's youngest brother, Richard, Duke of Gloucester, is often thought to have been the particular cause of this 'displeasure'. Margaret remained Edward's prisoner for four years, until in 1475 Louis XI of France ransomed her for fifty thousand crowns in exchange for her inheritance of Anjou, Provence and Lorraine.

Henry, unlike his Queen, was quite out of sympathy with the men of his time, and totally out of place in the rough, rancorous years that unwittingly he helped to create. He was a good man, whose gentle, scholarly disposition will always be remembered with gratitude by the thousands who have benefited from his two great foundations – King's College, Cambridge, and the King's College of our Lady of Eton.

The reigns of the first two Lancastrians were not a great time for works of art and architecture. There was no worthy successor to Yevele in the craft of architecture. Henry IV was too busy consolidating his position to give much attention to art and Henry V was looking over his shoulder at the continental dreams of his great-grandfather, Edward III. Henry IV did, of course, complete Richard's work on Westminster Hall, while Henry V endowed monasteries at Sheen and Brentford and enabled the rebuilding of the nave of Westminster Abbey to go forward, and his craftsmen made his father's tomb at Canterbury a splendid work. It is in connection with the growing school of English music that Henry V's patronage was of particular importance; leading composers of the century received pensions or grants at his hands. It is to Henry VI that we are indebted for King's College, Cambridge, and Eton College. In the early part of his reign his uncles, the Dukes of Gloucester and Bedford, gave special encouragement to musicians, and Archbishop Chichele led a wave of church building and collegiate foundations at the universities – in particular Chichele's All Souls College at Oxford was begun in 1438.

There are, however, many buildings directly connected with the Lancastrians, which still stand in part or in a slightly altered form, and which are well worth a visit.

Cambridge

King's College was founded by Henry VI and designed for the support of a rector and twelve scholars, a number that was increased to seventy in 1443. The King laid the first stone of the college on Easter Sunday 1441, and the first stone of the magnificent perpendicular Gothic chapel on 25 July 1446. The work begun by Henry VI was continued by Richard III, and brought to completion by Henry VIII. Evensong has been sung in the chapel every evening since its foundation, and an opportunity to attend this hour of worship, and to hear the beautiful singing in such a superb setting, should not be missed.

The Church of St Edward King and Martyr. Although taking its name from the boy-king who was murdered at Corfe Castle in 978, the church was built two centuries later, in 1175. When Henry VI demolished the Church of St John Zachary in order to make room for his magnificent foundation of King's College Chapel, he removed from Clare and Trinity Hall their place of worship. In March 1446 he obtained the living of St Edward's and gave it in perpetuity to the Master and Fellows of Trinity Hall. Some twenty years later both Trinity Hall and Clare added a chapel to the church, opening into the north and south sides of the chancel.

Canterbury Cathedral (Kent). (See also Chapters 4 and 5.) Henry IV died at Westminster in the Jerusalem Chamber, but his body was taken by river to Gravesend and thence to Canterbury Cathedral, where it now rests in a tomb surmounted by a fine effigy, just to the north of St Thomas Becket's shrine and facing the tomb of the Black Prince. Twenty-four years later, in 1437, his Queen, Joan of Navarre, was buried at his side.

Eton College (Windsor, Berks.) was founded by Henry VI for seventy scholars. Work on the site, which was immediately to the north of the parish church, was begun in the summer of 1441, and continued with various breaks until Henry's deposition in 1461. Thereafter building went on over many years. Lupton's Tower, for instance, between School Yard and The Cloisters, was built between 1517 and 1520. The fine Perpendicular chapel was commissioned in about 1483, when the parish church was demolished.

Falaise (Calvados, France). (See also Chapter 3.) Henry V took this fortress, the birth place of William the Conqueror, during his campaigns in Normandy.

Lancaster Castle (Lancs.). Although the keep of this castle, which Henry III gave to his younger son Edward of Lancaster, dates from the twelfth century, most of what can still be seen, including the gateway, was the work of Henry IV.

London
The Guildhall. The Guildhall, home of the Corporation of the City of London, is open every day throughout the year. It was in the great hall that Richard Whittington, Lord Mayor of London, received Henry V in 1419 to celebrate his French victories. No part of the 1411 building survives, but the hall, porch and crypt, built between 1425 and 1430, have been beautifully restored.

The Museum of London (London Wall) contains numerous objects of great interest that are connected with London over the centuries. In particular, for this period, there is an oak cradle that was said to have belonged to Henry V's mother, Mary de Bohun, and used by her for her eldest son. (N.B. Exhibits in this museum are not always on permanent display.)

The Tower of London. (See also Chapters 3–5.) On 21 May 1471 Edward IV rode into London in triumph after his defeat at Tewkesbury of Margaret of Anjou's army. A few hours later Queen Margaret's husband, Henry VI, was done to death in the Wakefield Tower. Every year on the anniversary of his murder the Provosts of Eton College and King's College Cambridge, the king's two great foundations, lay a wreath of lilies and roses respectively in the room in which he died.

Westminster Abbey. Henry V's Chantry Chapel was built in accordance with the King's directive in his will that a chapel be raised over his body at the eastern end of St Edward's Chapel. The Chapel is decorated with scenes from Henry's life, including his great victory at Agincourt. The King's tomb is of Purbeck marble, but the effigy has suffered badly over the years; the silver covering was stolen and the head was removed, but has recently been replaced in polyester resin. The body of his Queen, Catherine of Valois, rests beneath the altar in this chapel, while her very fine wooden funeral effigy is in the Abbey's Undercroft Museum. Also in the museum can be seen Henry V's shield, purchased specially for his funeral, and his tilting helmet.

Monmouth Castle (Gwent). Very little stands of this castle, which was the birthplace of Henry V in 1387, but the visitor can, in the summer months, walk round what is left of the keep and great hall. The castle was built in 1071, and it became an important fortress during Henry IV's battles with Owen Glendower. A short walk down the hill from the castle runs the River Monnow with its bridge on which was built the gate-tower to defend the town from Welsh raids from the west. The gate-tower has also been used as a toll house and prison, and it is the last remaining example of its kind in Britain.

Oxford
The Queen's College. Henry V was what we would call a graduate of this college, although in fact the term used for someone of his standing, who was barred from a fellowship because of wealth, or through being born in the northern counties, was *commensaliis*. The college had been founded in 1381 by Robert de Eglesfield who was chaplain to Queen Philippa, wife of Edward III.

The Bodleian Library. Henry V's youngest brother, Humphrey, Duke of Gloucester, gave some 280 volumes of his very fine library to Oxford University in 1439. On receiving this gift, the University decided to build a library worthy of such a fine collection of books and the magnificent room, known as the Duke Humphrey Library, with its beautifully painted ceiling, was completed in 1488. Unfortunately, through a subsequent lack of funds the University was unable to keep the library in a proper state of repair and most of the books were sold. In the late sixteenth century, Sir Thomas Bodley, a scholar and diplomat, rescued the library from its parlous condition and it now takes his name.

All Souls' College. Henry Chichele, Archbishop of Canterbury, founded All Souls' in 1438, so that the Fellows might 'pray for the souls of Henry V, and all those who fell in the wars for the Crown of France'. The front quadrangle, which was built between 1438 and 1444, still retains its medieval appearance.

Penshurst Place (Kent). The fortified manor house at Penshurst was built in the middle of the fourteenth century by Sir John de Pulteney. Its magnificent great hall, with its splendid chestnut-beamed ceiling, is the finest of its kind in the country. The house came into royal ownership when it was held by two of Henry V's brothers: first by John, Duke of Bedford; and then by Humphrey, Duke of Gloucester, who held it until his death in 1447. The manor was then given to Humphrey Stafford, first Duke of Buckingham. Penshurst is about eight miles south-west of Tonbridge, where the B2176 road meets the B2188.

Pickering Castle (North Yorks.). In 1267 this castle became a Lancastrian stronghold when it was conferred by charter to Edward Crouchback, Henry III's younger son, who was created Earl of Lancaster. It passed to Edward II, but was regained for the house of Lancaster by Henry IV, who stayed at Pickering on his way south to claim the throne after landing at Ravenspur in July 1399.

Pickering is a few miles north of Malton on the southern edge of the Yorkshire Moors, and at the crossing of what were once important forest routes. William I built the original castle, but the present ruins date from the end of the twelfth century.

Tutbury Castle (Staffs.). Henry IV inherited this castle from his father, John of Gaunt. Much work was done by Henry, and later by Margaret of Anjou from 1446 to 1461, when she held the castle as part of her jointure. The curtain wall and rectangular towers which still stand date from the fifteenth century, but the gatehouse is fourteenth century and the facade of the great hall seventeenth century.

Titchfield Abbey (Hants.) was founded as a house of Premonstratensian canons in 1232 by Peter des Roches, Bishop of Winchester, and in 1445, in the monastic church, Henry VI married Margaret of Anjou. At the Dissolution the Abbey passed to Thomas Wriothesley, first Earl of Southampton, who converted it into a private residence called Place House. He incorporated the nave of the church into the gatehouse range of his mansion, and, although much of the mansion was demolished in 1781, this part still stands to its full height. Titchfield is just a few miles west of Fareham in Hampshire on the A27 road.

Warwick
The Beauchamp Chantry Chapel, St Mary's Church. In 1439, Richard Beauchamp, Earl of Warwick, governor and tutor to Henry VI, and latterly his Lieutenant-Governor in France, died in Rouen. His embalmed body was brought back to Warwick and laid to rest in his chantry chapel. His fine tomb, with its bronze-gilt effigy, lies in the middle of the chapel, which is a gem of fifteenth-century architecture.

7

THE HOUSE OF YORK

The new King had been born at Rouen in April 1442 to Cecily Neville (daughter of the 1st Earl of Westmorland) and Richard, Duke of York, who had been executed, together with his second son, after the battle of Wakefield. Therefore at the change of dynasty Edward IV was only nineteen years old; but England now had a man on the throne cast in the true mould of a king. Tall (he stood six feet four inches), handsome and of a pleasing disposition, he was to prove himself a brave fighter and a very skilful general. Possessed of considerable intelligence, he was capable when exerting himself of governing wisely, but he had a broad streak of indolence and hedonism. In these early days he much preferred to leave matters of State to his cousin Richard Neville, Earl of Warwick, and to enjoy the fruits of his kingdom. It was a mistake that nearly cost him his throne.

Edward realized that with a large Lancastrian army still in the field there was no time for a coronation. In less than three weeks from being proclaimed king he left London for the north, and on 29 March 1461 he avenged the Yorkist defeats of Wakefield and St Albans at the battle of Towton. This battle, fought two and a half miles south of Tadcaster, was the bloodiest of all the battles of the Wars of the Roses; the Yorkists gained a complete victory in that part of the country where the Lancastrian strength was greatest. The numbers of those who perished on the field of battle, or in the pursuit, will never be accurately known, but it was probably in the region of twenty thousand, and the casualties in this one battle were almost a third of those suffered throughout the Wars of the Roses.

Edward spent the next three weeks in York, where there were plenty of Lancastrian heads to replace those of his father and others that had grinned down upon the city since Wakefield. In case lurking foes from across the Scottish border should decide to take advantage of this cataclysm that had befallen the English aristocracy and gentry, Warwick was left to guard the north, while Edward returned to London, where the usual coronation festivities and distribution of honours culminated in his crowning on Sunday, 28 June.

In spite of the great killing at Towton the war in the north was to drag on for a further three years with, as we have already seen, Queen Margaret getting what help she could from Scotland and France. But after the defeats at Hedgeley Moor in April and Hexham in May 1464, the Lancastrian effort in those parts was spent, and it only remained for John Tiptoft, Earl of Worcester, and Constable of England – a man as cruel as he was cultured – to bring their nobles and knights to trial by the score with a view to execution.

Edward was a valiant man of war, but he loved peace for what he could get from it by way of ease and enjoyment. For a little while he was content to allow the powerful Neville family to run the kingdom for him, and had he let matters go on in this way the Wars of the Roses might have been over. But the King had a will of his own; he would not be thwarted, and when he was he could quickly slough off his indolence and let it be known that he was the master and a man to be reckoned with. His quarrel with the Nevilles lasted six years, but in the end he triumphed.

The quarrel concerned first his marriage to Elizabeth Woodville, or Wydvile, which occurred on May Day 1464, and was for a time a carefully guarded secret. Edward's female entanglements were to cause him and others a great deal of trouble. It was later alleged, and with fatal consequences, that he had entered into a marriage contract with Lady Eleanor Boteler. Now here he was – because he could not get what he wanted otherwise – married to a lady five years his senior, the widow of a Lancastrian knight, and although her mother had first been married to Henry V's brother, Elizabeth was not considered queen material. To Warwick and other magnates the announcement came as an unwelcome shock (especially to Warwick, who had plans for a French bride), and shock turned to resentment when the King started to shower honours and wealthy marriages on his wife's many relations – including her younger brother, John, who drew the eighty-year-old Duchess of Norfolk out of the hat as a bride!

But a more damaging difference between the King and Warwick arose over foreign affairs, for here the matter was raised above a purely family quarrel. Warwick was convinced that a French alliance was essential to forestall any possibility of a Lancastrian revival borne upon French arms; while he was working hard to this end, Edward was all the time negotiating behind his back with the Duke of Burgundy. Just as Warwick was bringing his negotiations to a successful conclusion

Edward, in November 1467, announced his pact with the Burgundian court, which included the marriage of his sister Margaret to Charles the Bold.

Warwick was humiliated and deeply angered. He had made one king, why not another? He won over Edward's foolish and ambitious brother George Duke of Clarence with specious promises, and married him to his daughter and co-heiress Isabella. Next he stirred up trouble in the north, where his kinsman, Sir John Conyers, calling himself Robin of Redesdale, headed a troublesome insurrection. Edward, together with his brother Richard of Gloucester, moved north in a leisurely way to deal with this disturbance, only to find himself sandwiched between two hostile armies. Warwick (recently arrived from Calais) and Clarence were advancing from the south, and Robin moved round Edward's flank to cut him off from London. Reinforcements under Lords Devon and Pembroke were defeated by the northern rebels at the battle of Edgcote on 26 July 1469, and Edward, who was then at Olney and unable to rally his scattered forces, was made to realize that he was Warwick's prisoner.

For a short while England presented the ludicrous spectacle of a country with two kings, both of whom were in prison. But Warwick, in spite of his popularity, could not carry his schemes any further, and Edward played his hand craftily. He decided to dissemble, professing himself penitent and ready to mend his ways. In due course he was liberated; but the breach between these two powerful men could not be healed, and Warwick continued to plot. Another insurrection – this time in Lincolnshire – required the King once again to march north. In a battle near Empingham on 12 March 1470 – known as Losecoat Field from the way in which the rebels hastened their flight – the King defeated Sir Robert Welles, who before his execution confessed that Warwick was the instigator of the revolt and that he had intended to place Clarence on the throne. Warwick promptly fled to France, where Louis XI saw his opportunity.

Warwick's alliance with Margaret of Anjou has already been related; it was as strange as it was unfruitful, but at first there was a measure of success. His landing in Devon took Edward by surprise, and it was now Edward's turn to seek safety in flight. But when his brother-in-law, Charles of Burgundy, realized that Warwick's policy was to aid France against him, he readily lent Edward ships, mercenaries and money. In March 1471 Edward, following almost exactly in Henry IV's footsteps, landed at Ravenspur and overcame the sullen resistance of the Yorkshiremen by declaring that he came only to claim his paternal inheritance. His march south, gathering reinforcements as he went, was swift and skilful. At Nottingham he felt strong enough to resume the royal title, and a few days later he met Clarence, who reaffirmed his loyalty. Warwick was at Coventry and not disposed to give battle, and so on to London, where on 11 April the council opened the city gates and King Edward had come home in triumph.

His subsequent defeat of the Lancastrian armies, first at Barnet, where Warwick was among the slain, and then at Tewkesbury, did not end the Wars of the Roses; but for fourteen years there was peace, and when on 21 May 1471 Edward returned to his capital in the full panoply of victory, his second and more happy reign may be said to have begun. For the next twelve years Edward gave the country what it most needed – peace. Inevitably there were a few foreign and domestic disruptions, which Edward handled adroitly, showing himself to be a very sound man of business and administration. He realized the importance to the country of the merchant class, whose activities had been so greatly disrupted during the recent war, and he managed the Crown's finances well enough to refrain from taxation demands for several years. It is true that the Lancastrian sequestrations considerably helped to fill the royal coffers, but Edward and his beautiful wife held a court that was reckoned the most splendid in Europe. The magnificence of dress and furnishings was matched only by the lavishness of the hospitality and the excellence of the hunting.

Edward was not a benefactor of education (there was a time when he nearly closed down Eton), but he founded a permanent royal library, and together with his brother-in-law, Earl Rivers, encouraged and patronized William Caxton, who set up his printing establishment at the sign of the Red. Pale, near Westminster Abbey. Jewellers and goldsmiths, the weavers of tapestries and the illuminators of manuscripts, all benefited from the sumptuousness of Edward's court. Above all Edward was a great builder, and to him we owe St George's Chapel, Windsor, and the hall (recently restored) at Eltham Palace.

But this was still an epoch of divided loyalties and martial enterprise; three events were to occur to ruffle the tranquillity of ease and leisure. The first, which caused little more than a ripple, concerned the Earl of Oxford and probably the Duke of Clarence. Oxford made good his escape after Barnet and withdrew to France. In May 1473, backed by Louis and almost certainly with the connivance of Clarence, he landed a small force in Essex, but finding no support quickly re-embarked; he then hovered about the Channel before seizing St Michael's Mount, where he was cut off and in February 1474 surrendered. Edward, who was merciful more often than cruel, spared his life – an act that his brother, Richard, would live to regret.

In October 1472 Edward announced to Parliament his intention of invading France, and met with a most generous response, for Louis had been consistently hostile to the Yorkist cause. For more than two years the way was carefully prepared and military resources built up. The Dukes of Brittany and Burgundy were encouraged by treaty to ally themselves with Edward. However, Brittany faltered early in 1473, and although Charles of Burgundy signed a treaty of alliance in July 1474, when Edward arrived at Calais a year later with 1,500 men-at-arms and 11,000 archers Duke Charles was there to meet him but without his army, which was embroiled in another war many hundreds of miles away. Edward soon realised the futility of this task, and, finding that Louis shared his preference for peace to another ruinous war, was astute enough to strike a very favourable bargain. By the Treaty of Picquigny Edward was paid 75,000 crowns to leave the country, and an annual pension for life of 50,000. There were some, among them Burgundy and Richard of Gloucester, who felt that honour had been surrendered for the sake of peace, but Edward remained unmoved and unrepentant.

The Duke of Gloucester may have grumbled at what he considered was the King's pusillanimity, but he was throughout the reign both loyal and useful to Edward, which was a great deal more than can be said for his other brother, George Duke of Clarence. Clarence with a weak, shallow character, was unstable and unprincipled; capable of much charm, he could also be petulant and moody. For him the grass was always greener on the other side, and his loyalty was consistently in question. Edward showed the utmost patience towards the man who in 1469 had borne arms against him, and thereafter intrigued with his enemies and behaved abominably over the matter of his brother's marriage. The final rupture came when Clarence wanted to marry Mary of Burgundy, Europe's richest heiress, and Edward quite rightly forbade it. Clarence then behaved in an utterly irresponsible and brutal manner*, and ignored every warning that Edward pointedly gave him. Further evidence of treason and rebellion compelled Edward to arrest and arraign his brother, and after much heart-searching (urged on by his Queen and held back by Richard) ordered his execution. On 18 February 1478 the Duke of Clarence died; supposedly he had requested to meet his end in a vat of his favourite malmsey wine – perfectly possible, for he was a man with a warped sense of humour.

Edward's operations against Scotland towards the close of his reign more properly belong to the story of Richard, for by 1482, when the King had planned to lead the invasion, his consistent intemperance was beginning to weaken his constitution. In the end what little was achieved (and this did include the taking of Berwick, in Scottish hands since its surrender by Margaret of Anjou) was due to Richard and the

---

* In April 1477, taking the law into his own hands, he arrested his late wife's servant, Ankarette Twynyho, and had her hanged on trumped up charges.

Earl of Northumberland, his second-in-command. Both this invasion and a further one planned for 1483, but never to materialize, centred round King James III's brother, the Duke of Albany – sometimes described as a Clarence in a kilt – who was shifty and totally unreliable. James III was a weak King, but had Edward succeeded in putting Albany in his place, Scotland (although perhaps not England) would have been worse served.

While Edward was genuinely determined to pursue an aggressive policy towards Scotland, it is doubtful whether his plans of a further invasion of France were ever more than half-hearted. His risky foreign policy, based upon the friendship of Louis XI, finally broke down when Burgundy came to terms with Louis in December 1482, and Edward's pension was stopped. Greatly angered, he undoubtedly considered an invasion, but his health prevented it, and in the month before he died he had changed direction and was anxious to preserve the peace.

Edward died at Westminster on 9 April 1483; he was not quite forty-one. Since his restoration the country had prospered under his able administrations. In 1470 England was in dire distress; by his personality, determination and ever growing achievements, Edward saved his country from destruction and set her on the road to prosperity. He was buried in his splendid – but far from completed – new Chapel of St George at Windsor, and the throne passed to his son, an intelligent and sensitive boy of twelve, with his uncle, Richard, determined to control the destiny of the nation.

Edward V was never crowned, and his reign lasted for only eleven weeks. The sad story of the two sons of Edward IV belongs to the reign of their uncle, Richard III, and we can pass directly on to this King.

Richard Plantagenet was born at Fotheringhay Castle on 2 October 1452; he was the youngest son and eleventh child of the Duke and Duchess of York. As a child he was very delicate, but he was not the wicked monster distorted in body and mind that the tendentious writings of Tudor historians would have us believe. It is true that he was below average height and one shoulder was slightly higher than the other, but there is no reliable record of deformity. Indeed the Countess of Desmond, who lived to know Sir Walter Raleigh, and who had danced with Richard, reported him as being 'the handsomest man in the room, except his brother Edward, and was very well made'.

Richard was only eight when his brother was proclaimed King, and his early years were spent at Fotheringhay and under the protection of his cousin, the Earl of Warwick, at Middleham in Yorkshire – later to become his own most favoured residence. He accompanied Edward into exile, and as a young man of seventeen he fought with distinction at Barnet and Tewkesbury; in 1475 he was in France with Edward, but the principal service he rendered his brother was in the north of England, where Edward had given him vast estates. For thirteen years he virtually ruled, as the King's deputy but with his own council, those counties north of the Trent. As Warden of the West March he was constantly involved in military activity against the French-inspired raids of James III's Scots. In May 1480 he was created Lieutenant-General in the North, and although the planned invasion of Scotland for the following year never went further than a naval action, in July and August 1482 Richard invested Berwick, and at the head of a large army burned his way into Edinburgh without any serious fighting. It was a messy, inconclusive campaign with only the re-taking of Berwick to show for it, but the fault lay not so much with Richard as with Edward's indecisiveness.

Maybe it was the twists and turns of fortune's wheel during the early formative years that moulded a character very different from that of his elder brothers. Where Edward – and to a lesser extent Clarence – was gay and warm-hearted, making friends easily, Richard was taciturn, cold and withdrawn. He disliked dalliance and professed – not always convincingly – a high moral virtue. He kept his own counsel and went his own way; when he most needed friends he found that friendship, for him, was but a veneer on the harsh canvas of hatred and suspicion. But he was a sound commander and a courageous fighter, and in his short reign, although he made blunders, he proved himself to be in many ways an able and intelligent ruler. Though he was often accused of being a cunning schemer, it seems more likely that impetuosity, not guile, was the hallmark of his character.

In 1472 Richard married Anne Neville, Warwick's second daughter and co-heiress with Clarence's wife, Isabella, to the vast Beauchamp estates. It had been a stormy wooing, for Clarence – whose ward she was – raised considerable objections at losing half the inheritance, and even went so far as to spirit Anne away in the kitchen of a neighbour's house. However, the persistent Richard found her, and in their twelve years of married life – spent chiefly in the north away from the hurly-burly of court life – they were to know great happiness, marred only by the death of their ten-year-old son.

When Edward died his son, Edward V, was at Ludlow in the care of his uncle Anthony, Earl Rivers. The late King was fully aware of his wife's unpopularity – and more particularly of that of her Woodville relations – and although his will did not long survive, it is well established that in it he designated Richard of Gloucester Protector during the young King's minority. Richard was in the north, and the Woodvilles had a slender control of the council in London. Clearly they could not prevent the protectorship, but they hoped to establish a regency council to whom the Protector would be responsible. Towards the end of April 1483 the new King, accompanied by his uncle Rivers, his half-brother Sir Richard Grey*, his chamberlain Sir Thomas Vaughan, and an escort of some two thousand Welsh soldiers, set out for London. Richard started south at about the same time.

Lord Hastings, who at the time of Edward's death was one of Richard's principal supporters, sent couriers to warn him that the Woodvilles had no intention of allowing him. unfettered control. Richard therefore suggested to Rivers that the two parties should meet at Northampton and proceed to London together. At Northampton Richard was joined by the young Duke of Buckingham, a new and welcome, but somewhat surprising (for he came of ardent Lancastrian stock) recruit. Buckingham was all that Richard was not; loquacious, flamboyant – Richard probably realized that he was something of a *faux bonhomme*, but next to himself he was the senior peer of the realm with royal blood in his veins, and therefore an important acquisition. Rivers had left the King and his escort at Stony Stratford and ridden back to Northampton with Grey and Vaughan to meet Richard. After a convivial evening all retired to bed; next morning Rivers and his companions found themselves under arrest, and Richard with Buckingham rode into Stony Stratford, dismissed his nephew's Welsh escort, and with many protestations of loyalty accompanied the bewildered boy to his capital.

Edward V arrived in London on 4 May; his mother and other members of her family had sought sanctuary in Westminster Abbey on learning what had happened at Northampton. Richard may not have had designs on the Crown at this early stage, but he was determined to resist any opposition to his rule during the minority. The Duke of Buckingham, who was a man scarcely less ambitious than Richard, became the recipient of great riches and rewards, and for a time Protector and Duke worked closely together. Lord Hastings was their first victim. In spite of his intense dislike for many of the Woodvilles, jealousy of Buckingham had driven Hastings into their camp, and he had formed the foolish habit of holding, together with Lord Stanley and John Morton, Bishop of Ely, a rival council to the Protector's. At a council meeting at the Tower on 13 June Richard suddenly had these three and Thomas Rotherham, Archbishop of York, arrested, and

* Grey was Elizabeth Woodville's second son by Sir John Grey. He is sometimes designated Lord Richard Grey, a title he may have assumed when his brother was created Marquess of Dorset.

Hastings was summarily executed on Tower Green. This was the Protector's first blunder, for it was one thing to execute Rivers (which he did twelve days later at Pontefract), but another to execute Hastings, who was of the old nobility and whose death was to raise powerful antagonisms.

Three days later it became fairly clear that Richard was thinking in terms of the throne. He had probably realized that in order to rule unchallenged, which was what he intended doing, he would have to be king. He went with the Archbishop of Canterbury, and certain other nobles, to Westminster, where Queen Elizabeth was persuaded (the threat of force was clearly in the background) to surrender her second son, Richard Duke of York, from sanctuary. He joined his brother, who on Buckingham's suggestion had already been 'more comfortably lodged' in the Tower. Both boys were murdered there, probably in the autumn of 1483, and quite possibly at the instigation of Buckingham. But the exact circumstances of their death will for ever remain a mystery.

With the Princes safely in the Tower, it now became necessary for Richard to justify his intended assumption of kingship. There was no great problem here. The old canard was raked up that Edward's marriage to Elizabeth Woodville was invalid because he had been pre-contracted to Lady Eleanor Boteler, and that it had been celebrated in an unconsecrated place; therefore Elizabeth's children were bastards. Clarence's offspring were even more easily accounted for, because, since Edward had executed their father in 1478, they could be conveniently excluded from the succession under their father's attainder. This doubtful reasoning did not entirely convince the citizens of London that Richard was therefore the true male Yorkist heir, but Buckingham worked so skilfully for Richard's cause that on 23 June he was able to head a deputation that waited on Richard at his riverside home of Baynard's Castle, and swore allegiance to him as King Richard III. The new King was crowned amid the greatest splendour on 6 July.

In October 1483 Richard was faced with what could have been a most serious insurrection had he not got warning of it and struck before the insurgents were fully prepared. Buckingham, like Hastings before him, had suddenly veered over to the Woodvilles. The exact cause of his discontent is uncertain, but it seems that the higher his fortune the higher rose his ambition, and that he thought he could plot a course for himself through devious channels to the throne.

A large-scale revolt, aimed at restoring Edward V, had been smouldering in the southern counties before Buckingham, repenting of his recent past, announced his intention of joining the rebels, and at the same time declared that the Princes were dead. This news caused some consternation, but apparently all were agreed that Richard must go. The fact that the Princes were dead made no difference to Buckingham (although it enabled Elizabeth Woodville to support the revolt), but his intentions towards Henry Tudor, now the figurehead of rebellion, probably differed from those of the other participants.

The Woodvilles, presumably with Buckingham's knowledge and consent, were in touch with Margaret Beaufort (now married to Lord Stanley) and through her had arranged for her exiled son, Henry Tudor, to invade England with troops supplied by the Duke of Brittany. On the successful conclusion of the enterprise Henry was to marry Elizabeth of York, and through this union it was hoped that the two great houses of Lancaster and York would be able to live in peace with one another. As is well known, this happy event was deferred for three years, but Henry did make an attempt – if a somewhat belated one – to honour his side of the bargain. He encountered a severe storm, and by the time he was off Poole only two of his fifteen ships were still with him, Buckingham had already been executed and the insurrection in the west country had been suppressed. Henry returned to Brittany; but he had at least shown that he was a force to be reckoned with, and in the months ahead many were comforted – and others disturbed – by the thought of an alternative ruler ready to cross the sea.

Richard was well aware of the insecurity of his position. At home, in spite of all his efforts towards good government, he had many enemies, and across the Channel exiled Lancastrians schemed to place Henry Tudor on the throne. The death of the Prince of Wales in April 1484 was a bitter blow; now without an heir, and with a wife who could bear no more children, he knew that Henry, with his intended bride, would gain many fresh supporters. An attempt that summer to bribe the Duke of Brittany's treasurer to have Henry closely confined, if not delivered to Richard, almost succeeded, but Henry was warned in time and escaped to Paris. There he was shortly joined by the Earl of Oxford, whose gaoler had obligingly released him from the fortress of Hammes, where he had been imprisoned since his unsuccessful attempt to invade England.

As 1484 gave way to 1485 King Richard was pursued and haunted by a profound feeling that the very air he breathed was charged with treason. It came almost as a relief to learn that the Lancastrian invasion, so long threatened, was now definitely planned for the summer of 1485. Until the recent treaty of friendship with Scotland, half England had been under arms against possible invasion on two fronts, but now there was something positive against which to prepare. With the coming of the fighting season garrisons were strengthened and the commissioners of array were ordered to have their musters ready to march at a day's notice. No efforts were spared to portray through proclamations Henry

Tudor's bastard descent on both sides of his family, and to remind Englishmen that he would be carried to their shores in French ships crowded with foreign soldiers. Richard took up residence in Nottingham Castle during June, from where he could be kept in constant communication with his lieutenants through the method, first introduced by Edward IV, of posting couriers at twenty-mile intervals along the principal highways.

Henry sailed from Harfleur on 1 August. His small fleet carried nearly two thousand French mercenaries, and with him sailed his uncle Jasper Tudor, Lord Oxford and other knights, both Yorkist and Lancastrian, who had shared his exile. On 7 August the fleet entered Milford Haven, and the troops disembarked at Dale. From here he marched through Wales, where many of the Welsh gentry rallied to his red dragon standard, and it was significant that neither of Richard's lieutenants in the principality – Sir Walter Herbert in the south and Sir William Stanley in the north – hindered him. At Shrewsbury Sir Gilbert Talbot joined him with five hundred of Lord Shrewsbury's retainers.

The speed with which Henry marched clearly surprised Richard, who was still at Nottingham waiting for reinforcements to join him. However, when on 19 August he heard that Henry was at Lichfield, he realized that he could wait no longer. On the night of the 21st Henry's army camped at a place called White Moors, five miles from Atherstone, while Richard, marching west from Leicester, made his camp in the Sutton Cheyney area. The battle of Bosworth was fought the next day on Ambion Hill. The result of this fiercely contested fight is well known. Richard, the last English King to die in battle, scorned safety in flight and went down fighting in the best traditions of medieval chivalry; with him went the Duke of Norfolk and some thousand others. Lord Stanley and his brother William (arch-trimmers, both of them) held the key to success or failure; after some hesitation they opted for the Tudor. The Earl of Northumberland, in command of Richard's rearguard, refused at the critical moment to support his King.

The body of the last Plantagenet King was stripped naked and with a halter round its neck was thrown over a horse and taken to Leicester, where it lay for two days before burial in the chapel of the Grey Friars. 'The evil that men do lives after them, the good is oft interred with their bones.' And so it was with Richard. The Tudors made a very thorough job of besmirching his character and his record. He was, of course, a typical product of his time in that he was intensely ambitious and sufficiently ruthless to see that any obstacle to his ambition was swiftly removed; but had he reigned for longer than two years and two months he would very likely have found a niche among those rulers remembered for their justice, fairness and administrative competence. In the short time allotted to him Richard passed, through his only Parliament, an impressive list of legal reforms; he founded the Council of the North, which was to endure almost unaltered in composition for more than 150 years, and in general he showed that he had the ability to govern wisely and the will to work.

After his restoration in 1471, Edward IV had twelve years of comparative peace, and from the point of view of culture he made good use of them. He is principally remembered for his rebuilding of St George's Chapel at Windsor, but the literary, musical and architectural achievements of the reign were considerable. Edward was a voracious reader, as his specially commissioned books now in the British Museum testify, and he spent money liberally on the transcription of books in manuscript. He also patronized the arts and the splendour of his court was a curtain raiser to the full flowering of Tudor magnificence.

His brother had only two years on the throne, but Richard was a great lover of music, he raised the singing in the Chapel Royal to the highest level and both he and his Queen had very talented troupes of minstrels. The first laws to be written entirely in English were produced in Richard III's reign and Sir Thomas Malory published his *Morte d'Arthur*. Richard was also an enthusiastic builder, although most of his efforts in this direction went to improving and altering existing buildings; he carried out alterations at the Tower of London, Baynard's Castle, Windsor Castle and Westminster Palace, and made gifts of money towards the completion of King's College, Cambridge, and St George's Chapel, Windsor.

Barnard Castle (Co. Durham). This castle passed to Anne Neville from her father, the Earl of Warwick, and was used by her husband, Richard Duke of Gloucester, as one of his residences while he was Lieutenant-General of the North. Richard added to the buildings, and in particular the Brackenbury Tower dates from his time. The castle is situated on the north-west side of the town.

Cambridge
Queens' College. Margaret of Anjou wished to found a college to match, or rival, that of her husband, and later both Elizabeth Woodville and Anne Neville (queens of Edward IV and Richard III respectively) became actively interested in the college – the college thus gaining the plural designation. Of these three queens only Anne actually endowed the college. John Fisher, Bishop of Rochester, was a Master of the college, and during his mastership Erasmus was a member.

Eltham Palace (Kent). Edward IV built the very splendid great hall of this palace, the building being finished in 1480. It was the only part of the palace to escape destruction during the Commonwealth, but gradually fell into decay, being used at one time as a barn. Visitors to Eltham can now see it rebuilt in its pristine glory, using much of the old stone, and timber for the fine hammer-beam roof. This was the work of Mr Stephen Courtauld in the 1930s.

Other parts of this old palace, which was a favourite resort of many of England's sovereigns from the time of Edward II to that of Elizabeth I, are in the process of being excavated. The foundations of Henry VIII's chapel and royal apartments have recently been uncovered. Eltham is three miles south-east of Greenwich.

Fotheringhay (Northants.). In 1412 Edward Duke of York, grandson of Edward III, obtained a charter for the endowment of a college in this attractive Northamptonshire village. The college has long since disappeared, but the beautiful church with its memorial to the college's founder, who was killed at Agincourt, and the tomb of his nephew Richard, Duke of York, father of Edward IV, who was killed at the battle of Wakefield, still stands on the site. The church is usually locked when not in use, but the key is available in the village.

Fotheringhay Castle, like the College of the Blessed Virgin and All Saints, is now no more. But the site, marked by grass mounds, is clearly visible at the east end of the village. In this castle Mary Queen of Scots was executed on 8 February 1587. Fotheringhay is some twelve miles south-west of Peterborough off the A605 road, three miles west of Elton.

London
The British Museum. In the museum's Medieval Room can be seen the Sword of State which was carried before Edward, Prince of Wales, the son of Edward IV, and, for a brief period, King Edward V. It is thought that the sword was made in Holland or Germany, and it bears enamelled arms on the principal side and grip. Edward was made Duke of Cornwall at his birth, and in 1471 was created Prince of Wales and Earl of Chester, so it would seem likely that this sword was carried before him when he visited Chester in 1475. It could perhaps have also been used by another Prince Edward, the son of Richard III, on the occasion of his investiture as Prince of Wales and Earl of Chester at York in September 1483, by which time Edward V was a prisoner in the Tower.

Crosby's Place was built in Bishopsgate by Sir John Crosby in 1466. Crosby died in 1475 and his house, with its magnificent great hall possessing a richly carved ceiling and minstrels gallery, was either bought or rented by Richard, Duke of Gloucester, and served as his London residence until he became King. It may have been here and not at Baynard's Castle, which was the home of his mother, that Richard was offered the Crown. In 1908 the great hall was taken down, stone by stone, and re-erected in Cheyne Walk, Chelsea.

The Tower of London. (See also Chapters 3–6.) The Tower, for long the scene of judicial murder and torture, was in the reigns of Edward IV and Richard III witness to three particularly unpleasant, hole-and-corner, royal murders. In February 1478 Edward IV's brother, George Duke of Clarence, was done to death. Mystery still surrounds the manner of his dying, but he was probably kept prisoner in the Bloody Tower (some accounts have it as the Bowyer) and tradition, based on a near-contemporary account, puts the method as drowning – suitably enough, for he was fond of wine – in a butt of Malmsey.

In about the autumn of 1483 there probably occurred in the Bloody Tower (at that time called the Garden Tower) the double murder of Edward V and his brother, Richard Duke of York. Arguments still persist as to who perpetrated this crime; but it seems fairly certain that the three men who knew most about it were James Tyrell (temporarily in charge of the Tower at the time), Henry Stafford, the Duke of Buckingham, who had his eye on the throne, and the boys' uncle, Richard III, who had usurped it. Where the two princes were buried is uncertain, but the skeletons of two young boys were found in the reign of Charles II, under a staircase to the south side of the White Tower.

Ludlow Castle (Salop). The keep of this castle was one of the first of stone to be built in England, and dates back to 1095. Some parts of the Norman building survive, and in particular the delightful chapel in the inner bailey; but the castle's first direct connection with a ruling sovereign starts with Edward IV. The castle suffered considerable damage during the Wars of the Roses, but was evidently considered fit for occupation soon afterwards, because Edward IV sent his two sons there, and a Council governed the province in Prince Edward's name. It was from Ludlow in 1483 that Edward, now King, set off on his last fatal journey to London and the Tower.

Middleham Castle (North Yorks.). This castle, which is a few miles north of Ripon, is chiefly associated with Richard III. It became the property of the Neville family in 1270, and descended through that family to Richard Earl of Warwick, the Kingmaker. Richard III, who married Anne Neville, Warwick's daughter, had spent much of his youth at Middleham. When he became the King's Lieutenant-General in the North he used it as his principal residence – the castle had by then been given to him by his brother, Edward IV.

It is now administered by the Department of the Environment, and a good deal of it still stands. It is perfectly possible, with the aid of the guide book, to visualize its former splendour.

Sheriff Hutton Castle (North Yorks.). A small part of this famous castle, which was one of Richard III's favourite residences, still stands just outside a farmyard in the village. It is not under the care of any public body (which, in view of its former importance as the headquarters of the Council of the North, is unfortunate), but it can be viewed by the public, using two public footpaths which approach the ruins from different angles. Sheriff Hutton is twelve miles north of York off the A64 York to Malton road.

Battle of Tewkesbury (Glos), 4 May 1471. This was not to be the last battle of the Wars of the Roses, but it did decide which of two Kings were to rule England, for Edward IV gained a decisive victory over the Lancastrian army commanded by Edward Beaufort, fourth Duke of Somerset, and the most important casualty of the fighting was Henry VI's only son, Prince Edward. Three weeks after the batle, with the murder of Henry VI in the Tower, the legitimate Lancastrian line was extinct.

On Easter Sunday 1471 the Earl of Warwick, the Kingmaker, was killed and his Lancastrian army defeated at Barnet. On that same day Henry VI's Queen, Margaret of Anjou, landed at Weymouth from France, and was soon joined by a number of prominent supporters bringing with them troops. Edward IV waited at Windsor to see whether the Lancastrians would march on London, or strike northwards to join forces with Jasper Tudor across the Severn. The latter was Somerset's and the Queen's obvious choice, and when Edward learnt their decision, he set off in pursuit.

Edward's attempts to bring the enemy to battle were at first unsuccessful, owing to a very clever piece of deception by the Lancastrians. But he did manage to get a message through to Gloucester warning the Governor to be certain to deny them the city and therefore the river crossing. Eventually the Yorkists caught up with Somerset and Margaret at Tewkesbury; the Lancastrians by then had marched enough, and their decision to stand and fight was dictated more by exhaustion than by confidence in the outcome. Somerset chose to make his stand on ground just north of Gupshill Manor, with his left resting on the Swilgate brook, and his right stretching to the low ground west of the main road. The Yorkists prepared for battle some 350 yards from their enemy; the King commanded the centre, with his brother Clarence, Richard Duke of Gloucester took the left of the line and Lord Hastings the right. The battle was not of long duration, and the victory was completed - as is so often the case – in the retreat; much Lancastrian slaughter took place in a field still known as Bloody Meadow near the banks of the River Avon. The Duke of Somerset, and some other Lancastrian leaders, took sanctuary in the Abbey; but the victorious Yorkists, violating every canon of good faith, managed to get them out and to speedy trial and execution.

The site of the heaviest fighting is still open country. It lies to the west of the A38(T) road from Gloucester, about half a mile south of Tewkesbury Abbey. There are two principal vantage points: the high ground where the road passes Stonehouse Farm, and Tewkesbury Park, now the property of Tewkesbury Borough Council.

Battle of Towton (North Yorks.), 29 March 1461. The casualties at Towton were not only the highest of any battle fought in the Wars of the Roses, but in any battle fought on British soil. Polydore Virgil puts them at twenty thousand and in the Paston letters we get a total of twenty-eight thousand – probably the truth lies somewhere in between.

After the second battle of St Albans, Henry VI, against all advice, forbade his army to march on London, and commenced withdrawing north. The holocaust from which Henry had saved London was reserved for numerous smaller towns. Edward IV, following the trail of ravaged towns and burnt-out homesteads, caught up with the Lancastrian army in the heart of their country at Towton, after a successful skirmish in the Dintingdale Valley where two of the principal Lancastrian leaders, Lords Clifford and Neville, were killed.

Henry Beaufort, third Duke of Somerset, commanded the Lancastrian army, and he took up a position just to the south of the monument on the A162 road from Towton to Pontefract, and his line stretched from the edge of the high ground on the west to a little way across the A162. Edward IV and his Yorkists held the line on the cross ridge beyond the slight depression that runs directly in front of the Lancastrian position in an east–west direction. Most of the heavy casualties took place during the retreat of the Lancastrian army, especially while they were trying to cross the swollen Cock Beck by the small wooden bridge. Except for the fact that the ground is now well cultivated, the battlefield is very little changed, and can be viewed quite easily from the A162 road. There is a public footpath from Towton to Stutton, and about half a mile along it the Cock is bridged at the same spot where the great slaughter took place in 1461.

Warwick Castle (Warwicks.). This castle first became a royal possession after the execution of George Duke of Clarence in 1478, but much of what can be seen today predates that event to about 1345 when Thomas Beauchamp, eleventh Earl of Warwick, started his massive rebuilding. The Beauchamps played a prominent part in national affairs during the fourteenth and fifteenth centuries – the twelfth Earl of Warwick was one of the Lords Appellant in Richard II's reign. In 1450 the castle became a Neville stronghold when Richard Neville married the Beauchamp heiress, Anne. He took, as was the custom at the time, the Warwick title and is known to history as the Kingmaker. George Duke of Clarence married one of his two daughters, the other was married to Richard Duke of Gloucester, who, as Richard III, began building a great tower on the north side of the castle, but it was never finished.

Windsor Castle, St George's Chapel (Berks.). Edward IV decided to build a new chapel to replace the one erected by Henry III and enlarged and renovated by Edward III. Richard Beauchamp, Bishop of Salisbury, was appointed surveyor and after clearance of lodgings and other buildings, work commenced in 1477 on a site immediately to the west of the existing chapel. It was far from complete at the time of Edward's death in 1483, and his last contribution towards it was the arrangement for his own tomb, which is on the north side of the choir with its wonderful wrought-iron gates, said to be the work of John Tresilian. In 1484 Richard III removed the bones of Henry VI from Chertsey Abbey and caused them to be reinterred in St George's Chapel. Lord Hastings, Edward IV's great friend and councillor to Edward V, is buried in the Hastings Chantry. Building work continued through the next three reigns, until the vaulting of the whole chapel was completed in the time of Henry VIII.

8

THE TUDOR KINGS

Henry VII, the founder of the Tudor dynasty, was the nearest approach to a socialist king that England had had since the Conquest, and his friends – of whom there were few – probably found him something of a bore. Nevertheless he was just what the country needed, and in a reign of twenty-four years he served England well, for he was probably the shrewdest and certainly the hardest-working man yet to occupy the throne. In 1485 the country still suffered from the aftermath of internal strife. The peasantry were bewildered, while the magnates were unsettled and, through the pernicious Livery and Maintenance, wielded considerable power. The realm needed stability, both physical and fiscal; Henry VII, without a standing army (save only the Yeomen of the Guard, which he founded) and without undue bloodshed, provided both.

He had gained the throne by right of conquest, for his hereditary claim was almost non-existent. His father, the Earl of Richmond, was the offspring of an obscure Welshman called Owen Tudor (beheaded by Yorkists in 1461) and Henry V's widow, Catherine of Valois; and while his mother, Lady Margaret Beaufort, was descended from John of Gaunt, his blood flowed through a bastard channel in her veins. It is true that the Beauforts had later been legitimized, but they had been expressly excluded from the succession. Furthermore, Henry came to the throne without any training for the task and with no experience of government. He could never have succeeded had he not been strong, self-reliant, cautious and very vigilant. Little by little he rebuilt (for he was not an innovator) the existing departments of State to suit his and the country's needs, and always he brought to bear perseverance, coupled with an uncanny business and legal flair.

Henry entered London to a tremendous welcome on 3 September 1485, and was crowned on 30 October. It was a great pageant attended by the Pope and many of the crowned heads of Europe. Henry, so careful and parsimonious in many ways, was always prepared to open wide the purse strings for any ceremonial that might enhance the prestige of the monarchy. Nor would he have looked out of place among his fellow princes, for according to Polydore Vergil the King was above average height, strongly built and the possessor of a remarkably attractive and cheerful countenance – this latter attribute is scarcely reflected in his portraits.

Henry was in no hurry to honour his pledge to marry Elizabeth of York, for it must not be thought that he was king by right of his marriage to the Yorkist heir. But by January 1486 he considered his position sufficiently established, and the wedding took place that month amid popular enthusiasm. Elizabeth had inherited her mother's beauty, but fortunately not her passion for intrigue. Whereas Elizabeth Woodville was to cause Henry deep concern, her daughter had nothing but a beneficial effect upon the King. The match originated as a political one, but it quickly developed into one of companionship and love. Elizabeth made no attempt to influence her husband in affairs of State, and Henry for his part gave her no cause for suspicion or envy.

The greatly desired union of the two houses did not bring the country internal peace. The last battle of the Wars of the Roses had yet to be fought, and even after that the long and tedious business of Perkin Warbeck showed that there were powerful Yorkists at home and abroad anxious to destroy any Lancastrian usurper. There can be little doubt that Edward IV's two sons had died before Bosworth, but the mystery of their fate made it possible for imposters to be set up to baffle a credulous public. However, the first attempt of this kind sought to impersonate the young Earl of Warwick,* who was in the Tower but very much alive, and whom Henry was able to produce. Nevertheless, a formidable movement gathered around Lambert Simnel, an insignificant Oxford artisan, who had been groomed for stardom by a dissident and crafty priest called Simons.

Simnel was of no consequence, but others in the plot were. Probably Elizabeth Woodville was involved, and the Earl of Lincoln was either in it from the start or easily persuaded to join. When King Richard's young son died, Lincoln (who was Richard's nephew) had been nominated his successor, and although he was apparently loyal, Henry could never be sure of him. Now the chance to strike a blow, the fruits whereof might prove inestimable, could not be resisted. He obtained willing help from his aunt, the Duchess of Burgundy (a sister of Edward IV and Richard III) who paid for two thousand German mercenaries with whom he

---

* Warwick was the son of George Duke of Clarence, brother of Edward IV.

crossed to Ireland. After Simnel had been duly crowned King Edward VI in Dublin, the expedition, now increased by strong Irish contingents, crossed to Lancashire and moved south. Henry had taken up a central position in the midlands, and with his army divided into three 'battles', under himself, Lord Oxford and Rhys ap Thomas, met and defeated the rebels at East Stoke (which lies to the south-west of Newark), on 16 June 1487.

Few details are known about this battle. It lasted for three hours and the casualties are said to have been four thousand rebels and three thousand royalists. Henry, who was not noted for martial enterprise either on the battlefield or in the tiltyard, seems to have fought bravely; Lincoln and the German commander, Schwartz, were killed and the Earl of Kildare, who led the poorly armed Irish contingent, was captured. Neither Simnel nor Simons fought, but both were captured. Henry, with a pretty sense of humour, put Simnel to work in his kitchens, but Simons disappeared from history into a dungeon.

Four years elapsed between the battle of Stoke and the beginning of the Perkin Warbeck affair, which lasted almost ten years and was played out against a background of intensive and very complex diplomatic negotiations between Henry, the Emperor Maximilian, Charles VIII of France and the Spanish monarchs, Ferdinand of Aragon and Isabella of Castile. Perkin Warbeck was the son of a boatman on the Scheldt, who, when he was about seventeen entered the service of a merchant of Brittany doing trade with Ireland. Warbeck, who was conspicuous for his good looks, pleasing manner and elegance of dress, impressed the Irish Yorkists as being an improvement on Simnel, for he was better spoken, more dignified and more self-possessed than the latter. At first he shrank from impersonating the Earl of Warwick, but when pressure was brought to bear by important Irish lords, he went one better than Simnel and consented to assume the personality of Prince Richard, the younger of Edward IV's two sons. Soon he was writing letters to the English Yorkists and the Kings of Scotland and France, outlining his claim to the English throne. Predictably he was at once recognized by the Duchess of Burgundy, and in due course was to receive royal hospitality from many of the princes of Europe, always anxious to fish in Henry's troubled waters.

Henry at first treated the whole affair with scorn, but as the evidence of Warbeck's genuineness was carefully built up and seemingly accepted by other rulers, he may have harboured secret doubts, for the Yorkist Princes had disappeared without trace. In any event as the business dragged on it became more tiresome. From Ireland Warbeck went to France, having to leave that country when Henry, after his only foreign military adventure, made peace with Charles. In 1495, at Deal, his first attempt to invade England with only two hundred men was a complete fiasco, and a return to Ireland produced disappointing results. But in Scotland he received a warm welcome from James IV (particularly annoying for Henry, who was hoping to secure a permanent peace with Scotland through the marriage of his daughter, Margaret, to James), who gave him, among other things, a brave and charming wife in Lady Catherine Gordon. However, the brief Scottish invasion of England which he accompanied was totally unproductive.

After a further profitless period in Ireland Warbeck arrived with his wife in Cornwall on 7 September 1497, and met with remarkable early success in raising some three thousand Cornishmen, but after their failure to take Exeter he abandoned them on the approach of the royal army, and having taken temporary sanctuary in Beaulieu Abbey, he gave himself up. Henry was content to place him on parole and submit him to public humiliation, but on his attempting to escape he was confined to the Tower. From here, in November 1499 after a further conspiracy to rescue him and Warwick had been discovered, Perkin Warbeck was taken to Tyburn and hanged. He had richly deserved his fate; but the execution, five days later, of the feeble-minded Warwick did not redound to Henry's credit.

During these troublesome years there had been periodic rumblings at home against Henry's determined attempts to amass money through swingeing taxation. The men of Yorkshire, many of whom revered the memory of King Richard, showed open hostility to the tax gatherers in 1489 and 1491, while six years later a much more serious expression of discontent came from fifteen thousand Cornishmen, who under their leaders Flammock and Michael Joseph marched on London, only to be defeated in battle at St George's Field, Blackheath.

However, the rout of the Cornishmen and the capture of Warbeck marked 1497 as a turning point in Henry's reign. In this year it may be said that the struggle for ascendancy had been achieved, and the way was now clear for supremacy. There were, it is true, other plots and problems, for besides the one that led to Warwick's and Warbeck's deaths, Edmund de la Pole, Duke of Suffolk (Lincoln's brother) was a constant anxiety to the King until he was surrendered by the Archduke Philip in 1506. Nevertheless, in 1497, the Milanese ambassador was able to report, . . . that this present state is most stable . . . . With concord at home they have no occasion to fear'.

Parliaments did not play a great part in this reign, only seven being summoned in the twenty-four years, and only one in the last ten. Henry showed a remarkable shrewdness in choosing good men to serve him, and government was done chiefly in Council. The King's Council comprised a large body of men drawn from peers, courtiers, churchmen and lawyers, but it seldom, if ever, sat as a whole, and routine business under the firm hand of the King was conducted by a few, such as the Lord Chancellor, the Keeper of the Privy Seal, the Lord Treasurer and one or two judges, meeting in the Star Chamber – but not yet called the Court of Star Chamber. Conciliar government was extended to Wales and the Marches, where first Jasper Tudor (the King's uncle) and then Henry's son, Prince Arthur (until his death in 1502), held sway.

By the end of 1497 the same Milanese ambassador who had reported to his master on the stability of the realm, estimated the King's wealth to be around £6 million – an enormous sum in those days. Money flowed into the royal coffers along devious channels. There were the royal prerogatives, rigidly enforced, such as wardships, appointment of bishops and feudal dues; surplus money from taxes granted by Parliament for campaigns against Scotland and France; the income from customs duties in a country grown rich in trade; and the revenues from Crown lands. For many years the King's annual income considerably exceeded his expenditure, and he left his son a comfortable fortune in jewellery and plate. But the able men he employed to gather in these large sums were not popular; two in particular, Edmund Dudley and Richard Empson, men of comparatively humble origins who served the King faithfully, if perhaps ruthlessly, paid for their zeal with their heads in the next reign.

On 11 February 1503 Queen Elizabeth died. She had played her part nobly, bringing to the court a gaiety and splendour that without her would probably have been lacking. She shared with Henry a love of the chase, and her death – following upon that of their elder son a few months before and the recent departure of Margaret to become Queen in Scotland – left a sad void in Henry's life. But the business of kingship must go forward and before long he was thinking of the need to marry again.

In the closing years of his reign there were many nubile ladies in the courts of Europe, and a good deal of time was spent by the monarchs concerned in devising dynastic marriages. At home Prince Arthur's widow, Catherine of Aragon, languished in an impoverished and miserable state while Henry was continually arguing with her father over the balance of her dowry. At one stage, even though he was convinced that her marriage to Arthur had been consummated, Henry considered marrying her himself, but that was too much for Catherine's mother, Queen Isabella, who forbade any further thought of it. Two other princesses whom the prematurely aged Henry thought about were Margaret of Angoulême and Margaret of Savoy, neither of whom had any desire to fulfil his wish. A third possibility was the recently widowed Juana (Catherine of Aragon's sister), whom Henry had met after she and her husband, Archduke Philip (Emperor Maximilian's son) had been shipwrecked on the Dorset coast. But she was already showing signs of madness, and wherever she went the Archduke accompanied her – in his coffin.

Henry had made himself faintly ridiculous in his search for a bride, and all that he got from it was the ambassadorial reports on the ladies of his choice, giving such fascinating details as the shape of their breasts and the quality of their breath. Even the betrothal of his daughter, Mary to the Archduke Charles (later Charles V) failed to develop into marriage, but at least the promise to marry Catherine of Aragon, said to have been extracted from his surviving son, Prince Henry, as the King lay dying, was honoured.

Henry died at Richmond Palace on 21 April 1509, aged fifty-two. The magnificent funeral service in St Paul's Cathedral and Westminster Abbey was followed by interment in the same vault as his Queen. The beautiful tomb that adorns his chapel was completed by Pietro Torrigiano in 1517.

The achievements of the reign had been very considerable. A new dynasty had been firmly established in circumstances that were far from easy, for Henry had little to work on save the ruin and rubble of many wasted years. Cautiously and patiently he built up the realm; he curbed the power of the barons, improved internal communications, developed a flourishing commerce based upon an efficient mercantile fleet, and was responsive to the promotion of the arts, music and literature. He enjoyed the company of intellectuals such as Erasmus, and was at pains to give his children a thorough training in the arts, languages (he himself spoke Spanish, French, Latin and Italian) and theology. If Henry was a despot he was a moderate and capable one, who got the best results with little bloodshed – how much more profitable were heavy fines than the headsman's axe. When he died he left the kingdom united, rich and at peace with its neighbours.

Henry VIII, who succeeded his father when not quite eighteen years of age, was a self-willed, ebullient extrovert. He possessed charm, but it could quickly turn to rage; gifted and highly intelligent, he was yet unstable, and there was a strong streak of cruelty in his make-up. He must have been a thoroughly unpleasant man, but he was in many ways a great king.

When he came to the throne, and for some years afterwards, he was a magnificent man physically, endowed with both good looks and an athlete's strength and stamina, which enabled him to compete successfully in the jousts and spend long hours in the saddle. His clothes dazzled and his ego knew no bounds. His education had been excellent; he was musical and from early youth took a passionate interest in theological questions. A keen intellect remained unimpaired throughout the later, tyrannical years when the splendid body, afflicted by a brutalizing disease, had swelled to gross and unmanageable proportions.

In compliance with his father's request – and presumably because he fancied himself in love – Henry duly married Catherine of Aragon at Greenwich shortly after his accession, and there was a dual coronation on Michaelmas Day 1509. So far so good, but soon there was a conflict of opinion, for until the rise of Wolsey some four years after the reign began, the late King's councillors retained the position, but not the authority, that they had exercised in the previous reign. Henry's main desire to spend what his father had saved, his immediate thoughts of plunging England back into the years of strife with France, and the old claim of sovereignty, were not at all to their liking.

However, Henry brushed their protests aside. His first problem was a lack of allies, but this was overcome in 1511 when Henry joined Spain and Venice in the Holy League formed by Pope Julius II. A campaign during the summer of 1512 in Spain was a bitter failure – thanks largely to the indifference of Ferdinand, Henry's father-in-law; but nothing daunted Henry took personal command of a large army that landed in Calais the following year, which soon settled down to besiege Thérouanne. The only open engagement of the campaign Henry ironically missed, but the battle of the Spurs (16 August) was hailed as a great victory, and it certainly opened the way for the fall of Thérouanne. A few weeks later the defences of Tournai could not withstand Henry's very formidable artillery train, and the first royal campaign ended in a blaze of glory with the King's triumphal entry into Tournai on 25 September 1513.

While Henry was trifling in France more serious business was afoot in Scotland. The Holy League had drawn a tight band of steel round France, and Louis XII looked towards James IV to renew the 'Auld Alliance'. James was not anxious to engage in a full-scale war against his brother-in-law, even though Border raids, semi-official naval incidents and the retention by Henry of Queen Margaret's jewellery had produced a strained relationship; but the alliance was deep-rooted and in July 1512 James took the decision to renew it. He agreed to advance into England should Henry invade France, and when in the summer of 1513 the French were in grave peril, he prepared to honour his word. Henry, before he left England, had appointed the Earl of Surrey Lord Lieutenant of the North, telling him, 'My lord, I trust not the Scots, therefore I pray you be not negligent.' Although an old man of seventy, Surrey was neither negligent nor negligible, as the Scots discovered at Flodden Field, where on 9 September he won a decisive victory, leaving among the carnage of the battlefield almost the entire chivalry of Scotland, including their King, twelve earls, fourteen lords an archbishop and two bishops. The road to Scotland lay open, but Henry allowed the opportunity to pass, and for the rest of his reign Scotland was always an elusive will-o'-the-wisp.

Thomas Wolsey, whose humble origins spurred his ambition and made him cautious and mistrustful, had become a royal chaplain in 1507, and in 1509 he entered Henry's service as almoner and councillor. His competent handling of the administration of the 1513 campaign ensured him rapid promotion – Archbishop of York in 1514, and the next year a cardinal's hat, legate *a latere* and Lord Chancellor of England. For almost fifteen years the proud, vainglorious but shrewd and hardworking Cardinal presided over affairs, and for most of them Henry was glad to leave him in charge, while he enjoyed the pleasures of court and chase.

In 1515 Francis I, who lusted for glory as much as Henry, became King of France, and four years later the young Charles V was elected to succeed his grandfather as Holy Roman Emperor. For the next thirty years these two men and Henry were to dominate European politics. Henry hated the French; on the other hand, he would ally himself to Francis if there were any danger of the Empire becoming an overbearing power.

In 1519 both Henry and Francis expressed a desire to meet, and the next year Wolsey stage-managed one of history's best known extravaganzas. But the Field of Cloth of Gold had a serious political undertone, and although Henry, while making promises to Francis, was in close touch with Charles, the latter was for a time kept firmly in check, and it seemed as though Wolsey's policy for England to hold the balance of power might meet with success. But England's commercial ties with The Netherlands, Wolsey's need to enlist Charles's help for the papal tiara, and Henry's personal animosity (tinged with jealousy) of Francis, proved too strong. Before three years were out those two great commanders of the reign, the Dukes of Norfolk and Suffolk, were marching and counter-marching large armies across Picardy.

Henry's quarrel with the Pope, which in its wake brought about the downfall of Wolsey, originated from his desire to divorce Catherine and marry Anne Boleyn – a long, drawn-out affair known as the 'King's Great Matter'. His orthodox championship of the Roman Church against Protestant heresies had earned Henry the title of 'Defender of the Faith' from Pope Clement's predecessor, Leo X, and there is little doubt that his and Wolsey's constant importuning for a divorce from Catherine would have been successful were it not that by 1527 Clement was virtually the prisoner of Catherine's nephew, the Emperor Charles.

From this quarrel there developed, very gradually, the English Reformation.

By 1527 it had become· obvious that Catherine could produce no more children. Her only surviving child, Mary, had been born in 1517, but Henry above all else desired a male heir. His bastard son by Bessie Blount was no substitute – and anyway, as it happened, the Duke of Richmond died in 1536. The longing to perpetuate his dynasty was greatly strengthened by another longing – to possess Sir Thomas Boleyn's younger daughter. And Anne, unlike her sister, Mary, would settle for nothing short of marriage. Whether Henry really believed, or merely forced himself to believe, that in marrying his brother's widow he had offended against God's Law cannot be told, but his determination to get what he wanted hardened in each of the six long years of complex and bitter argument.

In August 1529 Thomas Cranmer, a young Cambridge scholar, came forward with the suggestion that the matter of Henry's legal marriage should be submitted to the universities of Europe. This proved a success, for most of those appealed to (including Bologna in the Papal States) pronounced in favour of Henry. Henry did not forget Cranmer. In January 1533 it was known that Anne carried Henry's child, and urgent action became necessary. The see of Canterbury had been vacant since the previous August, and Cranmer, although married and with views more in accordance with the Reformers than were Henry's, was nevertheless selected. The Pope – after thinly veiled threats to withhold the payment of annates – duly granted the bulls for his consecration, and in May 1533, at his court in Dunstable, the Archbishop pronounced sentence to the effect that Henry had never been legally married to Catherine.

Wolsey had fallen from power in October 1529. For some time an aristocratic clique led by Norfolk had been waiting an opportunity to bring down this base-born Cardinal, and his handling of the divorce, the collapse of his European policy and the machinations of Anne Boleyn did the work for them. The Great Seal was given to Thomas More, who was virtually forced to accept the position of Lord Chancellor. It was an unfortunate choice with sad consequences, for More was a man with deeply held conservative convictions, and Henry was now set upon his course for royal supremacy. More resigned after two and a half unhappy years, and when in 1534 Henry made his breach with Rome complete by a series of Acts, chief among them the Act of Supremacy, More and Fisher, Bishop of Rochester, refused to take the oath. Their subsequent execution was one of Henry's darkest deeds.

The way towards divorce and the royal supremacy was made much easier for Henry by the actions of the Reformation Parliament, which sat from November 1529 to April 1536, and although not 'packed' was usually amenable to royal influence. It also marked the beginning of the second great partnership of the reign, for in 1529 Thomas Cromwell became the Member for Taunton. Like Wolsey, under whom he served for some ten years, he was a man of very humble origin, and, also like the Cardinal, he was ambitious, clever and hardworking, but he was more ruthless, wielded more power and gained more substantial achievements than Wolsey.

On 15 January 1535 Henry assumed the title of Supreme Head on Earth of the Church, and declared himself 'not subject to the laws of any earthly creature'. Some of the power thus arrogated to the King rubbed off on his Vicar-General, and Thomas Cromwell found himself with immeasurably greater opportunities than ever Wolsey had. The latter had suppressed some minor religious houses to make room for his Oxford foundation, Cardinal College – later Christ Church – but Cromwell, when the finances of the realm became overstretched, resorted to despoliation on the grand scale, and with ruthless efficiency. In 1535 the *Valor Ecclesiasticus*, an inventory of all Church incomes, was completed in the amazingly short time of six months, and in the next year Parliament passed the first Act of Dissolution, which affected only the smaller monasteries. This and the second Act, which got under way a year or so later and which abolished the remaining monastic houses and the friaries, met with considerable approbation from the upper classes, who were envious of the Church's great wealth and very ready to purchase land from the Crown. The latter enriched itself by more than a million pounds, and although Henry made vague promises to use some of the money for endowing new bishoprics and for strengthening existing dioceses, not very much was done. Most of the displaced monks were pensioned or became parish priests, but the poor and sick undoubtedly suffered from the loss of succour and charity dispensed by most of the houses.

The dissolution of the monasteries was responsible for the one serious insurrection of the reign – a northern rebellion known to history as the Pilgrimage of Grace. Until after this trouble, when the King revived the Council of the North, the royal authority remained insecure in most northern counties, and there was much grumbling not against the King, but against his advisers, and in particular Cromwell, whose commissioners were proceeding with the dissolution of the smaller monasteries. Trouble first broke out in Lincoln on 1 October 1536, with the rebels making a number of demands, from the restoration of the dissolved monasteries to the banishment of Cromwell and certain bishops. A few days later another, and potentially more dangerous, outbreak occurred in Yorkshire, where the leader was a landowner called Robert Aske.

Aske had under his command a large, well armed body of men, and had matters been concluded by force the Duke of Norfolk's army might well have been defeated at Doncaster before Suffolk, who was dealing with the smaller Lincoln affair, could come to his aid. But Aske shrank from the responsibility of plunging the country into civil strife, and when Norfolk gave gages that there would be a free pardon and a free parliament the rebels agreed to disband. Henry renewed these pledges in person, but he had little intention of keeping his word, and further sporadic risings gave him the excuse for the destruction of the rebel leaders.

Cromwell, during his ten years of power, knew four queens, and the last of them, from his point of view, proved the least satisfactory. He had assisted in Catherine of Aragon's divorce, manipulated Anne Boleyn's execution, been a witness to Jane Seymour's death and was himself in part cast down through Anne of Cleves. The year 1538 saw Henry looking for a fourth wife, and in a European situation that was becoming dangerous Cromwell's policy of dividing France from the Empire would play an important part in the search. There was a fairly wide selection available, and so Henry was able to make overtures in both camps. Probably the most beautiful of the eligible princesses was Christina of Denmark – the Emperor's niece, and although the widow of the Duke of Milan a girl of only seventeen. However, Cromwell thought he saw a better chance of driving a wedge between France and the Empire, and at the same time strengthening the hand of the Reformers, through an alliance with the house of Cleves.

The strategic advantages of a marriage to the sister of Duke William, whose territories lay across the Emperor's communications between the Rhineland and the Low Countries, were very real, but unfortunately the Lady Anne of Cleves was decidedly unattractive, and Cromwell was foolish enough to assure his master that she outshone Christina, 'as the golden sun excelleth the sylvern moon'. It was a poignant period in the great minister's career, for there were many eager to pull him down should he make a false step. He survived this blunder, but it ripened him for the sickle. Less than a year later, having by now become obsolete so far as his King was concerned, Parliament, which had made him, took the opportunity to break him, and he perished at Tyburn on 28 July 1540. On the same day Henry – who had divorced Anne – married Catherine Howard. And two years later, again in July (Catherine having lost her head after eighteen unfaithful months), Henry married his sixth and last wife – Katherine Parr.

Since the end of 1541, Henry had been angling for a closer alliance with the Emperor, but it was not until February 1543 that a treaty with Charles was agreed upon. There could be no joint action against France that year, for Henry was fully occupied with Scottish problems, but plans were made for a two-pronged attack to take place not later than 20 June 1544.

The tangled skein of Scottish politics, during the minorities first of James V and then of his daughter Mary, is not easily unravelled. The rapid turns and reversals of fortune among the leading factions is bewildering, and Henry made matters no easier with his so-called English party. There were times when reason appeared to prevail and Henry's peace overtures had some chance of success; but after his break with the Pope the Scottish Churchmen, usually assisted by some of the nobles, managed to steer the country away from an alliance with England. Such obstinacy enraged Henry, and indescribable devastation along the Border was to result. After the Scottish defeat at Solway Moss in November 1542, and the subsequent death of James, Henry (as in 1513) lost an excellent opportunity for complete conquest. Instead he tried to gain control – and possession of the infant Queen Mary, whom he hoped to marry to his son Edward – through tortuous negotiations which, in spite of a treaty of peace in July 1543, achieved little, and Henry was wrong to think that he could turn his full attention upon France. In 1544 there was further trouble, and for the next two years a large army under the Earl of Hertford was fully occupied scarifying the Border.

The agreement with Charles stipulated that both monarchs would put into the field against France thirty-five thousand foot and seven thousand horse. Henry was to march through Picardy, while Charles, forming the left arm of the pincer, would advance from Luxembourg through Champagne. Thus the grand design; but events proved somewhat different.

The English army, under those seasoned veterans the Dukes of Norfolk and Suffolk, crossed to Calais in June 1544. But Charles, having met with early success, found unexpected resistance from the garrison of St Dizier, and his army was bogged down in a siege. Henry, therefore, considered himself justified in deviating from the plan and launching an assault on Boulogne. He himself arrived before Boulogne on 26 July and after a stout resistance to bombardment, mining and assault the Governor beat the *chamade* on 11 September, and a week later Henry entered the city in triumph.

Boulogne (which a few days later was all but lost through the ineptitude of Norfolk) was the only prize of a thoroughly muddled campaign, for on the very day that Henry entered the city Charles signed a separate peace with Francis. This he was perfectly entitled to do, but Henry thought otherwise, and in the ensuing months Anglo-Imperial relations were brought nearly to breaking point.

Henry died on 28 January 1547, and was buried next to Queen Jane in St George's Chapel. He had reigned for thirty-eight years. A gay and gallant extrovert became a powerful political schemer and ended an embittered, tyrannical invalid. He left Scottish affairs, which he had handled badly, in dangerous confusion, but on the Continent the unnecessary French wars had temporarily ceased. At home such achievements as an initiative in naval architecture, an improvement of the administrative machine and the advancement of the Commons had been somewhat overshadowed by the appalling state of the economy – due mainly to a damaging debasement of the coinage – and the beginnings of a religious discord of a kind that would build up into a roaring inferno.

Nevertheless, Henry had for the most part retained the affections of his people; he had become something of an institution, and they instinctively – and correctly – felt that without him times would become difficult, dangerous and very different.

Edward VI was crowned in Westminster Abbey on 20 February 1547. The great splendour of the occasion and the long drawn-out ceremony must have been something of an ordeal for a boy not yet ten years old. The new King had been born on 12 October 1537 to Jane Seymour, the third wife of Henry VIII. She had died shortly afterwards, and the first six years of Edward's life had been spent in a separate establishment of his own in the country, outside the range – it was hoped – of pestilence and disease, for it was only natural that the health of the long-awaited heir to the throne should be a matter of considerable concern. It was Katherine Parr who eventually persuaded Henry to unite his family and have his children more at court.

When it was time to move forward from his nursery education to more important studies, great care was taken over the appointment of his tutors, and in Richard Cox and John Cheke the boy was in the hands of the most brilliant humanists in England, and, what was more important for the destiny of the nation, both held staunchly Protestant views. Moroever, Edward's French tutor, the humanist Jean Belmain, was a stout Calvinist, and he also must have influenced the boy's religious thinking. It is possible that Henry, who lived and died a Catholic, made the appointments reluctantly, but his uncanny ability for feeling the pulse of the nation doubtless told him that, with most of the best brains belonging to men of Protestant persuasion, the country was set on course for a Protestant settlement.

Other tutors took care of Edward's musical instruction, his deportment and athletic exercises. Few princes could have received such an intensive, scholarly and humane education, and even fewer still could have achieved such intellectual maturity at so early an age. Edward took a delight in learning and had a naturally enquiring mind; early in life he had mastered languages and was well versed in the classics. There were signs of intellectual arrogance in this cold, dour youth, who seemed to lack spontaneity and any warmth of heart; only one - Barnaby Fitzpatrick - of the many specially selected playmates retained the affection and intimacy of this precocious and aloof young man. He grew up, as his tutors intended he should, an ardent Protestant; but religion and work did not entirely crowd out the pleasures of life, and later on - encouraged by the Duke of Northumberland - Edward enjoyed pageants, plays and masques as much as all his family did.

Until the last year of his life the King kept what would now be called a diary, or journal. It is a somewhat cold, hard piece of reporting. His entry recording the death of his uncle, Edward Seymour, who had shown him much kindness and served the State with tolerance and devotion, if not with great wisdom, simply read, 'The Duke of Somerset had his head cut of apon Towre hill betwene eight and nine a cloke in the morning.' His entry upon the well-deserved death of his other uncle, Thomas Seymour, the Lord High Admiral, was even more callous.

In a book on sovereigns and their doings Edward VI has little part, because most of his reign was dominated by two great noblemen, the Dukes of Somerset and Northumberland - neither of whom had the complete confidence of the King - and only when he was fourteen and considered himself ready to rule, did he play any part in government. Nevertheless, during his short reign some momentous events took place, and it is necessary just to touch on these and their origins.

When Henry died Edward Seymour, Earl of Hertford (Queen Jane's brother) had achieved a place of great prominence in the Council. He was a pronounced Protestant, and his path to ascendancy had been made easier by the humbling of the Catholic Howards. The old Duke of Norfolk had been caught in the web of treason woven by his son, Lord Surrey. Norfolk, who was saved from the axe by the death of Henry, was framed, but Surrey lost his head on merit. In any event, Henry had begun to turn against the Catholic faction in his Council. He had the idea that he could continue to rule England from the grave through the medium of his will, and of the sixteen executors whom he intended should control affairs during his son's minority, only four could be definitely labelled as Catholics.

In the event, two of the sixteen executors - Hertford and William Paget, principal Secretary of State - took such swift and masterly action that Henry's devise for the succession never materialized. It was agreed between them that Hertford (who promised to accept Paget's advice in matters of State) was to ride off immediately Henry died to fetch the new

King from Hertford Castle to London, while Paget, who was known to have been the closest of the executors to Henry, would endeavour to persuade the Council that, for the better governance of the realm, Hertford should be appointed Protector and Governor of the King's person.

Everything went very smoothly, and on 1 February 1547 – five days after Henry had died – the executors conducted Edward from the State apartments in the Tower to hear the Lord Chancellor declare that they all agreed to nominate Hertford Protector of the Realm. Oaths of allegiance were taken, letters despatched to foreign states, and the new government got down to business with Paget announcing certain honours and awards that the late King had intended to make. Among these Edward Seymour was to become Duke of Somerset. He had handled a delicate situation, and achieved a position under the King of the highest authority in the realm, with a speed and decisiveness that he was never to show again. Success soon bred failure and disillusionment. It is at least arguable that, had he adhered to his promise to abide always by Paget's advice, his fall from power might have been avoided.

Undoubtedly the most important event of the reign was the furtherance of the Reformation. Henry VIII, with great skill, had carried his subjects with him in his break with the Pope and his assumption of Head of the Anglican Church. He had instigated a revolution so gradually that most Englishmen, including most Churchmen, scarcely realized that the whole basis of their faith was being altered. A political convenience was not seen to be a matter of conscience. Nor was it so long as Henry lived, for although evangelical Protestantism was on the march, Henry's orthodox Catholicism could and did (the Six Articles Act) apply the brake.

But with the new reign the Reformers got the encouragement they wanted. Somerset as Lord Protector wielded immense power, which could include the settlement of Church affairs. His personal faith was therefore important, and he was a Protestant; but he was also a very tolerant man, who simply did not believe in the use of force for religious purposes. In the two and a half years that he was at the head of the nation's affairs he was able – often with much difficulty – to guide through Parliament the successive measures towards reform that were mainly the inspiration and faithful industry of Thomas Cranmer.

Perhaps the greatest impetus to the English Reformation came from the continent of Europe. England had lacked the enthusiasm of the great European dissenters such as Luther, Zwingli, Calvin and their disciples; but when the Emperor won the battle of Mühlberg in April 1547, and Germany was at his mercy, his religious settlement, known as the Interim of Augsburg, drove many famous Lutheran preachers from their pulpits. Cranmer óffered a number of these Protestant leaders hospitality in England, and undoubtedly their thinking and disputations, and above all their differing approaches to the central dogma of the Church – the doctrine of the Eucharist – deeply impressed the Archbishop, and two of their number in particular (Peter Martyr and John à Lasco) were influential in the liturgical changes incorporated in the Second Prayer Book.

The long story of the Reformation, with its stormy debates in Parliament, the ordering of services, the visitation of the Commissioners, and all the problems and passions of the time, cannot be entered into here. But in two respects at least this great religious revolution brought a measure of comfort to many of the living and joy to generations yet unborn. The Chantries Act, expropriating some two thousand chantry foundations, although intended to put funds hitherto misapplied for ignorant and superstitious purposes to wiser use, caused a considerable social shock that stimulated much charitable giving. Chantry grammar schools were refounded as Edward VI grammar schools, and large sums of money were subscribed privately and by the government towards education and various social needs. Another and more lasting benefit was Cranmer's Book of Common Prayer, which endowed the English people with a consoling liturgy in prose of incomparable beauty. By the end of the reign England was in theory, and largely in practice, a Protestant State. Many there were who rejected the new creed; their brief moment of triumph lay immediately ahead.

In Scotland the uneasy peace which prevailed at Henry's death drifted on, until the situation was dramatically altered when Henry II ascended the French throne. Encouraged by his enthusiasm for their cause the Scots hardened in their attitude, and made it clear that they had no intention of honouring the treaty of 1543 (confirmed by the treaty with France of 1546) binding their Queen in marriage to the English King. This union of the two crowns in one empire was the keystone in Somerset's foreign policy. Although fearful of antagonizing Henry II (who made no secret of his determination to get back Boulogne before the treaty date) and therefore having to fight on two fronts, he went to war with Scotland after despairing of getting his way through conciliation.

Somerset was by inclination and training a soldier; he had fought with distinction in France and Scotland in the last reign, and on 10 September 1547 he decisively defeated the Scots at Pinkie Cleuch, near the present town of Musselburgh. But this victory achieved virtually nothing. The war in Scotland dragged on for two years, with the English fighting not only large numbers of determined Scotsmen, but an army of six thousand well-equipped Frenchmen. Gradually the firm grip achieved after Pinkie Cleuch had to be relinquished. Any chances of seizing the young Queen were greatly reduced when the Scots took her to the island of Inchmahone, and vanished completely when she landed safely in France in August 1548. A year later, French pressure on Boulogne and the threat of rebellion at home forced Somerset to pull out of all but a few of the more important Border towns. The Scottish saga was at an end, with more than twenty thousand soldiers lying buried beneath the peathags.

To add to the Protector's many difficulties, there were two rebellions in 1549; they were in no way connected, and although they overlapped the government was able to contain them locally and so avoid a rising *en masse*. In the west it was in the main a revolt against the reformed religion, but Kett's rebellion in Norfolk took the form of an agrarian rising. However, in each case there were many underlying causes, and both rebellions had in common a hatred of the gentry, for there was much social and economic inequality springing from rising costs, inflation, increased rents and, above all, enclosures.

The Western Rebellion started in the tiny Devon village of Sampford Courtenay on Whitsunday 9 June, the day the new Prayer Book was to be introduced into all the churches of England. Soon the Devonians were joined by a large Cornish contingent, and from Bodmin and Exeter sets of articles, or demands, were sent to London. Negotiation was never seriously contemplated by either side, and before the revolt was finally crushed in mid-August by the combined armies of Lords Russell and Grey and Sir William Herbert, at least three thousand misguided west countrymen lay dead.

Kett's rebellion, which was mainly centred on Norwich, and the result of many years of landlord and tenant disputes, was a more orderly affair. Here again articles were submitted, some of which Somerset was in sympathy with, for he realized that he was dealing with a sorely oppressed people; but with between fifteen and twenty thousand rebels under arms on Mousehold Heath, it took only a small incident to cause an explosion. On 12 July Norwich was under attack, but just over a month later it was all over. At the battle of Dussindale on 25 August Lord Warwick*, at the head of English and German troops, killed more than two thousand rebels. The brothers Robert and William Kett were later hanged from the top of Norwich Castle and Wymondham steeple respectively.

These two rebellions gave a powerful lever to the faction, headed by Warwick, which was determined to bend and break Somerset. This was accomplished in a very underhand way in October 1549. Somerset was

* John Dudley, Earl of Warwick, was the son of Edmund Dudley, Henry VII's minister, who was executed in 1510.

1 Egbert, King of Wessex, who by 839 had gained supremacy over all the English kingdoms. This illustration is taken from an illuminated roll at Hatfield House, tracing the genealogy of Elizabeth I.

2 The Alfred Jewel, made of gold and cloisonné enamel. The figure is presumed to represent the Saxon King, and around the top runs the inscription. 'Aelfred mec heht Gewyrcan', 'Alfred ordered me to be made'.

3 King Canute and his wife, the redoubtable Emma of Normandy, presenting a charter to the Church.

4, 5, 6 Three scenes from the Bayeux Tapestry. Above: Edward the Confessor's body being taken for burial in his recently consecrated West Minster in January 1066; below: Harold II being crowned King by Stigand, Archbishop of Canterbury; above right: William I in conference with his two half-brothers, Odo of Bayeux and Robert of Mortain.

ET·HIC·EPISCOPVS·CIBV·ET   ODO·EPS   ROTBERT·ISTE·IVSSIT·VT·LODERETVR·C
POTV·BENEDICIT   WILLELM

7 Miniature of Lanfranc from *De corpore et sanguine Domini*, *c.* 1100 (Ms Bodley 569, f.1). A native of Pavia in northern Italy, he became abbot of St Stephen's Caen, and, after Stigand's deposition in 1070, William I appointed him Archbishop of Canterbury.

INCIPIT LIBER LANFRANCI VENERABILIS
ARCHIEPI CANTVARIENSIS AECCLIAE DE
CORPORE ET SANGVINE DOMINI CONTRA
BERINGARIVM·

LANFRANCVS MISERICORDIA DEI
catholicus beringerio catholice ecclie aduersario.

Si diuina pietas cordi tuo inspirare dignaret. quatinus respe

8, 9 Henry II's long and bitter quarrel with his Archbishop, Thomas Becket, culminated in Becket's murder in December 1170. Above left: a fourteenth-century miniature showing the King and prelate in conflict; above right: Reginald Fitzurse striking down Becket in his cathedral at Canterbury.

10 The keep at Orford Castle in Suffolk, built between 1165 and 1173 by Henry II as part of his system of defence for the kingdom.

12 King John stag hunting, from a fourteenth-century manuscript.

11 In 1192 Richard I left the Holy Land to return to England. He chose to take the overland route and fell into the hands of Leopold, Duke of Austria, who kept him in the mountain fortress of Durnstein. This illustration, from the Chronicle of Petrus of Eboli, shows Richard being arrested by Leopold's soldiers, and at the feet of the Holy Roman Emperor, Henry VI.

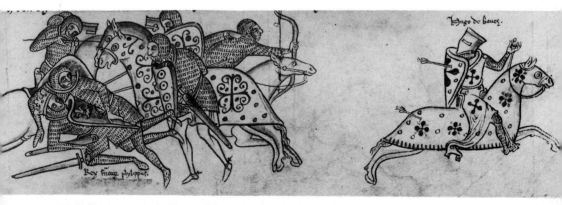

13 Philip Augustus, the French King, being unhorsed at the battle of Bouvines on 27 July 1214. Despite this incident, the battle resulted in the complete defeat of John's allies.

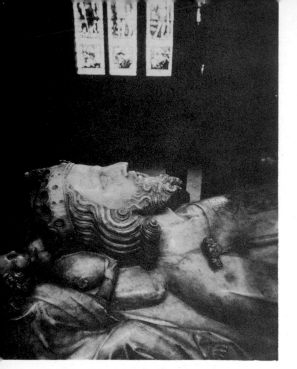

14 A detail from Edward II's magnificent marble effigy in Gloucester Cathedral.

15 The head of Edward III, from the gilt-bronze effigy executed by John Orchard for his tomb in Westminster Abbey.

16 Edward III assuming the royal arms of France and quartering them with those of England, thus making claim to the French throne and instituting the Hundred Years War. A miniature from Froissart's Chronicles.

17 One panel of the Wilton Diptych, showing Richard II with his patron saints: Edmund, the English King who was martyred by the Danes in 870; Edward the Confessor; and John the Baptist.

18 John of Gaunt, Duke
Lancaster, Edward III
third son and father of Hen
IV, In this miniature fro
Jean de Wavrin's *Chroniq
d'Angleterre*, John of Gaunt
being entertained by John
of Portugal.

19 Henry IV, the tall figure with a black hat at the top
of the picture, claiming his throne from Parliament on
6 October 1399.

20 Portrait of Henry V by an unknown artist.

22 By the Treaty of Troyes, concluded on 30 May 1420, Henry V gained the hand of the French Princess Catherine, and through her the Crown of France for himself and his heirs on the death of Charles VI. This silverpoint drawing, from *The Life of Richard Beauchamp*, shows the marriage of Henry and Catherine in Troyes Cathedral on 2 June.

21 Henry V riding in triumph on the field of Agincourt, a carving in stone from his chantry chapel in Westminster Abbey.

23 When Henry V died in 1422, he entrusted his infant son, Henry VI, to the care of Richard Beauchamp, Earl of Warwick. In this drawing from the Rous Roll, Beauchamp carries the child king on his left arm, and in his right hand holds his chantry chapel at St Mary's Warwick.

24 Henry VI became King of England at the age of nine months; a few months later his maternal grandfather, Charles VI, died and he became King of France as well. In 1430 Henry was taken to France and this drawing shows his coronation in St Denis: the one sovereign to be crowned both in England and France.

25 Henry VI with his Queen, Margaret of Anjou, surrounded by their courtiers.

26 The battle of Tewkesbury, 4 May 1471, one of Edward IV's most decisive victories over his Lancastrian opponents in the Wars of the Roses. Edward, Prince of Wales, the only son of Henry VI, was slain in the battle, and with Henry VI's murder shortly after, the legitimate Lancastrian line was extinguished. This miniature illustration is taken from *Historie of the Arrivall of Edward IV*.

27 Richard III, portrait by an unknown artist.

28 Lady Margaret Beaufort, Countess of Richmond, the mother of Henry VII. This portrait now hangs in St John's College, Cambridge, which Lady Margaret helped to found.

29 Torrigiano's magnificent gilt-bronze effigies of Henry VII and Elizabeth of York, which lie on a black marble tomb in the King's great chapel at Westminster Abbey.

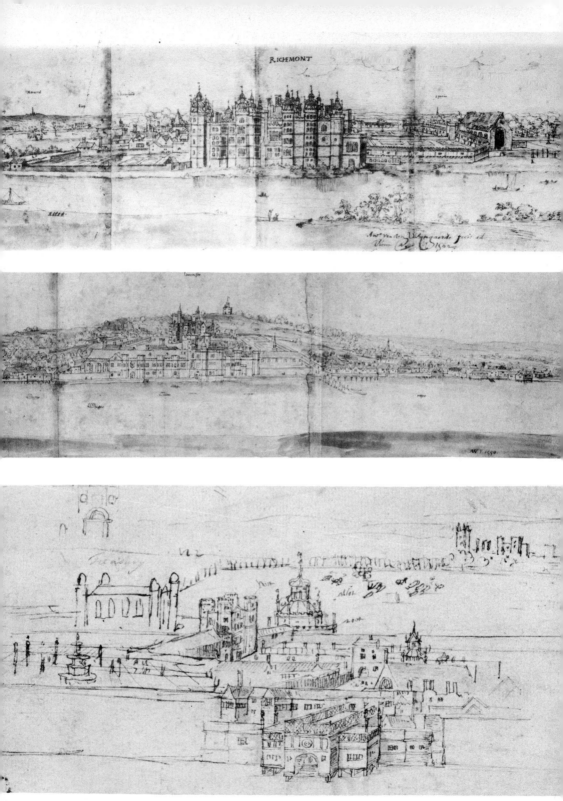

30, 31 and 32 Anthony van Wyngaerde's drawings of three Tudor palaces in 1555. Top: Richmond, rebuilt by Henry VII after Sheen Palace was burnt out. Distinctive features of the new palace were high towers surmounted by ornate cupolas, and complex bay windows. Centre: Greenwich Palace, formerly Margaret of Anjou's Placentia, which Henry VII refaced and refurbished. Bottom: Whitehall, formerly York Place. Cardinal Wolsey converted the medieval house into a splendid mansion, and at the prelate's fall Henry VIII took over the buildings and incorporated them into his palace at Whitehall.

33 Henry VIII with his family by an unknown artist. The King is depicted sitting under his canopy of State with his third Queen, Jane Seymour, and their son, Edward. Flanking them are Henry's two daughters, Mary to the left and Elizabeth to the right.

34 In February 1512, Catherine of Aragon gave birth to a son, Henry, but tragically he lived for less than two months. This detail from the Great Tournament Roll of Westminster depicts the King as 'True Heart' jousting before the Queen and her ladies to celebrate the birth of his son.

35 An anti-papal allegory of the death of Henry VIII, showing the King pointing to his successor Edward VI. To Edward's left are the Protector Somerset and the Council, the Duke of Northumberland, Archbishop Cranmer and the Earl of Bedford.

36 Mary Tudor, from a portrait by the Habsburg court painter, Antonio Moro.

37 Philip II of Spain, Mary Tudor's consort, from a portrait by Titian.

38 Mary Queen of Scots, from a portrait painted during her captivity in England.

39 Henry Stuart, Lord Darnley, with his younger brother, Charles. In July 1565 he married Mary Queen of Scots, thus uniting the two Stuart claims to the Scottish throne.

40 Detail of a painting attributed to
Robert Peake, showing Elizabeth I being
carried by her courtiers.

41 The ceiling of the Banqueting House at Whitehall, painted by Rubens to
portray the apotheosis of James I and the allegory of the birth of Charles I.

42 George Villiers, Duke of Buckingham, favourite of James I and of his son Charles. This portrait was painted by Anthony van Dyck after Buckingham's assassination at the hands of an aggrieved naval lieutenant, John Felton, in August 1628.

43 Detail from Mantegna's *Triumphs of Caesar*. This series of paintings was purchased by Charles I from the impoverished Gonzagos of Mantua in a transaction that was regarded as a major coup in the art world, because the paintings were much coveted. When the King's great collection was dispersed after his execution, Cromwell saved the *Triumphs* for Hampton Court, where they are still to be seen.

44 Charles I with Henrietta Maria and their eldest children, Charles, Prince of Wales (later Charles II), and Princess Mary (the mother of William III). Portrait by Anthony van Dyck.

45 An engraving by Godfrey Kneller of the execution of Charles I outside the Banqueting House at Whitehall, 30 January 1649.

46 Charles II, the 'Black Boy', from a miniature by an unidentified artist.

47 Catherine of Braganza, Charles II's Portuguese Queen, from a miniature by Samuel Cooper.

48 Barbara Palmer, Countess of Castlemaine, Charles II's mistress at the time of his marriage. This portrait by Lely is one of a series of the court ladies commissioned by Anne Hyde, Duchess of York, and known as the Windsor Beauties.

49 James, Duke of York, with his wife
Anne Hyde and their two daughters, Mary
and Anne. Portrait by Lely.

50 Dutch print showing Titus Oates in the
stocks, surrounded by portraits of the men
that he incriminated in the Popish Plot.

51 Allegorical Dutch engraving with Britannia welcoming William and Mary to England on 5 November 1688, while James flees the country.

52 James II being welcomed by Louis XIV at St Germain-en-Laye in January 1689. Mary of Modena is shown awaiting her husband in her bedchamber.

53 Kip's engraving of Kensington Palace, with the formal gardens laid out in the Dutch style by George London and Henry Wise for William III.

54 A birds-eye view of Hampton Court painted by Knyff during the reign of Queen Anne. The south and east fronts and the Fountain Court had just been rebuilt by Wren, but behind can be seen the remains of the Tudor palace.

55 Queen Anne at the time of her accession in 1702, dressed in her robes of State.

56 Marlborough's victory at Blenheim in 1704, recorded in tapestry at Blenheim Palace.

58 Sophia Dorothea, the unfortunate wife of George I, with their two children, George (later George II) and Sophia Dorothea.

57 Portrait of George I painted just after his accession in 1714.

59 and 60 George II and his charming and cultivated Queen, Caroline of Anspach, painted at the time of their coronation in 1727.

61 Frederick, Prince of Wales, for once in accord with his sisters in a music party. In the background can be seen the Dutch House at Kew. Painting by Mercier, 1733.

62 Rowlandson's drawing of George III returning from the hunt, with Windsor Castle, his favourite home, in the background.

63 On 15 December 1785, George, Prince of Wales was married in secret to Mrs Fitzherbert. This caricature shows Charles James Fox holding Mrs Fitzherbert's left hand, while Lord North sleeps through the ceremony.

64 George IV, from a portrait painted by Matthew Brown in 1790, when he was Prince of Wales.

65 Portrait of George III as an old man, living out his days in solitary seclusion in Windsor Castle.

66 Princess Charlotte, only daughter of George IV, with her husband Prince Leopold of Saxe-Coburg, later King Leopold I of the Belgians. Charlotte's death in 1817 was to cause panic within the royal family and an undignified flurry of marriages to produce an heir to the throne.

67 Cartoon showing George IV's desperate efforts to get himself divorced from Caroline of Brunswick.

68 Victoria and Albert at Windsor Castle in the early 1840s, with their eldest daughter, 'Vicky'. Painting by Landseer.

69 Photograph of Queen Victoria, in deepest mourning, with the Prince of Wales and Alexandra an hour after their wedding on 10 March 1863. The spirit of the Prince Consort dominated the occasion.

70 The Blue Room at Windsor, in which Albert died on 14 December 1861. The room was left exactly as it had been during the Prince's last illness, until the Queen's death in 1901.

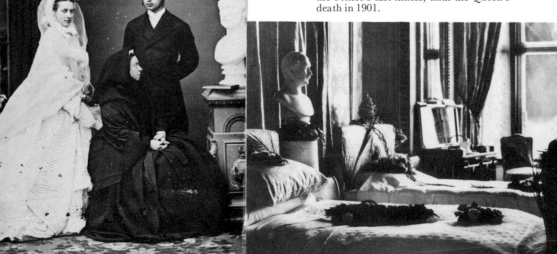

72 Four generations of British monarchy: Queen Victoria with her son, the future Edward VII, her grandson, the future George V, and her great-grandson, the future Edward VIII.

71 The uneasy relationship between Victoria and her eldest son is epitomised in this cartoon by Max Beerbohm, entitled 'the rare, the rather awful visits of Albert Edward, Prince of Wales, to Windsor Castle'.

73 If Queen Victoria was the grandmother of Europe, then Edward VII was the uncle, linked by kinship to most of the crowned heads. In this group, taken at Windsor in 1907, the King is shown with his relations, including the Queen of Norway, the Emperor and Empress of Germany, the King and Queen of Spain, the Grand Duke Vladimir of Russia, Prince Johann of Saxony, the Duchess of Aosta, and the Queen of Portugal.

74 The Duke and Duchess of Windsor on their wedding day, 3 June 1937, at the château of Candé in France.

75 George VI and Queen Elizabeth celebrating their silver wedding at Buckingham Palace on 20 April 1948.

76 The present royal family celebrating the silver wedding of Elizabeth II and Prince Philip at Balmoral, 31 October 1972.

sent to the Tower, and although he regained his freedom the following February, and a place on the Council, he no longer influenced events. Warwick never attempted to assume the outward trappings of power (he scorned the title of Protector), nevertheless he quickly set about gaining the confidence of the young King and taking the reins of government into his own ruthless hands. He was a vindictive man, totally devoid of scruple, and he was determined on Somerset's death. This he brought about through trumped-up charges, when on 22 January 1552 Somerset was executed on Tower Hill.

Even before Somerset's fall the King had begun to be present at Council meetings, and under the guidance of Warwick (created Duke of Northumberland in 1551) his attendance was not uncommon. He took a lively and enquiring interest in political and religious matters of policy, and it would seem that from 1551 onwards – when important events began to be entered quite frequently in his chronicle – his personal decisions had to be taken into account. It is, however, unlikely that he had any say during the disastrous non-policy months between the fall of Somerset and the time when Warwick felt himself firmly in control; months that saw the complete withdrawal from Scotland, and in April 1550 a treaty with France, which gave her back Boulogne and acknowledged her influence in Scottish affairs.

Apart from a nasty bout of fever when he was four, Edward was not an unhealthy child, but in April 1552 he quite suddenly fell very ill. However, by the end of that month he had recovered and was well enough until the onset of his final illness somewhere about February 1553. He suffered from acute tuberculosis, a disease that in those days was apt to give the patients a series of false dawns before extinction. Edward rallied from time to time during the early summer, only to die at Greenwich on 6 July.

It is possible that by Edward's death before his sixteenth birthday, England lost a potentially great King. Edward's early promise was immense. His learning was profound; his understanding of people was for his years exceptional; and he had already disciplined a cool, rational mind to long hours of work.

The first two Tudor Kings were great builders and renovators, although it can be argued that Henry VIII was responsible from 1536 onwards for despoiling more beautiful buildings and treasures than ever he created or restored.

Henry VII had too many problems to tackle during the first ten years of his reign to think much about building. But before he died he had built extensively at Greenwich, rebuilt Sheen Palace and in its grounds encouraged the siting of Richmond Friary, and paid for the erection of the conventual buildings. His further works of piety included the Savoy Hospital, built on the site of John of Gaunt's palace and the largest institution of its kind in England; the Westminster almshouses, modelled on those of St Cross, Winchester; and, of course, his lovely chapel in Westminster Abbey. In addition he brought almost to completion, on a scale more lavish than the founder had ever contemplated, King's College Chapel, Cambridge. Although begun in 1448, the Chapel was far from finished at the time of Bosworth, and indeed had to wait until 1508 before Henry VII could take full interest in its building, and work continued after his death.

Henry VIII also spent much money on repairs and extensions to Greenwich, Windsor, Richmond and Eltham. In 1515 he acquired Bridewell from Cardinal Wolsey, and began to rebuild the palace, which stood close to the present Ludgate Circus. His work of embellishment at Hampton Court can still be seen, but nothing remains of another great house that he secured from Wolsey, York Place (later known as the Palace of Whitehall), where work of enlargement and alteration commenced only four days after it had been taken from the Cardinal in November 1529. The gatehouse and chapel of St James's Palace in London, which Henry built between 1532 and 1540 on the site of a former leper hospital, still survive; but nothing now remains of Oatlands, a palace he built near Weybridge, nor of his most ambitious work, the great palace of Nonsuch, which stood some eight miles from Oatlands and not far from Epsom.

Apart from the money Henry VIII lavished on his many palaces, he also spent liberally on military fortifications in England and in France. Some of these are still in excellent condition: Dover, Deal, Sandgate, Walmer, and in Cornwall Pendennis and St Mawes were fortresses built or strengthened against the fear of a French invasion. Work on the fortifications at Calais went on intermittently during the reigns of all three Tudor kings, and Henry VIII took a personal interest in the designs for both Calais and Boulogne, which, with its neighbouring outposts of Ambleteuse and Blackness, required much work to restore military efficiency after their capture in 1544. The great castle at Boulogne still dominates the Basse Ville as it did in Tudor days, but Ambleteuse and Blackness are now ruins.

Cambridge
Christ's College. This college was founded in 1505 by Lady Margaret Beaufort, mother of Henry VII, on the instigation of her chaplain, John Fisher, Bishop of Rochester. Much rebuilding has been done since the foundation, but Lady Margaret's armorial bearings still hang over the college gateway and above the door of the Master's Lodge.

St John's College. The hospital of St John formerly occupied the site of this college, but by the sixteenth century it survived only in a very dilapidated state. John Fisher persuaded Lady Margaret Beaufort to refound the hospital as a college; this she agreed to do, but died before the plans had progressed. The charter of the college was eventually granted by Henry VIII on 9 April 1511, after two years hard work by Bishop Fisher. It is one of the most beautiful of the Cambridge colleges, with its splendid main gate of 1516, and the First and Second Courts.

Trinity College. In 1546 Henry VIII united King's Hall and Michaelhouse to form Trinity College. It has the largest court of all the Cambridge colleges, and in its centre stands the fountain, added in Elizabeth I's time, that once supplied the college with its drinking water. The Great Gate, with its statue of the King, predates the founding of Trinity, being finished in 1535. It was originally adorned with a statue of Edward III, the founder of King's Hall in 1337, but this was removed in the early seventeenth century to the clock tower of the chapel, and replaced by a statue of the founder.

Church of St Mary the Great. This very lovely church, which is the principal parish church of the town, was begun in 1478 and completed in the early years of the sixteenth century. Henry VII made a gift of timber for the church roof in 1505, and it is interesting that, when the roof had to be repaired in 1726, the architect preferred to preserve the old timbers rather than replace them, by building a supplementary roof above and tying the old one into the new:

Henry VII's body lay in state in this church, and the coffin was covered by a beautiful hearse cloth. For many years this magnificent pall of Florentine black silk velvet on a cloth of gold was on view in the Fitzwilliam Museum, but it has recently been returned to Great St Mary's, where it properly belongs.

Compton Wynyates (Warwicks.). This Tudor house was begun by Edward Compton in 1480, on the site of an earlier dwelling, and has remained in the family ever since. Edward Compton died in 1493, leaving as his heir, his eleven-year-old son, William. Henry VII offered him a place at court as page to Prince Henry, who later became Henry VIII. William and Henry spent much time together, and when Henry became King he gave many valuable presents to William and often stayed with him at Compton Wynyates, and the house still retains much evidence of those visits. Elizabeth I, who was a friend of William's grandson, was also a visitor to the house. Compton Wynyates is some three miles north-east of Shipston on Stour off the B4035 road.

Battle of Flodden (Northumberland). On 9 September 1513 the English army, commanded by the veteran general Thomas, Earl of Surrey (later second Duke of Norfolk), not only defeated at Flodden a Scottish army commanded by their King, James IV, but virtually annihilated a complete generation of that country's nobility. For besides the King, the Scots lost some two dozen earls and barons, the King's bastard son, an archbishop, two bishops and many knights.

The battlefield is one of the few in Britain that is still very much the same as it was at the time of the battle. The curious position of the two armies at the start of the battle is the result of some abortive Border raids that took place during the previous month, and the fact that Surrey carried out a daring manoeuvre to march his half-starved army round the flank of the enemy, and put it between that enemy and home, in order to deceive James and tempt him from a strong position. The Scots' final position was on Branxton Hill, and stretched for two thousand yards. Surrey had marched in two columns to the east of the Scots, and, crossing the River Till and Pallins' Burn, took up a position on the ridge immediately to the south of Branxton village, where the monument (possibly the site of King James's death) now stands.

The battle was fought on a very wet, murky afternoon, with the southerly wind blowing the rain into the faces of the English. It was a desperate affair once James – apparently unable to control the Scotsman's inherent desire to be always, and immediately, at the throats of the enemy – ordered his army to abandon their strong position and close with the English. For two hours or more the combatants were locked together in a grim and deadly struggle on the English ridge, until, with most of their leaders slain and the carnage on the field appalling, the Scotsmen gave way.

Branxton is about three miles south-east of Coldstream and to the south of the main Morpeth-Coldstream road. The land is all privately owned, with the exception of a public footpath to the monument However, a good view of the ground can be obtained from the top of Branxton Hill.

Hampton Court Palace (Middlesex). In 1514 Thomas Wolsey, Archbishop of York (to become a Cardinal and Lord Chancellor in the following year) leased Hampton Court, together with two thousand acres of land, from the Knights Hospitallers of St John of Jerusalem. He immediately set about converting the old manor house into a magnificent palace, emparked the grounds and laid out the gardens. In 1525, Wolsey deemed it politic to give Hampton Court to Henry VIII, but it was not until after Wolsey's fall and death four years later that Henry entered into full possession and immediately set about enlarging the house, which already rivalled most royal palaces for splendour and size.

Additions, improvements and embellishments went on during most of Henry's reign. Although many of the Tudor buildings were demolished during the reign of William and Mary, the entrance Court and closet from Wolsey's original palace, and the clock tower, great hall with its kitchens, Chapel Royal and Great Watching Chamber from Henry VIII's palace, still remain. Edward VI was born at Hampton Court, Jane Seymour died there, and Catherine Howard was arrested in the Palace. The Haunted Gallery gets its name from the legend that Catherine, having temporarily escaped from confinement, ran down the gallery to the doors of the chapel while Henry was hearing Mass; intercepted by the guards and dragged back to her room screaming, she can still be seen and heard by those with psychic powers.

Henry VIII's Coastal Defences. To meet the danger of a French invasion in the late 1530s, Henry VIII set about building new castles and blockhouses from

Hull to Milford Haven. **St Mawes,** Cornwall, was begun in 1540 and completed in 1543, and is one of two castles constructed at the mouth of the Fal estuary; on the opposite side of Carrick Roads there stands **Pendennis Castle**. St Mawes has a low, round keep with the entrance gate on the north-east side in the form of a hexagonal guardhouse. The entrance is onto the first floor and from there a staircase ascends to a second floor, and another descends to the ground floor and basement. The garrison varied between twenty and one hundred men.

Deal and Walmer Castles (Kent). These castles, together with **Sandown** (of which little remains) were built during the 1530s on orders of Henry VIII as part of his coastal defence system. They were, for the English, revolutionary in design and their fortifications were built to take account of the latest developments in artillery.

Hever Castle (Kent), which is situated south-east of Edenbridge, may have been the birthplace of Anne Boleyn. Alternatively, she might have been born at Rochford Hall in Essex. The castle was owned by her father Sir Thomas Boleyn, who was created Viscount Rochford, and later Earl of Wiltshire, by Henry VIII. Anne certainly spent most of her childhood at Hever, and here it was that Henry came to court her. After her execution, the property remained in her father's possession, but when he died it became a royal residence and Henry granted it to another of his queens, Anne of Cleves, until her death in 1557. It contains, many documents, pictures and furniture of the Tudor period.

Kimbolton Castle (Cambs.). The façade of the great house was remodelled by Vanbrugh in 1707 for the first Duke of Manchester, and the outer gatehouse and gateway on the north side are the work of Robert Adam in about 1766. The house has, therefore, been greatly changed since the days when Catherine of Aragon was confined within its walls from 1534 until her death in 1536. A part of the old castle was incorporated in the rebuilding, and the Queen's Room, where Catherine died is still to be seen. Kimbolton is ten miles south-west of Huntingdon on the A45 road.

Knole (Kent). The magnificently imposing home of the Sackville family, has comparatively few royal connections. Thomas Bourchier, Archbishop of Canterbury, first transformed the building into a palace in the middle of the fifteenth century, and succeeding Archbishops (particularly John Morton) carried on the work of construction and embellishment. When the palace was in the occupation of Archbishop Cranmer it came under the covetous eye of Henry VIII, who decided to take it for himself; but although he spent a considerable amount of money on the building, he did not make much use of it and his son, Edward VI, assigned it to John Dudley, Duke of Northumberland.

Linlithgow Palace (Central Region, Scotland), stands on a high promontory on the southern shore of Linlithgow Loch; a royal abode has stood here since the twelfth century, and Edward I spent some months at Linlithgow during his Scottish wars. But the present building was commenced by James I of Scotland in 1425, and had been developed into its quadrangular form by the end of the fifteenth century. The north quarter, which had collapsed through decay, was rebuilt in 1618.

Linlithgow was the most beautiful palace of its day in Scotland, and became the favourite residence of Henry VII's daughter, Margaret, who married James IV. Here, in a chamber at the top of the palace, Margaret waited for news of her husband's fight at Flodden against her brother, Henry VIII. The battle was to end in James's death.

'His own Queen Margaret, who in Lithgow's tower
All lonely sat, and wept the weary hour.'

Linlithgow is fifteen miles west of Edinburgh on the A9080 road, and the palace, picturesque and proud, and full of grace and dignity, is well worth a visit.

London
Henry VII's Chapel, Westminster Abbey. (See also Chapters 4–6.) This was first intended to house the remains of Henry VI, for the first Tudor sovereign wished to honour his father's half-brother. However, in the end Henry VI's bones never left Windsor, and the beautiful chapel, with the tombs of Henry VII and Elizabeth was built upon the site of the crumbling and ancient Lady Chapel. The foundation stone of this chapel was laid by the King on 24 January 1503, although the chapel was not completed till 1519. The great fan-vault is a supreme example of medieval masonic craftsmanship. The magnificent tomb of Henry and his Queen, with their effigies in gilt-bronze, was designed in the High Renaissance style by Pietro Torrigiano, a Florentine sculptor. He was also responsible for the lovely effigy, again in gilt-bronze, of Henry VII's mother, Lady Margaret Beaufort, which lies in one of the side chapels.

St James's Palace. In what used to be a very desolate spot near a swamp bordering the Tyburn stream, there stood a hospital for female lepers, called the Sisters of St James in the Fields. By 1532 it had only four inmates and Henry VIII gave them pensions and dissolved the foundation. He pulled down the hospital and built the palace around four courts, having previously enclosed St James's Park. This became St James's Palace and Henry's Gateway leading into the Great Court (now Colour Court) still stands on the north front of the palace, at the bottom of St James's Street.

The Chapel Royal, which is the only part of the palace open to the public (for morning service from October to Easter) dates from about 1540. It is a very beautiful, plain rectangular building with a superb ceiling, the design for which is attributed to Holbein.

Syon House. Syon monastery was suppressed in 1534 and became Crown property. Queen Catherine Howard spent the last three months of her life as a prisoner in Syon from November 1541 to February 1542. On the accession of Edward VI, Edward Seymour became Duke of Somerset and Protector of the Realm, and he also became the owner of Syon, and much of the outside of the present house was built by him, and he also laid out the gardens. Queen Mary re-established the monastery, but Elizabeth I dissolved it again – after much wandering the nuns came to rest at Syon Abbey in Devon. Syon House is on the north bank of the Thames opposite Kew Gardens.

The Tower of London. (See also Chapters 3–7.) Henry VIII's association with the Tower is chiefly remembered from the use he made of the block; from the very first year of his reign to the last, the headsman was in fairly steady demand. Henry, however, did build what is now the Queen's House for Anne Boleyn, although she never occupied it until the last few days of her life while awaiting execution. And, although there had been a chapel on the site of St Peter ad Vincula (for the use chiefly of prisoners, as its name suggests) at least since the time of King John, much of the present building dates from the reign of Henry VIII. In the armouries can be seen many weapons and pieces of armour from the Tudor period, notably Henry VIII's armour and that of his horse dating from about 1514, and his armour for field and tournament 1540, and a splendid helmet given to him by the Emperor Maximilian I.

Ludlow Castle (Salop). (See also Chapter 7.) Henry VII's elder son, Prince Arthur, brought his bride, Catherine of Aragon to this castle after their wedding in 1501, and it was here that he died in 1502. By this time the State apartments had been made very imposing, having, besides the great hall and all the usual rooms, kitchen, garderobes, armouries, etc., a solar chamber for the ladies – much of which still exists. In Henry VIII's reign Princess Mary occupied the castle, and in Elizabethan times, when it became the administrative centre for the Council of the Marches, the judges' lodgings were added.

Oxburgh Hall (Norfolk). This enchanting moated house had been in the ownership of the Bedingfeld family ever since Edmund Bedingfeld was granted permission by Edward IV in 1482 to build a fortified manor. Edmund became in due course a staunch supporter of Henry VII, who made him a knight banneret on Stoke Field, after that King had won the last battle in the Wars of the Roses. Henry VII subsequently visited the house and slept in the room now known as the King's Room. One interesting exhibit in the house is the beautiful needlework worked by Mary Queen of Scots and the wife of her captor Bess of Hardwick. These magnificent embroidered hangings were once a family possession, and have now been returned on loan from the Victoria and Albert Museum. Also on display is a most interesting collection of letters from Henry VIII, Mary and Elizabeth. Oxburgh is eight miles south-west of Swaffham, and north of Stoke Ferry off the A134.

Oxford
Christ Church. Cardinal Wolsey, who began his career as Fellow and Bursar of Magdalen College, originally founded what is now called Christ Church, and which he called Cardinal College. At Wolsey's fall in 1529, much of the

college, including the great hall, was completed, but his cloister was not finished and still remains unfinished as Tom Quad. In 1532 King Henry VIII refounded the college as 'King Henry VIII's College', an ecclesiastical foundation divorced from university teaching; but in 1545 he dissolved this foundation and a year later re-established it by uniting the college and Osney Abbey and calling it the Cathedral Church of Christ in Oxford.

Pembroke Castle (Dyfed), stands on a promontory almost surrounded by the Pembroke River, whose steep banks aided its defence. In this castle, in January 1457, Lady Margaret Beaufort gave birth posthumously to the future Henry VII in the tower next to the gatehouse. At that time the castle was in the possession of Jasper Tudor, Henry's uncle. The castle was an important strategical point as far back as the twelfth century, and its great tower, which is one of the two most impressive cylindrical great towers to survive in Britain, dates back to that period.

Richmond Castle (North Yorks.). Edmund Tudor, Earl of Richmond, father of Henry VII, held this castle from 1453 until his death in 1456. On his father's death the future King took the Richmond title, and on his succession to the throne he became the owner of the castle. The castle, which stands in the middle of the lovely old town of Richmond, was Norman in origin and called Richemont by its builder. Perched high above the River Swale, it must have been both beautiful and almost impregnable, but it was never besieged nor involved in much warfare. Two Scottish kings were imprisoned within its walls – William the Lion in 1174, and David II after his defeat at Neville's Cross in 1346. During the Wars of the Roses the castle changed hands according to which faction held power, but Henry VII finally regained it for his family after the battle of Bosworth. The tower has been preserved in a remarkably good condition, and it has some fine features that can no longer be found in many medieval castles; but unfortunately little else, save parts of the eastern wall, still stand.

Richmond Palace (Surrey). The other royal Richmond possession was at Sheen. Here the great palace, partly demolished by Richard II and rebuilt by Henry V, was destroyed by fire in the reign of Henry VII. He rebuilt it around two courtyards with an exciting, high-towered silhouette in the prevailing style, and called it Richmond Palace. But nothing of this Tudor palace remains beyond the main gateway, with the arms of Henry VII above it, and three houses that once formed a part of the Great Court.

Sudeley Castle (Glos.). This castle, which was built principally in the fifteenth century by the Boteler family, became Crown property in the reign of Henry VIII, and was given by Edward VI in 1547 to his uncle, Thomas Seymour, who was Lord High Admiral of England. Thomas had married Henry VIII's widow, Katherine Parr, who died in childbed at Sudeley and is buried in the chapel.

Winchester Castle (Hants.). The castle's great hall was the scene of a magnificent entertainment that Henry VIII arranged in honour of the Emperor Charles V in 1522. Mounted on the west wall of the hall is the huge round table, which, although made many years before Henry VIII's reign, was redecorated on his orders in its present Tudor colours of green and white for Charles's visit.

The hall, which is said to be the finest medieval hall in England after Westminster, was built for Henry III between 1222 and 1236. Now it is the only part of the castle still standing, and has been associated with the administration of justice from at least the sixteenth century until the present day.

Windsor Castle, St George's Chapel (Berks.). (See also Chapters 3–5 and 7.) In 1528 Henry VIII brought to completion what Edward IV had begun fifty years earlier. The central boss of the vault over the crossing between the choir and the nave displays Henry's arms and the date. The King was buried in the centre of the choir alongside his third wife Jane Seymour.

Worcester Cathedral (Worcs.). (See also Chapter 4.) On the south side of the high altar, Henry VII's eldest son, Prince Arthur, was buried. Onver the grave Henry built a chantry chapel, in the middle of which stands the Prince's monument.

9

THE TUDOR QUEENS

When Edward VI died his half-sister Mary, who under Henry VIII's will was the rightful heir to the throne, was staying at Kenninghall in Norfolk. She learned of the King's death on 9 July 1553, and at once despatched a letter to the Council in London commanding them to recognize her as Queen. But the Council refused, having been prepared by the Duke of Northumberland to acclaim the Lady Jane Grey. Mary, whose main support at the time came from the gentry of East Anglia, then removed herself to the greater strength of Framlingham Castle and prepared to assert her rights, or if the support she received was insufficient, to withdraw overseas to her cousin the Emperor Charles's domains.

Towards the end of Edward's reign the Duke of Northumberland, who had virtually ruled the kingdom since the death of the Duke of Somerset, was a tired, sick and disappointed man; he would probably have been very glad to hand over power to the young King within another year or two. But when it became obvious that Edward was dying, matters took on a different aspect. Even then it is likely that it was Edward who pushed Northumberland into a trap from which he was unable to escape. It is true that Northumberland had married his son, Guildford Dudley, to Jane Grey, who, being the great granddaughter of Henry VII (through Princess Mary's marriage to Charles Brandon, Duke of Suffolk), was heir to the throne if Mary's claim was set aside, but the marriage had been planned some time before it was known that Edward was dying.

Both Edward and Northumberland were determined that Mary should not succeed; Edward because he desired the country to remain Protestant, and Northumberland because he could expect no mercy from Mary. If Edward himself was not the actual instigator of the devise for the Crown, he very readily agreed to Northumberland's suggestions.

Edward made the fatal mistake in thinking that, because Henry VIII changed the succession in his will, he could do the same; but whereas Henry had obtained this power through an Act of Parliament, Edward had not.

The hapless Lady Jane was duly brought to the Tower and proclaimed Queen. Nine days later she was Mary's prisoner. Support for Mary, both Protestant and Catholic, was overwhelming; from her base at Framlingham Castle in Suffolk she could soon command a sizeable army with which to meet the two thousand men that Northumberland led against her. There was to be no bloodshed, for Northumberland's men began to desert, and his Council in London forsook him and Queen Jane. On 24 July he was arrested in Cambridge; on the evening of 3 August 1553, Queen Mary rode into London in triumph.

Mary, the first Queen to rule England since the brief, unhappy days of Matilda, had had her full share of troubles before she came to the throne. The only daughter of the rumbustious Henry VIII by his devout Spanish wife, Catherine of Aragon, she was old enough to understand and to share the suffering of her mother at the hands of her father; a father who first created Mary Princess of Wales and then bastardized her. Like all the Tudors she was immensely stubborn, and, unlike them, completely honest to herself and to others; she was utterly irreconcilable to her father's schismatical breach with the Church of Rome, and her half-brother's conversion of England to a Protestant State. For her Catholic principles she was content to suffer humiliations and insults. In her loneliness and desperation she would lean upon her cousin, the Emperor Charles V, to whom on one occasion she planned to escape; he did what he could for her, but even he in the end was powerless to prevent her brother's government from prohibiting her the mass.

It is perhaps small wonder that her reign was such a sad one, for a wretched childhood and a persecuted adolescence left her at thirty-seven prematurely aged, slightly embittered, unwell in body and unhappy in mind. Moreover, she had a mission – divinely ordained – to bring back her people into the fold of the true faith. Here lay her tragedy and failure, for in attempting to fulfil this mission Mary not only turned the love and respect of her people into hatred and fear, but far from re-establishing the old religion she ensured that England became again and remained a Protestant State.

Known to every schoolchild as Bloody Mary, this Queen gained the epithet through the fires that consumed 283 martyrs in less than four years. But the name belies a character that, although lacking sparkle and charm, was not unpleasant. To those who served her Mary was always loyal, kind and affectionate; she was absolutely sincere, charitable and in the face of danger most courageous. There were flaws, of course, but these militated against her more as a ruler than a person, for she was easily swayed, almost incapable of making a decision and possessed no political aptitude or intuition.

Her coronation took place on 1 October 1553, and as she rode from the Tower to Westminster, seated in a 'chariot of tissue drawn with six horses all bestrapped with red velvet', she must have looked every inch a Queen, for although not beautiful she possessed the regal dignity of a Tudor, and she was very fond of jewellery and fine clothes. She had already released from the Tower the principal men imprisoned there in the previous reigns for their religious or political beliefs, and had made Stephen Gardiner, Bishop of Winchester, her Lord Chancellor. Now she was resisting pressure from him, and in particular from the Imperial ambassador (Simon Renard, who quickly became her *eminence grise*), for stern justice against those who had tried to debar her from the throne. But she insisted on clemency; only Northumberland and his two principal henchmen – Gates and Palmer – should die. Jane Grey and her husband remained prisoners, but with much freedom, while Jane's father, the Duke of Suffolk, was permitted to go free. Mary's first Parliament reflected this mood of mercy by repealing the treason and felony laws passed in the two previous reigns; they also repealed the Acts of Edward in respect of the Prayer Book, the sacraments and married priests, but they could not be moved on the matter of the Royal Supremacy, for too many Members held abbey lands and these they refused to be parted from.

Even before Mary's coronation the question of her marriage had been under consideration. Her personal inclination was to remain single, for she was not only totally uninterested in but slightly nervous of the sexual relationship of marriage. However, she reluctantly admitted the necessity for ensuring the Catholic succession, and Simon Renard, who on behalf of the Emperor master-minded the whole affair, used all his undoubted skill and cunning to arouse her interest in the Emperor's son, Prince Philip, both as a man and as a brilliant political match. Philip, a widower, was equally reluctant, for Mary was eleven years his senior, and plainly looked it; but he was quick to see how useful England could be to him in his Continental designs. The only difference between them was that whereas Mary promised that if she married Philip she would love him dearly – and she more than kept that promise – Philip gave no such assurance, and while he respected his wife, and usually treated her with affection, he never loved her.

Throughout all England the marriage was extremely unpopular. Many Protestants had openly supported Mary in her bid for the throne, but they most certainly would not tolerate a Spanish marriage. In January 1554 plans were laid for a large-scale rebellion and leaders emerged in Devon, Kent, Wales and Leicestershire, with French aid in the background as soon as success appeared evident. But in the event it was only in Kent that the plans were translated into action. Here Sir Thomas Wyatt, at the head of some two thousand men, scattered an army sent against him, and was soon besieging London from Southwark. Council and City were in panic, but Mary bravely rose to the occasion. On 1 February she went to the Guildhall, and in her deep, commanding voice she delivered the citizens a spirited and morally courageous address. It was as magnificent as it was unexpected, and it gave fresh heart to all. Crossing the river at Kingston, Wyatt attacked London from the west, but at Ludgate Hill he was overwhelmed, and after a fortnight of considerable danger it was all over.

As a result of this rebellion Mary lent a willing ear to Gardiner's and Renard's entreaties for sterner measures. The brief trial of clemency had, she was persuaded, failed. Those ringleaders of the rebellion who had not escaped the country could expect short shrift. One of them was the Duke of Suffolk, who richly deserved to die; but through his folly his daughter, Jane Grey, and her husband, both entirely innocent of the plot, were brought to the scaffold. It had been a useless demonstration and waste of life, for with her obstinacy and lack of judgement Mary pursued her chosen course and married Prince Philip (recently created King of Naples by his father) at Winchester on 25 July 1554.

Chief among those whom Gardiner and Renard were determined should be executed was Princess Elizabeth. Mary's relationship with her half-sister Elizabeth was ambivalent; as the daughter of Anne Boleyn she hated her; as a Protestant she distrusted her; but as her younger sister she shrank from taking the decisive step. Nevertheless, Elizabeth spent two anxious months in the Tower after Wyatt's rebellion, and but for her popularity and personal skill her life might well have been forfeit.

In the autumn of 1554 Cardinal Pole (Mary's cousin) returned from a long exile in Rome. Mary greeted him with great joy, and made him Archbishop of Canterbury. He had been empowered by Pope Julius III to secularize the confiscated Church lands, leaving them in the permanent possession of their owners, and thus enable Parliament to repeal the Act of Supremacy. This was done on 29 November, and the next day at a ceremony in Whitehall the Cardinal officially absolved the realm from the sin of schism. England was once more a Catholic State.

From there it was but a short step to the revival of the heresy laws, and in February 1555 the burnings began. Of the prelates Hooper, Bishop of Gloucester, was the first to burn; his execution in Gloucester on 9 February was a particularly cruel one, for he took three quarters of an hour to die. Ridley and Latimer suffered at Oxford on 16 October, and Cranmer, who at first recanted but later died courageously, was kept alive until 21 March 1556. The burnings in London and south-east England were on such a vast scale as to cause horror and resentment among all classes of a people not unaccustomed to public executions, and certainly not particularly squeamish. Many linked them, unfairly as it happened, to the presence of a Spanish King, others to the supremacy of an Italian Pope.

There has been much controversy about who was chiefly responsible for the holocaust. The names of Bonner, Gardiner and Pole are closely associated with this singularly foolish and ferocious policy, and none of them can be exonerated. But surely the principal blame must lie with Mary, for she alone had the power to cry halt. It was not so much that she was cruel, but that she had come to believe with a consuming passion that the Lord God had delegated to her the awful yet inescapable duty of purging the realm of heretics.

For most of the summer of 1555 the Queen went into retirement at Hampton Court, for she had become convinced that she was pregnant and that the child had quickened in her womb at the very moment that Cardinal Pole had first greeted her. 'The Queen's lying-in is the foundation of everything', reported Renard, adding that if there was no child matters would be so grim that 'a pen would hardly write them.' And soon his foreboding came true, for in August the Queen abandoned hope and dismissed the bevy of flattering doctors and other false prophets. At the end of the month her beloved Philip left her – ostensibly only for a fortnight to see the Emperor, but most people knew that once at home in Spain he would be in no hurry to return.

Later that year Gardiner died, and Mary must have felt very much alone. In failing health and worried about money – for she had long since returned what was left of the Crown's pickings from the monasteries – this grimly pious, melancholy lady had only Cardinal Pole to lean on. His charm, courtly manner and sagacity had, from the moment of his arrival, earned him a pre-eminent influence, but he could never make up for the loss of Philip. However, there was to be one more flash of happiness, for the King was to return for a brief and final visit.

Philip was always suspected – rightly – of wanting to use England for his greater European designs, and his initial efforts to ingratiate himself by bribes of money, gold chains and generous pensions had met with little response. Nevertheless, undeterred by the malice of his enemies this highly sensitive, intelligent man had always taken the keenest interest in the country's affairs, and even when abroad he insisted on reading the Council's minutes. But the reason for his return in March 1557 was certainly not in England's best interest.

Although Mary would do almost anything for her husband there were some things that she knew to be too dangerous. She had procrastinated over the matter of his coronation; she had refused to compel Elizabeth to marry his friend the Duke of Savoy, and now, when he desperately wanted to bring England into his war with France, he found the Queen and Council writing their excuses. And so he returned to see what bribery and his personal influence could accomplish. At first he met with no success, for although Henry II was prepared to aid English rebels, he did not want war with England, nor did the English want war with him.

But Philip was to get what he wanted through a foolish escapade on the part of Thomas Stafford – a scion of the house of Buckingham and therefore related to the royal family. There had been a plot to murder Mary in 1556 with French backing, and then at the following Easter Stafford mounted an attack from French ships on Scarborough. He was soon rounded up, but when it was learnt that there were three thousand French troops in Scotland ready to support him, a badly frightened Council became favourably disposed to war.

In July Philip, his object achieved, left England for ever. His sorrowing wife accompanied him to Dover. The war started well; Philip gained a resounding victory before St Quentin in August. But the French then recalled the Duc de Guise (Europe's greatest captain) from Italy, and the position altered dramatically. The English had done little over the years about strengthening the Calais defences, and the whole pale – a strip twenty-five miles long and some six miles wide – was very vulnerable. Lord Wentworth surrendered Calais after very little fighting on 6 January 1558, but Lord Grey, in command of Guisnes, put up a magnificent fight. The loss of Calais was considered at the time to be irreparable, and it was the death knell to Mary's prestige. Undoubtedly England was humbled by its loss, but apart from the trade and maritime value, this small English foothold on the Continent had already ceased to have much political relevance.

Another false pregnancy indicated that something was very wrong with the Queen, and by the late summer of 1558 it was fairly clear that she was dying. Philip did what he could to persuade her to nominate Elizabeth as her heir; but not until 9 November would she reluctantly concur with what the Privy Council, at the absent Philip's bidding, had approved. Early in the morning of 17 November, Mary died at St James's Palace; twelve hours later her cousin and confidant, Cardinal Pole, died at Lambeth. She was buried, on Elizabeth's orders, with full Catholic rites in Westminster Abbey. As a Queen Mary had been a disaster, but as a woman she had many endearing qualities – and above them all she placed truth and honour.

On 17 November (a day long commemorated by the English people)

Princess Elizabeth was at Hatfield, when the news was brought to her that her sister was dead and she was Queen of England.

Elizabeth – even more than Mary – had had to endure a childhood and adolescence that could easily have destroyed a weaker character. When she was only two her mother, Anne Boleyn, was executed, and she was declared illegitimate by her father, Henry VIII, who took little interest in her and inspired not love, but fear. Until the arrival of her last stepmother, Katherine Parr, she was lonely and neglected; during her brother's reign she survived a dangerous flirtation with the un-scrupulous Thomas Seymour, brother of the Lord Protector, and during that of her sister she came close to the block more than once. However, her courage, cunning, sharp wits, equivocation and feminine artifices – characteristics that were later, at times, to drive her ministers almost to despair – steered her safely along the perilous paths that led to the throne.

At twenty-five she arrived there untutored in the ways of kingship, but well tutored in the classics, languages and arts. Her excellent mind and keen intellect had been shaped by her brother's preceptors, Richard Cox and John Cheke, as well as the great Greek scholar William Grindall, and Roger Ascham. In addition to her academic achievements, Elizabeth had inherited much from her father – those flashes of rage, to which she added a tongue that could be vituperatively unleashed, but also the gaiety of his youth and his love of music and the chase. Above all, she came to the throne on a current of immense popularity – which she carefully fostered throughout the reign – for her people sensed that in this regal-looking, auburn-haired Princess they had got a genuine chip off the old block.

Almost the Queen's first act was to have Sir William Cecil sworn as a member of her Council. Cecil, now a man of thirty-eight, had been secretary to the Dukes of Somerset and Northumberland in Edward's reign; the possessor of vast knowledge and unfailing industry, he became the lynchpin in that magnificent Elizabethan coach of State, and the most brilliant statesman of the century.

Having carefully selected the members of her Council, Elizabeth and they turned their attention to the religious problem. Elizabeth's first care was to gain the goodwill of her people, and by the time of her coronation on 15 January 1559 she felt her grip, at any rate among the Londoners – whose Protestant complexion was beyond doubt – to be sufficiently firm to enable her to unfold her religious Settlement. The Royal Supremacy Bill was to be re-enacted, but it was her wish to avoid the extremes of the last two reigns, and to steer a middle course, whereby Catholics, provided they conformed outwardly to the Anglican service, might hear the Roman mass in the privacy of their homes. Even this much needed courage in the face of a hostile Pope and the two great Catholic nations that bestrode her realm, for at this time Elizabeth presided none too securely over a country that was financially crippled and by no means united.

From the start this golden mean ran into difficulties. On the one hand the Marian bishops (the bench was fortunately diminished by recent deaths) preferred resignation to acceptance, while for the Commons – and in particular the dozen or so Marian exiles in that House – the Settlement did not go nearly far enough. Elizabeth would not be stampeded by her Parliament, but eventually a compromise with a very liberal doctrinal base was agreed upon. The Queen had made many concessions to the radicals, but as Supreme Governor of the Church of England she was in later years to oppose vehemently and successfully the Puritan challenge to the Royal Supremacy. For the time being the Catholics, without leadership or much spunk, were quiescent, with only a small minority of diehards outwardly dissatisfied.

Elizabeth was annoyed at having to make concessions to Parliament, and determined that in future, policy and important legislation would be initiated by the Crown. She would listen and consider, but she would not be driven. Thus it was that when the next important issues were raised – marriage and the succession – the Queen would not be persuaded.

We cannot be certain whether Elizabeth ever wanted to marry. Possibly she never intended going beyond flirtation, but unless her acting was of a deceptively high standard, it would seem that, had she been able to subordinate the needs of State to those of the flesh, she would have liked to marry and have children. But her sense of duty and her love for England made the decision a very difficult one – and throughout her life she hated taking decisions.

Many of the greatest men of that brilliant age, both at home and abroad, contended for her hand, for she was Europe's most desirable match. To marry a foreigner meant to become involved in his country's affairs (her sister's example was always before her), to marry an Englishman could be to set one faction against another and possibly weaken her own position. This was made clear to her in the one courtship that really had a meaning in her life. Undoubtedly she loved Robert Dudley, whom she made Earl of Leicester and who was to become one of the principal participants in the glories of her reign, but the tragic death of his wife, Amy Robsart, and other problems made marriage impossible. The cluster of foreign suitors (which included her brother-in-law, King Philip) she treated with feminine charm and equivocation. The Duke of Alençon came the closest of these 'potent princes' to success, perhaps because in his second suit he represented the

Queen's last chance, but his religion (if not his looks) was a deciding factor.

In 1562 the Queen nearly died of smallpox, and the thought of the chaos and bloodshed that could have ensued terrified the country and led her ministers to implore her to name a successor. Undoubtedly Elizabeth was worried; but she would not be rushed, and resorted to skilful evasion and procrastination. As with marriage, so with the succession, there were difficulties. To name a successor could make him or her a rallying point for the discontented, and bring about the bloodshed that all were anxious to avoid. And so no successor was ever named.

The most obvious one, but for the religious and political bar, was Mary, Queen of Scots, a great-granddaughter of Henry VII. She was married to the French Dauphin (soon to be King), and although after his death she petitioned Elizabeth to be named her successor, she lost any chance there might have been when she disdainfully refused Elizabeth's magnanimous suggestion that she marry Lord Leicester.

The long road to Fotheringhay virtually began when in 1560 Mary and her husband refused to ratify the Treaty of Edinburgh which, inter alia, removed French troops from Scotland, recognized Elizabeth's right to the English throne and debarred Mary from using the English royal arms. Just conceivably the story might have had a different ending had Elizabeth acted more generously when Mary, now a widow, requested a passage through England on her way home. A meeting between the two Queens might have reduced subsequent misunderstanding, mistrust and malevolence. But this chance and two others were missed.

In July 1565 Mary made the mistake of marrying her shallow-minded, charmless cousin, Lord Darnley. Nothing but trouble resulted from this ill-considered match. Mary, soon tiring of her despicable husband, took for adviser, and perhaps lover, her Italian secretary, David Rizzio. Darnley murdered him; Mary found another paramour, the Earl of Bothwell, with whom she conspired to blow up Darnley in a house at Kirk-o'-Field. Nobody much regretted the demise of Darnley; but there were many not prepared to tolerate the manner of it, and still less the rise of Bothwell, whose reward for regicide was the Queen and the kingdom. In a battle at Carberry Hill, the Protestant Lords of the Congregation defeated Bothwell, who fled the country. Mary was captured, and on 24 July 1567 forced to abdicate in favour of her fifteen-months-old-son, James, with her half-brother, the Earl of Moray, as regent.

Elizabeth was an anxious observer of these bizarre events. She championed Mary and roundly condemned the Protestant Lords for their behaviour towards the Queen. When, ten months later, Mary escaped from Lochleven, Elizabeth wrote encouragingly; however, the defeat of Mary's troops and her subsequent escape to England, a fugitive from her people, posed a serious problem for Elizabeth. To bring her to court would be folly, to return her forcibly to Scotland meant the overthrow of the Protestant regime there, and to leave her at large to solicit allies would be dangerous. And so Mary was to be kept in honourable custody.

Her presence in England made her the natural focus for Catholic plots, and particularly was this so in the north, where Popery was still strongly rooted. Moreover, in this year – 1568 – two other events occurred to foster Catholic revival. William Allen founded his college at Douai for the training of Catholic missionaries, who in a few years were to start infiltrating throughout England; and Philip strengthened his grip on the Netherlands, thus providing a springboard for the Counter-Reformation backed by the presence of a strong Spanish military threat from across the Narrow Seas.

In 1569 the first of many plots engineered by the Catholics, the Northern Rebellion, was quickly suppressed, but two years later a Florentine banker called Ridolfi – to whom in 1570 the Pope had entrusted copies of his Bull of Excommunication against Elizabeth – was the agent for a potentially more serious attempt to impose (with the aid of the Duke of Alva and six thousand Spanish soldiers) Mary and the Catholic religion upon England. But Cecil (now Lord Burghley) learnt of the plot, and the Duke of Norfolk, who had been implicated in the Northern Rebellion and far more deeply in this affair, was beheaded.

Inevitably, after the discovery of this plot, Elizabeth's attitude hardened; honourable custody for Mary was replaced by captivity, first under Lord Shrewsbury and then the Puritan Sir Amyas Paulet, at Sheffield, Wingfield, Tutbury and Chartley. Two further plots, in which Mary was heavily compromised (Throckmorton's of 1582 and Babington's of 1586), and which were cleverly and patiently exposed by that austere personality Francis Walsingham, led to Mary's removal from Chartley to Fotheringhay, and to her execution there on 8 February 1587. Elizabeth suffered agonies of conscience before signing the death warrant, and having done so took care to place the onus of dispatching it upon her councillors. But it had to be done; there was no room for two queens in England.

The Queen's life was frequently in danger, not only indirectly through plots to put Mary on the throne, but from individual assassins motivated by religious madness. Such threats did not, however, deter Elizabeth from her normal rounds of duty and pleasure. Ever anxious to see and be seen by as many of her people as possible, she much enjoyed –

although it is doubtful whether all of her hosts did – her celebrated progresses. Her court was gay and colourful; music and dancing she especially loved, and the public had the chance to watch many of the ceremonial processions and duties performed in the palaces.

The upkeep of a court on such a lavish scale was costly, and Elizabeth, like her predecessors, was usually short of money. The country's merchants were doing excellent business, London was an international port, and the export trade – mostly broadcloths – was booming. But taxation was not heavy, and the Queen gained little revenue from this source. She did, however, take her cut in the substantial illicit gains brought into the ports through the genius, daring and energy of that remarkable band of Elizabethan sea-dogs.

John Hawkins, whom the Queen made treasurer of the navy in 1578, was responsible for new ideas in shipbuilding. His fighting galleons, in the hands of such men as Drake, Frobisher, Grenville, Ralegh and Humphry Gilbert could outmatch anything that the Spaniards put against them. These men were not only superb seamen and brave fighters, but in the interest of their financial backers they needed to be diplomats with a dash of business acumen. Hawkins, Grenville, Drake, Gilbert and Ralegh had at various times in their colourful careers sat in the House of Commons. Gilbert and Ralegh (Captain of the Guard and a great favourite of the Queen) gave their private fortunes, and in the case of Gilbert his life, in the discovery of new lands and those mixed blessings, the potato and tobacco.

Elizabeth's handling of the Commons was masterly; she flattered them, flirted with them, coaxed, cajoled or commanded as occasion demanded. They adored her, and they admired her sagacity and breadth of view, but at times, along with her ministers, they were baffled by her whims and foibles, her hesitations and procrastinations. Her policy, for instance, towards William of Orange and his struggling United Netherlanders was tortuous in the extreme. She hated war – indeed she hated all bloodshed, and was an exceptionally merciful ruler – and strove to avoid committing the country; but after William of Orange's murder, and with France and Spain united in destroying his revolt, she was forced to change from unofficial to official help. In 1585 she sent Leicester with an army to aid the Dutch; there followed an unhappy two years for both Leicester and the Queen, with little more than the gallantry of Sir Philip Sidney at Zutphen to raise the morale of the English.

Elizabeth's decision to help The Netherlands was accompanied by an increase of naval hostility towards Spain – Drake being sent off on one of those marauding expeditions against the Spanish West Indies treasure fleet. She did not consider herself at war with Spain – the Netherlands invasion being but an act of defence. However, Philip's patience had been tried too far; the long projected English Enterprise must become a reality.

Naval preparations for this inevitable trial of strength had been going on for some years in both countries. England had fewer ships; but, thanks to Hawkins, their speed and greater gun range gave them the advantage over the cumbersome Spanish vessels, with their high castles and short-range guns designed principally for a grappling fight. Drake's famous raid on Cadiz in 1587 had so damaged the Spanish fleet as to keep it from sailing until the spring of the next year. But on 28 May, one hundred and thirty ships carrying thirty thousand men sailed from Lisbon to hold the Narrow Seas, while the Duke of Parma's army, carried in barges, invaded from The Netherlands.

The Armada immediately ran into rough weather and had to put into Corunna to refit, but by 23 July it was in the Channel. The English refused to close, and battered the Spaniards with long-range fire, driving them up the Channel and into Calais. From here they were smoked out by fireships and forced to give battle. Had there not been a providential change of wind, the Spanish fleet might have been annihilated by England's seamen. As it was they fled before the wind, making for home round the north of Scotland and west of Ireland, harassed and hampered for much of the way; crippled, wounded and defeated for all of it. This great victory was noted in Lord Burghley's diary with commendable brevity and modesty. The entry for 29 July simply reads, 'The Gr Navy of Spayn forced into ye North seas and so with Grt. wrack passed homewards about Scotl. and Irland.'

The threat of invasion was not believed to have ended with the defeat of the Armada. The anti-invasion army, assembled under Leicester at Tilbury, was not immediately stood down, for it was feared (quite unnecessarily) that Parma might still attempt a landing. At the threat of invasion, Elizabeth's courage rose to its greatest height. No thought of danger would prevent her from reviewing her troops; wearing steel armour 'like some Amazonian empress' she rode through their ranks, and delivered that marvellous speech, 'I know that I have but the body of a weak and feeble woman; but I have the heart and stomach of a king, and a king of England too, and think foul scorn that Parma or Spain, or any prince of Europe should dare to invade the borders of my realm . . .'

The last years were in many ways years of sadness. Raised to the pinnacle of Europe through the success of her arms and her personal courage and wisdom, Elizabeth had now to witness the departure of many of those who had made this such a great era of prosperity and glory. The first to go was 'Sweet Robin' Leicester, her 'eyes', and his death in September 1588 was followed in the next year by that of her

personal treasurer, Sir Francis Knollys. In 1590 Blanche Parry, a
gentlewoman of the Privy Chamber whom she had known since
childhood, Walsingham and Lord Shrewsbury took their leave; and in
1591 the Queen, with that tender kindness that she was to show again
when the great Lord Burghley lay dying, brought 'cordial broths' and
comfort to the mortally ill Lord Chancellor, Sir Christopher Hatton –
her devoted 'lids'.

One last star was to shine briefly in this brilliant galaxy – the
flamboyant, conceited, sulky and turbulent Robert Devereux, second
Earl of Essex. Undoubtedly he irradiated at least a part of Elizabeth's
closing years, but she was now too old to tame him and bend him to her
will. For a decade Essex was the gallant soldier, sailor, courtier *par
excellence*; he served in France (1591) and with greater distinction at
Cadiz (1596). Master of the Horse, Knight of the Garter, a Privy
Councillor and friend of the Bacon brothers – there seemed no end to the
heights he might have climbed. But like most Tudor courtiers he was
racked by envy and ambition, and a prey to the swift turns of fortune
that these vices could induce. He quarrelled with the intellectually
superior Ralegh, and with Robert Cecil, brilliant son of a brilliant
father; he all but lost Ireland for the Queen, and in the end his
ingratitude, boorishness and matchless folly brought him to the block.

The end came with painful slowness; propped up with cushions in her
room, the Queen lay for days '*mortua sed non sepulta*'. When Cecil told her
that to content her people she must go to bed, some of the old spirit
returned with her reply, 'Little man is "must" a word to use to princes?'
Death came on 24 March, and with it the end of the greatest dynasty yet
to occupy the English throne.

The two Tudor queens did not themselves commission any new buildings of
note, although Elizabeth's passion for progresses kept her wealthier subjects on
their toes, and many of their beautiful houses which still stand were built, or
added to and embellished, for the pleasure of the Queen. Mary had little time to
spend on the arts and architecture, nor did she have much money, for the royal
treasury had been exhausted by the extravagancies of the past two reigns,
ending with the profligacy of the Duke of Northumberland.

Elizabeth's reign was chiefly notable for martial enterprise and exploration.
The great achievements on land, and particularly on the seas, established
England as a world power. To her soldiers and sailors the Queen was a great
inspiration, for her patriotism was unbounded. But she left the patronage of
artists and writers mostly to her principal courtiers. English painting in

Elizabeth's time was largely confined to miniature portraits, but in the field of literature the English were well served by men of genius. Shakespeare performed his plays before the Queen, but there is no evidence that she showed much enthusiasm for the entertainment. Her chief recreational pursuits were music, masques and merriment.

Bolton Castle (North Yorks.). This castle, much of which still stands, commands wonderful views over Wensleydale. It was built by the first Lord Scrope during the last quarter of the fourteenth century, more as a residence than a fortress, for although on one side it is fairly inexpugnable, from the north it is open to bombardment. Its principal historic interest is that from July 1568 until January 1569 Mary Queen of Scots was kept there in 'honourable custody'. It is situated seven miles north-west of Middleham, north off the A684 road.

Bradgate Park (Leics.). Thomas Grey, Marquess of Dorset had Bradgate, an imposing semi-fortified country house, built at the end of the fifteenth century. He was the great-grandfather of Lady Jane Grey, Queen of England for nine days, who was born and brought up in the house. Very little now remains of it, although three towers and parts of the southern wall still stand; the most complete part of the ruin is the chapel which is well preserved. The beautiful park, in which this mansion was set, contains several gnarled oaks which are some of the oldest in the country and may well have been there when Lady Jane Grey lived in the house. Bradgate is five miles north-west of Leicester, and can be reached by leaving the M1 at Junction 22.

Buckland Abbey (Devon). Originally a Cistercian monastery, the present imposing mansion was largely the work of Elizabeth's sea-captain, Sir Richard Grenville, the hero of the *Revenge*, immortalized by Tennyson. The property was later bought by Sir Francis Drake, and now contains a wide range of memorabilia connected with both Grenville and Drake. Buckland is eleven miles north of Plymouth, west off the A386 road at Yelverton.

Burghley House (Northants.). This great Renaissance house was built towards the end of the sixteenth century by Queen Elizabeth I's Chief Secretary and later Lord High Treasurer, William Cecil, Lord Burghley. The Queen visited the house on more than one occasion, and, in addition to the magnificent collection of pictures, tapestries, furniture and silver, the Queen's bedroom and some of the original Elizabethan furniture can be seen by visitors.

Edinburgh
Palace of Holyrood House. The original palace was begun by James IV of Scotland in 1501. The buildings were extensively altered in the seventeenth century, but the north-west tower still remains. The murderers of David Rizzio, Mary Queen of Scots' Italian secretary, made their way up the spiral staircase of this tower in 1566, and a tablet marks the spot where his murder took place.

Framlingham Castle (Suffolk). In July 1553, a few days after the death of Edward VI, Princess Mary was at Kenninghall, but, advised that the house was indefensible, she removed to the Duke of Norfolk's castle at Framlingham. From there, having been informed by letter from the Council of her proclamation, she set out for London in triumph and vindication of her just and lawful claim to the throne.

Framlingham had been built about 1190 by Roger Bigod, son of the Earl of Norfolk who had rebelled against Henry II. Although a royal possession for a short period in the 1300s, for most of its active history Framlingham was owned by the Earls and Dukes of Norfolk, until it was sold in the seventeenth century. It was one of the earliest castles built to the pattern of a massive curtain wall with flanking towers – Framlingham had thirteen such towers. Framlingham is eight miles west of Saxmundham, and close to the castle is the church, which is also of great age and interest. The Howard tombs – in particular that of the poet Earl of Surrey, executed in 1547 – are very beautiful. Henry VIII's illegitimate son by Bessie Blount, Henry Fitzroy, Duke of Richmond, is also buried amongst the Howards. When he died in 1536, the Duke of Norfolk, who was his father-in-law, was ordered by the King to wrap his body in lead, and secretly to take the body to Suffolk for burial. Henry feared that there would be trouble if Richmond's death was widely known, for Mary and Elizabeth had both been declared illegitimate. Henry Fitzroy now lies in a fine Renaissance tomb.

Gloucester Cathedral (Glos.). (See also Chapters 3–5.) To the west of the cathedral, in a small square leading off Palace Yard, stands the statue of Bishop Hooper, on the site where in 1555 he was burnt to ashes – one of the earliest of the Marian martyrs.

Hardwick Hall (Derbys.). Hardwick was the family home of Bess of Hardwick, who married George Talbot, Earl of Shrewsbury, as her fourth husband in 1568. Soon after their wedding, Shrewsbury became the custodian of Mary Queen of Scots, and although she never was kept at Hardwick, the house has many objects connected with her. By 1584, Bess, jealous of her husband's fair prisoner, left him and returned to Hardwick, where she began to rebuild the house. It was well under way when Shrewsbury died in 1590, leaving her a very rich woman. She abandoned the house and began a new, even more ambitious one – the great mansion with its huge windows that dominates the skyline. Hardwick remains very much as Bess planned it, with its plasterwork, tapestries and furniture giving an unparalleled record of a large Elizabethan house. It has been suggested that Bess planned the series of state rooms as a suitable residence for her granddaughter, Lady Arabella Stuart, who was heir to the English throne after her cousin James, and whose life ended in tragedy as a result of her claim to the throne.

Hardwick Hall is two miles south of the A617, Chesterfield to Mansfield road.

Hatfield House (Herts.). On the morning of 17 November 1558, Princess Elizabeth was sitting under an oak tree in Hatfield Park when news was brought to her that her accession had already been proclaimed in London. What remains of that tree (a hollow trunk, seven feet high) has recently been lifted from its original site and placed under cover in the Old Palace Yard. Three days later, on 20 November 1558, Elizabeth I held her first Council in the Old Palace at Hatfield. When James I exchanged Hatfield for Robert Cecil's house Theobalds, Cecil decided to pull down the old house, and build at a little distance the present imposing mansion. Only that wing of the fifteenth-century Old Palace containing the banqueting hall still stands (and is still used for banquets), but in the present house visitors can see a number of very fine pictures, including three famous portraits of Elizabeth, and many items of interest belonging to or connected with her.

Hayes Barton (Budleigh Salterton, Devon). Sir Walter Ralegh was born in the farmhouse in 1552. His family leased the property, and when Ralegh, in the days of his fame, wished to buy it, the owner refused to sell. The house is little changed, especially its interior, from the time when Ralegh knew it as a boy.

Ingatestone Hall (Essex). Ingatestone was built by William Petre, Secretary of State to four Tudor sovereigns. In July 1561, on one of her royal progresses, Elizabeth I visited her minister at his house at Ingatestone and was entertained there for three days. The present Lord Petre has leased part of the house to the Essex County Council, and the long gallery and garden chamber, which are open to the public, are very much as they were at the time of Elizabeth I's visit. Ingatestone Hall is half a mile south-east of Ingatestone, off the B1002.

Kenilworth Castle (Warwicks.). (See also Chapters 4 and 5.) John Dudley, Duke of Northumberland, had obtained Kenilworth after he had succeeded the Duke of Somerset in all but name as Protector of the Realm during Edward VI's reign; but he was executed by Queen Mary. However, her successor, Elizabeth I, restored the castle to the family in the person of Northumberland's fifth son, Robert, who, as Earl of Leicester, became her most cherished servant and friend. Leicester carried out extensive work at Kenilworth between 1570 and 1575, making it a fit place in which to entertain his sovereign in magnificent style – the most famous of her visits lasted for nineteen days, with much feasting and merriment. His gatehouse, stables and some of his State apartments form a prominent part of the present ruin.

London
The Tower of London. (See also Chapters 3–8.) Sir Thomas Wyatt's rebellion at the beginning of Queen Mary's reign sealed the fate of Lady Jane Grey, and on the same day that this seventeen-year-old girl was beheaded on Tower Green, Mary's half-sister, the Princess Elizabeth, left Ashridge under guard first for Whitehall Palace and then the Tower. On Palm Sunday 1554, Elizabeth entered the Tower by Traitors' Gate, and although her famous exclamation on arrival, 'Here landeth as true a subject, being a prisoner, as ever landed on these stairs . . .', may well have been correct, it did not prevent her spending two very perilous months confined in the Bell Tower.

The Victoria and Albert Museum. The museum holds many items of interest connected with the reign of Elizabeth I: in the musical instrument gallery are the Queen's virginals decorated with the Boleyn arms; the work of the two great miniaturists of the reign – Nicholas Hilliard and Isaac Oliver – includes portraits of the Queen; there is a fine display of Elizabethan furniture, with the gigantic Bed of Ware; and the beautiful Armada Jewel, that was given by Elizabeth to Sir Thomas Heneage to commemorate the defeat of the Spaniards.

Westminster Abbey. In the north aisle of Henry VII's Chapel lie, in somewhat uneasy alliance; the two granddaughters of the first Tudor king. Elizabeth I's dramatic effigy in white marble was carved by Maximilian Colt and completed in 1607. Elizabeth's half-sister, Mary, also lies in the vault, but there is no representation of her upon the tomb, only an inscription, 'Here sleep Elizabeth and Mary, sisters, in hope of resurrection'. In the south aisle of Henry VII's Chapel is the tomb of Mary Queen of Scots – her body was brought from Peterborough Cathedral to the Abbey in 1612, and her life-like effigy was carved by William and Cornelius Cure. Next to her tomb stands the colourful monument to her mother-in-law, Margaret Countess of Lennox. Margaret's children are depicted along the side of her tomb, led by Henry Lord Darnley, kneeling, with the Crown of Scotland, which cost him his life, hanging over his head.

Westminster Abbey (Norman Undercroft Museum). (See also Chapter 6.) In this museum can be seen the illuminated service book used by Queen Elizabeth I during her coronation in 1559, a ring said to have been given by her to Robert Devereux, Earl of Essex, and the effigy carried at her funeral.

Loseley House (Surrey). This Elizabethan house was built in the 1560s by Sir William More, a kinsman of Sir Thomas. Elizabeth I visited the house more than once on her royal progresses, and her bedroom, in which she stayed in August 1569, still has its sixteenth-century furniture and furnishings. Loseley House is two and a half miles south-west of Guildford.

Penshurst Place (Kent). (See also Chapter 6.) From 1521, when the third Duke of Buckingham was beheaded, until 1552, Penshurst was a royal manor. Edward VI then gave the property to Sir William Sidney. There is much royal history connected with the Sidney family – who still own Penshurst. On the death of the gallant Sir Philip Sidney on the battlefield of Zutphen, the property passed to his younger brother Robert, who built the splendid long gallery.

Queen Elizabeth's Hunting Lodge (Chingford, Essex). This very unusual timber-framed survival from Tudor times is said to have gained its name after Elizabeth I rode up its staircase on a white palfrey after the defeat of the Armada. Certainly there was a hunting lodge there in the time of Henry VIII and Elizabeth carried out extensive repairs there. The lodge fulfilled the unusual function for those days (now a common practice wherever wild game abounds) of providing a viewpoint from which to scan the forest. For this purpose the space between the studs on the two upper stories was left open. The hunting lodge is now the Epping Forest Museum. Chingford is ten miles south of Epping, a short distance west off the A11 road.

Sherborne Castle (Dorset). In 1591 Queen Elizabeth I gave Sherborne to her favourite, Sir Walter Ralegh. Soldier, adventurer, author, philosopher, one of the great men of a great age, Ralegh decided to abandon the old Norman castle in favour of a new building on the other side of the beautiful lake. The centre block of the existing castle was his creation,* and to this house of happiness he brought his wife Bess Throckmorton, whom he had recently married, to the fury of his Queen. Much of Ralegh's building, and the rooms associated with him, still remain, and in his great kitchens can be seen traces of the original hunting lodge, whose foundations he built upon.

Sherborne is situated between Shaftesbury and Yeovil in Dorset, and the castle lies off the New Road, one mile to the east of the centre of the town of Sherborne.

Sudeley Castle (Glos.). (See also Chapter 8.) The castle has been owned by the Dent-Brocklehurst family for many years, and in the last century Mrs Emma Dent made several valuable collections, among which is Queen Elizabeth I's christening robe. When the castle was owned by Thomas Seymour and his wife, Queen Katherine Parr, the young Princess Elizabeth would have known it well, so it is very fitting that her christening robe should now be displayed in this castle, which is situated at Winchcombe, near Cheltenham.

Tutbury Castle (Staffs.). (See also Chapter 6.) For most of 1569, and again in 1585, Mary Queen of Scots was a prisoner in this castle. During the year immediately prior to her occupation, the castle had been used as the administrative centre of the Duchy of Lancaster estates. It was beginning to fall into disrepair; however, a good sum of money was spent on it before Mary was incarcerated, but apparently not enough for Mary's liking, because she was constantly complaining of the cold and of its dilapidated condition. She occupied the first floor on the south-east side of the castle, where it was considered the best rooms were situated, but Mary's complaints were probably justified. Tutbury is five miles north of Burton-upon-Trent on the A50 road.

10

THE FIRST STUARTS

From Scotland to Scaffold

James VI of Scotland, later to become James I of England, was born in Edinburgh Castle on 19 June 1566 to Mary, Queen of Scots, and Henry Stuart, Lord Darnley. A year later Darnley was dead, Mary was in captivity and on 29 July 1567 James was crowned King of the Scots. For the next ten years Scotland was governed by a series of regents, two of whom were assassinated and a third beheaded.

James's education was principally in the hands of the brilliant scholar, George Buchanan, a short-tempered martinet with a pathological hatred of the King's mother. That he did his work well is amply testified by the deep learning displayed by his pupil when only eight years of age. James's schooling ceased abruptly at fourteen, by which time he had mastered a considerable amount of the Old Testament, spoke Latin, Greek and French and was well versed in such abstruse subjects as cosmography and astronomy. There was forged in this stern schoolroom a young polymath, soon to become a pedant.

A keen, sharp mind, elevation of thought and breadth of view were not matched by a perfect physique. James was certainly no weakling, but his slight body was ill-supported on spindly legs, and, with a tongue that was too large for his narrow jaws, he was given to slobbering. He was ungainly and unmannerly, but not deformed beyond an awkward foot. There was no meanness about the boy or man – in fact his love of giving was carried to excess. Like all his family he lived for the chase, and indeed he enjoyed most forms of physical exercise.

In 1560 the Scottish Protestants had severed all connection with Rome, and under John Knox had established their Calvinist-inspired Reformation. James was therefore brought up a member of the reformed Presbyterian Kirk, with whom he was very early at loggerheads, greatly preferring a form of Episcopalianism. Throughout his life religious and mystic questions fascinated him, and in particular witchcraft, on which he wrote a treatise, *Daemonologie*, and which he was inclined to regard as a branch of theology.

When James was only twelve, the Earls of Atholl and Argyll persuaded him to dispose of the regency and govern through a Council, and a year later he fell totally under the spell of a cousin newly arrived from France. Esmé Stuart, Seigneur d'Aubigny, was the first person to give James any sort of love, and the boy responded with an unnatural passion. There was probably no sexual relationship between these two very different men, but Stuart's influence, and that of the French courtiers in his train, was wholly undesirable, and seeds were sown at this time which produced a crop of moral and mental instabilities.

It was perhaps natural that James should shower honours and promotion upon his favourite, and Stuart was soon created Duke of Lennox. In a society that had scarcely emerged from the cocoon of a primitive life, and in which many clan chieftains aspired to political power, the French Stuart's rapid rise was bitterly resented, and ended in the extraordinary Raid of Ruthven, in which the King was captured and held prisoner for ten months in the home of the Earl of Gowrie. During his captivity he was forced to issue a proclamation acknowledging the freedom of the Kirk and – what was even more galling and psychologically disturbing – another proclamation banishing Lennox, whom he was never to see again.

A French marriage having been considered and rejected, James married in November 1589 Anne, daughter of the King of Denmark. This marriage brought a gleam of sunshine into a life that had hitherto been drab and full of troubles, for although James was to reserve his deepest affections for those of his own sex, there is no doubt that at least in the early days of their marriage he loved his wife, was proud of her beauty and tolerant of her shallow brain. They had seven children, but only three survived infancy; the eldest, Prince Henry, a youth of exceptional promise, was to die in 1612, aged eighteen.

James's task as a ruler was more difficult in Scotland than it was to be in England; it is true he was not so tightly trammelled by Parliament, but these were fierce and hectic times in Scotland with a militant Church, and every family cultivating its vendetta. For much of the time the King was prey to a deep, unrelenting fear of physical violence, which, if his own account of his amazing second brush with the Ruthven family is correct,* is understandable. From an early age he was a sincere

---

* In August 1600 the King was lured from Falkland Palace to Gowrie House by the Master of Ruthven, on the pretence of examining and acquiring a pot of gold coins. According to the King, after dinner he was taken up to a turret room, where the Master attempted to murder him. But as both the Master and his brother, Lord Gowrie, were killed in the ensuing fracas, there was no one to contradict his story.

believer in the sanctity and absolute supremacy of kings. Such a view inevitably produced irreconcilable differences of opinion with the Church, and dangerous difficulties with the nobles, who were apt to regard their king as no more than first among equals. It says much for his skill and perseverance – and indeed for his courage – that in the end James achieved a measure of peace, and governed the country through his chosen Council with considerable ability.

The Crown of England had long excited James's cupidity and ambition; he thought of England as a richer land and Englishmen as being more civilized than the 'barbarous and stiff necked people' who were his present subjects. But the prize could not be taken for granted (for one thing, although in direct descent from Henry VIII's sister, as an alien he was debarred under Henry VIII's will); there were other candidates in the field, although James's credentials were certainly the best, and Elizabeth, while retaining her enigmatic silence, obviously favoured him.

James left nothing to chance; he wooed Elizabeth, the Pope and the English Roman Catholics. He kept a foot in the Irish camp with Tyrone, but he very nearly ruined his chances by misjudging the strength of Essex, with whom he was in correspondence. However, after Essex's execution a near miracle occurred for James. Robert Cecil, with whom James had been on the very worst of terms, now saw that the Scots King represented his best chance, and he began a secret correspondence with him in which he attempted to prepare the King's mind for his new task. With Cecil transformed from enemy to friend, success was assured, and on 5 April 1603 – a fortnight after Queen Elizabeth had died – King James left Scotland on the road leading south, where he confidently hoped he would find greater erudition, security and wealth. But, as is so often the case, the promise of enduring happiness proved illusory.

First impressions of their new King were entirely favourable; Englishmen, high and low, were apprehensive of the future when their great Queen died and an era passed away. They liked James for his quiet, homely manner, his apparent simplicity and good nature; they were prepared to ignore his lack of courtesy and they even admired his physical appearance and mode of dress. For his part, James was delighted to exchange the rough-tongued, bawdy behaviour of his Scottish lairds for the obsequious flattery of the English courtiers. His reputation as a poet and writer had gone before him, and his latest book, *Basilikon Doron* (fortuitously published at the time of his accession), was an immediate success. The fact that both this work and his earlier, *The Trew Law of Free Monarchies*, attempted to justify his belief in absolute kingship, was for the time overlooked.

James rightly regarded himself as King of Great Britain, but neither

Parliament nor the Estates would have parliamentary union. James continued to govern Scotland through a small Privy Council, and his promise to return there every three years was soon forgotten. In fact he returned but once, in 1617, when he unsuccessfully attempted to impose Anglican ceremonies on to a thoroughly resentful Presbyterian Church.

In England the new King soon found that life was not going to be all that he had hoped for; he inherited a large debt and a Parliament that had been kept in leash too long, and which (especially its Puritan element) was not going to be easy to handle. Moreover, James had no experience in manipulating an English Parliament, and he made mistakes from which his son never learnt. The country was still officially at war with Spain, but in 1604 James made a wise peace treaty, and thereafter his policy was always to favour Spain.

Perhaps James's most difficult Elizabethan legacy concerned religion. The country was sadly divided, with Anglicans, Puritans and Catholics all centring their hopes upon James. He felt himself well qualified to mediate, and always delighted in disputations on Church matters; but at his conference in 1604 at Hampton Court he found himself unable to fulfil any of the demands put forward by the Puritans, and came down firmly on the side of the High Church bishops. In the succeeding years the Puritans became the party of dissent, and in 1620 a hundred of them sailed in the *Mayflower* to seek that freedom of worship denied to them in England. A Virginian company had already formed a settlement around Jamestown in 1606, and the Puritan migration of the 1620s and 1630s, when twenty thousand Englishmen crossed the Atlantic, is one of the great sagas of our history.

It was not the Puritans, however, but the Catholics who caused the first great upheaval of the reign. James, before he ascended the English throne, had given leading Catholics vague assurances of toleration, and it was certainly his hope that he could be instrumental in easing their burden, but he found Cecil adamant. In their disappointment at getting no relief from the strict laws that encompassed them, some Catholics hatched the famous treason plot of November 1605. Cecil and his colleagues were almost certainly aware of the conspiracy before it was leaked to Lord Monteagle, and the dramatic timing of its discovery was well calculated to have the maximum effect on James's innate fear of assassination.

James was perhaps the most learned King to sit on the English throne; he saw himself as the schoolmaster of the nation. The universities, institutions and the Church were all subjected to his drastic precepts, and on the whole his royal patronage was beneficial and well received, for undoubtedly his interest in learning and learned men was sincere. The greatest achievement of the reign was the production in

1611 of the Authorized Version of the Bible, and much of the credit must go to James, for it was he who favoured the idea and fostered the work of the various committees who drafted and scrutinized the text.

In 1611, when James created his current favourite, Robert Carr, Viscount Rochester (later Earl of Somerset) the King's homosexual propensities took on a more sinister aspect, for Carr, through his constant attendance upon the King, wielded considerable power, if in an unofficial capacity. Unfortunately (like Buckingham who followed him), Carr lacked political acumen and judgement, and his position of trust was sadly abused. The ultimate degradation in this affair occurred after Cecil's death,* when the thoroughly nasty Henry Howard, Earl of Northampton, gained power and succeeded in marrying his great-niece, Frances Howard, to the favourite. But this attempt to advance his family miscarried, because the young lady caused such a scandal by poisoning the one man who stood against her, Sir Thomas Overbury, that it was all James could do to save her and her (probably innocent) husband from the scaffold.

Marriage of the favourites did not disturb their relationship with the King, but, as it happened, Carr was on the way out before his wife resorted to murder. The last, and greatest, favourite, George Villiers, was by all accounts a veritable Adonis, who excelled at every manly sport. Moreover, he was a master at obsequious grovelling, which he knew was the surest path to power and glory for himself and his family. His rapid rise to the dukedom of Buckingham and important offices of State was predictable, as was its consequence. He became vain and arrogant; he brought corruption and debauchery to an impoverished court, and his influence on the King, whom later he treated disgracefully, was disastrous.

James, like most of his predecessors, was not free of Irish problems – and he made certain that his successors would not be. He had a chance to make some improvement when those two powerful chieftains, Tyrone and Tyrconnell, were forced into exile. Large tracts of Ulster then became available for resettlement, and had James agreed to the Lord Deputy's plan of giving the fortified lands first to the native inhabitants and then to the English and Scottish colonists, instead of first to the colonists and what little was left over to the native Irish, much future trouble might have been avoided. Furthermore, he embittered the southerners with his attempts to force them into the Anglican Communion. His only Irish Parliament of 1613 to 1615 was chiefly occupied in heated debate on this religious measure – which James had to abandon.

* Robert Cecil was created Viscount Cranborne in 1604, Earl of Salisbury in 1605 and a Knight of the Garter the next year. He died in 1612, and his death removed a valuable brake on the use of the royal prerogative, for James held him in considerable awe.

At home, too, as the years went on he became more estranged from his own Parliament, largely because the Commons, and the Bench, led by the Chief Justice, Sir Edward Coke, found the King's use of the royal prerogative threatened their independence. In theory – and to a great extent in practice – the King was still supreme in that he could call and dismiss Parliaments at will, and his only real need for Parliament was when he required money. But unfortunately he very often did require money, and occasionally, to his disgust, after bitter wrangling on matters such as foreign affairs, which he considered to be outside their province, the Commons refused to vote a subsidy.

There were, however, other possible means of improving his treasury, and one such intimately concerned Sir Walter Ralegh. Ralegh had been imprisoned at the beginning of the reign for favouring the claim of Arabella Stuart to the throne, but in 1616 James released him to voyage to the Orinoco River, where Ralegh was quite certain there were gold deposits. The expedition was a total failure; no gold was found and, worse than that, Ralegh was foolish enough to assault the Spanish-held San Thomé. On his return James had Ralegh executed, chiefly to placate the Spanish ambassador, Count Gondomar. James's pro-Spanish policy was much to the dislike of the majority of Englishmen, and the sacrificing of Ralegh was extremely unpopular.

The last years of the reign were clouded by a crisis that closely involved the King's family. James had always been a man of peace, partly because he was by nature timid, but also because he knew that the country could ill-afford to launch out into expensive wars. Therefore, when his son-in-law, Frederick V, Elector Palatine, accepted the crown of Bohemia in defiance of the Emperor Ferdinand, James was alarmed to find himself involved (if only on the fringe) in what proved to be the beginning of the Thirty Years War.

James's dilemma was most painful. Spain would almost certainly side with Austria, throwing into jeopardy not only the Spanish alliance, but James's well advanced arrangements for the marriage of his son, Prince Charles, to the Infanta Maria. James showed every sign of sacrificing his family in order to keep the peace with Spain, but when in August 1620 a Spanish army from The Netherlands marched against Frederick, feeling ran so high in England that James was forced to call a Parliament to vote money for a campaign. In fact, Frederick was defeated at Prague before Parliament met, and chased out of Bohemia and the Palatinate.

Matters went from bad to worse. Throughout 1621 James and his Parliament were constantly bickering, and when at the end of the year he dissolved Parliament, having obtained only two small subsidies, any hope of saving the Palatinate for Frederick had to rest with the Spanish government, who were still not fully committed. Here the marriage negotiations dragged on, with Charles and Buckingham, who had become firm friends, visiting Madrid. In the end both the Infanta and Charles became disillusioned, the Spaniards – backed by the Pope – proposed unacceptable terms, and no Spanish help was forthcoming for the Palatinate. Negotiations for the marriage were eventually broken off, and in 1624 Buckingham, against the King's wishes, started others with the French for the hand of Henrietta Maria, the daughter of Henry IV of France.

Queen Anne died in 1619; James took her death philosophically, which is understandable, for they had seen little of each other for some years. From 1623, his own health deteriorated quite rapidly; he was crippled with arthritis, and had become flabby and debauched-looking. The problems of Parliament and the Palatinate weighed heavily upon him, and Buckingham, who was gaining increasing control of policy, treated him with unforgivable contempt.

In 1607 James had exchanged Hatfield for Theobalds with Robert Cecil – recently created Earl of Salisbury – and here on 27 March 1625 he died. He was buried, as was fitting, alongside the founder of the previous dynasty, after one of the most magnificent funerals ever accorded a sovereign. James was what we would now call an intellectual, who took a long time to learn that most human beings are more often swayed by prejudice than motivated by reason. He was clever enough to temper absolute monarchy with compromise in the face of his Parliament's growing influence; an influence that his son failed to recognize.

James was succeeded by his second son, who had been born in Dunfermline Palace on 19 November 1600. When Prince Henry died in 1612, Charles became heir to the throne, and was created Prince of Wales four years later. Unlike his brother he was not a strong lad, being particularly weak in the legs, and having a stutter. His mother, who died when he was eighteen, declared that from an early age he was wilful and obstinate. He grew to be a man of short stature, only five feet four inches, but well proportioned and not unattractive. His portraits show him neatly but not flamboyantly dressed; looking out at us with eyes that are usually, and perhaps understandably, pensive and sad. In manhood he overcame his physical weakness, but never completely mastered his stammer, and his obstinacy flourished to the end. His learning was sound, but never impressive like that of his father; he was from early days serious- minded, deeply religious and dedicated to the Anglican Church.

Charles married Henrietta Maria, the fourteen-year-old sister of Louis XIII of France, on 12 June 1625. For the first four years the marriage was constantly on the rocks, owing to the child-queen's understandable homesickness, and the bondage of Buckingham. But after the Duke's assassination in 1628, Charles soon shook off the chains of infatuation that had bound him so disastrously, and discovered in a wife, grown to be a beautiful girl, a mutual love, which grew in strength over the years. Charles was a person who constantly needed affection and guidance; from 1629, so long as she was in England, Henrietta Maria supplied both – the first with entirely beneficial results, the second usually with disastrous consequences.

But Buckingham's influence at the beginning of the reign was more disastrous, because it was more complete, than ever was the Queen's in later years. He involved the country in war first with Spain, and then with France in support of the Huguenots at La Rochelle. In both cases his personal leadership was inept, and a furious Parliament would have impeached him had not Charles dissolved it to save him in August 1625, and again a year later. It was largely the fault of Buckingham that the King was faced with such contumacious Parliaments in his first years, but his own arrogant handling of them made matters worse.

Elizabeth had formed a very successful working partnership with her Parliaments, which James had failed to maintain – although he realized the need for compromise. Charles from the very first was obstinate (over Buckingham) and tactless (over his prerogative), and was soon in conflict with the Commons on questions of foreign policy, religion and taxation. As a result, both Houses devised a Petition of Right in which they laid out a whole chapter of grievances. The Petition, among other things, declared the illegality of arbitrary imprisonment, compulsory billeting of troops without payment, and taxation without the consent of Parliament. Charles did his best to wriggle out of signing the document, but his word as a King was not acceptable, and in June 1628 he signed. The most important consequence of the Petition of Right was that it put a financial stranglehold upon the King, for he had been granted the revenue for tonnage and poundage (customs dues) for only a year, instead of the usual span of a lifetime, and no longer could wealthy subjects be imprisoned for failing to pay forced loans.

This same Parliament found fault with the King's attitude towards the Church. Calvinist theology dominated the Church of England, and although the doctrine of the Dutch theologian, Arminius, with its leaning towards certain aspects of Roman Catholic ritual, was beginning to gain ground, in most country churches there was neither surplice nor church music, while the altar occupied a central position. Charles was a sincere Protestant, but he favoured a more elaborate ritual than did most of his subjects. His appointments of William Laud, a convinced Arminian, first to the Privy Council and as personal adviser, and in 1633 to be Archbishop of Canterbury, was most unpopular and opened the way to a doctrinal split, and to the so-called Bishops' Wars of 1639 and 1640 in Scotland.

The assassination of Buckingham by John Felton, a dissatisfied and slightly mad army officer, in August 1628, resulted in peace abroad but no respite for Charles in his constant conflict with Parliament. Matters came to a head in the 1629 Parliament, when the Speaker was forcibly held down when rising to adjourn the House on Charles's orders. In the resulting scuffle and disorder, Members passed by acclamation three resolutions. The levying of tonnage and poundage without authority of Parliament was forbidden, as was the paying of the same by any person when Parliamentary sanction had not been granted, and it became illegal to introduce any innovation into religion. But to many it seemed that the opposition in Parliament had gone too far, and when Charles dissolved it and started on his eleven years of personal rule, some of his erstwhile opponents – including Thomas Wentworth, who was to become his most able servant – came over to his side.

The next few years were probably Charles's happiest as King. Not nearly as shy and retiring, and with a wife who gave him great joy, he became the archetypal seventeenth-century prince – courtly, cultivated and chivalrous. But his dogmatic and inflexible approach to political questions led inexorably to the flashpoint of civil war. He presided over a Council of courtiers who were sometimes corrupt and nearly always factious, while he himself strove to perform conscientiously, if often misguidedly, the God-given duty of absolute arbiter over people and events in a society where 'a subject and a sovereign are clean different things'.

The system of absolutism that now ensued first hit serious trouble in 1635 with the reintroduction of ship money. This was an old tax which in Elizabeth's time had been imposed only on the coastal counties and sea ports for the benefit of the navy; Charles attempted to extend it to inland counties, which was not unreasonable but deeply resented. It brought to the fore a Buckinghamshire landowner called John Hampden who was singled out for prosecution. The judge upheld the legality of ship money, but it was a hollow victory for the King, for by 1640 resistance to the tax was almost nationwide.

More serious than this affair was the religious agitation fostered by the Parliamentary party, and which centred chiefly round Archbishop Laud, who had foolishly reintroduced the obligation for all to attend divine worship, with a fine for those who refused, while in Scotland the National Covenant was drafted in protest against his imposition of the new Prayer Book. The subsequent First Bishop's War led Charles to recall Thomas Wentworth from Ireland, where since 1633 he had administered that country with strength and success as Lord Deputy. He was now to become, until his execution a year later, Charles's principal adviser.

In April 1640 Parliament was again, after eleven years, summoned. But Wentworth (now Earl of Strafford) had miscalculated the mood, and whereas he had successfully manipulated the Irish Parliament, he found men in the Commons who were too strong for him, and who had come to Westminster determined to plunge Parliament into constitutional assertiveness. Charles after three weeks dissolved the Short Parliament; but the disastrous result of the Second Bishop's War, in which the English were routed, necessitated the calling of what became known as the Long Parliament. The man who, until his death in 1643, dominated this Parliament was John Pym, who stood out above all his colleagues for his intellect, eloquence and cool judgement.

Almost the first step taken by Parliament was to set up a committee to deal with what they considered were the misdemeanours of Wentworth. Unable to topple him through impeachment, Parliament resorted to a bill of attainder, and the King found it necessary in the interests of peace to bow to the inevitable. On 12 May 1641 this loyal servant was sacrificed on the block. Others of the King's Council fled the country to escape impeachment, but Laud disdained flight and was imprisoned; four years later he too was beheaded.

Charles had now reached the cross roads, and he took the wrong turning. Absolute monarchy was a closed road; but the King, deprived of his able advisers, increasingly turned towards his wife, and her advice was to make no concessions. She urged the resumption of absolutism, with or without foreign intervention. There could be little hope of reimposing his authority by force, and his occasional attempts to resolve matters by conciliation were patently insincere. The deadlock between himself and Parliament grew, and the stepping-stones to war became clearly defined.

In January 1641 Parliament passed the Triennial Act, and followed this up with a bill to ensure that it could not be dissolved without its own consent. Ship money had already been declared an illegal tax, and in July the prerogative courts were abolished. The King had by now reluctantly given his assent to most of the important measures that Pym had included in his programme. There followed in October of this year the revolt of the Irish Catholics against the English and Scottish settlers. An army had to be sent to quell the rebellion, and this led Parliament to challenge one of the last of Charles's remaining prerogatives – the control of the armed forces.

By this time Parliament was no longer unanimous in its thinking. Some of the moderates had come to dislike Pym's methods, and a royalist party began to emerge. Measures such as the Militia Bill and the Grand Remonstrance – the most damaging indictment that foe and faction could possibly devise – passed the Commons by the narrowest of margins. War was still not inevitable, although Charles, who had utterly refused to give up control of the army, did his best to make it so. In January 1642 he came to Westminster, accompanied by three hundred troopers, to arrest five Members of the Commons. Warned of trouble, the five had escaped by river, leaving Charles looking very foolish and his opponents greatly strengthened. On 10 January he and his Queen slipped furtively out of London. When he next entered his capital it was as a prisoner on trial for his life.

From London he went to Hampton Court, from there to Windsor and then to York. For the country it was a period of agonizing suspense; for the royalist faction a period of advice and counter-advice. The Queen and certain hotheads of the court constantly advised the King to sever the last hopeful strands of peace; the moderates, who comprised Charles's few remaining friends in Parliament, urged him to negotiate while there was still time. But the country was sliding, with gathering momentum, towards civil war. The Queen was to go overseas, taking the crown jewels with which to buy foreign aid. In March 1642 the Commons passed the Militia Bill as an ordinance, and in June Pym produced his nineteen propositions, which made religious as well as secular demands on the King. Had Charles accepted these he would have become little better than the puppet of Parliament. The choice before him was to surrender or to fight. Charles chose to fight.

The First Civil War lasted from 1642 until 1646. During that time there were fought eight major battles – Edgehill (October 1642); Roundway Down (July 1643); two battles of Newbury (September 1643 and October 1644); Cheriton (March 1644); Marston Moor (July 1644); Lostwithiel (September 1644), and Naseby (June 1645). In addition, including the important victories gained by the great Montrose in Scotland, there were twenty-eight other engagements of importance.

In 1642 there was no standing army as such, and the build-up in the first instance was from volunteers, which in the early days presented no problem, although the men were without experience and lacking discipline. In manpower, and in the important matter of finance, Parliament always had an advantage over the King. Their London 'trained bands' of eight thousand well-disciplined troops were superior fighting material to the county militia (with the exception of the Cornishmen), and the professional soldiers that Charles's nephews, the Princes Rupert and Maurice, brought over from Holland were small in number. Geographically Parliament's support came mostly from the rich eastern and south-eastern counties, and they held London and Hull; they could, therefore, levy customs duties and borrow from the London merchants, whereas the Royalist strongholds in Wales, the north, the western midlands and the south-west of the country offered few facilities – other than rich landowners – for raising revenue.

Leadership was something of a problem. On the three occasions that Charles actively commanded in a major battle (Edgehill, Lostwithiel and second Newbury) he showed, especially at Lostwithiel, a fair grasp of tactics. Strategically he suffered too often from indecision and failure to back his plans against the less sound ones of his generals. To finish the war quickly was his main hope, and he might well have accomplished it if, after the indecisive battle of Edgehill, he had pressed home his march on London, instead of withdrawing after the skirmish at Turnham Green. Prince Rupert, who had command in many of the major operations, was a dashing cavalry leader, but too impetuous to make a good army commander. On both sides, and for most of the war, there was a constant obfuscation of command, due largely to jealousy and petty squabbling – and the Parliamentary generals had the added disadvantage of control by committee.

In the first two years the honours of war were fairly evenly divided. On balance the Royalists may have had the better of 1643; certainly in the first half of that year, with victories in the north for Lord Newcastle and the west for Sir Ralph Hopton, their fortune was at its zenith. But in 1644 there was a swing towards Parliament. The influx of eighteen thousand Scots under Lord Leven in January of that year gave them a very considerable advantage in the north, where in July they won the decisive victory of Marston Moor. In the south, their victory at Cheriton earlier in the year gave their generals much needed confidence. At the end of 1644 Oliver Cromwell, almost the only senior officer who had hitherto imposed a strict and impressive discipline on the troops under his command, persuaded Parliament to raise the New Model Army, that élite force and efficient fighting machine which was the precursor of our regular army, and which under Thomas Fairfax sounded the death knell of the King's war at Naseby.

With the defeat of Lord Goring at Langport in July 1645 the only good news for Charles came from Scotland, where in August Montrose won the last of his victories at Kilsyth. For the rest it was mostly mopping-up operations by the various Parliamentary armies, and in May 1646 Charles stole out of Oxford (which had been his 'capital' throughout the war) and placed himself in the hands of the Scottish army, which was still in the north. Here he found that he was no guest, but a carefully guarded prisoner, and for almost a year he engaged in argument with Parliament and the Scots. Charles's main hope from now onwards was that his foes would fall out among themselves; meanwhile he resisted and procrastinated over attempts to get him to accept the Covenant in Scotland and Presbyterianism in England. Negotiations ended when Parliament raised enough money to buy the Scots out of England and to obtain the return of the King.

For the next eighteen months Charles, now as a prisoner of the English, continued his attempts to play off one faction against the other, and indeed there were grounds for cautious optimism, because Cromwell and Ireton were not in agreement with the uncompromising demands of the army Levellers, and favoured coming to terms with the King. But Charles made it difficult for them; with the attitude of the army hardening and the country coming more under the rule of the sword, the King chose this moment to escape from the relatively mild restrictions of Hampton Court to the Isle of Wight, where he was much more strictly confined in Carisbrooke Castle. Then, in the summer of 1648, the Scots – indignant at the treatment accorded their King – entered England and there began the brief Second Civil War. But Parliament's soldiers were far too strong; they beat the invaders decisively at Preston in August, and suppressed with considerable severity local risings in Cornwall and East Anglia.

Even before the Second Civil War Cromwell and Ireton, alarmed by Charles's Scottish negotiations, had veered away from an agreement with the King. Now there seemed but one solution, to prevent 'the Man of Blood' from ever again having the chance to interfere with the designs of the ruling military clique. At the end of 1648 the King was brought – under the close surveillance of Colonel Harrison and his troopers – from Carisbrooke to the mainland at Hurst Castle, and from there to Windsor and finally to St James's. Here in London the last scenes were to be played out; some fortunate members of the public were to be given the chance to witness the might and authority of their new masters.

At his trial in Westminster Hall for waging war on the people, the King conducted himself with great dignity, merely contending that the proceedings had no legal basis, and refusing to acknowledge the authority of the tribunal. The verdict and sentence were never in doubt, for the 135 commissioners were there for the express purpose of killing a king. But by his dignified behaviour in Westminster Hall, and his steadfast courage on the scaffold at Whitehall, Charles more than atoned for his grievous mistakes, and made it certain that in the course of time a king would once again rule in England.

James I was not particularly notable for his love of art, although his wife was passionately fond of pictures, but his two sons, the Princes Henry and Charles, were outstanding in their knowledge and appreciation of what was, or could be made, beautiful. Prince Henry died before his father, but his brother Charles, and his wife, the French Princess Henrietta Maria, presided over a court that for dignity, grace and gentleness had not yet been seen in England, nor was to be seen again for a very long time.

In the field of architecture Inigo Jones was outstanding; Prince Henry, from 1611 until his early death in 1616, employed Inigo Jones as his surveyor, and he went on to be the Surveyor of the King's Works until 1643. During this time such lovely buildings as the Banqueting House at Whitehall, the Queen's Chapel at St James's Palace, and the Queen's House at Greenwich were created, and work went on at many other places – Theobalds, Oatlands Palace, Newmarket, Somerset House and Old St Paul's, to name just a few – that are no longer standing.

Charles I's great favourite, the Duke of Buckingham, had a bad influence over him save in one respect – collecting works of art. When they were in Spain in 1623, Charles failed to collect a bride, but he did make a fine collection of pictures. Perhaps his favourite painter was Titian, a choice favoured by Van Dyck, who was to create his principal masterpieces for Charles in the 1630s. Rubens also worked at the English court, first for James and then for Charles. It was to be the King's practice (and that of his court circle) to encourage craftsmen from far afield to come to England, and conversely to instruct his representatives abroad to be always on the look out for suitable purchases. In the arts, these were certainly years of exquisite refinement.

Aston Hall (Birmingham). Charles I was entertained here in October 1642, a week before the battle of Edgehill. On the first floor, immediately over the chapel and leading off the great dining room, is the King's bedroom. The King's host was Thomas Holte, created a baronet in 1611, and builder of the house between 1618 and 1635.

Battlefields of the Civil War. Several of the battlefields, where major engagements were fought, are still relatively unspoilt. In particular Edgehill, Cheriton, Marston Moor, Auldearn and Naseby have good viewpoints from which the ground can be studied. But no Civil War battlefield has, at the time of writing, any museum or audio-visual exhibition, such as can be found at Bannockburn, Bosworth, Killiecrankie and Culloden; it is therefore necessary to go armed with a book which describes the battle and battlefield in detail. Recommended books for this purpose are: John Adair (*Cheriton 1644*); A.H. Burne (*Battlefields of England*); H.C.B. Rogers (*Battles and Generals of the Civil War*); Peter Young (*Edgehill 1642, Marston Moor 1644*); Peter Young and John Adair (*Hastings to Culloden*); William Seymour (*Battles in Britain* Vol. II); and C.V. Wedgwood (*The Great Rebellion Vol. II, The King's War*).

Edgehill (Warwicks.) 23 October 1642. This was the first major engagement of the Civil War, and ended indecisively so far as the fighting was concerned. If there was a victor, it was the King, because Lord Essex, commanding the Parliamentarians, completely failed to achieve his objective, which was to put his army between the royalist force and London. The tragedy for Charles was that he subsequently failed to pursue the advantage he had gained, and was never to come so close to London again. Edgehill is about seven miles north-west of Banbury, off the A422. Just opposite the Castle Inn there is a public footpath that leads to fields immediately above Radway Grange, from here there is an uninterrupted view across the battlefield. But unlike the other battles mentioned above, it is not possible to walk over the ground where the main fight took place, because it is Ministry of Defence property; however, those with a special purpose or interest can apply for a pass from the headquarters of the C.A.D. Kineton.

Cheriton (Hants.) 29 March 1644. Cheriton is two and a half miles south of New Alresford, and a few miles east of Winchester. There is some dispute as to the exact site of the battle, but it is only a matter of which of two ridges, that encompass the site in the form of a horseshoe, was occupied by the royalist army. This does not affect the visitor's general appreciation, in fact, it makes a study of the ground more interesting. The importance of this battle was that it was the first decisive major victory gained by the Parliamentarians: there had been minor successes, but here was defeat, naked and brutal, for a royalist army that had sought battle. Sir William Waller was one of Parliament's greatest generals, and in defeating Lord Hopton at Cheriton (Hopton was nominally under Lord Forth, but the latter was incapacitated by gout) he got his revenge for the battle of Lansdown, where he was unable to stem the attack of Hopton's Cornishmen. The battle took place to the east of Cheriton, between that village and Cheriton Wood, and the whole area is easily viewed from public footpaths.

Marston Moor (North Yorks.) 2 July 1644. This battle, which was fought first in a violent thunderstorm and then by the light of the moon, took place on ground immediately to the north of the Tockwith–Long Marston road (Long Marston is situated about five miles west of York, on the B1224 road leading to Wetherby), and the best view of the battlefield is obtained from the high ground to the south of the road in the vicinity of Cromwell Plump. In the battle the royalists, under Prince Rupert and the Earl of Newcastle, were defeated by a mixed English and Scottish Parliamentarian army, whose two outstanding generals were Sir Thomas Fairfax and Oliver Cromwell. Rupert, always impetuous, soon left his command post to lead his cavalry against Cromwell's troopers, with a result that he got unhorsed and took no further part in the battle. The outstanding feature of the fight was in the last glorious phase, when Newcastle's Whitecoats, having run out of ammunition after inflicting grievous casualties on the enemy, disdained to surrender, and fought furiously to the last with butt and pike.

Auldearn (Nairn, Grampian Region, Scotland) 9 May 1645. In his *annus mirabilis* the Marquess of Montrose won three great victories, and the greatest of them was at Auldearn, a small Scottish town which lies just over two miles south-east of Nairn. Greatly outnumbered in foot and horse, Montrose skilfully laid a trap for the Covenanter Commander, Colonel Hurry, and in spite of the fiery impetuosity of Alasdair Macdonald and his Irishmen, who through a gallant, but misplaced, charge nearly lost Montrose the battle, the plan succeeded and in the victory, which was complete, it is estimated that between two and three thousand Covenanters perished. There is a natural viewpoint just to the west of Auldearn church, and here the National Trust for Scotland have put an excellent plan and description of the battle.

Naseby (Leics.) 14 June 1645. This was the last major battle of the First Civil War, and is notable chiefly for two things. First, it saw the New Model Army in battle for the first time under its able commander, Sir Thomas Fairfax, and its equally able lieutenant-general of horse, Oliver Cromwell. Second, the disaster it inflicted on the royalist army (which it outnumbered by nearly two to one) sounded the death knell of the King's military machine. It was one of the hardest fought engagements of the war; the royalist foot, led by the stout-hearted veteran Jacob Astley, fought superbly against odds that were too great, and the deciding factor was undoubtedly the Roundhead cavalry and Colonel Okey's mounted dragoons. Prince Rupert, in nominal command under the King, once again insisted on leading the cavalry in person and once again through his impetuosity left his infantry with too much to do, and at the mercy of Cromwell's thrust from the flank. Towards the end the King took personal command of the reserves, but the Earl of Carnworth seized his bridle, and exclaiming 'Will you go upon your death?' prevented him from entering the fight. One wonders whether Carnworth acted for the best.

Naseby, which is some six miles south of Market Harborough, is perhaps the least spoilt of all the Civil War battlefields, and although the ground over which the battle was fought is all privately owned, both the original positions of the rival armies and the actual scene of the fighting can be very easily seen from the undulating Naseby-Sibbertoft road.

Carisbrooke Castle (Isle of Wight). In 1647 Colonel Hammond, whose brother was chaplain to Charles I, was the governor of the castle. Perhaps because the King felt that here he would find a friend in need, he decided to make for the Island when planning his escape from Hampton Court. Hammond, however, proved loyal to those who employed him, and would have no part in any ideas of escape to France. Charles was kept in the castle at first with few restrictions, but later he was more closely confined. Two escapes were attempted, and one might well have succeeded had the King co-operated more intelligently. Charles left the castle in September 1648, having been a prisoner there for ten months. Two years later his younger children, Henry Duke of Gloucester and Princess Elizabeth, were brought to the castle, where Elizabeth soon died, aged thirteen. She was buried in Newport church, while her brother was released in 1653, and sent to Holland. The governor's house, where Charles was lodged, is now the Isle of Wight Museum.

Chiddingstone Castle (Kent), stands to the west of the ancient and beautiful village of Chiddingstone, with its Tudor half-timbered houses. The castle is of little historical importance, but its late owner, Mr Denys Bower, devoted most of his life to collecting objets d'art, pictures, miniatures, historical documents, Japanese and Egyptian antiquities, and these are beautifully displayed. The whole collection is exceedingly interesting, but for the student of British sovereigns it is the Stuart room that will appeal most..Here can be seen original letters of the Stuart royal family (including Monmouth's last letter to James II); superb miniatures of the Stuarts by Nicholas Hilliard, Matthew Snelling and Samuel Cooper; Lely's portrait of the nude Nell Gwynne, memorabilia, such as Charles I's embroidered handkerchief, many boxes, badges, lockets, etc., that were in the possession of the family, and the much prized silver reliquary containing a part of James II's heart, brought from France at the time of the Revolution.

Dover Castle (Kent). (See also Chapter 4.) King Charles I spent large sums of money in bringing the royal apartments of the castle to a fit standard to receive his bride, Henrietta Maria, who arrived at Dover in June 1625. Later, in 1642, the King and Queen were to reside in the castle again, but this time as refugees from their capital. The castle came into Parliamentary hands by subterfuge that same year, and royalist attempts to recapture it failed.

Edinburgh Castle. (See also Chapter 5.) Most of the royal apartments date from the fifteenth and early sixteenth centuries, and in them much history has been enacted. Mary of Guise, widow of James V and Regent during the stormy years of civil war and Church Reformation, died in an upper room of the castle. Her daughter, Mary Queen of Scots, gave birth to James VI of Scotland and I of England in another small, curiously shaped room that can still be seen. In the great hall, where Scottish Parliaments used to meet, Charles I attended a banquet given by the Earl of Mar, and not long afterwards the man who brought about his death, Oliver Cromwell, was fêted in the same room by Alexander Leslie. In the Crown Room is kept the Scottish regalia – the crown, dating from 1540, sceptre and sword of State. On the ramparts of this great fortress there stands the cannon that was the wonder of its day, Mons Meg, which accompanied James IV when he besieged and took Norham Castle in August 1513, a few days before his defeat and death at the battle of Flodden.

Falkland Palace (Fife), belongs almost exclusively to Scottish history, in which it is steeped, but it touches upon the English scene first in the time of James IV, who entertained Perkin Warbeck there and married him to Lady Catherine Gordon, and again in the reign of James VI, who became James I of England.

The Castle of Falkland (as it was then called) was in the twelfth century the home of the Earls of Fife, and came to the Stuarts through the childless Isabel, Countess of Fife in her own right, who left it to her brother-in-law, Robert Stuart, in 1371. From then on it became the home of the royal Stuarts for nearly three hundred years, and when James II came into possession of Falkland he raised it to the dignity of a palace in 1458, and made the small town a royal burgh. The palace still belongs to the Sovereign, but has not been occupied by one since Charles II, and is left in the custody of hereditary keepers.

In its long royal history Falkland has seen much tragedy. Many of the early Stuarts met violent ends – some of them at Falkland – and James IV left Falkland to find death on the battlefield of Flodden, while his son James V (who reconstructed the palace to give it its present outward appearance) died there after the defeat of his army at Solway Moss in 1542. But for James VI, once he had survived an armed assault on the palace, it held happier memories, and until he left Scotland it became a favourite home and hunting place. The great bed, which forms the centrepiece of the King's bedchamber, dates from reign and the room has been restored in line with the original interior decoration.

This enchanting palace, with its haunting memories of the stormy periods of Scottish history, and its beautiful garden now laid out in its ancient form, lies in the centre of the town between Kinross and Cupar on the A912 road.

Hampton Court Palace (Middlesex). (See also Chapter 8.) During the reign of Charles I, many of his works of art adorned the palace and gardens at Hampton Court; one example was the great equestrian portrait of the King by Van Dyck, now in the National Gallery, which hung at the end of the Prince's Gallery. After the King's execution, his magnificent collection was broken up and sold. However, Cromwell, as Lord Protector, chose Hampton Court as his residence and retained some of the King's works of art for the palace. Foremost amongst these were the Raphael Cartoons, now in the Victoria and Albert Museum, and a series of paintings by the Mantuan artist, Andrea Mantegna, known as the *Triumphs of Caesar*. The Mantegna Triumphs still hang at Hampton Court, in a special gallery in the Orangery, while other works from Charles's collection, saved at the Restoration, hang in the state rooms of the palace.

Jedburgh (Roxburgh), as an important Border town, was constantly under attack during the Border raids of the fifteenth and sixteenth centuries, and when the castle was razed by order of the Scottish government, six 'Castel-houses' were built round the town (in the fashion of peel towers) for the town's protection. One of these, a turreted building three storeys high, still survives almost unchanged in appearance and architectural structure from the time in October 1565, when Mary Queen of Scots lay desperately ill in the bedchamber above the banqueting hall. The house at the time was owned by Lady Ker of Ferniehurst, to whom the Queen paid £40 in rent. There are a number of extremely interesting pictures, objects, documents and personal letters connected with the Queen that are undoubtedly authentic. However, the communion service and the death mask may not have the contemporary connections attributed to them.

Linlithgow Palace (Central Region, Scotland). (See also Chapter 8.) The palace had close associations with James VI of Scotland and I of England, and it was he who had the north quarters rebuilt in 1618. His mother, Mary Queen of Scots, had been born there in December 1542. Charles I, who stayed in the palace in July 1633, was the last sovereign to sleep there. From then on it was allowed to fall into decay, and it was left to the Duke of Cumberland's men to put the seal on this neglect when, billeted there in 1746, they carelessly set the place alight.

London
The Banqueting House, Whitehall. The original banqueting hall in the Palace of Whitehall was destroyed by fire in 1619, and the present masterpiece is the work of Inigo Jones. It is the only part of the Palace of Whitehall that survived the disastrous fire of 1698. Inigo Jones modelled his building on that of a Roman basilica as interpreted by Palladio. The beautiful ceiling, representing the apotheosis of James I and an allegory of the birth of Charles I, was painted by Rubens. The Banqueting House was used for State banquets, receptions of ambassadors, etc., and is still used for certain receptions. From one of the windows in the Banqueting House, Charles I stepped on to the scaffold to be executed.

The Queen's Chapel, St James's Palace, was designed and built by Inigo Jones and commenced in 1623. It was originally meant for use by the Infanta Maria of Spain, who was Charles I's intended bride, to comply with a clause in the treaty of marriage. This marriage having fallen through, it was completed, after some delay, in 1626 for the use of Charles's French bride, Henrietta Maria.

Originally the gallery was full of pictures by such masters as Titian and Van Dyck, but during the Commonwealth, when the chapel was closed, it was robbed of everything of value.

Services are now held there every Sunday at 11.15 a.m. from Easter until the end of July, when the public are admitted. On festival days the beautiful Restoration silver-gilt plate adorns the altar.

The Queen's House (Greenwich). This house was begun by Inigo Jones for James I's Queen, Anne of Denmark. It was built in the shape of an H over the Deptford–Woolwich road, which then divided the park from the palace gardens. Queen Anne died before the building was completed, and James I took no further interest in it. But work was resumed in 1629 by Charles I for his Queen, Henrietta Maria, and she used it as a residence up to the Civil War, and for a time afterwards. A number of very interesting pictures hang in the many beautiful rooms, most of which are on the first floor.

The Tower of London. In the Armouries (see also Chapter 8), is a suit of armour worn by Charles I, which was probably of Dutch origin and made about 1625. It is interesting to compare it with the armour belonging to Henry VIII, as an indication of the size of the two men.

The Victoria and Albert Museum. (See also Chapter 9.) In the various rooms of this museum (it is not possible to be precise, for they are occasionally changed around) can be seen: a room taken from a house at Bromley-by-Bow that was probably used by James I as a hunting lodge; a suit worn by that King; a scarf said to have been worn by Charles I at the battle of Edgehill; an embroidered doublet also worn by him; and the chair used by the King at his trial. As well as these personal items, the museum houses the Raphael Tapestry Cartoons, which were purchased by Charles I when he was Prince of Wales. They were painted by Raphael in 1515–16 as designs for a set of ten tapestries commissioned for the Sistine Chapel.

Oxford

Christ Church College. (See also Chapter 8.) During the Civil War the University was staunchly royalist, but the Town favoured Parliament. After Edgehill, in October 1642, Charles I made Oxford his headquarters for the rest of the war. He himself was quartered in Christ Church, and his Queen in Merton College. Part of the defence works of Oxford at this time can still be seen in the grounds of Mansfield College.

Stirling Castle (Central Region, Scotland) (See also Chapter 5.) Like Edinburgh Castle, this impregnable Scottish fortress is perched on the top of a precipitous rock, and it became one of the principal royal residences for the Stuart dynasty in Scotland. Much of the present building dates from the fifteenth and sixteenth centuries, and many important events have taken place within its formidable walls. James III was born in the castle, and later built the Parliament Hall; Mary Queen of Scots was crowned in the castle; her son James VI spent much of his childhood in its precincts and was also crowned there, and when his elder son, Prince Henry, was born in the castle in 1594, King James had the Chapel Royal (which stands virtually unaltered) specially built for his christening. It ceased to be a royal residence when James succeeded to the Crown of England.

Traquair House (Peebles), has been the home of the lairds of Traquair since it was given to James Stuart in 1491. It is perhaps the oldest inhabited house in Scotland, and certainly its ancient walls enshrine eight centuries of Scottish history. Sir John Stuart, a sixteenth-century laird of Traquair, was Captain of the Queen's Guard to Mary Queen of Scots, and later to James VI. In 1566 the Queen and Lord Darnley visited the house, and left behind them the cradle used for her baby son. This can be seen in the room that the Queen occupied, and on the bed in this room is a beautifully embroidered quilt worked by the hands of the Queen and her three ladies-in-waiting – 'the Four Maries'. The house, which is one mile from Innerleithen off the A72 road from Edinburgh, is full of exciting and interesting Stuart memorabilia both of this period and from other centuries.

Wilton House (Wilts.). During the reign of Henry VIII, Sir William Herbert began to build at Wilton, and part of his Tudor house stands at the very heart of the seventeenth-century building. William Herbert, third Earl of Pembroke, was Lord Steward to Charles I. He was persuaded by the King to build a new south front and to lay out formal gardens. Inigo Jones was asked to do this but was too busy with the Royal Works, so the additions were made by Isaac de Caus. In 1647, the house was badly damaged by fire, and Philip Herbert, the fourth Earl and Lord Chamberlain to the King, commissioned John Webb to repair and complete the house. He incorporated both the Tudor east front and de Caus' south front into a fine seventeenth-century house built around a central courtyard. His magnificent state apartments reflect the taste of the court, with their painted ceilings and rich plasterwork. In the Double Cube room hang a series of Van Dyck paintings, including those of Charles I and Henrietta Maria and their children, and William and Philip Herbert in their court robes.

The house stands in the town of Wilton, two and a half miles west of Salisbury on the A30, Exeter road.

The Interregnum

King Charles I was executed on 30 January 1649; on 17 March the Long Parliament (or what was left of it after Colonel Pride's purge, and known as the Rump) passed an Act abolishing the office of king, and England became what her new rulers called a Commonwealth. In April 1653 Oliver Cromwell dismissed the Rump, and by the Instrument of Government a new constitution was devised with a Protector, Council and single-chamber legislature of 460 members. Oliver Cromwell was nominated Lord Protector for life, and the Protectorate lasted officially from December 1653 until May 1660.

On 3 September 1658 Cromwell died and was succeeded by his son Richard, a pleasant enough man, but entirely ineffectual, who, on realizing his limitations, soon retired. There followed a period of dissension with the army leaders falling out among themselves, and the army itself falling into disrepute. But with General Monck's arrival in London at the head of his regiment, on 3 February 1660, the way ahead seemed clearer. The Long Parliament at last dissolved itself and a new one was elected in April, whose members wanted nothing so much as the return of the monarchy. Charles Stuart, from his headquarters in Breda, issued a document drawn up by Edward Hyde and known as the *Declaration of Breda*, by which he promised pardons, a fair settlement of disputes relating to property, and the settlement of all arrears of pay due to army officers and men. These promises proving satisfactory, Charles was proclaimed King on 8 May, and on 25 May (his birthday) he entered his capital amid the greatest rejoicing.

11

THE MIDDLE STUARTS

From Restoration to Revolution

༄

On his thirtieth birthday, Charles II entered London. He had been restored to the throne by the will of Parliament and people, and the resolution of General Monck – whom he created Duke of Albemarle. It was 25 May 1660, and the nation gave itself over to rejoicing, free at last from the strait-jacket of Puritanism. The 'Black Boy' had come home to begin a reign that was to last almost twenty-five years, and to take his place in history as one of the most successful sovereigns to sit upon the English throne.

But his nominal reign had begun in very different circumstances – an exile at the head of an impecunious, dejected group, dependent on charity and the whims of foreign governments. During the Civil War the young Charles had been given his own Council, and was for a time in nominal command of the west. When ordered to go to France by his father, it was some time before he complied; on 2 March 1646 he sailed for the Scilly Isles, and then after two months in Jersey he joined his mother in France in June of that year. In such times of stress and strain there was little chance of a formal, academic education. The Earl of Newcastle had been appointed his Governor, and Charles built upon and benefited from that nobleman's maxim that he would learn more from men than from books.

The first important adventure of his life began in shame and ended in glory. On the death of Charles I the Scots had proclaimed his son as King, but while they were still endeavouring to get him to Scotland on their terms, the Marquess of Montrose, who in 1646 had been ordered by Charles I to disband his army and leave Scotland, returned there in April 1650 at the head of fifteen hundred men. It was a forlorn adventure from the start – and Montrose knew it – because Charles, for the sake of a Crown, was practising a piece of duplicity. If Montrose could successfully dominate Scotland, and allow Charles to break the promises he had made to the Covenanters,* well and good; but if Charles could come to Scotland only on Covenanter terms, then Montrose might have to be sacrificed. In the event Montrose was defeated and executed, and by the Treaty of Breda Charles agreed to take the Covenant, to embrace Presbytery himself, to enforce it upon his English subjects and to root out episcopacy – for which his father had died.

There followed for Charles almost a year of interminable sermons, privations, restrictions and mortifications at the hands of the Kirk and Covenanters, led by the infamous Marquess of Argyll. After Cromwell's victory at Dunbar in September 1650, matters improved somewhat for the royalist faction, for the Kirk realized that Charles must play an important part in raising any new army. On 1 January 1651 he was crowned at Scone – a mockery of a coronation at which prayers were offered seeking God's forgiveness for the sins of the King's family! And later that year the new army under Charles and General Leslie made its wild dash into England; this advance was to end abruptly in September at the battle of Worcester.

For six weeks after Worcester, Charles, with a price on his head, made a perilous journey across half of southern England. The pages of history are enlivened by the tribulations of the 'tall, black, man, two yards high' (as the posters described Charles), and the courage and devotion of a few staunch royalists – mostly Catholics with convenient priest holes in their houses. There were the humble Penderels; Father Hudleston – who guided Charles to safety while he lived and to salvation when he died; Colonel Lane, and his intrepid sister Jane, whose servant Charles became and who carried him pillion across the Cotswolds; Colonels Wyndham and Phelipps; and always that faithful, foolhardy Cavalier, Lord Wilmot. Hugging the country lanes for greater safety, fugitives of the night and October mists, the faithful few, carrying the future of England in their hands, passed Charles from house to house until at last a ship from France was found at Shoreham. It was 15 October 1651: nine years later they would all be remembered by a grateful sovereign.

For those long years the small band of down-at-heel, penniless exiles lived alternatively in hope and despair. There was little for them to do save plot, quarrel and beg first from one country and then another. But of all these companions in adversity, Charles stood out for his courage and cheerfulness. His perils and wanderings in Scotland and England, and the hardships of exile worked only to toughen the fibres of his

* In 1638 the Scots, provoked by Charles I's and Archbishop Laud's attempt to Anglicize the Scottish Church, drew up the National Covenant. In September of that year the General Assembly abolished episcopacy and re-established Presbyterianism.

character; he emerged from his ordeal untouched by rancour or resentment, and he was always prepared to take his pleasures where he could find them and enjoy life to the full. Many of these pleasures were to be found among the ladies, and not always of the court (even before Scotland he had become enamoured of Lucy Walter, and in April 1649 that child of woe, who was to become the Duke of Monmouth, was born), but there was also his boyhood friend the Duke of Buckingham, who, according to Edward Hyde – Charles's Chancellor – was 'good for nothing'. There were scandals, but he overcame them; and when in England they buried Oliver Cromwell and a royalist reaction began slowly to set in, Charles was ready to step out of the nightmare and into the proffered dream, shabby and in debt, but wise, understanding and enlightened.

For almost a year the honeymooon lasted; King and nation gave over to rejoicing. Once more there was singing, dancing, whoring, cock-fighting and many other comparatively harmless pleasures so long restricted or forbidden. Crowds flocked to see the King dine in Whitehall, to kiss his hand and to cheer his coming in and going out. The blood of the regicides was demanded, and it seemed that only Charles was anxious to be merciful; in the end no more than ten of the living were executed, but the tombs of the leading men (Cromwell, Ireton, Bradshaw and others) were desecrated and their bodies hanged in their coffins at Tyburn.

Problems were soon to crowd in upon Charles. In September 1660 his brother, James, Duke of York, the heir-presumptive, married a com-moner, Anne Hyde (the Chancellor's daughter), a few weeks before the birth of their son – who, like five others of their eight children, was to die in infancy. Amid the furore and royal recriminations, only the King, with his never failing kindly tolerance, remained calm. There were enormous debts to be met, and no money to meet them with. Petitioners came thick and fast; some were purely place-hunters, others wanted restitution of cash, and yet others the return of confiscated land. Few could be satisfied, and Hyde – whom they thought responsible – bore the brunt of their fiercely expressed dissatisfaction.

Nor was there any relief for Charles in the matter of religion. He himself kept a completely open mind on the sectarian problems that beset him. His personal preference was probably always for the Roman Catholic faith with its more elaborate ritual, and certainly after his Scottish ordeal he could not be expected to look too favourably on Presbyterianism. But if his outward expressions on religion inclined to the cynical, he sincerely believed that no one creed had a monopoly of truth, and he vastly preferred the personal virtues in a man to any expressions of his religion. He therefore opted for tolerance – almost one might say indifference – and tried through his Declaration of Indulgence to ease the penal laws against dissenters, and to moderate the Act of Uniformity, which had deprived almost two thousand ministers, who had refused to comply, of their livings. But in neither instance was he successful, and from the squabblings of the clergy there was to emerge, after its many years of suffering, a golden age for the Anglican Church.

Charles was crowned on 23 April 1661 – and a little over a year later, in May 1662, his Portuguese bride, Catherine of Braganza, landed at Portsmouth. There are some who think that with his many mistresses Charles treated Catherine most cruelly; but while it is true that the pursuit of pleasure was always to the fore in Charles's court, and there had been a considerable moral decline among those now at the top, the keeping of mistresses – even in such a flagrant manner as Charles kept his – was an accepted practice. There are, furthermore, many actions throughout their married life to illustrate Charles's deep love and concern for Catherine. She was a quiet, kindly person and by no means unattractive – save that her teeth stuck out a little.

At the time of Catherine's arrival the reigning beauty (although in May 1662 expecting a baby) was Barbara Palmer, Countess of Castlemaine (later Duchess of Cleveland), a tiresome termagant who probably gave Charles almost as much trouble as she did pleasure. Other ladies had preceded Barbara into the royal bed and more would follow. They were drawn from no particular strata of society, for so long as they were beautiful, and preferably witty, the King was indifferent to their social background. The exquisitely lovely Frances Stewart and the dark, delicately featured Louise de Kéroualle (Duchess of Portsmouth) were both accustomed to court life, but to Nell Gwynn (the 'Protestant whore' and probably the wittiest and most lovable of all the royal mistresses) the surroundings were unfamiliar and very exciting.

In the bedroom Charles certainly gave the lie to his father's dictum that 'subject and sovereign are clean different things'. But in politics neither concubine nor consort had any place. There were two sides to Charles's character; the frivolous, indolent, pleasure-loving prince; and the ruler, who, when the pressure was on, showed himself to be an astute and able politician with an uncanny gift for knowing what his country most needed, and the patience and tenacity of purpose to hold faction at bay, and steer his countrymen safely through the perils that were mostly of their own making.

Foreign affairs during the first few years of the reign were dominated by Anglo-Dutch trade rivalry. Acts of brigandage at sea were constantly occurring, and by 1664 almost everyone in the country – save Charles – was clamouring for war. The mighty Cromwellian navy had become sadly run down both in regard to ships and sailors, but Charles did his best with limited resources to restore it – and when they saw what he could do from borrowing and begging, Parliament voted the King two and a half million pounds. In August 1664, before war was actually declared, an English expedition seized New Amsterdam in North America and renamed it New York. Throughout that autumn open warfare at sea was taking place, but it was not until 22 February 1665 that the Second Dutch War* officially began.

The Duke of York, Lord High Admiral of England, put to sea in the *Royal Charles* at the head of a fleet of some 150 ships mounting 5,000 guns, and met the Dutch east of Lowestoft. It was a fiercely contested fight with heavy casualties on both sides. Eventually the Dutch withdrew, battered but not beaten. James, who had shown great courage and skill during the battle, was deprived of victory when his Secretary counter-manded the order to pursue the crippled Dutchmen. This was done while James was asleep.

The war thus begun was to drag on until 1667 with fluctuating fortunes. In 1666 the French joined the Dutch, and their combined fleets got the better of a stiff fight of four days off the North Foreland; but in August of that year it was the turn of the English to gain the victory. While the nation's seamen were engaged in battle and blockade, the country as a whole – and London in particular, where seventy thousand out of a population of about half a million died in one year – was afflicted by the Great Plague of 1665, which was followed the next year by the Great Fire of London. These calamities took much strength out of the war effort, and matters were made no easier for Charles by Parliament's refusal to vote sufficient financial aid. Both sides were eager for peace by the summer of 1667, but the Dutch had one further most humiliating blow to deliver. Lulled into carelessness through thoughts of peace, and lacking money to keep the fleet at sea, the English were unable to prevent the ships of Admiral van Ghent from sailing up the Medway, breaking the boom that guarded Chatham, burning several ships and towing away the *Royal Charles*.

Peace was obtained on fairly favourable terms, with England retain-ing New York. But the country had been frightened; Charles did not escape censure, although the chief recriminations centred round Hyde (whom Charles had created Earl of Clarendon in 1661). This most able man, who had served both the Charleses so faithfully, had become old, cantankerous and out of touch; he constantly condemned the court (not without some justification) as being profligate, incompetent and cor-rupt. His enemies were numerous – not least among them being the powerful Lady Castlemaine – and Charles, having failed to get him to

* The First Dutch War was fought during the Protectorate between 1652 and 1654.

retire, was forced to take the Great Seal from him.

Government now passed into the hands of five ministers with widely differing principles and ambitions, whose initials made up the word CABAL. Thomas Clifford was a Roman Catholic and a hard tough man of the extreme right, who favoured an anti-Dutch, pro-French policy. Arlington, distinguished by a black patch across his nose to conceal a war wound, was an old and devoted friend of Charles, and ready to follow his policies without question. Buckingham did well as a play-boy, but was no politician. Ashley (soon to become Earl of Shaftesbury) was probably the most able and certainly the most unreliable of the five, for he dwelt almost exclusively on the welfare of Ashley. He changed sides whenever it best suited his purpose; he was a Whig* who believed in monarchy, but only when it was subservient to Parliament; and he sought popularity, for it satisfied his vanity. Lauderdale, a somewhat cruel, ruthless man, who had ruled Scotland with a rod of iron ever since the Restoration, was the fifth member of this ill-assorted team.

The Cabal started off on a note of high Protestant fervour when they concluded a triple alliance with Holland and Sweden against France, which put Louis XIV in check for a while and forced him to make peace with Spain. But Charles was soon to embark upon a great piece of legerdemain – the *grand design*, by which he hoodwinked his countrymen, most of his ministers and eventually the other principal participant, the French King.

Desperately short of money, and fearful of summoning another Parliament, who he felt sure would not have obliged, Charles had, since 1668, been in secret correspondence with his youngest sister, Henrietta, whom he called Minette and who was the one woman in his life that he really adored. Minette was married to Louis's unpleasant brother, Monsieur, and she was given the task of preparing the way for the notorious Treaty of Dover, which was signed in May 1670. The unpopularity of a French alliance would have been troublesome enough, but should some of the proposed terms be leaked, Charles could well have been faced with a revolution. The utmost secrecy was therefore essential, and at first only Arlington was privy to the plan, although later Sir Richard Bellings and the Catholic peers, Clifford and Arundel of Wardour, were taken into Charles's confidence. Used as intermediaries, they signed the Treaty, which had been finally agreed upon and brought to Dover by Minette.

The Treaty contained many clauses. The two most important of

* The terms Tory and Whig began to come in at this time, and were at first used in a pejorative sense; a tory being an Irish Catholic brigand, and a whig a fanatical Scottish Covenanter.

which were: first, that Charles would make a public declaration of his conversion to the Roman Catholic faith as soon as affairs would permit, for which Louis would pay two million livres (about £166,000), and if this declaration should result in rebellion, Louis would assist Charles with six thousand troops; and second, that both sovereigns were to wage war on the Dutch, with the Dutch interests of the Prince of Orange, Charles's nephew, being guaranteed.* The colossal deception came with a second, or simulated, treaty which differed from the first in that there was no reference to the royal conversion, and the £166,000 was to be treated as a war subsidy. Buckingham, quite unaware that he was being fooled, was sent to France to negotiate this *Traité Simulé*, which was signed in December by the entire Cabal, who were thus committed to Charles's foreign policy.

It is difficult to say to what extent Charles was indulging in a confidence trick purely to get money – and in the event what he received was quite inadequate – or how much he was in earnest with the terms. Dutch maritime supremacy was probably a greater threat to England at that time than French expansionism. Neutrality might have been best, and in fact between 1674 and 1678 it was a policy that paid off and brought considerable revenue to Charles through customs dues. It is unlikely that he would want to fool Minette, and so probably he would have been prepared to declare himself a Catholic, although he must have known that the opportunity would not arise, and he procrastinated over this with great skill. His first cautious steps towards honouring the religious clause, the Declaration of Indulgence in March 1672, met with no success at all. It was probably no more than a test of public opinion, for it must be emphasized that Charles never in the Treaty promised the forcible reconversion of England.

His brother, James, had been made aware of the secret negotiations in 1669, and was delighted, for although he did not openly declare himself a Catholic until the Test Act of 1673, he was by then converted. His chance came in March 1672, when Louis called upon Charles to fulfil his pledge against the Dutch, who were most reluctantly provoked into war, and James was again made Commander-in-Chief of the fleet. The Third Dutch War lasted two years, and redounded greatly to the credit of the Republic. Between the hammer and the anvil of two formidable sea and land powers they fought back most tenaciously under their famous Admiral de Ruyter, and on land William of Orange, whom the embattled nation turned to in their peril, hurled defiance at

* The Dutch Republic had refused to recognize William III of Orange as Stadholder on his father's death; this war gained him the position, but what Charles really wanted was that his nephew should become the sovereign ruler of the United Provinces – preferably as Charles's puppet. William would have none of that.

the French invader. But there was heroism in plenty for England. At the indecisive battle of Sole Bay, James and his sailors showed great courage; Lord Sandwich in the *Royal James* perished, and James had to transfer his flag from the *Prince* to the *St Michael*, and when that was sunk under him to the *London*.

But the war against Protestant Holland was very unpopular; nor could it be financed by Louis's subsidies. Parliament had to be called, and their terms were harsh: no money unless the Declaration of Indulgence was withdrawn; and a Test Act whereby no man could hold office who would not deny the doctrine of transubstantiation. Aimed at James, the Test Act forced him to declare his faith and resign his command; but it also sounded the death knell of the Cabal. Buckingham, Clifford and Arlington withdrew from public affairs; Lauderdale stayed on in Scotland; but Shaftesbury, who was dismissed from the office of Lord Chancellor and who might by now have learnt of the secret clause in the Treaty of Dover, went into opposition, and until his exile eight years later was to cause Charles considerable trouble.

The man who now came to the fore was Sir Thomas Osborne (soon to be created Earl of Danby). As he was a sound business man, shrewd and experienced in public affairs, his appointment as Lord Treasurer was a wise one, and Charles came to rely on him implicitly. He sought peace to reduce expenditure, set about restoring the country's finances, and attempted to cool the religious climate by forbidding Catholics the court and enforcing laws against recusants. Charles himself further enhanced the Protestant cause when, in October 1677, he arranged the engagement of his niece Mary (James's elder daughter by his first wife, Anne Hyde) to William of Orange, the cold, proud, but clever Dutchman, and now that country's Stadholder.

The marriage had the immediate effect of stopping Louis's payments, which left Charles free to break his side of the agreement and summon a Parliament. The next few years showed Charles at his very best. Beset on all sides by unscrupulous and difficult people, sects and institutions – Louis, the States-General of Holland, Shaftesbury and his Country Party, narrow-minded Catholics, fiery Puritans – he retained that sense of calm and power which was his aura, gave little or nothing away, and through his skill and cunning rose superior to his enemies and kept his head and Crown.

Throughout 1678 the political atmosphere gradually, but noticeably, became charged with the presage of storm. The last few years had been ones of tension and strain for all, and nerves wore frayed; it needed only the smallest spark to set alight Protestant passions. That spark was applied by two arrogant, unscrupulous liars – Titus Oates and Israel Tonge. Oates, the more frightening of the two, who thundered his venom and scurrility in the fashion of the comminatory utterings of the ancient prophets, had been in trouble with the law since boyhood, and was the worst type of charlatan. Tonge at least possessed a genuine Oxford degree, and may even have believed in his cause. These men let loose upon the country two years of terror, persecution and execution, in what was known as the Popish Plot.

The plot, which purported to be a Jesuit one to assassinate the King, murder all Protestants and put James upon the throne, was of course fictitious. Charles saw through it at once, for he personally examined Oates and constantly detected his falsehoods; but certain parts of his testimony disclosed a knowledge of affairs that was surprising in a man of his background, and when, with the acquisition of greater confidence, Oates started laying charges of treason against certain Catholics by name, the Council began to take the matter seriously. Soon a gullible public became convinced of this sinister plot, and the flames of their understandable terror were fanned by such acts as the stage-managed 'Catholic' murder of the popular magistrate, Sir Edmund Berry Godfrey. By now no Catholic was safe upon the London streets; arrests were made on the evidence of any scallywag who wanted to earn a dishonest penny. Charles did his best to save the accused from the clutches of a biased and infuriated jury, but he realized that the whole affair – with Oates getting the active support of Shaftesbury's Green Ribbon Club, and the City – had become too big and too dangerous for him to handle personally.

Events moved forward remorselessly. Shaftesbury, now the Protestant champion, did his best to discredit Danby and gain the dismissal of James from the Council. But Charles, unlike his father, staunchly supported his minister, and although eventually Danby was sent to the Tower this, for him, was safety. Parliament insisted on the disbandment of the standing army, and when Charles had solemnly declared his son, the Duke of Monmouth, to be illegitimate, James consented to go abroad until passions cooled. Charles himself calmly went off to the pleasanter atmosphere of Windsor with his wife, who, poor lady, had not escaped the lash of these demagogue slanderers.

Gradually the reaction against Shaftesbury and Oates set in, considerably helped by Charles's two serious bouts of fever (incidentally, said to have been cured by Jesuits' quinine!). In their anxiety the people showed clearly how deeply they regarded the King. But the fight with Shaftesbury was still on, and by now centred on the Exclusion Bill to prevent James from coming to the throne. This bill was thrown out by the Lords after a marathon debating match between Shaftesbury on behalf of the bill and Lord Halifax (the Great Trimmer) against it. An infuriated Commons tried to bribe the King with promises of money if he would agree to exclusion, but nothing would induce Charles to swerve from the rightful succession.

Shaftesbury, equally furious, considered urging Monmouth into rebellion, but he was too late; by 1681 Charles had not only got the measure of Shaftesbury, but through his well-timed Declaration had now become complete master of the situation. This Declaration, read from every pulpit in the country, criticized the recent actions of the Commons and set out the steps that Charles had taken to defeat the aims of his enemies. It produced immediate demonstrations of loyalty, and cleared away the last wisps of the lightning-charged clouds that had hung over the Popish Terror.

In November 1682 Shaftesbury slunk away (disguised as a parson) to Holland. Charles had undermined the source of his strength in the City, when by issuing new charters he made it possible to break the Whig monopoly of the City Corporation. Of all the discontented Whig mandarins Shaftesbury alone might not have stopped short of actual murder to achieve his ends. But as he died in exile in 1683, he avoided being directly involved in the one further act of criminal stupidity (fortunately unsuccessful) needed to consolidate the popular image of royalty – a popularity that was even extended to the Duke of York. However, other former colleagues of his somehow became unwittingly involved with a bunch of assassins (headed by a Cromwellian soldier called Rumbold) to murder not only James, who had recently returned from a second semi-banishment to Scotland, but also the King, as they returned from Newmarket in April 1683. Luckily a fire at Newmarket caused the royal brothers to return earlier than was anticipated, and they passed the Rye House, Hoddesdon, where an ambush was planned, before the plotters were ready. In June the plot was betrayed, and two leading Protestant exclusionists (Lord Russell and Algernon Sidney) were beheaded for their part in the affair, and lesser fry suffered the full rigours of a traitor's death; but Monmouth, who was implicated, was forgiven by an indulgent father. It was the last upheaval of the reign.

Charles died, on 6 February 1685, in the Catholic faith with Father Hudleston to administer the last rites. In the last three years he had been given the peace for which he had throughout his reign so earnestly striven. He had defeated most of what the Civil War and Interregnum had stood for – in the end he was an absolute monarch ruling without a Parliament. He had routed his enemies and firmly re-established the monarchy and the High Church. He died greatly mourned; his people loved him for his friendliness and tolerance, his lack of malice, his courage in misfortune, his magnanimity in success, and even for his very human peccadilloes.

Charles left his brother, who came to the throne aged fifty-one, a goodly heritage. It would seem that James had every opportunity that fortune could offer a king. It is true that his Catholic convictions made him unsuitable to wear a Protestant Crown, but this little difficulty he quickly brushed aside with reassuring promises. Who would have thought, in February 1685, that in less than four years James would undo almost all that his brother had done? And yet Charles, who knew him best, clearly saw the possibility when he confided to Sir Richard Bulstrode that he himself was 'resolved to go abroad no more. But when I am dead and gone, I know not what my brother will do: I am much afraid that when he comes to wear the crown he will be obliged to travel again.' Prophetic words indeed.

By the time James succeeded, he had left behind what little glory there was destined to be in a life overshadowed by failure and sadness. But there had been a few golden moments. In his youth the new King had much in his favour – good looks, charm, courage and intelligence. His period of exile was in fact a more satisfactory one than his elder brother's, for he was happily employed. He learnt soldiering under the great captain of the age, the Vicomte de Turenne, when in 1652 he joined the French King's army, in the war of the Fronde,* and four years later, when Charles was forced to leave France and ordered James to join him, he fought for the Spaniards when they were defeated by Turenne at the battle of the Dunes. Renown gained upon foreign battlefields was later enhanced upon the quarter-deck of his brother's men-of-war.

In his salad days James had much admired the ladies. He may not have wooed them so ardently as his brother, but he was said to have been 'perpetually in one amour or another', and there were illegitimate children by Arabella Churchill. However, with his conversion to Rome, things of the spirit gradually came to mean more than the lusts of the flesh – although his mistress, Catherine Sedley, kept a precarious foothold right up to the Revolution. Also, and more damagingly, with age his character changed for the worse. Much of his early charm and great courage, and almost all of his resolution, disappeared; he became impatient and arrogant, and he was to do some very foolish things.

In 1673 James married, for the second time, a tall, dark and beautiful girl from the duchy of Modena, called Mary Beatrice d'Este. She loved him dearly and amid many trials was always devoted to his interest, and for that reason it is unlikely that she was responsible for letting him think

---

* The Fronde was the name given to the civil war that broke out at the beginning of Louis XIV's reign between the royalist party and the party of the princes, or Frondeurs, from the word for a sling used by the urchins of Paris. James fought in the Second Fronde, which began in 1651, when Louis was thirteen, and ended in 1653.

that his duty to his creed was more important than his kingship. This piece of insidious teaching was more likely to have come from his egregious Jesuit priest, and confidant, Father Petre.

James's Tory, land-owning Parliament was both reactionary and loyal. They voted him for life the same revenue as the last King, and were very generous in the matter of his Queen's jointure. There was, of course, some anxiety about his Catholicism, but he told them that it was his intention to keep the government 'in Church and State, as it is now by law established . . .', and his coronation – which, like his brother's, took place on St George's Day – was conducted in accordance with Anglican rites, save that the King and Queen did not receive the Sacrament. He told them some other less palatable things – that he expected total obedience and that calls for money were not to be countered with requests for the redress of grievances. But his religious assurances and the rumblings of Whig-inspired rebellion – the Earl of Argyll had already left Holland to lead Scottish dissidents in revolt – were sufficient to ensure him their almost unanimous support. The arrival of the Duke of Monmouth in Dorset a month later sealed their loyalty.

Monmouth, as already observed, had been indirectly concerned with the Rye House plot, and the once popular 'Protestant Duke' now found himself the fugleman for that party of discontented Whigs who were determined to unseat Catholic James. When Charles died, Monmouth was an exile at The Hague, but he could not stay there, for William of Orange found it expedient to placate his father-in-law, although he proved extremely negligent in keeping watch on the movements of his guest. Nor is this surprising, for if Monmouth was to gain the English throne there would be a Protestant ally in William's quarrels with Louis, and if he failed (which William thought and hoped would be the case) the succession of William's wife, the Princess Mary, became less complicated.

Monmouth's circumstances had undergone a change; now that he was enjoying the pleasure of a devoted mistress it is probable that his ambition to become King of England had faded. Furthermore, his not inconsiderable experience in command of troops enabled him to realize the military advantage James had with his large standing army. However, as his uncle said, when at the end of the venture he refused to pardon him, 'Poor Monmouth, he was always easy to be imposed upon', and a few fellow exiles persuaded him to head a rebellion in the Protestant west to synchronize with Argyll's landing in Scotland.

Monmouth, with eighty-two companions and some arms and armour, landed unopposed near Lyme Regis on 11 June. News of the landing soon reached James, and he despatched Lord Churchill with six troops of horse and five infantry companies to keep watch on the rebels.

No one in Whitehall was unduly alarmed, nor had much doubt of the result of the affair, for although Monmouth managed to enrol a large number of misguided yokels, there were not enough arms to go round, and many went into battle carrying nothing but a scythe blade on an eight-foot pole.

He was proclaimed King at the market cross in Taunton, but his army – through his lack of resolution – failed to take Bristol. It did, however, have a small measure of success at Philips Norton, through the ineptitude of Lord Feversham, who had taken over command from Churchill. But this did little to raise morale, for by now Monmouth was beginning to lose heart. He had learnt of Argyll's execution, and there had been no encouraging signs from the north or from London.

At the beginning of July it was the intention of the rebel army to march north to join up with a supporter (Lord Delamere), but getting news while at Bridgwater that the royalist army was encamped near-by at Westonzoyland, Monmouth decided to hazard all on a surprise night attack. On the night of 6 July a long and difficult approach march over boggy ground was carried out with great skill, but surprise was in the end lost, and the result was more of a massacre than a battle.

Had Monmouth died on the battlefield he would have become a hero, but unfortunately he took the advice to save himself and abandon his troops. After being picked up in a ditch some sixty miles from his defeat at Sedgemoor, there was a shaming and undignified scene before an unforgiving uncle, followed by a recovery of his courage on the scaffold, where he died horribly at the hands of a bungling executioner. The defeat of Monmouth was a catalyst in the shaping of James's reign. For now he proceeded to act as though his throne was completely secure, and in doing so lost first the goodwill of the most loyal Parliament that a sovereign could wish for, and in the end the confidence and affection of almost the entire nation.

'Liberty of Conscience' was James's constant cry, and there is no doubt that he genuinely wanted religious toleration – probably for all dissenters. But the argument that this was all that he aimed at is very difficult to sustain in the face of his ever increasing promotion of Catholics to important posts not only in the civil administration, but in the services as well. His Declaration of Indulgence and repeal of the penal laws meant that by 1687 religious toleration was in theory complete, but the Ecclesiastical Commission (set up to prevent the Anglican clergy from attacking the Roman faith) and above all the abolition of the Test against Catholics, enabled him to give preference to his co-religionists, where promotion and appointment was open, again in theory, to all. An alarmed Anglican Church quickly appreciated that their main props (so painfully built up) were being shorn from under them, and indeed in a kind of opinion poll, which James ordered his Lords Lieutenant to conduct, the country as a whole was shown to be against the repeal of the penal laws.

In just nine months after he came to the throne James had succeeded in alienating his Tory Parliament. Always uneasy over his decidedly pro-Papist designs, they raised difficulties when James asked them for additional revenue for the expansion of the army: an army already enlarged by an influx of Catholics – some from Ireland – for the Monmouth rebellion, and whom he refused to demobilize at its completion. James, whose impatience to opposition contributed to his undoing, prorogued Parliament in November 1685, and it was not to meet again in his reign. By 1687, when he dissolved this Parliament, he had accomplished the incredible feat of driving the Whigs and Tories into something of a coalition, ranged against his own Papist and Nonconformist alliance, which vainly sought for support from an army already wavering in its loyalty.

In this same year, 1687, the King decided to make changes in his ministry. His brothers-in-law, the Hydes, Halifax and most convinced Anglicans disappeared; in their place arose Robert Spencer, Earl of Sunderland, as James's chief minister. He was a timid sycophant, who changed his religion to please his King. This in itself was fairly harmless, but his introduction to the Council of Father Petre was certainly not.

During 1688 matters began to get totally out of hand. James decided to quicken the pace, and committed two further blunders. He and Sunderland stirred up a hornet's nest in Oxford, and succeeded in alienating that bastion of the royalist cause, when an attempt was made to overrule the election by the Fellows of a new President of Magdalen College and to substitute a most unsatisfactory candidate of James's choosing. This was followed by an Order in Council making it obligatory for the clergy to read James's second Declaration of Indulgence from every pulpit on 20 and 27 May. The Archbishop of Canterbury (Sancroft) and six bishops presented an address stating that in their opinion this order was illegal. James was furious, and ordered the seven to be put on trial for seditious libel. Not for years had bishops been so popular, and there was much jubilation, expressed not only in the streets of London, but more ominously in the army camp at Hounslow, when a jury acquitted them.

It is possible that a long-suffering people, staunchly monarchist and intensely patriotic, would have been content to suffer Catholic revival under an ageing James, with the knowledge of better Protestant days to come. But when, on 10 June 1688, Mary Beatrice gave birth to a son the Catholic succession seemed assured. The Queen had given birth to three daughters and a son, all of whom had died in infancy, and had had four miscarriages, but she had not been pregnant for some years. This, and the fact that the birth was attended mostly by Catholics, gave rise to the story of a supposititious baby. This was not the case, and the King's daughters, Mary of Orange and Anne, could well have behaved with greater decorum.

James had been visiting his army at Hounslow on the day that the bishops had been acquitted, and the cheering that he had heard unnerved him. He decided to bring in a strengthening of Irish troops; this and the appointment of the Catholic Admiral Sir Roger Strickland to command the fleet only increased the tension in the services, and undermined the loyalty of senior Protestant officers. The popular song of the day, Lilliburlero, admirably expressed the pent-up fury of the soldiery, and indeed of the people, for even Catholics – except the diehards – began to realize the insecurity of their position. As the hopes of Protestantism for England faded, some people started to cross over to Holland, where William was waiting upon events.

Assured of support, the ambitious Prince proceeded to pour out propaganda to strengthen his cause in England as the protector of Protestants. In July 1688 he had received a formal invitation; of the seven signatories the principals were the Earls of Shrewsbury and Danby and Bishop Compton. As a result, if he could be assured that his own frontier was safe from French attack, William had agreed to bring his army into England. Not until September did James give credence to the Dutch threat and realize his son-in-law's intentions. Now – far too late – he attempted to undo the harm he had done. He dismissed the panic-stricken Sunderland; he declared himself ready to reverse his policies and disavow his designs. But on 19 October* William, finding Holland safe from invasion – Louis having sent his army from the Dutch border to invade the Palatinate – launched out upon the hazardous enterprise to which he had been called, at the head of an army of fourteen thousand soldiers.

The Dutch fleet ran into foul weather and was forced back to port. But nothing daunted, William put to sea again, and slipping past the faithful Lord Dartmouth – who had replaced the Catholic Strickland in command of the fleet – disembarked his troops off Torbay on 5/15 November. The original intention to land in the north might have been better, for the west country still had memories of many gibbets; William advanced cautiously and uncertainly, for at first there was some passive hostility and no sign of the promised support.

* England did not adopt the Gregorian calendar until 1752. In the seventeenth century the difference between England, still using what was known as the Old Style, and the Continent was ten days (eleven days in the eighteenth century), and so, according to William's dating, he sailed for the first time on 29 October.

James had two obvious choices before him – to negotiate, or to fight. To have done either might possibly have been to save his throne, for no one had promised the Prince of Orange the kingdom (although he had undoubtedly promised it to himself); he had been asked over to save Protestantism for the country. And had it come to fighting, James had a considerably larger army, and was himself an experienced soldier. But when he was betrayed by those he had trusted and favoured – including his unpleasant daughter Anne – his courage faltered, his resolution foundered, and he decided to adopt the one course that must lead to extrusion, for in flight he would appear to his countrymen as futile and even contemptible.

Back in London from the army's advance base at Salisbury, where instead of animating his troops he had been kept indoors by a severe haemorrhage and nose-bleeding, James made plans for his wife and son to leave the country. This accomplished (the poor Queen had a terrible journey and behaved with much fortitude) he slipped away from Whitehall in the early hours of 11 December, and crossing the Thames deposited the Great Seal in its dark waters. He had actually boarded a customs vessel at Elmley Ferry in Kent, but while waiting for the tide was captured by a party hunting for escaping recusants, and by 16 December was back in London to an unexpectedly loyal welcome. But his mind was made up, no less than was William's, and he was off on his travels again by the 18th, and this time no hindrance was put in his way. James arrived in France on Christmas Day. The Glorious Revolution had been accomplished, and the Jacobite legend begun. Louis XIV, both now and for the rest of James's life, showed him much kindness and hospitality. He was given a fairly generous pension, and he and Mary Beatrice maintained a modest court at the Château Neuf, St Germain-en-Laye. There were, of course, political advantages to be obtained by Louis; nevertheless there was also genuine friendship.

James, recapturing briefly some of his former confidence, felt that Ireland or Scotland held the key to a successful return. In Ireland his Lieutenant, Richard Talbot, whom he had created Earl of Tyrconnel, had a formidable army on paper, but although brave and enthusiastic they were undisciplined and untrained. In Scotland his main hopes lay with the gallant Viscount Dundee, who had stood by him so faithfully in England before his flight, and who was to die so gloriously in his cause in the Pass of Killiecrankie in July 1689.

At the time of William's landing, Louis had offered material assistance to James, which was refused; now in a different situation, James was eager for what he could get, and probably hoped for more than what Louis was prepared to give. Nevertheless, in March 1689 he was enabled to sail for Ireland in ships provided by the French King and with sufficient money and arms to pay and equip a sizeable army. Landing at Kinsale, James marched to Dublin, where he held court for some months, before going north to confront his old companion in arms – now William's general – Marshal Schomberg. But he considered the opposition too strongly entrenched for his somewhat unreliable troops to assault, and returned to Dublin for the winter.

In June 1690 William himself landed with reinforcements at Carrickfergus, and on 1 July uncle and nephew did battle on the River Boyne. James, whose performance as a commander was hopelessly inadequate, watched his troops fight well – but not well enough – from a distance. William, as in the previous year in England, was not anxious to capture his uncle, and James embarked once more for France. Two years after the defeat on the Boyne another grand attempt was to be made by James to regain his kingdom. This time Louis provided ten thousand French troops and ships to transport them; but as the large armada assembled off La Hogue the English navy got among it, and shattered the expedition before it had even sailed. In 1697, by the Treaty of Ryswick, Louis recognized William as King of England.

The year previous (1696) James had been offered the Crown of Poland, but he refused it lest it be thought that he had renounced all claim to his former dominions. Besides, he had by then lost much of his worldly interest. It is true that until almost the end he enjoyed his favourite sport of hunting, but his last years were increasingly occupied by religious devotions. He paid frequent visits to the convent of La Trappe, where the strict regime seemed to suit his melancholy mood. This sad man died on 16 September 1701. On his death-bed he tried to comfort his distraught wife with the words, 'Madame, do not afflict yourself, I am going, I hope, to be happy.'

In the summer following Charles I's execution there commenced at Somerset House what became known as the Great Commonwealth Sale, which successfully disposed of most of the wonderful collection of royal treasures. Pictures, furniture, jewellery, plate, tapestries, etc., all came under the hammer, and the royal regalia was destroyed at about the same time.

Charles II, therefore, when he came to the throne could not expect to find his palaces so richly embellished as when his father had left them. But no sooner was the Restoration a *fait accompli* than great efforts were made to recover the King's treasures, and the committee set up to organize this work soon had some remarkable successes. Moreover, the Dutch made Charles a handsome gift of pictures and sculptures on his return to England.

Neither Charles II nor his brother James II possessed their father's great knowledge of art, or his enthusiasm as a collector; but Charles, in particular, was certainly not ignorant of the finer points of art and architecture. He took a great personal interest in the work of Christopher Wren, and especially in the designs for a new London after the Great Fire of 1666. Not many royal foundations survive from this period, but the Royal Hospital at Chelsea is a notable exception, and Charles II was also responsible for making Newmarket the headquarters of racing, which it has remained until this day. He was also a great patron of the theatre, and played a prominent part in the foundation of the Royal Society. During his reign men like Purcell, Newton and Dryden enriched posterity with their work in music, science and poetry. James II's reign was too short for him to have left any great impression on Britain's heritage, but, as the Duke of York he commissioned Sir Peter Lely to paint a number of portraits, some of which now hang in the National Maritime Museum at Greenwich.

Audley End (Essex). Charles II bought the great mansion in 1669 for £50,000, and called it New Palace. The court was often in residence there during his reign and that of James II, for it was very convenient for Newmarket. It continued to be used as a royal residence until 1701, when it was returned to the Howard family, who had owned the property since the death of Lord Audley in 1544. However, the present house is a mere fragment of a very much larger building designed by Bernard Johnson in the early years of the seventeenth century. Only three sides of the inner court remain, the rest having been demolished at various times, notably when, in 1721, the seventh Earl of Suffolk consulted Vanbrugh, who pulled down the outer courtyard, kitchen, chapel and some other parts of the house, and made his own additions. Audley End is just west of Saffron Walden, off the A11 road.

Boscobel House (Salop), played a most important part in Charles II's escape from the battlefield of Worcester in September 1651. After the defeat of his army, Charles rode north with Scotland in mind, and came first to White Ladies, which at that time – like nearby Boscobel – belonged to Frances Cotton the daughter of John Giffard, who was probably the builder of Boscobel House. A poor Catholic family of woodcutters called Penderel were tenants of Boscobel, and on being sent for and told who the principal fugitive was, they took full charge of the King for the next six days. Changing his mind about the Scottish venture, Charles made to cross the Severn at Madeley, but finding the crossing too well guarded, returned to Boscobel House. The house is very much as it was in 1651, and it is easy to imagine what discomfort Charles must have suffered from hours in the attic priest-hole, although the panelled rooms were comfortable enough, and the long attic gallery gave Charles a good view of the road. On his first day there Charles moved out from the house, for greater security, to the adjoining wood and hid in an oak tree. An old oak tree is preserved quite close to the house, which may have been a sapling when the King hid in the wood, but it certainly is not the same tree that gave him shelter on that memorable day, for that tree was described three hundred years ago as old and partly hollow. Boscobel is four miles east of Tong off the A41.

Bowhill (Selkirk). Bowhill is one of the seats of the Duke of Buccleuch and Queensberry, who is indirectly descended from the Duke of Monmouth through the latter's marriage to a Scott heiress in 1663. This lady, who was called Anne, became Duchess of Buccleuch in her own right, and so her titles and lands were not attainted after Monmouth's execution. In the Monmouth Room, and elsewhere in the house, there are many fascinating relics of Charles II's natural son, such as his saddle and equippage, cradle, and nightshirt, and a full-length portrait of the Duke in Garter robes.

Bowhill, which mainly dates from the beginning of the nineteenth century, stands between the Ettrick and the Yarrow Rivers in some of the finest Border country scenery. It is just south of the A708 Selkirk to Moffat road, some four miles from Selkirk.

Dover Castle (Kent). (See also Chapters 4 and 10.) Charles II held a magnificent court in the castle in honour of his sister Henrietta (Minette) of Orléans when she came to England in 1670 for proceedings connected with the signing of the Treaty of Dover. In June 1672 the Duke of York (later James II) was at Dover Castle to meet his bride, Mary of Modena. James II was the last sovereign to use the castle as a royal residence.

Drumlanrig Castle (Dumfries and Galloway Region), was built by the first Duke of Queensberry between 1679 and 1691, and passed to the Scott family in 1810 when the third Duke of Buccleuch succeeded to the Queensberry title on the death of the fourth Duke of Queensberry. Besides being the centre of a large and thriving agricultural estate the castle contains a superb collection of pictures, furniture, objets d'art, and many pieces of great historical interest. In the beautiful drawing room, with its lovely Grinling Gibbons carvings, stand two magnificent French cabinets, which were the gift of Louis XIV to Charles II, who gave them to his natural son, James Crofts, Duke of Monmouth, as a wedding present on the occasion of his marriage to Anne Scott in 1663 – the couple on that day being created Duke and Duchess of Buccleuch. Above these cabinets are portraits by Lely of Chalres II and Monmouth.

The castle, which lies to the west of the A76, four miles north of Thornhill, has had many associations with royalty over the years. Mary Queen of Scots, King James VI and I, and Prince Charles Edward Stuart all stayed there.

Edinburgh
Palace of Holyrood House. (See also Chapter 9.) Charles II ordered the building of the present palace behind the façade of the sixteenth-century one, although he never visited Scotland after the Restoration. However, his brother James, when Duke of York, lived in the palace from October 1672 to March 1682, when he was Lord High Commissioner in Scotland.

Ham House (Surrey). Ham was originally built in 1610, but was completely refurbished and enlarged by the Duke and Duchess of Lauderdale in the 1670s. Lauderdale was the fifth minister of the Cabal, and Charles II's Secretary for

Scotland, and was thus able to draw upon court artists for work on his house. By good fortune, the house retains much of its original hangings and furniture, providing an excellent record of courtly life during the reign of Charles II. Amongst the rooms is a suite for Queen Catherine of Braganza; her bedroom very suitably once held 'a Portugal bedstead'.

Ham House is on the south bank of the Thames, opposite Twickenham.

Hampton Court Palace (Middlesex). (See also Chapters 8 and 10.) In the palace hang two famous series of portraits of court beauties. The first was commissioned by Anne Hyde, Duchess of York, from Peter Lely to hang in her rooms at Whitehall. They are known as the Windsor Beauties, but are now at Hampton Court. Amongst them are two ladies much admired by Charles II: Barbara Villiers, Duchess of Cleveland, who became his mistress at the Restoration; and Frances Stuart, Duchess of Richmond, the one lady who spurned the King's advances. When William and Mary were rebuilding Hampton Court, the Queen commissioned Godfrey Kneller to paint portraits of her court ladies, now known as the Hampton Court Beauties.

Knole (Kent). (See also Chapter 8.) In the reigns of Charles II and James II, Knole was a centre of court life, for its owner, Charles Sackville, the sixth Earl of Dorset, was a close friend of both sovereigns. There can still be seen in the house beds certainly used by, and probably made for James, together with other very fine pieces of period furniture, both in the King's bedroom and elsewhere.

London
Greenwich Palace. (See also Chapter 10.) When he came to the throne, Charles II pulled down the old and derelict Tudor palace by the Thames, and in its place commissioned John Webb, a pupil of Inigo Jones, to build a new palace to be called the King's House. The original idea was that it should form three sides of a square with the river forming the fourth, and soon the east part of what is now called the King Charles block began to rise. But the money ran out, and only one side of the intended square was completed. However, at this time the park was laid out to a design that is still retained. Charles had hoped to entice over from France, Louis XIV's great garden designer, Le Nôtre, for this work, but although there is a plan of his extant, it is probable that Mollet – who worked with Le Nôtre – was chiefly responsible for the layout, with the planting being done by John Evelyn's friend, William Boreham.

National Maritime Museum, Greenwich. James II, when he was Duke of York, was in command at the naval battles of Lowestoft, 3 June 1665, and Solebay, 28 May 1672, and in this museum – among many other interesting exhibits – are paintings of these two engagements. After Lowestoft, the Duke of York commissioned Sir Peter Lely to paint a series of portraits of his commanders, and these included such well known men as George Monck, Duke of Albemarle, and Edward Montagu, the first Earl of Sandwich. These portraits, collectively known as the 'flagmen', can also be seen in the National Maritime Museum.

The Queen's Chapel, St James's Palace. (See also Chapter 10.) On 21 September 1662, the chapel was reopened by Charles II for his Queen, Catherine of Braganza, who housed a number of resident priests (among others Father Hudleston) in buildings on the site now occupied by Marlborough House. It continued in use as a Roman Catholic chapel until the accession of William and Mary, and in 1685 the Host was secretly fetched from the chapel and administered to the dying Charles II by Father Hudleston in accordance with the Romish rites, and with the Papal Nuncio representing the Pope.

The Royal Hospital, Chelsea, was founded by Charles II in 1682, as a home for veteran soldiers who had become unfit for duty after twenty years' service, or from wounds. Its inspiration almost certainly came from the Hôtel des Invalides, founded by Louis XIV in 1670. The influence of Nell Gwynne in the foundation can be discounted.

To reach the great hall and chapel, visitors have to pass through the Figure Court, in which stands a statue of Charles II by Grinling Gibbons. The chapel was completed by Wren in 1687, and consecrated in August 1691. The great hall has now reverted to its original purpose and is the dining hall of the pensioners.

Wren's buildings were originally set off by his magnificent gardens that stretched down to the river, but these were removed to make way for the Embankment in the middle of the last century. However, the present gardens laid out by John Gibson in about 1860, although not so extensive or so formal, are very pleasant and are open to the public.

St Paul's Cathedral. On the morning of 2 September 1666 Charles II received news that a fire which had broken out in Pudding Lane the previous night was sweeping on an easterly gale into the heart of the City. Charles went down that evening to take personal control, but to no avail and by the next day the great Gothic cathedral of St Paul's with its tall central tower was enveloped in flames. It was in fact already in a sad state of repair and some years earlier Christopher Wren had put forward plans for extensive repairs and alteration. Now, as Surveyor-General of the King's Works, he was called upon to make plans for a new cathedral. The King was actively interested in the whole series of designs that Wren made for the superb building that we now know with its massive dome, Grinling Gibbons' beautifully carved choir stalls and Jean Tijou's magnificent ironwork. But Charles did not live to see much of the work, for the choir was not ready until 1697, and although by 1711 the cathedral was virtually complete, work still went on beyond that date.

The Tower of London. (See also Chapters 3–9.) The royal apartments, which adjoined the White Tower on its southern side, were destroyed during the Commonwealth. Nevertheless Charles II, in accordance with ancient custom, rode from the Tower through the City to the palace of Whitehall on the day before his coronation. Charles was the last sovereign to uphold this glorious pageant, in which the streets were specially gravelled, the balconies of houses hung with colourful carpets, and at strategic points were positioned jugglers, *tableaux vivants* and fountains that flowed wine.

During the Commonwealth the Crown Jewels – some of which dated back to the early Middle Ages – were systematically destroyed. It was therefore necessary to replace the regalia, and much of the present beautiful display that can now be seen in the Jewel House of the Tower dates from the time of Charles II. Of the thirteen silver-gilt maces usually to be seen, two bear the royal cipher of Charles II, two of James II and three of William and Mary. There have been a great many additions to this glittering collection of jewels and plate over the centuries – including a number of crowns made for use in this century – but the swords of State, St Edward's Crown (the coronation crown), the Sovereign's Orb, St George's spurs, the Sceptre, and much of the Communion Service, all date from the coronation of Charles II. Only the Ampulla and Spoon actually escaped destruction and may date back to the fourteenth and twelfth centuries respectively.

An interesting sideline to the replacement of the Crown Jewels, was the attempted theft of them from the Martin Tower by a ruffian calling himself Colonel Blood and two associates in May 1671. Disturbed at their work, they managed to get the Crown and Orb as far as an outer gate before being overpowered. The amazing and unexplained sequel to this daring robbery and criminal assault was the free pardon – and indeed pension – given to Blood by Charles II.

In **the Armouries** (see also Chapters 8 and 10) are two suits of armour made for Charles II, one English and one Dutch, and harquebus armour that belonged to James II. Harquebus armour consisted of breast, back and pot (helmet), and was designed for mounted wear, and the carrying of a harquebus, or broadsword.

Moseley Old Hall (Wolverhampton). On the night of 7 September 1651, which happened to be very dark and stormy, the Penderel brothers brought King Charles II, riding on Humphrey Penderel's old mill-horse, the eight miles that separated Moseley from Boscobel. Here the owner of the Hall, a Roman Catholic and staunch royalist called Thomas Whitgreave, and Father Hudleston who lived there, welcomed their footsore and weary King. Lord Wilmot, another fugitive from Worcester, was also there and he it was who led Charles through the hall and up the staircase to a panelled room, where the King was to sleep in the same four-poster bed as can be seen there today. Opening off this room is the small, secret hiding place where Charles spent an uncomfortable hour when soldiers came to the house.

Moseley Hall dates from about 1600, and, although it has been restored, the main rooms are much as King Charles knew them. They are furnished with seventeenth-century pieces, and the paintings and engravings depict personalities and events of the time. There is also on display a letter written by Charles in his own hand from Paris in 1652 to Jane Lane, expressing his regret at not being able, at the time, to reward her for the great service she had done him.

Moseley Old Hall is now almost encroached by the suburbs of Wolverhampton, being four miles north of the town centre off the A460 road.

The Garrison Church (Portsmouth), was originally the thirteenth-century hospital of St John the Baptist and St Nicholas, and the foundation of Bishop des Roches. The nave, which was the hall of the hospital, suffered damage in the war, but the chancel, which was originally the hospital chapel, escaped. Charles II married Catherine of Braganza in this church on 21 May 1662.

Sizergh Castle (Cumbria). In the seventeenth century, the castle was owned by Sir Thomas Strickland, Keeper of the Privy Purse for Catherine of Braganza. His second wife, Winifred, was a member of the household of Mary of Modena, and attended the controversial birth of the Old Pretender. When James II and Mary decided to flee from England and take up exile at St Germain, the Stricklands chose to join them, and remained at their court for the rest of their lives. Lady Strickland acted as governess to Prince James, and was given many personal relics and portraits of the Stuarts by Mary of Modena, which now are to be seen at Sizergh.

The castle lies three and a half miles south of Kendal, north-west of the A6/A591 interchange.

Windsor Castle (Berks.). (See also Chapters 3, 4, 5, 7 and 8.) Between 1675 and 1683 King Charles II, with his architect Hugh May, replaced the work of Edward III in the Upper Ward with a palace in the grand baroque style. The exterior was kept plain, almost to the point of ugliness, to retain the medieval character, but inside the splendour and loveliness of what are now the State apartments were the work of such brilliant craftsmen as Grinling Gibbons and Antonio Verrio. Sadly, only three of the rooms have retained their full Caroline interiors – the Queen's Audience Chamber, the Queen's Presence Chamber, and the King's Dining Room. Charles II also laid out the Long Walk, an avenue three miles long, lined with four rows of elms.

Battle of Worcester (Worcs.), 3 September 1651. For any student of the battle of Worcester who is as energetic and fit as Charles II proved himself on that day, the best vantage point is the top of the tower of Worcester Cathedral. Charles, before taking personal charge of the fighting round the river, spent some time observing the battle from this tower, from where he could see such important tactical features as Red Hill, Perry Wood, Fort Royal and the confluence of the Rivers Teme and Severn. So much of the battlefield is now built over, but from the Cathedral tower these places can still be discerned by anyone who has a map of the city with him. The verger will unlock the door leading to the steps and the stiff climb to the top.

12

THE LAST STUARTS
From Holland to Hanover

⟨∞⟩

In November 1677 Mary Stuart, the elder daughter of the Duke of York (later James II) by his first wife, Anne Hyde, married William, Prince of Orange. Mary was, after her father, heir presumptive to the English throne. William had been born in 1650 (he was eleven years older than his wife) to William II of Orange and his wife, another Mary Stuart, the daughter of Charles I. William II had died shortly before his son's birth, and the latter did not succeed to his father's title of Stadholder.* However the House of Orange occupied a prominent position in the seven Provinces; they were wealthy landowners and sovereign princes in their own right, and since William the Silent (1533–84) members of the family had held the greatest offices of State in the new Republic. William's education and upbringing, therefore, were aimed at equipping him for the high office that many felt was his by right.

He was not a sturdy lad, being thin and pale with a slightly warped frame, and he suffered from asthma all his life. But what he lacked in physique he made up in toughness of fibre; and a love of fresh air and a passion for hunting proved an antidote to lurking ill health. He had been soundly educated in religion (he was, of course, a Calvinist), languages, history and the military arts. He quickly proved himself a courageous fighter, a good leader of men (although he was never a great commander), and he was to become the foremost diplomat of his time. He was proud of his House, a great patriot with an overriding ambition to break the power of France. It was not surprising, therefore, that in 1672, when his countrymen faced the full fury of Louis XIV's France,

---

* In the United Provinces at that time the title of Stadholder was not hereditary, and, in theory at least, the powers were somewhat circumscribed. The Stadholder could not, for example, declare war, levy taxes or impose the death penalty.

they should turn to him. The unpopular government of Johan and Cornelius de Witt was overthrown, and on 4 July William was proclaimed Stadholder of Holland and four days later confirmed as Captain-General and Admiral-General of the whole Republic for life. In 1674 the post of Stadholder was made hereditary.

Such was the man who, principally to strengthen his hand against the hated French, sought to marry the niece of Charles II, who warmly approved of the match. Mary was only fifteen, and she wept bitterly at the thought of being taken from home to live in a strange land with this taciturn, aesthetic, unattractive man. The contrast was startling indeed. Where William was short, Mary was tall; where he was an introvert, reserved and formal, she was a gay extrovert; her clothes were always fashionable and well fitted, his were drab and inelegant; she was beautiful, he was ugly. And yet she very quickly came to love her difficult, unpredictable husband, who seemed far happier in the company of men and was so often away from her fighting or hunting. She was always miserable when he left her, and moreover, when the time came for her to leave Holland, she was as sad at departing as the Dutch were to see her go.

William's affections for Mary are less easy to define. What started as a political match, moved through a *modus vivendi* to what in the end was undoubtedly a great love. Mary was always there in the background to understand and to cherish; they shared a strong religious faith and a delight in building and embellishing their many homes, to which William brought a fine collection of pictures. And although Mary realized that there was no place for her in the political and military side of William's life, she was of considerable help to him as regent in England during his annual campaigning in Holland. When she died in 1694, his tremendous display of grief could not have been anything but absolutely genuine. In a fit of remorse he even gave up his mistress, Elizabeth Villiers, although Mary some time before had accepted that situation.

During most of James's reign an uneasy relationship was maintained between the English King and his daughter and son-in-law. William had not been too vigilant in preventing Monmouth's invasion, but he did at least send over the English and Scottish regiments in the Dutch service. There was some friction over Whig refugees in Holland, and James's attitude to Mary was often rather petty, but William had no designs on the kingdom – which it seemed certain would anyway fall to his wife – until in 1687 it became clear that James was bent on changing the established religion; and then in 1688 came the birth of James's son, whose legitimacy Mary was loath to recognize. With the Catholic succession seemingly assured, William was now ready to take action upon the invitation of the seven spiritual and temporal lords, which he had obtained that summer.*

A large army had to be assembled and equipped and the navy made ready for sea in an incredibly short space of time, and no definite plan could be put into operation until it was seen that Louis XIV had more urgent matters to attend to in the Palatinate, and would not attack the Dutch Republic that year. William had little doubt how the invasion, if successful, would end, but he felt the need for deception. When asking permission from the States-General to embark an army, he told them that he 'did not intend to dethrone the King nor to conquer England, but only to ensure that by the convocation of a free Parliament, the reformed religion will be secure and out of danger'.

An army of between twelve and fifteen thousand soldiers was ready to sail in 225 transport ships, protected by a naval force of forty-nine men-of-war and ten fireships, by October, and on the 19th of that month (old style) the fleet put to sea. However, a violent storm forced it back into port with the loss of only one ship, but thirteen hundred horses. The damage was soon made good, and when by 1 November a steady east wind (or Protestant wind, as it was called) set in, the armada put to sea once more. The original intention was to land in the north, where greater support was assured; but the wind, which also hampered the designs of the English fleet, took William's ships with their banners 'for Religion and Liberty' through the Strait of Dover, past Beachy Head and down Channel to Torbay, where on 5 November the troops disembarked.

The first few days were not happy ones. The roads across Devon to Exeter were in a very bad condition for the transport of so much baggage, and the Seven had not honoured their promise to be in attendance at the landing. But in Exeter the first important landowners and noblemen joined the Prince. The progress from there onwards was satisfactory and, with the exception of a small skirmish at Wincanton, unimpeded. At Hungerford, which was reached on 7 December, William met James's Commissioners, who informed him that the King had summoned a Parliament and that the elections would be free. But William was not impressed, and laid down a number of conditions to which James must accede. These, as William well knew (for had James accepted them, the Dutchman's mission would have been at an end) proved too humiliating; and sickened by the many desertions of those whom he trusted most, James made arrangements to leave the country,

* For a further account of the birth of the Prince of Wales, and the invitation to William, see previous chapter.

which he finally succeeded in doing on 23 December 1688.*

William, guarded by his famous Dutch Blue Guards, was now securely ensconced in Whitehall. Matters had gone surprisingly well for him; he had been careful to preserve the myth that he had not come to conquer, but merely to put the English house in order. However, England was unsettled, with anti-Catholic feeling running high, and William was just about the only man who could sort things out. A Convention Parliament was elected in January 1689, and its primary duty was to decide the position of the monarchy. The Whigs saw William's accession as the keystone of their revolution; but the Tories, with their majority in the Lords, were loath to abandon the principle of hereditary monarchy. When Mary let it be known that she would not rule alone (and anyway William had made it clear that he would not be subordinated to her), a regency for King James was proposed, and defeated by a narrow majority. The only practical solution therefore was for William and Mary to rule jointly, and the interregnum came to an end on 13 February when William and Mary formally accepted the Crown, it being agreed that William alone should exercise the regal power of the joint sovereigns.

The Whig triumph was almost complete; it required only safeguards to ensure that the monarchy in future should rule through Parliament, and that there could be no return to absolute power. The first important step was the Declaration of Rights (which in December 1689 came on the statute book as the Bill of Rights), that accompanied the offer of the Crown; and the Coronation Oath by which the sovereigns swore to govern according to the laws and customs of Parliament, and to uphold the Protestant religion. The Declaration of Rights was drawn up as a practical document to introduce certain important safeguards on a change of monarchy; it was never intended to be a permanent charter enshrining the principles of parliamentary sovereignty. However, its conditions, together with the Coronation Oath, went far to ensure that William and Mary would rule as constitutional monarchs.

There was much trouble in the early months. When Mary arrived from Holland in February 1689, she was appalled to see how ill William looked. His asthma was very bad in English winter conditions, and he had moved out of London to Hampton Court; for almost a year he remained aloof and ungracious to all but his Dutch friends. He had been greatly angered when Parliament refused to grant him a revenue for life; this took away his independence and ability to wage war without their approval. The golden years of the Anglican Church had been eclipsed by the Toleration Act of 1689, and William's leaning towards the

* See previous chapter.

Presbyterians further embittered the High Anglicans. There seemed much support for an opinion openly expressed, that James would be welcomed back if he would renounce Catholicism. And maybe at this time William would not have been sorry to go, for he was at loggerheads with both Whigs and Tories, and his presence in Holland was necessary. Nor was Mary free from censure, and she later confessed that she found her first year as Queen to be a great trial.

But in reality the English knew that they must keep William, and he had every intention of mending his ways and of keeping England. And when his father-in-law tried to regain his kingdom through Ireland, the English were glad to have a leader capable of giving the military machine the drastic overhaul it needed, and after early failures and disappointments take personal charge of full-scale military operations. He took to Ireland thirty-five thousand infantry and nine thousand cavalry, and on 1 July 1690 defeated James on the River Boyne. But William, like many before and after him, found Ireland something of a military graveyard. He failed to take Limerick, and on 3 September embarked for England.

During his absence Mary had acted as regent, and gained well-deserved praise for the cool and competent way she assumed control in a difficult situation. The Anglo-Dutch fleet had been defeated by the French off Beachy Head, and with the army away in Ireland the country was vulnerable to a French invasion; but the danger passed and the English navy shortly regained command of the sea. Two years later Beachy Head was avenged at La Hogue. The return of William to England and his entry into London with Mary, which was greeted with great acclamation, marked a notable swing in popularity towards the monarchs, and enabled William to make plans for a visit to Holland, where in his absence the campaign against France had been disastrous.

Campaigning in Holland became for William a seasonal affair, and he was often away for most of the summer, facing, usually with indifferent success, the French onslaughts of Marshal Luxembourg in the Spanish Netherlands. During these absences Mary acted as regent, and her most notable achievements were her practical capacity to take a leading role in Church matters, and her progress towards improving the moral tone of the court, and indeed of her subjects generally. Never entirely happy when William was away, she found consolation in her work of improving and beautifying the garden and rooms of Hampton Court, and of Kensington Palace, which she and her husband had bought from the Earl of Nottingham in 1689. The great sorrow in her life was the worsening relationship with her sister, Anne. Their characters were very different; Anne was stolid, none too clever, obstinate and dull, while Mary was good-looking, intelligent and ebullient. It is possible that their relationship would not have fallen apart so completely had not Anne been a tool in the empoisoned hands of Sarah Churchill; but it has to be admitted that both William and Mary sometimes behaved very boorishly towards Anne.

William's Continental wars. were a heavy drain on the English exchequer, which had to pay and maintain English troops in The Netherlands. This brought to the fore two able financiers, Charles Montagu (later Earl of Halifax), Chancellor of the Exchequer, and a Scottish banker, William Paterson. Between them they devised in 1694 the Bank of England, and carried out a complete overhaul of the coinage. Their success in fiscal reconstruction enabled England to play her part in·William's wars, and later in the War of the Spanish Succession.

William was very knowledgeable about political affairs on the Continent, but in England he was far less sure and less interested. His lack of interest in, and understanding of, Scottish affairs was probably responsible for his signing the order that led to the treacherous slaughter of the MacDonalds of Glencoe by troops under the command of Captain Robert Campbell of Glenlyon in February 1692. The Scots knew well enough that the Earl of Stair was the principal offender, and they blamed William far less for the massacre than for the loss of so many of their soldiers in his Continental campaigns.

On 28 December 1694 Mary died of smallpox. William's grief was terrible to witness, as well it might be, for apart from their love, which had grown with the years, he owed so much to this wife, who at only thirty-two had now left him. She had brought him the throne that he had coveted, and although without his political ability – politics bored her – she was his constant support in good and bad times. She was universally mourned, not only in England (where she had always been more popular than William), but in the United Provinces too.

At Mary's death William became reconciled to Anne, although the Churchills had to wait a further four years before Marlborough took his rightful place as William's military deputy. This might have occurred earlier had not William, in 1695, gained his only military success in the capture of Namur, which led to the Treaty of Ryswick in 1697. William knew very well that the ambitions of Louis were still unsatisfied, but for the moment the truce he had gained gave him some short-lived popularity.

Peace did not suit William; he was never so happy as when on campaign. It was noticeable that in the last years of the century his austere mode of life had gradually changed to one bordering on debauchery. He spent long hours drinking with his latest favourite, Arnold Keppel, whom he created Earl of Albemarle. This man, amid unedifying scenes of jealousy, had replaced Bentinck (Earl of Portland) as William's principal confidant. These two, and other Dutch cronies, were not only unpopular in themselves, but made William unpopular too, both with Parliament – with whom he was always at variance – and with the nation as a whole. In the end Parliament presented him with an address asking him to remove all foreigners except Prince George of Denmark (Anne's husband). Many of them stayed, but even William's undoubtedly sincere threat of abdication could not save the disbanding of his Dutch troops and their compulsory return to Holland.

Parliament's insistence on the reduction of the armed forces would seem shortsighted in view of the trouble that was now brewing over the Spanish Succession. The demise of the childless, feeble-minded, sickly Charles II of Spain had been a long-expected event in the chancelleries of Europe, and the future of the huge Spanish Empire was of considerable concern to the Emperor Leopold I of Austria, Louis XIV and William. Leopold and Louis had candidates (Leopold's second son, the Archduke Charles, and Louis's grandson, Philip Duke of Anjou), with equal hereditary claims from Philip III of Spain. There was also a third contender in the Emperor's grandson, the Electoral Prince of Bavaria. Neither Louis nor William was ready in 1698 for more fighting, and they agreed upon a plan (resented by the Emperor and the Spanish people) of partition. By the Treaty of Partition the young Electoral Prince was to get Spain and the colonies, with territorial concessions going to Austria and France.

This plan was thrown into disarray by the unexpected death in 1699 of the seven-year-old Electoral Prince, and a second partition treaty of 1700 dividing the Empire between Archduke Charles and Philip of Anjou (and not recognized by the Emperor), collapsed when in November of that year Charles II died, and by his will left the entire Empire to Philip. Louis decided to abide by the will, and was soon at war with the Empire, but at first William got little support from Parliament in his wish to take up the cudgels against his life-long foe. However, Louis's foolishly provocative actions, culminating in his recognition of James II's son as James III when his father died in 1701, made it inevitable for the Commons (equally·divided between Whigs and Tories) to prepare for war. By the beginning of 1702 war with France was inevitable, but for William it came too late.

When the Duke of Gloucester, Anne's only surviving son, died in 1700 at the age of eleven, there was left no direct Protestant heir after Anne. On 12 June 1701 William gave his assent to the Act of Settlement, naming the House of Hanover, in descent from James I's fascinating daughter, Elizabeth (the Winter Queen), heirs to the Crown. Parliament, having experienced the difficulties connected with a foreign-born sovereign, took care to wrap the Settlement in eight articles imposing certain military, religious and personal limitations on future monarchs. If this was a last hit at William, it missed its mark, for by now he was too ill to worry much about his successors – so long as they were Protestants and Francophobes.

For much of 1701 his health had been in steep decline. He suffered continuously from badly swollen legs, and only his robust constitution kept him alive that winter. On 21 February 1702 his horse, Sorrel, stumbled on a molehill in the park at Hampton Court, and William broke his collar-bone. More swelling, fever and lung trouble followed, and on 8 March he died.

The Revolution of 1688 had as great an effect on the future of England as the Reformation, and a far greater one than the Civil War. Without William, James could not easily have been dethroned, and without Mary, William would have had no justification to act. William was the first European in English politics; he brought England into a close political and military involvement with Europe. And even if some of the great legal measures introduced in his reign – the Bill of Rights; the Toleration, Civil List, Triennial and Settlement Acts – were enacted in opposition to his wishes, they were important stepping stones in English constitutional history, for which he is owed, if indirectly, a debt of gratitude.

When Anne came to the throne in 1702 she was thirty-seven years old. In 1682 she had married Prince George of Denmark, an amiable nonentity who had little ambition and less ability, but a kindly man who knew how to appreciate the good things in life. He had given Anne six children before she became Queen, of whom only one, William, Duke of Gloucester, survived infancy. Anne had also suffered no fewer than twelve miscarriages between 1687 and 1700.

Her education had been extremely scanty; in her youth the prospects of her becoming Queen were slender, and anyway girls were no longer educated to the high Tudor standards. Some attention was paid to the courtly accomplishments of music (for which Anne had a good ear), dancing and French, and a lot to religious studies. These latter were principally in the hands of Bishop Compton, for Charles II had insisted on a Protestant education. There was in her make-up a lot of good common sense, which served her well in a reign that produced some great men who, under a patriotic Queen, were responsible for great achievements.

Anne was fairly tall and well proportioned, but she was not beautiful (except for her hands), nor did she make any attempt to enhance her appearance by elaborate clothes and jewellery – the latter she would wear only on State occasions. Although she had undoubtedly behaved extremely badly to her father, who was devoted to her, she was not by nature unkind – in fact the reverse, and she was generous to a fault. It must be remembered, in judging her character, that for much of the time Anne was in bad health, and often in considerable pain. Ever since childhood she had suffered from poor eyesight, and by the time she became Queen she was a martyr to gout – being the only sovereign who had to be carried to her coronation. She had inherited the Stuart love of the chase, although her frequent attacks of gout often made it necessary for her to follow the sport in an open calash.

Anne came to the throne entirely inexperienced in affairs of State. She may not have been confident of her ability to rule, but she had no qualms concerning usurpation. At heart she probably believed in the legitimacy of the half-brother she had scarcely ever seen, but he was a Catholic and her England must be Protestant. Although she was to revive the curious practice of touching for the 'King's Evil', she was later to disclaim the theory of divine right, and she probably accepted her position as being the natural heir to her brother-in-law under the Bill of Rights.

The two-party system, although in its infancy, was rapidly becoming the accepted form of government; but in the first half of the eighteenth century there was no party discipline with members owing allegiance to a given leader. Instead, a party would comprise a loose band of men sharing the same principles and political views, which could very quickly be changed. It was a time when the great families of the realm were beginning to be associated with one or other party. However, Anne would have nothing to do with parties, and no matter how much pressure was brought to bear she liked to choose her ministers irrespective of their party's majority in Parliament. This often proved a serious embarrassment to them.

In March 1702, when Anne succeeded, the country was on the verge of war with France. John Churchill (now created Earl of Marlborough) was England's and Holland's chosen champion – although Anne would dearly have liked her husband to be made Commander-in-Chief of the allied land forces. Marlborough at this time was a lukewarm Tory; his wife (as Sarah Jennings, an old childhood friend of Anne's) was a fervent Whig. In the happy days of the Cockpit,* Anne, the Marlboroughs and Sidney Godolphin had formed a close and intimate association, corresponding freely with each other on personal and political matters, using pseudonyms. The Marlboroughs were called Mr and Mrs Freeman, Godolphin was Mr Montgomery, Anne herself was known as

---

* Before Mary died Anne had lived in the Cockpit at Whitehall.

Mrs Morley, and King William was accorded the unpleasing epithet of Caliban.

It was only natural that on Anne's accession the Cockpit circle should find themselves in positions of honour and authority. Marlborough, besides becoming Captain-General of the Forces, was given the Garter; Godolphin (who shared with the Queen a great love of racing) gained the foremost political post of Lord Treasurer; and Sarah Marlborough became Mistress of the Robes, Keeper of the Privy Purse and Ranger of Windsor Park, while her two married daughters became Ladies of the Bedchamber. Such honours only encouraged Sarah to think that she could impose her will upon the Queen; she lost no time in trying to persuade Anne of the benefits to the nation of Whiggism, and constantly put pressure on her in the interest of her Whig cronies. But here she failed, for the Queen was stubborn and had a will of her own; indeed we can only marvel at Anne's patience and tolerance, because for many years she endured with few complaints impertinences that no other sovereign would have suffered from a subject.

On 4 May 1702 England, Holland and the Empire declared war on France. This Grand Alliance, as it was called, had been fashioned in the last two years of William's reign, and he and Marlborough had been the principal architects. The war was to drag on for eleven years; but the courage of the Queen's soldiers and the military prowess of her general, ably supported by the brilliant warrior-prince (Eugene of Savoy) who commanded the Imperial armies, brought victory in many battles. Blenheim, Ramillies, Oudenarde and Malplaquet immortalized the name of Marlborough and altered the political fulcrum of Europe. In 1702 a grateful sovereign made her friend and Captain-General a duke, and two years later granted him the Crown's interest in the royal manor of Woodstock, where Vanbrugh, frequently harassed by Sarah, was to build the magnificent Blenheim Palace.

For nearly the whole of Anne's reign the country was at war, and inevitably many of the problems that faced the Queen were connected with the war. The other great issue was the Church. In the matter of the war, the Whigs favoured an all out offensive on land against the principal enemy, France. The Tories, on the other hand, wanted a limited land war and a concentration of naval effort towards colonial expansion. Nor were they averse to operations in Spain – which was never a fruitful theatre of war for the allies – from which they hoped to obtain Spanish colonies. 'The Church in Danger' was their cry at home, and in their opposition to Dissenters they had the support of the junior clergy, but not the majority of the Bench of Bishops, whose views were more broadly based and in line with those of the Whigs.

It was the Tories, therefore, who in 1702 (and several times thereafter) introduced the bill to abolish the practice known as Occasional Conformity. The Test Act required that all those who held important offices of State must be communicants of the Anglican Church. But under King William, and with the full assent of the Whigs, it had become a habit for some Dissenters to take the sacrament once and then to worship in their own church or chapel. The Bill was constantly thrown out by a Whig majority in the Lords, until in 1711 it was allowed to pass – in somewhat discreditable circumstances – as part of a bargain concerning the peace campaign. Anne favoured toleration in religious matters, but she was behind the Tories at this time over the Occasional Conformity Bill, probably because she considered occasional conformity to be hypocritical, and also through a dislike for Whigs and their policies.

Anne's preference for the Tories is understandable, for they were the party of the Church, and although some of them had Jacobite leanings they were also predominantly the royalist party; moreover, they had come to her help in the last reign over the matter of her revenue. The Whigs she was inclined to regard as republicans, and the more Sarah pressed their cause the stiffer became the Queen's resistance. Personalities also entered into it, for she cordially disliked all five of the so-called Lords of the Whig Junto – Halifax, Orford, Somers, Sunderland and Wharton. Anne knew little about politics on ascending the throne, but if not a great ruler she was a most conscientious one, and she took immediate steps to improve her knowledge, being the last sovereign to attend the debates in the Lords.

These were still the days when a comparatively small ruling caste could impose its will on a much larger unprivileged, and in the main uneducated, majority. The men that Anne came to rely upon in the first years of her reign were Marlborough, Godolphin, Robert Harley and – to a lesser extent – Harley's young protégé, Henry St John. Marlborough had always tendered Anne sound advice, and although abroad most of the time he continued to do so; in Godolphin he had the perfect colleague to further his aims – which were, of course, the successful prosecution of the war – at home. Godolphin, a moderate Tory and a man of the centre, was an able financier and an administrator with a clarity of vision greater than that of most of his colleagues. Harley, once a Whig and now an ardent Tory, was a more complex character and a man of contradictions. At heart a pacifist, he now championed the war and at first worked closely with Marlborough and Godolphin; he was a very able parliamentarian. St John came to prominence through his brilliant oratory, and in 1704 was made Secretary-at-War. A flamboyant roué of much charm and intelligence, he was ambitious and unpredictable. There was more quicksand in St John, more solid earth in Harley.

In the five crowded years between 1706 and 1711, people and events passed in rapid succession upon the English political stage. Except for some nine months after the death of her beloved Prince George, in October 1708, when she scarcely left St James's Palace, Queen Anne was always at the centre of affairs. She had her likes and dislikes among her ministers, and she showed these very plainly. By present standards many of her acts were unconstitutional, and in some instances her good faith might be called in question; but in Anne's day a sovereign, if not above reproach, was, within wide bounds, above constraint, and those who caught the rays of the royal light were for a time above competition.

In May 1707 the Queen went in State to the House of Lords to give the royal assent to the Act of Union, and in October of that year she opened the first Parliament of Great Britain. Negotiations with the Scots Commissioners had been in progress for many months previous, and the Whigs, who by the end of 1706 were at the head of affairs, gained much credit for the successful outcome. This emboldened the Lords of the Junto to press the Queen for important ministerial appointments. One such was for Lord Sunderland (whose case was championed by his father-in-law, Marlborough). Anne thoroughly disliked Sunderland, as she had his father before him, and she gave way only after many months and under extreme pressure.

Even more traumatic for Anne was the case of Harley, to whom she had taken a strong liking. Many of his actions – not least his backstairs intrigues with the Queen, made possible through her dresser, and Harley's cousin, Abigail Hill – had by 1707 estranged him from Marlborough and Godolphin, and at the end of that year a breach of security in which he was involved gave ammunition to his many Whig opponents. Faced with the resignation of both Marlborough and Godolphin, and indeed the break-up of the entire ministry, Anne had to dismiss Harley. She never really forgave Marlborough and Godolphin for forcing this course upon her, and she continued consulting Harley in secret.

A month after the Queen had parted with her favourite minister the country was shaken by an invasion scare. In March 1708 a French fleet carrying the Pretender (as Anne now called her half-brother) sailed from Dunkirk, and reached the Firth of Forth; troops were rushed north, but the English navy under Admiral Byng prevented a landing. The Whigs took advantage of this hour of crisis by staging a popular display of patriotism, which was reflected in the result of the election that summer. But Harley was almost as dangerous to them out of office as in it, and his attempts to undermine the ministry had the backing of the Queen when she emerged from her period of mourning in the summer of 1709.

During 1709 and 1710 the Tories strengthened their position throughout the country. The Whigs were divided, and their cause was gravely damaged through their folly in impeaching the bombastic Oxford divine, Henry Sacheverell. His sermon condemning their attitude to the Church, the Revolution and the Toleration Act would have been soon forgotten had they not staged a State trial in Westminster Hall, from which the Doctor emerged with the reputation of a hero quite out of proportion to his merits, and the Tories with an electoral certainty.

Godolphin, who through force of circumstances found himself increasingly in the Whig camp, had by now lost the confidence of the Queen. He did not help matters by treating Anne in a surly, offhand manner; nevertheless, his dismissal – which took place in August 1710 – after many faithful years as her principal minister was ill-conceived and shabbily executed. Harley came back to power as Chancellor of the Exchequer, and that autumn there was a Tory landslide at the polls. He had been in office only a few months when in March 1711 he was stabbed by a French adventurer called the Marquis de Guiscard, who was being held for high treason. The injury was not severe, but Harley became the recipient of much national solicitude; he took his time convalescing, and in his absence the direction of affairs passed to St John, who having messed up a combined operation against Quebec, lent his not inconsiderable weight towards ending the war.

During these years of testing warfare on the Continent and political upheavals caused by rival factions at home, Anne was constantly subjected to the stresses and strains imposed upon her relationship with Sarah Marlborough. Sarah, as we have seen, received many honours upon Anne's accession, and she carried out her duties entirely to Anne's satisfaction. If she had a fault it was that she kept the strings of the Privy Purse too tightly drawn. The trouble lay in the fact that the beautiful Sarah had not the sense to realize that the old Cockpit days of easy familiarity had gone. Anne was Queen now, and Sarah should show proper respect to her anointed sovereign. She did not do so; she frequently behaved badly towards the Queen in public; she took to absenting herself for long periods from court, and she persistently importuned Anne for favours.

By 1705 the long friendship between the two women was showing signs of breaking, but Anne's wonderful patience was still not entirely exhausted. In 1707 another link in the chain that still bound them was severed when Sarah discovered she had a rival to Anne's affections. Before Anne became Queen, Sarah had introduced into her service an indigent relative called Abigail Hill, to whom Sarah had been extremely kind. Abigail was not beautiful, but she was entertaining and sympathetic, and became the sort of person that Anne needed to have about her. In 1707 she married Samuel Masham, a member of Prince George's household. Anne attended the wedding, but Sarah knew nothing about it. Sarah became embittered, and her subsequent hatred of Abigail was founded upon the latter's base ingratitude and strengthened by jealousy. Moreover, Harley, who owed his position with the Queen in great measure to Abigail, stood for everything in politics that Sarah detested.

Matters went from bad to worse; Anne charged Sarah with 'inveteracy against poor Masham' and of desiring her cousin's ruin, and Sarah retaliated with wild statements of how she had 'set and kept the crown upon her [Anne's] head'. And for good measure she referred to the Queen as a 'praying godly idiot'. The end came in January 1711, when amid painful scenes, and a personal plea from Marlborough, which Anne ignored, Sarah was dismissed from all her offices.

Almost exactly a year after Sarah had been deservedly dismissed, her great husband was hounded into the shadows in circumstances as shabby as those that had attended Godolphin's departure. For some time the Queen and the majority of the nation had grown weary of war, and in 1710 secret negotiations for peace had begun. St John, when he stepped into the place of Harley (created Earl of Oxford and Mortimer after the Guiscard affair), worked hard for peace, but the Whigs, headed by Marlborough, were dissatisfied with the terms – which in fact gave England all and more than she had fought for – and the cry went up 'No Peace without Spain'. With the unexpected death of the Emperor Joseph I and the succession of his brother the Archduke Charles ('King Charles III of Spain') the Tories, who were fed up with pursuing the elusive goal of 'no peace without Spain', had the opportunity they wanted. The danger of adding Spain to the already vast Habsburg possessions gave them a powerful lever for making peace, leaving Philip V on the Spanish throne.

The Whig motion was defeated in the Commons, but in the Lords matters were different. The Whigs at last allowed Nottingham's Occasional Conformity Bill to go through in exchange for his support, and through the efforts of Marlborough, Halifax and one or two others the motion 'No Peace without Spain' was carried. Oxford, now back in business, and St John went to work on the Queen at once, and without too much difficulty – for peace was her greatest desire – persuaded her that in failing to dismiss Marlborough she would be abandoning her ministers and even jeopardizing her Crown. On the last day of 1712 she wrote a letter (the contents of which we do not know, for in a rare burst of temper Marlborough burnt it) dismissing her Captain-General, whose genius had procured the principal glories of her reign. Shortly afterwards she reluctantly agreed to the creation of twelve new peers; a Tory majority was secure, and peace with France was eventually signed on 11 April 1713.

But for Anne the last year of her life was not to be one of peace. The Tories gained another victory at the polls at the end of 1713, but now a widening breach between Oxford and St John cast a deepening cloud over the political scene, and with the Queen's health rapidly failing the question of the succession – always anathema to Anne – came into. prominence in spite of the Act of Settlement.

Oxford was also now in ill-health, and with it he became unreliable and at times unpleasant. St John was the man of the moment, but Anne never wholly trusted him, and frowned upon his loose morals. Whether she knew the extent of his Jacobite designs is uncertain, but her dislike for the House of Hanover (shortly before both of them died, there was acrimonious correspondence between her and the Electress Sophia*) was put aside after her half-brother's categorical announcement that he would not change his religion, for the Protestant succession was her paramount consideration.

As the Queen's life moved towards its close, the bitter wrangling between Oxford and St John worsened; accusations of peculation were levied against St John (as they had been, most unjustly, against Marlborough), who now had Abigail on his side and against Oxford, although much of her influence at court had been superseded by that of the Whig Duchess of Somerset. Oxford had to go, but his replacement by St John would have spelt disaster. The Privy Council recognized this, and as Anne lay dying they persuaded her to dismiss Oxford, and give the Lord Treasurer's staff of office to the well-trusted Duke of Shrewsbury.

Anne died on 1 August 1714. Politically hers had been a turbulent reign; she had done her best to keep the Crown above party politics, and if she had her likes and dislikes she made certain that they did not impinge upon the nation's welfare. Shortly after her accession she had said, 'As I know my heart to be entirely English . . . there is not one thing you can expect or desire of me which I shall not be ready to do for the happiness or prosperity of England.' Within her limitations she kept her word, and she left her country on the threshold of stability and achievement.

---

* The Hanoverian claim came through the Electress Sophia, who was the daughter of Elizabeth of Bohemia and therefore the granddaughter of James I.

William III and his wife Mary II both had a great interest in architecture, interior decoration and gardening, and the work that they ordered to be carried out at Hampton Court and Kensington Palace was on a large and impressive scale. Queen Mary took particular interest in the layout and stocking of the gardens at Hampton Court and Kensington Palace and built up a magnificent collection of oriental porcelain. William was a connoisseur of pictures, and acquired a fine collection. Grinling Gibbons, who had been active in the last two reigns, continued his decorative wood-carving in the reign of William and Mary.

Queen Anne was the least inspiring of the Stuarts in most ways, and certainly in so far as interest in, and acquisition of, works of art were concerned. She contributed very little to the wonderful royal collections that had been skilfully assembled since the Restoration. However, it is often said that the beginning of the Augustan age coincided with her reign, and certainly literature, music, painting and architecture flourished at this time with men such as Pope, Handel, Kneller and Vanbrugh all at work. Many splendid private houses – Chatsworth, Blenheim and Castle Howard among them – were either started or rebuilt in the period covered by this chapter, many of the late Classical churches of Wren and Hawksmoor also date from this time.

Blenheim Palace (Oxfordshire).

In 1705 work was started to the designs of Sir John Vanbrugh on this vast and imposing palace, the gift of the nation and of Queen Anne to John Churchill, first Duke of Marlborough, for his famous victory over the French and Bavarians at Blenheim in 1704. There had been a royal palace in the manor of Woodstock since the time of Henry I. By 1705 it was nothing but a ruin, which the Duchess of Marlborough insisted should be pulled down to make way for the splendid new building. The great Baroque house was not completed until after the Duke's death in 1722, and after much of the family fortune had been poured into it. Vanbrugh was unable to come to terms with Duchess Sarah's tantrums, and threw in his hand in 1716, and the work was continued by Nicholas Hawksmoor, with Michael Rysbrack designing the chapel, in which are the tombs of the first Duke and his Duchess. The grounds were landscaped by Lancelot (Capability) Brown.

Hampton Court Palace (Middlesex).

(See also Chapters 8, 10 and 11.) Between the death of Henry VIII and the accession of William III and Mary, every sovereign, with the exception of James II, resided – with varying frequency – at Hampton Court. Alterations and repair work were constantly in progress; Charles II in particular was very active, although nothing remains of his work. But it was not until the reign of William and Mary that extensive rebuilding took place. Sir Christopher Wren was given the task of pulling down the old Tudor buildings and erecting a new Baroque palace. Wren produced several ambitious schemes for the new palace, but eventually financial expediency and speed forced him to compromise. In the event, only the Tudor state apartments of Cloister Green Court were demolished, leaving largely untouched Base and Clock Courts, the great hall and the kitchens. Wren used brick with stone dressings on the new state apartments around Fountain Court, to fit in with the old palace. His craftsmen from the Office of Works were brought in to provide the decorative work: Grinling Gibbons executed the woodcarving inside the palace as well as some of the carved stonework of the exterior; Jean Tijou wrought the iron balustrades; and Antonio Verrio embarked upon a series of allegorical paintings for the walls and ceilings of the state apartments.

While the work was carried forward, Wren transformed the Tudor water gallery into an apartment for the Queen, so that she could watch the progress of the palace and the gardens. In this gallery special cabinets were provided for the Queen's magnificent collection of Oriental porcelain. Although the water gallery was demolished on Mary's death, her collection was transferred to the new palace and still adorns the state apartments.

The beautiful gardens at Hampton Court were laid out by Henry Wise and George London. Although they have been altered over the years, many features of the late seventeenth-century formal gardens remain.

London

Kensington Palace. William III bought Nottingham House at Kensington from Daniel Finch, second Earl of Nottingham, in 1689. It soon became his main London residence, for he found Whitehall, with its fogs from the Thames bad for his health, and St James's Palace too uncomfortable. Nottingham House was, however, too small for a royal residence and the King commissioned Wren to enlarge and embellish the house, transforming it into Kensington Palace. William and Mary together began the improvements and alterations to the garden, which were brought to fruition by Henry Wise and Charles Bridgeman in the reigns of George I and II.

Anne, whose earlier memories of Kensington Palace may not have been too happy, for it was here that she had most of the difficult interviews with her sister that led to their estrangement, was to live in the palace for much of her reign and she died there in 1714. Building continued in her reign under the direction of Nicholas Hawksmoor, who designed the splendid Cupola Room, and also in the reign of George I. The Broad Walk and the Round Pond, with its radiating avenues, date from the reigns of the first two Georges, and the *route du roi*, now the Rotten Row, was the main approach to the palace from the east. After George II's death, it was never again occupied by a reigning sovereign, but it has continued to have royal associations up to the present day.

The Royal Naval College (Greenwich). (See also Chapters 10 and 11.) William and Mary founded by a charter, dated 25 October 1694, the Royal Hospital at Greenwich, which was to be the naval counterpart of Charles II's Chelsea Hospital. The work was undertaken by Christopher Wren and he completed what John Webb had always intended, a pair for the Baroque palace he had built on the west side of the great courtyard. Webb's original 1660s building is called the King Charles block: its pair is known as the Queen Anne block. Two other blocks, those of King William and Queen Mary, were both begun by Wren, but finished some years after his death by Nicholas Hawksmoor and Sir John Vanbrugh. Greenwich is still a building without a middle, as Queen Mary refused to close the vista from Inigo Jones's Queen's House to the river. In the King William block can be seen the Painted Hall, decorated by Sir James Thornhill between 1707 and 1727. In 1869 the hospital was closed and became the Royal Naval College.

Syon House. (See also Chapter 8.) At the end of the seventeenth century Syon House had returned, through marriage, from the Percys to the Seymours, in the person of Charles, sixth Duke of Somerset (the Proud Duke). He had been President of the Council in the early days of William and Mary's reign, but he found himself more in sympathy with Princess Anne in her quarrel with her sister than in William's court, with his many Dutch favourites. When the Princess wished to retire from court, he placed Syon at her disposal, and while she was living there she gave birth to a son who only lived a few hours. Shortly after the event, the Queen came to Syon not so much to commiserate with Anne, as to repeat her demands, which Anne refused, to cease her friendship with the Duchess of Marlborough.

13

THE HOUSE OF HANOVER

The First Three Georges

The first three Hanoverian kings presided over British affairs for almost one hundred years – excluding the years of George III's final illness. It was an era of much magnificence and glory for Britain. During these years a dynasty was secured, an empire was lost and another gained, and the nation was engaged – on the whole successfully – in three long wars. Beautiful houses, bold landscaping, marvellous music, painting, poetry and prose, fine furniture and prosperous farming were all features of these golden years. Everything that wealth and good breeding could create, or collect, pullulated in these one hundred years. But the reverse side of the coin was not so pretty. The sun shone brightly on Reynolds' superbly dressed men and Gainsborough's ladies apparelled in beauty. In the shadows however, was a world vitiated by human selfishness, cruelty, hatred and aggression: greed and corruption at the top; a mindless inanity in the middle; and the horrors of a struggling, moiling mob (who loved nothing so much as a public execution or whipping) at the bottom.

When George I entered upon this scene in 1714 he was fifty-four years old. The Act of Settlement of 1701 had declared that the Electress Sophia should succeed Anne on the throne of England. She died shortly before Queen Anne, and her son, George Lewis, became the heir.* He spoke virtually no English, and he greatly preferred his native Hanover to his adopted country. But it is not true to say that he never wanted the throne and would have preferred to stay in his Electorate. George was not a clever man, but he had much sound sense and he saw very clearly that his position as sovereign of a rich and powerful nation would immeasurably enhance his prestige with his fellow electors, and greatly assist in the aggrandizement of his beloved Hanover.

* See Chapter 12.

The new King was in no hurry to exchange the delights of Herrenhausen, and a country where his every word was law, for a court full of strangers and a constitution that would keep him tightly trammelled; it was not until 18 September that he stepped ashore at Greenwich – some seven weeks after Anne had died. But the succession was absolutely peaceful; the Tories were in disarray at the time of the Queen's death, and a Council of Regency consisting almost exclusively of Whigs, aided by George's personal representative, Graf von Bothmer, faced no serious problems pending the King's arrival.

George came to England without a wife, who was languishing a prisoner in the Castle of Ahlden, where he had confined her after an understandable, but ill-advised, affair with a Swedish Colonel of Dragoons, Count von Königsmarck, and where she was to remain until she died. But he did bring his son, who hated him for what he had done to his mother and for much else besides. The King was not a very pleasant man; he had inherited none of his mother's pleasing characteristics, for she would have made a good queen. He could be cruel, was sensual, greedy, mean and avaricious. His coldness, it was said, would freeze his surroundings. Nor was he good to look upon, being short with a sallow complexion and the blue bulbous eyes characteristic of his ancient Guelph family. He had, however, displayed much courage on the battlefield, and although not clever he was nobody's fool. He possessed a strong will with the determination to exercise it, and he was endowed with the usual Teutonic thoroughness.

Besides his son the King brought to England a household numbering almost a hundred. They included his Chief Minister in Hanover, von Bernstorff, and his secretary, Robethon – both, with Bothmer, to play an important role in English affairs. He also brought two hideously ugly mistresses: one tall, thin and angular called Ehrengard Melusina Schulenberg,* whom he eventually made Duchess of Kendal; the other large and very fat (who some say was his illegitimate half-sister by the odious Countess von Platen) called Charlotte Sophia Kielmannsegge, whom he created Countess of Darlington.

No sooner had George arrived in England than the Council of Regency ceased to function, and the King announced his list of ministers. The list was mainly the work of the two Hanoverians, Bothmer and Robethon, and not surprisingly, for they had always been the party to champion the Hanoverian succession, greatly favoured the Whigs; only one Tory name (Nottingham) was on the final list. The fact that the names were accepted with scarcely a protest in the face of a Tory

---

* To be accurate, Baroness von Schulenberg, George's *maîtress en titre*, arrived somewhat later.

parliamentary majority, shows that the King, although bound quite fully by the constitution, still wielded considerable power.

The ancient and powerful post of Lord Treasurer was abolished, for although collective responsibility by Cabinet lay in the future, it was hoped to avoid the concentration of too much power in the hands of one man. This, of course, was wishful thinking. The man who came to the fore in George's first ministry was a general – James Stanhope, who was appointed Secretary of State for the Southern Department. Lord Townshend was given the Northern Department, usually considered the more important; but Stanhope, a forceful character and undoubtedly without equal in foreign affairs, was in the Commons – until being ennobled in 1717 – and quickly arrogated to himself the principal power. Marlborough was reinstated as Captain-General, and for a year retained some influence in the ministry, but Lord Sunderland, much to his annoyance, was fobbed off with the political consolation prize of Lord Lieutenant of Ireland. A man who was appointed to the minor post of Paymaster (and raised to the Exchequer a year later) was Townshend's brother-in-law and fellow Norfolk landowner, Robert Walpole.

George's coronation took place on 20 October 1714, and was the occasion of the usual pomp and ceremony so beloved of the English people. But for the King it was something of an ordeal; he disliked ceremony intensely, and always preferred a quiet, simple life. When he went to the opera (music was his one concession to culture) he avoided the royal box, and at St James's Palace he occupied only two rooms, spending much of his time in the suites of his German mistresses, who wielded considerable power, and whose venality and greed made them most unpopular, and a favourite target for Lady Mary Wortley Montagu's scalpel pen.

At the beginning of 1715 the Tory majority of the past four years ended with a Whig victory at the polls, and there followed the all-too-familiar witch hunt. Of the principal offenders singled out for persecution, Bolingbroke, and a little later the Duke of Ormonde, took flight to James III's – the Pretender's – court, but Lord Oxford stood his ground and did a spell in the Tower. Had the Pretender taken the political advice of Bolingbroke, and the military advice of his half-brother the Duke of Berwick, instead of relying on mediocrities such as Ormonde and Mar, the course of history might well have been different, for in spite of the death of Louis XIV (the Pretender's most important supporter) on 1 September 1715, the Stuart chances of success were greater in 1715 than they were in 1745.

The Earl of Mar had been peremptorily dismissed from the office of Secretary of State for Scotland, and being a man perfectly prepared to turn his coat according to circumstances, decided that his best interests lay now with the Stuarts. At Braemar on 6 September 1715 he raised what was called the Restoration Standard, that symbol of hope intended to replace the constant round of intrigue and diplomacy in the council chamber with courage and skill on the battlefield. The First Jacobite Rebellion had officially begun, and very soon almost all Scotland north of the Tay was under Jacobite control.

For a brief period Mar moved with speed, and quickly occupied Perth. Edinburgh, with its prestige value and important arsenal, was his for the taking; but by now he had started to dither, failing to recognize that if rebellions are to succeed they must be prosecuted with ruthless vigour. This was particularly important for the Jacobites, for their cause in England had at best lukewarm support, but continuing success in Scotland might well have had sympathetic repercussions in England, and even persuaded the Regent of France to be more co-operative.

Mar held all the cards, and had he been a man of action and played them with determination he might have gained the kingdom for his new master, for with his superior numbers he could have swept the Duke of Argyll (the loyalist commander) and his troops out of existence, and joined hands with the rebel forces on the Borders and in northern England. But it was not to be. The Government got wind of the Duke of Ormonde's projected landing in south-west England and forestalled it; and in the north disaster struck almost simultaneously on a lonely moor near Stirling on 13 November, and at Preston a day later. Both Argyll and Mar claimed the victory at Sheriffmuir, but in fact it was an untidy, inconclusive affair, and for the Jacobites tantamount to defeat, for they needed more than that to preserve morale, and to prevent many of the clansmen from going home. At Preston, defeat of the combined Anglo-Scottish troops was decisive.

By 1716 King George was firmly established on the throne, and felt himself able to pay what he considered to be a long overdue visit to Hanover. It was assumed that in his absence his son would act as regent, but the first three Georges shared a common characteristic in that they hated their eldest sons (George IV did not have a son, but not to be outdone, he quickly developed a dislike for his son-in-law), and so only after much difficulty was the King persuaded to allow George Augustus limited powers as Guardian of the Realm. This dislike, leading to much bitterness and quarrelling between father and son, had a number of repercussions, some of them important. At the start of his reign George attended the meetings of his ministers, and although he could not understand what was being said (in private he would converse with them in French or dog-Latin) the Prince of Wales acted as interpreter. When the latter was banished from St James's, George gradually gave up attending the meetings, although decisions had to be submitted to him for approval. As a result there developed, very gradually, a true parliamentary monarchy with decisions taken in Cabinet by ministers working under a Prime Minister.*

The Prince of Wales was in many ways his father's son. He had shown great courage at the battle of Oudenarde; he was not very clever, had a nasty temper, was inclined to pettiness and could be most obstinate. But he liked England; he was not so shy as the King and he enjoyed a social life; moreover he had married a lady of great charm and considerable intelligence in Caroline of Anspach, and when the couple were expelled from St James's and moved to Leicester House their court was much sought after. It was to a great extent through Caroline that Robert Walpole arrived at the top, for they were to establish a close relationship based on ambition. But that was in the future, and meanwhile during the King's first absence in Hanover the Whig ministry was split down the middle.

Stanhope had accompanied the King to Hanover, and Sunderland, who by now had left Ireland and, chiefly through his ability to converse in perfect French, had gained George's confidence, found an excuse to join the royal party there. Townshend and Walpole, left in charge of affairs at home, mistrusted Sunderland, as well they might, but thought that they had a staunch friend in Stanhope. Here they were mistaken, for both Stanhope and the King listened very readily to Sunderland's subversive stories of how the two yeoman-ministers were undermining the loyalty of the Prince of Wales. As a result, shortly before the King's return in March 1717, Townshend found that it was his turn to be sent to Ireland, and not long afterwards Walpole joined his brother-in-law in the political wilderness, where they made a considerable nuisance of themselves in opposition.

While in 1717 no one would have cared to predict that Robert Walpole would rise to be the King's first minister for a longer period than any other man in our history, it was obvious that neither he nor his, at this time more highly regarded, brother-in-law could be kept from office for long. And indeed within three years a number of circumstances – chief among them being Walpole's successful efforts at a reconciliation between royal father and son – saw them back in uneasy harness with Stanhope and Sunderland. How long they would have survived is problematical, but shortly after their reinstatement came the second great crisis of George's reign – the bursting of the South Sea Bubble.

The South Sea Company had been granted a charter in 1711 by

---

* The First Lord of the Treasury did not become officially known as Prime Minister until the time of the Younger Pitt.

Harley; it never did much trading with the South Seas, and was in fact a finance company which did extremely well, even though the directors, motivated by greed, ignored obvious fmancial safeguards. In 1720 a proposal to take over a large part of the National Debt was sanctioned by Parliament in April – despite the attack on the bill by Walpole – and this sparked off a speculation bonanza. Already those in high places, including the King, his mistresses and many of his ministers, were heavily involved financially, and others from all walks of life poured money into the mass of small companies that now sprang up overnight to trade in almost anything. Parliament took action against the proliferation of these companies, and this caused a loss of public confidence and a rush to get out of the main company. Prices plummeted and thousands were literally ruined overnight. So great was the crisis that George was forced to tear himself away from the pleasures of Herrenhausen.

Someone had to be found to take control of a dangerously worsening situation. Walpole seemed the obvious man. He was out of office when the plan to absorb the National Debt was put to Parliament, and at the height of the crisis he had calmly gone off to his native Norfolk, from which rural retreat he surveyed the damage, until popular demand necessitated his return. On this occasion it was not his financial but his political acumen that was required, for the country was still financially buoyant. What Walpole succeeded in doing was to restore confidence and, at some personal cost to his reputation, rescue the King and his ministers from the mess they had got into. It did not immediately lead to promotion, but it helped him at court, and within a year or two accidents of death (including those of Stanhope and Sunderland), and a minor Jacobite plot, opened the door through which he went.

The remaining years of George I's reign were comparatively uneventful. Walpole and Townshend came to the top, and brought peace and prosperity. They even allowed Bolingbroke to return from exile, although they kept him pinioned, and his opposition – chiefly confined to vituperative attacks on Walpole through the medium of his paper *The Craftsman* – was largely unproductive. The King went on what was to be his last visit to Hanover in June 1727, taking with him the Duchess of Kendal and Mustapha, one of his two Turkish servants who had come to England with him in 1714. On the journey, in his brother the Duke of York's Castle at Osnabrück – indeed in the very room in which he had been born – he died from a stroke on 10 June. He was interred at midnight on 3 September near where he had died. And so George passed from this world a German by birth, inclination and burial.

His death caused little stir in England, for although he had been tolerated he had never been loved. His shy, retiring nature, his dislike of ceremony and his inability to communicate in the English language, were not likely to endear him to a people in whom he took little interest. But for all that he was not a bad king, even if his frequent absences in Hanover made difficulties for his governments. He was blessed with some very able ministers, and he had the good sense not to interfere with them; he was Britain's first constitutional King, and by his strict adherence to the terms of the Act of Settlement he greatly assisted the establishment of a parliamentary monarchy.

George Augustus was forty-three years old when Robert Walpole roused him from an afternoon nap at Richmond Lodge to tell him he was King. Unable to believe his good fortune he is alleged to have said, 'Dat is von big lie'. He probably said no such thing, but it may give some indication of his command of the English language. George II could, however, speak English quite adequately, and he came to the throne with a very fair working knowledge of the English political scene. Nevertheless, he remained a devoted Hanoverian; one of his first acts was to suppress his father's will, because it contained a scheme to dissolve the personal union of Britain and Hanover, and although he did not bother to go to his father's funeral, he visited the Electorate every other year.

The King, as we have seen, had as a wife a lady who was capable, cultivated and charming. Although there were occasional unseemly quarrels, George was much in love with Caroline, and she with him. He relied on her superior intelligence implicitly, even to the extent of consulting her over his mistresses. Walpole was right with one of his earthy bucolic remarks that he had 'the right sow by the ear', for with this King there was little to be gained through his mistresses, as long as Caroline lived.

The King and Queen had a family of two boys and five girls. The elder boy, Frederick, Prince of Wales, was born in February 1707 and spent his early years in Hanover; the other children – apart from a dismal period between 1717 and 1720, when George I forbade their parents to have custody of them – lived quietly at Leicester House until their father succeeded. George, and to an even greater extent Caroline, developed a paranoic hatred of Frederick (or Fretz as they called him), which made the relationship between George I and his son seem positively cordial. Frederick's arrival from Hanover in 1728 to live in England ushered in a deplorable relationship between parents and son, which lasted until the Prince's death in 1751, when his father shed a few crocodile tears (Queen Caroline had died in 1737).

George II was to reign for thirty-three years, and they were momentous years in the history of the nation. The ministry of Walpole; the War of the Austrian Succession; the second Jacobite rebellion, and the Seven Years War, during which Pitt laid the foundations of empire, were all a part of this important epoch. These great events touched the King very closely, although for others going on during his reign, such as the religious revival inspired by the Wesleys, the development of industry and the improvements in agriculture, he evinced little enthusiasm. His prime bent was military, and he possessed considerable knowledge of army uniforms and weapons; he much enjoyed reminiscing over his part in the battle of Oudenarde, and later that of Dettingen, where he was the last British King to lead his troops in battle. His formidable knowledge of the royal houses of Europe was of value to his ministers in foreign affairs, and although he often gave way only with bad grace – for he lacked confidence, and could ·be bullied into submission, but was too pig-headed to admit it – he was most careful, like his father, never to overstep his constitutional mandate.

The first important event of the new reign was the rise to prominence of Robert Walpole. This ugly, coarse, outspoken and grossly large man had proved his high capabilities in the last reign, and although George I never liked him he came to realize his ability. But Walpole's monopoly of power and his brilliant handling of the Commons made him many enemies among the opposition, who thought they now saw their chance to be rid of him, for it was well known that George Augustus was no longer his friend. And indeed Walpole was dismissed at the beginning of the reign, when the Government was entrusted to Sir Spencer Compton; but George soon saw that Compton was in no way fitted for the task, and Walpole's standing with Queen Caroline was sufficient to get him reinstated in a very short time. The relationship between Queen and first minister was a very happy one (although Caroline would argue fiercely with the great man on certain matters, such as the appointment of bishops), and before long George, too, came to regard Walpole as indispensable.

For fifteen years he held sway – derogatorily called Prime Minister by his many enemies – adroitly parrying the many assaults on his position, carefully manipulating the Commons, feathering his nest as occasion permitted, dismissing troublesome ministers, protecting the King's Hanoverian patrimony, and keeping the Government running peacefully on an even keel. In 1733 he was nearly unshipped over his most unpopular Excise Bill, and although with his famous remark, 'This dance it will no longer go', he withdrew the bill and survived, the opposition kept after him. Either one of two requirements could bring him down from his eminence – forfeiture of the King's confidence, or that of the people. Walpole had enemies at court, but not at the fountain-head; it was the public's chauvinism that eventually brought his long and fruitful ministry to a close.

Walpole was essentially a man of peace. In the same year as his unlucky Excise Bill he resisted strong pressure for the King to go to the aid of the Emperor Charles VI in the War of the Polish Succession, but when in 1738–39 British merchant vessels trading (for the most part illicitly) off the Spanish Main were subjected to seizure and search, the howl for war, strongly supported by the King and the Prince of Wales, was too great for the Government to ignore. War against Spain (sometimes known as the War of Jenkins Ear, after the shrivelled organ allegedly sliced off by the Spaniards and produced in a bottle to the Commons by the sea-dog of that name) was declared in October 1739. It was but the beginning of a long series of wars that were to occupy almost the whole of the remaining years of the reign. The opposition, who had forced this war on Walpole, did not rest content until in February 1742 they brought down his ministry.

What was called the War of the Austrian Succession was caused by the death of the Emperor Charles VI and the subsequent invasion of Silesia by Frederick the Great. France supported Frederick, and the English Government – now in the hands of Henry Pelham and Lord Carteret – seeing the danger to Europe in general and Hanover in particular from this formidable alliance, decided to stand by the Emperor's daughter, Maria Theresa. Thus a mainly naval war with Spain had quickly escalated to encompass military operations on the Continent.

In June 1742 a British, Hanoverian and Hessian army of some thirty thousand men assembled in the Low Countries under the command of the Earl of Stair – until the King, with his younger and much loved son, the Duke of Cumberland, arrived a year later. When George reached the army he found it encamped on the right bank of the River Main, endeavouring to keep the French from joining their Prussian allies. But the French commander had virtually succeeded in surrounding the British force, cutting them off from their base at Hanau. In the ensuing fight for survival near the village of Dettingen on 27 June, the great courage of the soldiery (and not least that of the King and his son) overcame the handicap of bad generalship, and the army extricated itself with honour from the trap. George is rightly given high praise for his gallantry, but often criticized for not taking Stair's advice to pursue the beaten enemy. Criticism comes easily, but pursuit must be rapid, and after a hard-fought battle lasting until 10 pm it is not lightly undertaken.

The war was to last nine years before France and Spain signed the Treaty of Aix-la-Chapelle in 1748, and little material gain, save maritime supremacy and a new song called 'Rule Britannia', came from it. Cumberland's fight at Fontenoy in May 1745 (in which he was wounded) could be termed an honourable defeat, and it marked the end of the British effort on the Continent; for, encouraged by English involvement in a major war the Jacobites, now led by Prince Charles Edward (the Young Pretender), decided that this was a favourable time to strike, even though French aid would be negligible. In July 1745, after an eventful and exciting sea journey, the Prince with a handful of companions, set forth upon a venture that was hazardous in the extreme. But the Jacobites knew that their time was running out: the Stuart flame was flickering, and might soon be extinguished.

The red and blue silk standard was broken at Glenfinnan on 19 August, but the immediate response of the Highlanders was not encouraging. However, an early display of loyalty by Lochiel and two other Chiefs had the desired effect, and soon the Prince had a fighting force of some two thousand; five hundred men, and the march to Edinburgh and the south was under way. General Cope, with an army of three thousand, was defeated at Prestonpans on 21 September, and although Edinburgh Castle held out, Charles was now recognized throughout most of Scotland. In London there was consternation, and the Government hurried troops over from Europe; in Scotland General Handyside replaced Cope, and in England the Duke of Cumberland and General Wade stood ready to block an advance upon the capital.

In November Charles, now with an army swelled to five thousand troops, crossed the Border and, on the 14th, Carlisle surrendered; soon Penrith, Lancaster and Preston were occupied, but the English response to the Jacobite cause had been disappointing. At Derby the momentous decision to turn back was taken, and the Highlanders – closely pursued by Cumberland – re-crossed the Border on 20 December. In January 1746 the Prince and his men won another resounding victory at Falkirk. But it was to be the last, for now the tide began to turn. There was dissension among the leaders about what course to pursue; some Highlanders began to desert, and those who remained steadfast found that success in a few minor raids was little compensation for the hardships to be endured in the cold and hungry winter months.

Brought to battle at Culloden on 16 April by the Duke of Cumberland (who the day previous had celebrated his twenty-fifth birthday) the clansmen, in a short fight contested with fearful savagery, found the odds against them too great, and the last chances of a Stuart restoration vanished in the mists of Drummossie Moor. The carnage of the field was appalling, for Cumberland ordered his men to slay the wounded.

When Walpole's ministry came to an end in 1742, the man who in practice assumed control was Lord Carteret, while serving as Secretary of State first under Lord Wilmington and then Henry Pelham. The King liked Carteret, who had a sound grasp of foreign affairs. However, he constantly made himself obnoxious to his colleagues, and after much complaining the King was eventually prevailed upon to dismiss him.

One of Carteret's most vociferous opponents was William Pitt, who had begun his political career among those Whigs in opposition to the Government, and who was very soon *persona non grata* with the King. The Prince of Wales had married Princess Augusta of Saxe Gotha in 1736, and his court at Leicester House (which he leased from 1743) inevitably became the centre of opposition to his father's ministers, and for a time Pitt was among those who looked to the heir for political advancement. However, the Prince's death in 1751 was a setback for this faction, although Pitt found favour with the King's mistress, Lady Yarmouth.*

But while royal patronage was a prerequisite to success for some, Pitt's greatness shone like a beacon amid the surrounding murk, and he achieved power not because of royal favour, but in spite of it. His genius was to make the last years of George II's reign exciting and rewarding, for although nominally he was under the Duke of Newcastle, his was the skill that turned disaster into triumph during the Seven Years War, and broke the power that France had built up before and after Aix-la-Chapelle.

Nevertheless, his path to success was not an easy one, and made no easier by the fact that he suffered severely from gout, and at times from fits of deep depression. The vicissitudes of his career illustrate very clearly the degree of influence and the ability for interference that the Crown still retained. Persuaded by the Pelhams to take Pitt into the Government in 1746 as Paymaster – where his refusal to accept the usual rich emoluments of that office gained him the trust and admiration of an important section of the community – the King did his best to edge him out in favour of Henry Fox, whom he liked, after Henry Pelham's death in 1754. He was not successful until November 1755 when, following a particularly brilliant speech in which Pitt attacked the treaties made to secure the defence of Hanover, the King – touched on a most sensitive spot – demanded his dismissal.

But the early disasters in the Seven Years War gave Pitt a further chance, and he was back as Secretary of State in 1756, only to be dismissed again the following year, partly because the King was angered at his attempts to save Admiral Byng from execution after the loss of Minorca, but chiefly because the Duke of Cumberland, who disliked Pitt even more than the King did, refused to take command of the allied army in Germany while Pitt was Secretary of State.

It is scarcely to be wondered at that with such fickleness at the top the war got off to a bad start. But Pitt was a man who could rise above the

---

* Amelia von Walmoden, whom he created Lady Yarmouth.

passions of the hour; he is said to have told the Duke of Devonshire, 'I know that I can save this country, and that no one else can.' If he did actually say it, his performance over the next few years amply fulfilled the promise. The immediate period after Pitt's second dismissal was called by Horace Walpole an 'inter-ministerium', which clearly could not last for long, and after a break of only three months the country at last got a strong, workable war administration, nominally under Newcastle, but with Pitt directing the war policy. It was a policy that did not neglect the principle of engaging the foe on the mainland of Europe, but looked for its chief success through the blockading of the French naval ports, so that troops could be sent without interference to attack and seize the enemy's possessions in North America, India and other parts of the world. Moreover, it was a policy carried through with all the ruthless, strong brilliance of a successful military dictator – for that is virtually what Pitt became. He would brook no opposition or interference from his colleagues; he yielded power to no man, but assumed control of all the important departments of State. Incompetent generals and admirals he dismissed, and put in their place brilliant young men of his own choosing.

Success was not universal; there were operations launched against the coast of France that were expensive failures, but there were enough victories in 1759 alone to keep the church bells busy – the capture of Guadeloupe, Ticonderoga and Fort Niagara, the winning of Canada at Quebec and the triumphs of Minden and Quiberon Bay. Before and after that year Robert Clive (of whom the King had a very high opinion) had defeated the French in India, and gained the East India Company two rich provinces; in 1760 Lord Amherst captured Montreal, and a little later Martinique, Dominica, St Lucia and Grenada fell to British arms. Thus did Pitt, with leadership that inspired the whole nation, with commanders who displayed great daring, and with soldiers and sailors who showed great courage, gain the victory and an empire.

George Augustus did not live to see the concluding triumphs of the man he could never like, but whom in the end he had sufficient sense to come to terms with. Nevertheless, he had lived long enough for the Great Commoner – as men called Pitt – to give him, now at seventy-seven and in declining health, that which he most coveted for his kingdom – military glory. At about 7.30 on the morning of 25 October 1760, King George II died from a heart attack in his water-closet, brought on – it is said – from overstraining. The place and manner of his death are often considered undignified. Maybe, although sudden death is seldom dignified, and there must be worse places than the privacy of the lavatory for the departure of the soul from the bondage of the body.

George II was the last King to be buried in Westminster Abbey. If his death had been undignified, his burial was infinitely more so, with everyone jostling for a better position in the Henry VII Chapel, and the Duke of Newcastle alternating between tears – he could be relied upon for a good cry whenever the occasion demanded – and running around the Chapel quizzing the mourners, and then keeping his feet warm by standing on the Duke of Cumberland's robe.

George III's long reign (it was the second longest in British history) divides itself, in so far as the King was concerned, into three phases: the years of apprenticeship, the years of fulfilment and the years of decline and oblivion. He came to the throne aged twenty-two, a slightly priggish young man, totally inexperienced in affairs of State, but when he left it sixty years later he was loved as a man and honoured as a King, for he had raised the dignity of the Crown to a high pinnacle – from which, during the last ten years of his reign, his feckless son, as Regent, did his best to dislodge it.

George William Frederick was born on 4 June* 1738, at Norfolk House, where his father – forbidden the royal palaces – had temporarily settled. When Prince Frederick died George was thirteen years old, and a shy rather backward boy – until he was eleven he could scarcely read. Now, with his grandfather the King into his late sixties, the education problem became an urgent one. The old King was quick to ensure that George's tutors were changed from those that his father had appointed, and who were sympathetic to the late Prince's politics. The results were not at first satisfactory, but by the time he was eighteen the new Prince of Wales had a working knowledge of French, German and Latin, knew some Greek, had a broad understanding of science, mathematics and history, and had developed a lifelong interest in astronomy.

His mother, Princess Augusta, played little part in her son's education, except to introduce into his life her close friend, the handsome, worldly, well cultivated and ambitious Earl of Bute. In Bute the lonely and uncertain boy found a confidant whom he felt was the only person – outside his family – that he could trust. From the age of eighteen until a few years after his accession, when he came to realize Bute's political limitations, he relied entirely upon the Earl, whom he insisted upon appointing Groom of the Stole when, in 1756, he was granted his own establishment.

George grew to be fairly tall, and he carried himself with poise and dignity. He had inherited the family's protruding eyes, but these did not

---

* In fact he was born in May according to the Julian calendar still in use in Britain, but when the Gregorian calendar was adopted in 1752 his birthday fell on 4 June, a date celebrated annually by Eton College in memory of his active interest in the school.

affect the general impression of a strong, quite handsome face. Bute paid much attention in his teaching to the advantages of a morally healthy life, the dangers of allowing women to meddle in politics, and the need to avoid some of the worse follies of his grandfather. On the whole George was an obedient pupil. There had been an early affair with a little Quaker girl from Wapping, and more serious intentions towards the beautiful Lady Sarah Lennox. But when Bute said 'no' to any thoughts of marriage, George was sensible enough to heed the warning of his 'dearest friend'. He learnt through Bute many of the responsibilities of a constitutional monarch, and he had the strength of character to accept them.

Soon after his accession, and with the love for Lady Sarah thrust aside, George dutifully looked towards the eligible princesses of Germany for a bride. Bute was his mentor in this, as in all things, and the lady eventually selected was Charlotte of Mecklenburg-Strelitz – a plain girl from an unimportant duchy, who spoke no English and seemed to have few advantages, although in her younger days (and she was only seventeen when she married) she was gay and vivacious. George may have regretted her plainness, but his high sense of morality forced him to be absolutely faithful to her, and she bore him no fewer than fifteen children, of whom only two died in infancy. She lived to be seventy-four, and had much to put up with; nevertheless the marriage was a happy one, and George undoubtedly loved her. Charlotte had no wish to meddle in affairs of State (and anyway, true to Bute's tuition, George never confided in her), but she ruled her daughters with a rod of iron, and if she was in awe of the King, they were certainly in awe of her. On 22 September 1761, a fortnight after their marriage, the King and Queen were crowned in Westminster Abbey.

The first ten years of the reign – the years of apprenticeship – were most unhappy ones for the King, and the popularity of the Crown was at a very low ebb. It was axiomatic in the eighteenth century that at the beginning of a reign the ministry could expect to undergo changes, for the King still exercised a personal choice of those who were to govern his kingdom. In the case of the Georges it was usual for the heir to have been in opposition to the policies of his predecessor. This was less so at the accession of George III on account of his youth; nevertheless, the new King had no great liking for his grandfather's ministers. Changes there would be, but there was no question – as is sometimes asserted – that the King wished to arrogate power to himself and rule despotically. George III had stricter principles than either of his two predecessors on the throne; the trouble was that he was inclined to confuse principle with prejudice.

Bute was destined for high office as soon as his protégé succeeded.

This got the reign off to a bad start politically, for Bute was as unsure of himself as was the King at this time, and would have been far more at home in a university than in the Cabinet. His advice was taken on everything; both he and the King were anxious for peace with France at almost any price, and this at once got Pitt into opposition. Furthermore, Pitt had the support of the City merchants and professional classes, all of whom feared that an inexperienced King and an irresolute minister would lose all that had been gained in the war. In October 1761 Pitt resigned, followed a few months later by Newcastle, which left the way open for Bute to become First Lord of the Treasury with George Grenville leader of the Commons.

Bute's year in office was disastrous; the ridicule and opposition that he met with in Parliament, and the oft-expressed hostility of the London mob, was directed as much against the King as against himself, for it was known that George still gave Bute his full confidence. Between them they managed to get the peace ratified by Parliament, and immediately afterwards – in April 1763 – Bute resigned. His resignation coincided with the notorious issue No. 45 of *The North Briton*, whose author, John Wilkes, had for some time been lampooning Bute, and who in this issue got himself involved in lengthy proceedings for seditious libel. This and his later expulsion from the House of Commons only indirectly affected the King, but rabble rousers were anathema to George, and he heartily approved of the action taken against Wilkes. He saw his flaunting of authority as the sole cause of the unpleasant and dangerous riots of the London mob – whereas such riots were endemic and sprang from the appalling poverty of the people, who took every opportunity to express their resentment against authority.

Between Bute's resignation and North's appointment there were five first ministers. Grenville held sway for the longest time, and during his two years in office he submitted the King to interminable lectures on how he should conduct business with his ministers. Grenville did in fact have some cause to complain, for although George no longer relied implicitly on Bute, he was – until the final break in 1766 – inclined to consult him behind his first minister's back. Grenville ran into difficulties over the Regency Bill, which the King felt was necessary after his illness at the beginning of 1765 – it was not a very serious illness, and probably in no way connected with his later troubles – and in June of that year George turned to his ailing uncle, the Duke of Cumberland, who briefly took charge of affairs, and was appointed Captain-General during this period of ministerial uncertainty. Cumberland died that October at the age of forty-four, and was succeeded by the Marquess of Rockingham, Pitt (now Lord Chatham), whose broken health verged on insanity, and then the Duke of Grafton. In January 1770 the King asked Lord North to form a government; he was to remain in office for twelve years.

A young and inexperienced King had had to learn his craft from scratch. Many mistakes were made, but there might have been more and they might have been worse. He had been called upon to play a very personal role in the perilous politics of the time, and George had learnt a lot and gained confidence. In Lord North he had found a man who could relieve him of much of the wearisome task of everyday politics. North received harsh treatment from Junius (the brilliant contemporary journalist), and in subsequent years has been constantly vilified. In fact he was an excellent House of Commons man, and had won his way up the political ladder through hard work and sound sense. But he was a dangerously useless war leader, and as an eighteenth-century Prime Minister became vitally necessary only in time of war, his ministry has been condemned as an utter failure.

The King and North worked happily in tandem; they shared the same views on the role of the monarchy, financial matters, the tiresome business of Wilkes, and the problems arising from the taxation of the American Colonies. A more confident and mature George proved on many occasions to be the dominant partner, which gave the impression of a King interfering too much in affairs of State. The attempts to tax the American Colonies – starting with Grenville's Stamp Act, which had to be repealed – and their general subjection to the mother country, met with almost universal approval in England; but the subsequent mismanagement of the drift into war and the war itself by North's ministry backed by the power of the throne, brought the King's popularity to its nadir. The fall of North was inevitable, as was the granting of independence to the colonists; but both were matters of the greatest sadness for George, who in a moment of utter dejection drafted his abdication. He thought he saw in the loss of the Colonies a betrayal of his trust as his people's sovereign.

It seemed impossible that he could weather the storm, but through a fine display of political adroitness and courage he succeeded. The King was forced to take back Rockingham in succession to North, which in itself was an unpleasant pill to swallow, for Rockingham soon set about introducing legislation to reduce the King's influence in politics; but when he suddenly died, worse was to follow. For the man who now came to the top was the brilliant, but erratic, Charles James Fox, who shared the leadership with the discredited North. George detested Fox (who proceeded to make even more astringent curtailments of the royal prerogative), and once again thought of abdication, but instead he meekly gave way to these unpleasant impositions, and bided his time. He had not long to wait for Fox to overstep the mark in introducing the unpopular East India Bill, which seemed to give to Fox the patronage he had taken from the King.

George was ready; and interfering, for the first time, unconstitutionally he killed the bill in the House of Lords. He followed this by dismissing Fox, and asking William Pitt, a younger son of Chatham, to form a minority government. For three months, backed by the power of the Crown, Pitt hung on, and in the 1784 election the people showed their approval for the King's action. George had acted with courage and political acumen, while Fox had failed to realize the strength of the monarchy.

In Pitt the King had found an outstanding young minister who did much to raise the prestige and popularity of the throne. However, George was not the man to sit quietly in the wings; until his health finally broke down his sense of duty kept him in daily touch with his ministers and left him little time for a family life, which, like his regal duties, had its problems.

The King and Queen spent much of their time at Buckingham House, which George had bought in 1762. It was far too small for his huge family, but most of what little money he was prepared to spend went on Windsor Castle, which became his favourite residence, and so there was little left for this house or his two Kew residences – Kew Palace (the White House) and the Dutch House. After his illness in 1788 the King visited Weymouth (such was his popularity by then that the town went *en fête*, and the whole tour was a triumphal progress), and liked it so well that he started the fashion for seaside holidays by making regular summer visits there. George III never visited Hanover; at the beginning of his reign – largely because he wished to differ from his grandfather – he would speak disparagingly of the Electorate, but he sent his sons to be educated there, and took considerable interest in the regency that governed for him.

George was a kind parent – perhaps too kind – although his love for his daughters was too possessive, resulting in his keeping them spinsters as long as he could, and far longer than he should. His seven sons were much more of a problem; the combination of paternal indulgence and educational methods that did not work, proved disastrous. Almost all the sons ran into debt frequently and behaved badly, and most of them managed to get themselves into a series of unsavoury scrapes – 'the damndest millstones about any government', is how the Duke of Wellington described them. George Augustus Frederick, because he was the heir, caused the King the most anxiety. He was generous and kindly, but his character was weak, and he thought of little but his own pleasures; he became an easy prey for calculating courtesans and actresses – such as 'Perdita' Robinson – and the natural figurehead for unscrupulous politicians, such as Charles James Fox.

A great deal has been written about the King's illnesses, and this is no place to continue the debate. The present Prince of Wales, in the foreword to John Brooke's book on George III, is of the opinion that there was nothing wrong with the King's brain *before* the onset of his illness, and the author of the book writes, 'On the basis of our present evidence we can say that the King was not mentally ill',* and he thinks that the diagnosis satisfies the requirements of porphyria. They may well be right, and the outward signs of insanity in the later illnesses are very understandable when we consider the brutal treatment the poor patient was constantly submitted to at the hands of the aptly called 'mad doctors'.

The first illness (if we exclude that of 1765) came in June 1788, just after the King's fiftieth birthday, and lasted off and on until February 1789. By November, with no telling for how long the King would remain incapacitated, Pitt was forced into considering a Regency Bill, and there began a fearful wrangle as to the power of the Regent, who would of course be the Prince of Wales. The Prince was genuinely moved by his father's plight, which is more than can be said for Mrs Fitzherbert, whom he had married illegally in 1785, or Fox, his chief political supporter. Both saw golden prospects, and together with the Prince insisted on full powers. Fortunately the King's recovery came in time, bringing with it much discredit to the Prince and Fox for their behaviour, and a realization by the public of the true worth of the King they had so nearly lost.

George had not long recovered before Europe was shaken by the cataclysmal events in Paris. As the Terror increased its senseless bloodletting, the more horrified and alarmed became the English establishment; no one doubted but that it could happen in London; the Gordon Riots† were still fresh in many people's minds. One effect of the Revolution was to draw the King and the Prince of Wales closer together, and another – more important and more lasting – was the declaration of war against Revolutionary France in 1793. The King interested himself closely in military matters at the beginning of the war, and was pleased to appoint his favourite son, the Duke of York, Commander-in-Chief in 1795. He did not fare too well, but the fault was

---

* *King George III*, by John Brooke. Constable, 1972.

† In June 1780 the eccentric and unreliable Lord George Gordon, at the head of a band of Protestant supporters, petitioned Parliament to repeal the Roman Catholic Relief Act of 1778. The London mob, who needed little encouragement to riot, got out of control and quite a few people were killed and many houses, chapels, shops, etc., were sacked before order was eventually restored by the army.

certainly not entirely his. The fact is that the broad-bottomed Pitt–Portland coalition was incompetent at waging war.

Between 1793 and 1800 the Government were faced with a number of unpleasant situations. The British army was forced to evacuate The Netherlands; the King's coach was pelted with stones by a hungry mob; there was a serious financial crisis; the navy mutinied; and the French, ever quick to pierce Britain's Achilles heel, attempted a landing in Botany Bay and stirred up Irish nationalism into open rebellion. Pitt's solution for the Irish troubles was union, and the Act of Union was passed in 1801; but when he attempted to introduce Catholic Emancipation the King was adamant, regarding it as a violation of his Coronation Oath, and Pitt had no alternative but to resign.

In February 1801, while Pitt's successor, Addington, was endeavouring to form his ministry, the King again became seriously ill. This illness was of shorter duration than the 1788 attack, but more serious than the third illness, which was to occur in 1804; more than anything the comparatively rapid succession of the attacks caused concern for the future, and were disconcerting for a government engaged in the prosecution of a major war. It is true that Addington had negotiated a peace with Napoleon in 1802, but everyone knew that it was nothing more than an armistice, and indeed war broke out again a year later.

From 1804 (which was also the year that saw the resignation of Addington and the return of Pitt) the King's long twilight can be said to have begun. His illness of that year was of very short duration, but his eyesight began to fail, and his constitution was being weakened by the ravages of his malady. But his brain remained very clear, and until his final illness he still ruled as well as reigned. It must have been with very mixed feelings that on Pitt's death in 1806 he found it necessary to include Fox in Lord Grenville's so-called Ministry of all the Talents, but when the old reprobate died shortly afterwards the King admitted that the country could ill afford so great a loss at so perilous a time.

On 25 October 1810 the King had ruled for fifty years, and his popularity reached its zenith with the celebrations for the event, But his last illness was upon him, although it was not until the following July that the doctor's hopes and expectations of recovery were finally shattered, and George III sank sadly, but slowly, into oblivion. On 5 February 1811 the Prince of Wales (with irksome limitations to his power for a period of one year) was proclaimed Regent, and the last years of the reign are his story.

The old King lingered on, very much alone, shuffling about in the cold north rooms of Windsor Castle that were his prison, wearing a violet dressing-gown to which was pinned the Garter star. His face, now adorned with a magnificent beard, could occasionally be seen at the window, and in his better days he was known to acknowledge the salute of the ensign of the guard. Relief from the long vigil he had kept with death came on 29 January 1820.

George III was the only one of the first four Georges to achieve more than fleeting popularity. It was in a way a negative popularity, based on what had gone before and what was known to be coming. Nevertheless, it was sincere and spontaneous (as was very evident when the mad James Hadfield took a shot at the King at Drury Lane Theatre in May 1800); and in part at least it sprang from the recognition that here was a God-fearing, good, honest and humble man, who according to his lights and within his limitations had done his best to be a just and fair King. Posterity owes George much, for he founded the Royal Academy; he was a great collector of books (at his death he had sixty-five thousand) and his son, fulfilling his father's wish, gave this fine library to the nation, where as the King's Library in the British Museum it can be enjoyed by all; and in the realms of science his patronage of William Herschel and the pension he gave him, enabled the great astronomer to build his telescopes and produce his important observations on the universe. All that George III did for the arts, and it was much, he paid for out of his own money. If these were the actions of a mad King, it is a pity that more sovereigns were not similarly afflicted.

The reigns of the first three Georges were years of great promise for the arts, for building and landscaping, and for discoveries in science, chemistry and philosophy – for this was the Age of Enlightenment. And yet the first two sovereigns, although like George III delighting in music, contributed practically nothing to this golden era. What aesthetic enjoyment George I and II obtained, came mostly from their beloved Herrenhausen in Hanover, and they were obsessed with matters military and inclined to be frugal, obstinate and suspicious, which are characteristics unlikely to promote patronage. George II's son, Prince Frederick, broke this philistinism and became a well-informed collector of pictures and patron of the arts, and his son, who became George III, left much that the public can still enjoy. He made an extremely valuable collection of pictures from Italy of the standard set by Charles I, and he commissioned many portraits from Allan Ramsay, Gainsborough, and Johann Zoffany, although Reynolds was not a favourite with him. George III was also deeply interested and closely involved in agriculture. And although there is now nothing to be seen of his farming activities in Windsor, the public in general and the wool trade in particular have benefited from his introduction of merino sheep into Britain.

A procession of talent paraded across the hundred years. Isaac Newton was at work throughout the reign of the first Hanoverian, and, like him, he died in 1727. Handel played himself back into court favour (there had been some displeasure in Hanover) with his Water Music, as George I was rowed down river from Whitehall. Chippendale was busy making his beautiful furniture, Josiah Wedgwood his porcelain, and in 1768 Sir Joshua Reynolds became the first President of the Royal Academy, which he had helped to found. Among the giants in the field of architecture were Robert Adam (the best of four brothers), William Chambers, who designed Somerset House where the Academy opened its rooms in 1780, James Wyatt and his nephew Jeffry Wyatville. Landscape gardening reached its zenith through the genius of William Kent, Capability Brown and Humphry Repton.

Battle of Culloden (Inverness), 16 April 1746. Prince Charles Edward Stuart's hopes of regaining the throne of his forebears vanished for ever in the mists of Drummossie Moor, when his army of Highlanders was decisively beaten by William Augustus, Duke of Cumberland ('Billy the Martial Boy'), the second son of King George II. The defeat of the Young Pretender's troops, and the subsequent appalling carnage of the field, effectively put an end to further Jacobite attempts to upset the Hanoverian dynasty. The battlefield is very accessible, being only a little east of Inverness, off the Inverness–Perth road (A9). The National Trust for Scotland have a useful information centre on the site of the battle.

Eilean Donan Castle (Ross and Cromarty), featured prominently in the abortive Jacobite rising of 1719. The prime mover in this rising was the Spanish Cardinal Alberoni, who organized two simultaneous invasions of Scotland's west coast. The main one under the Duke of Ormonde failed to reach the south-west coast, but a small subsidiary landing, by Jacobite leaders and 307 Spanish soldiers, was made from a fleet that entered Loch Alsh on 2 April (o.s.) and made Eilean Donan the main arms and ammunition base. On 9 May, three government warships appeared in the Loch, and the small garrison left in the castle (the remainder of the force had marched to join the clansmen and give battle at Glenshiel) of two officers and forty soldiers was forced to surrender, and the castle was destroyed.

At the beginning of the century the castle was carefully and skilfully restored to its original condition, and is a beautiful and fascinating place to visit in the summer. It is situated some twenty miles west of Fort Augustus. The A87 runs through Glenshiel (the site of the battle) and on to Eilean Donan.

Hampton Court Palace (Middlesex). (See also Chapters 8, 10, 11 and 12.) When George I arrived in England in 1714, the interior decoration of William and Mary's new palace at Hampton Court remained unfinished. The King commissioned Sir John Vanbrugh to supervise the completion of the Queen's state apartments and the little rooms in the north-east corner of Fountain

Court. Their boldly moulded ceilings and massive fireplaces echo Vanbrugh's country house interiors.

By 1732, the old Tudor block on the east side of the Clock Court had fallen badly into decay. George II therefore commissioned the Palladian architect, William Kent, to rebuild the range in Tudor Gothic style to match the flanking buildings. Within these new buildings, Kent created a new set of state apartments, now known as the Duke of Cumberland's Suite.

Houghton Hall (Norfolk). The home of George I's and George II's First Lord of the Treasury, Robert Walpole, was built between 1722 and 1735. For more than twenty years (the longest period of office held by a First Minister), Walpole governed England under the first Hanoverians, and the beauty of this house and the treasures it contains gives the lie to the occasionally expressed description of the great statesman as having been little more than a rather bucolic Norfolk squire. Apart from many fine portraits and the lovely Kent furniture and room designs, there are some magnificent tapestries depicting the Stuart sovereigns. Houghton Hall is two miles north of the A148, almost exactly midway between King's Lynn and Fakenham.

London
The British Museum (see also Chapter 9), acquired George III's magnificent library in 1823 through the munificence of his son, George IV. The printed books were housed in the King's Library, where they are still kept and can be viewed by the public. They are also available for consultation and research, but for this a reader's pass to the British Library's Department of Printed Books is required.

The Dutch House at Kew was built in about 1631 by a prosperous London merchant called Samuel Fortrey. George III and his family moved into it while his vast castellated palace was being built on the banks of the river. In this house the Dukes of Kent and Clarence were married on the same day in 1818, and Queen Charlotte died in it. It is a beautiful miniature palace, with an interesting collection of memorabilia connected with George III and his family.

The Dutch House stands quite close to the main gate of Kew Gardens. George III's large family occupied many residences in and around Kew Gardens and the Green, but most of them have now gone. The White House, which stood very close to the Dutch House, was demolished in 1802, and the vast Gothic folly by the river was pulled down in 1828 without ever being occupied; much of the flooring and staircases was used in the reconstruction of Buckingham Palace. But some twenty minutes' walk from the Dutch House, at the south-west corner of the Gardens, there still stands Queen Charlotte's Cottage, which is open to the public in the summer months. It was used for picnics and as a shooting lodge in Queen Victoria's time, and she gave it to the nation to commemorate her Diamond Jubilee in 1897.

Visitors to the Dutch House should linger in the lovely Kew Gardens, with the magnificent collection of shrubs, trees and herbaceous plants, which reflect the interest that first Augusta, and then her son, George III, had for the beauty of the land and for rare species of plants. In 1760 Kew Gardens consisted of only about nine acres, but the King enlarged them when he took land previously belonging to Richmond Park. Many of the exotic species came from the expeditions of the distinguished botanist and biologist, Sir Joseph Banks, who for many years was George III's principal adviser. When Kew ceased to be Crown property in 1841, the Gardens had extended to fifteen acres, but the first Director, Sir William Jackson Hooker (to whom we are indebted for the importation of many delightful Himalayan rhododendron species) soon extended them to some 250 acres, and built the Palm House. The Great Pagoda was built by Sir William Chambers to commemorate the marriage of George III and Queen Charlotte.

National Maritime Museum, Greenwich. Prince Frederick's Barge, designed by William Kent in 1732, is on display in the Barge Room. In the eighteenth century, barges were a very important means of transport, for the sovereigns and their courtiers used the river for getting to their riverside palaces and houses. The Queen's Shallop, built in 1689 for Mary II, can also be seen in the Barge Room, and the museum is full of the most beautiful and interesting pictures, memorabilia, and many models and objects of interest.

Royal Mews, Buckingham Palace, contains, among the other royal coaches, the **Gold State Coach** which was built to the design of Sir William Chambers and used for the first time by George III to open Parliament in November 1762. This gorgeously gilded juggernaut is embellished on the sides, front and back with panels painted by Giovanni Battista Cipriani, and on the roof stand three cherubs supporting the Crown; these represent the genii of England, Scotland and Ireland. The coach was used by George IV for his coronation, and by every other sovereign since that time.

The Tower of London. In **the Armouries** (see also Chapters 8, 10 and 11) can be seen the two-handed State sword of James Francis Edward Stuart, known as the Chevalier de St George and James III by his supporters, and the Old Pretender by his opponents. It was carried before him at his State entry into Dundee after he had been proclaimed James VIII of Scotland and III of England in January 1716.

The Royal Naval Museum (Portsmouth), George III's State Barge, a thirty-seven-foot-long oak boat, was also used to convey Lord Nelson's body from Greenwich, where it had lain in state, to Whitehall for burial in St Paul's Cathedral. It was recently found to be infested with woodworm, and has been very skilfully restored.

Battle of Sheriffmuir (Stirling, Central Region, Scotland), 13 November 1715. When George I ascended the throne in 1714, the Jacobites – now owing allegiance to James II's son, known to his enemies as the Pretender – enjoyed a considerable following. Their fugleman in Scotland was John Erskine, sixth Earl of Mar, but he proved himself irresolute and incompetent. In the first Jacobite rising, three battles were fought at Preston, Sheriffmuir and Glenshiel. The most important of the three was Sheriffmuir, where John Campbell, second Duke of Argyll, had slightly the better of an inconclusive and untidy battle against the greatly superior (numerically) force under the Earl of Mar. The defeat at Preston on the same day as this fiasco, and the disheartening performance of James Stuart who came to Scotland shortly after Sheriffmuir for a brief spell, tore the entrails out of the Jacobite movement for the time being. An attempt three years later to rekindle the flames of rebellion ended in defeat at Glenshiel.

The battlefield of Sheriffmuir remains very much as it was more than two hundred and fifty years ago. It lies about five miles north of Stirling, between the two minor roads that run from Dunblane and Bridge of Allan to Blackford. In fact, the present Dunblane-Blackford road runs through the site of the rival positions at the outset of the battle (Argyll's line probably crossed the road near the site of the MacRae Cairn, and Mar, whose right overlapped Argyll's, had much of his force north of the road and some seven hundred yards east of Argyll), and from the Gathering Stone, just north of the MacRae Cairn, there is a good view of the battlefield.

Traquair House (Peebles), (see also Chapter 10), has been owned by the Stuarts from 1491 until the present day. In the middle of the seventeenth century, it became one of the great strongholds of the Catholic faith, where mass was celebrated in secret at the top of the house in a tiny chapel approached by a concealed staircase. In the two Jacobite risings the Stuart Earls of Traquair, as might be expected, supported the Pretenders but the fourth and fifth Earls found time to carry out alterations and in 1737 the Bear Gates, which stand at the end of an imposing avenue of sycamores, were erected. Tradition has it that the last person to pass through them was Prince Charles Edward Stuart in 1745, and the fifth Earl swore that they should remain closed until a Stuart restoration. They have never been opened since that time.

Windsor Castle (Berks.). (See also Chapters 3–5 and 11.) The first two Hanoverians scarcely ever came to Windsor, but George III lived there from November 1804, off and on, for the rest of his life, and made some modest alterations to the castle. One of these was the introduction of Gothic windows in the Upper Ward building to replace Hugh May's round topped ones. His architect James Wyatt replaced the two Charles II staircases, with their walls and ceilings painted by Antonio Verrio, with a straight-running one that opened at the top into the King's Drawing Room. George III was also responsible, through the demolition of Charles II's chapel, for making a passage way round all the State Apartments; to do this, he roofed in what was then an open courtyard, and now forms the Waterloo Chamber.

14

THE HOUSE OF HANOVER

George IV and his Brother William

⟨✦⟩

George Augustus Frederick was born at St James's Palace on 12 August 1762; he was, therefore, fifty-seven when he became King in January 1820, and the oldest monarch until that time to have ascended the throne. But for the past eight years he had experienced full regal powers, and so his fancies and foibles (and they were varied and many) were well known to his ministers, and indeed to the public.

What a very strange person he was; although not, as is sometimes made out, an entirely bad one. It is a small recommendation to say that he was probably the best of George III's seven sons, for most of the others were disastrous, and even the Dukes of Clarence and Cambridge might be contenders for that doubtful honour. But certainly he suffered, in the eyes of the public, from being associated with their dull brains and coarse habits, from both of which he was free. However, he was no paragon of virtue and filial piety. As a young man he was always heavily in debt, he drank deeply and fornicated frequently (usually in dubious company), and although he may have been no more than typical of the young bucks of his time, he always contrived to go one better than most of his cronies among whom, of course, he occupied a more elevated position. His relations with his father ran true to Hanoverian form. George III, understandably, thoroughly disapproved of his debts, his heavy drinking and extravagant living; but later the Prince became very close to his mother, and was a most solicitous and generous head of the family.

Vanity and selfishness could be added to his faults, as they could be to those of many of his predecessors, but there was much to like about the man. In his early days he was handsome, elegant and suave, and although his continual heavy drinking and consumption of gargantuan meals was to play havoc with his figure and render him gross and unwieldy outwardly, he always remained possessed of an inner charm

275

and graciousness to which many were to pay tribute. He was undoubtedly the most intelligent of the Hanoverians, and the country owes him a debt of gratitude for his planning of many beautiful buildings and vistas, for although he spent prodigiously it was not always for himself. He was a connoisseur of pictures and furniture, but in building up his superb collection (much of which is now enjoyed by countless thousands) he was not averse to taking expert advice.

When the Prince was little more than twenty, his uncle of Cumberland (George III's egregious younger brother) introduced him to Fox, and immediately George became Fox's devoted friend and follower. It would be untrue to say that he became a Whig, for although when Fox joined the Ministry of All the Talents in 1806 the Prince attained political importance, he really had little use for politics and he was diametrically opposed to much that the Whigs stood for. But in the early days his devotion to Fox (a further cause for his father's displeasure) was such that he would accept any of his policies.

Until he became too corpulent, George enjoyed an outdoor life of riding, shooting and sailing, and seemed to live in a man's world, nevertheless, throughout his life he relied upon his many mistresses to give him that comfort and understanding that he never properly obtained (until the closing years with Knighton) from any of his male companions. Understandable perhaps, for men like Beau Brummel, Philip Francis and Sheridan were not made to be soul-mates. From an early age there was a constant procession of ladies. One or two he loved and left with children; others he merely loved and would (so he thought) have liked to marry, but none of them – Mary Hamilton, 'Perdita' Robinson and Lady Melbourne – was suitable, and 'Perdita' cost his father a lot of money. But in 1784 he met the desirable widow, Maria Fitzherbert, and immediately succumbed to her charms far more seriously than with any of his other paramours.

For more than a year he followed her around, and when she went abroad he plied her with passionate love letters. In vain did Fox, and many others, try to persuade him that marriage would be disastrous, and indeed, under his father's Royal Marriage Act of 1772, illegal. But it was marriage or nothing, for Mrs Fitzherbert was a devout and highly respectable Roman Catholic, who would not become his mistress. So, on 15 December 1785, the Prince married her in the drawing-room of her London home. He loved her to the end, and when he died her locket was round his neck; but the ardent passion of the early years did not last, and the grace and loveliness of Lady Jersey was to tempt him from Mrs Fitzherbert's bed before the break in 1794. But while they were together he insisted on her being treated with the courtesy and respect due to a princess, and his extravagances in Brighton, which led to the Pavilion, first took shape round her humble home there. In London he set her up in a splendid house close to his own Carlton House, which he had been given in 1783, and on which he had already spent more than £50,000.

In August 1794 the Court of Privileges declared the Prince's marriage illegal, and although – in spite of his new love – he was probably sorry to sever his connection with Mrs Fitzherbert, he had come to realize the necessity of having a suitable and legal wife. He was driven to this course partly because it seemed possible that none of his brothers would produce an heir, but largely because his father agreed to settle his debts when he was suitably married.

The totally unsuitable choice of a bride was due chiefly to his utter indifference about whom should be the lady once the decision to marry had been taken, but his father must share some of the blame for the unfair condition he imposed upon him. Princess Caroline of Brunswick was the Prince's first cousin, being the daughter of George III's sister, Augusta. She was unattractive, coarse in her behaviour, and dirty in her person. She was certainly vivacious, but possessed most of the defects and few of the charms of vivacity. Furthermore, she was often high-handed, sharp-tongued and insensitive, and her whims and foibles were of the kind that could do nothing but irritate her husband.

From the start the marriage was a complete disaster. It was un-necessary and unkind to attach Lady Jersey, who was well known to be the Prince's current mistress, to Caroline's suite on arrival, but it made little difference to the immediate feelings towards each other that the bride and bridegroom exhibited. Caroline complained that George's portrait greatly flattered him, and George took one look at Caroline and called for brandy. The wedding took place on 8 April 1795, and for a few months the couple tolerated each other's company, and a girl, Charlotte, was born in January 1796. But before long the Prince's dislike turned to hatred, and Caroline moved out of Carlton House. However, the King and Queen – who in the early years sided with their niece and daughter-in-law – insisted that she keep her apartments there. Mrs Fitzherbert was back again, having triumphed over wife and mistress.

King George made Caroline, Ranger of Blackheath, and she even-tually settled there in Montague House, where her behaviour gave rise to such scandal that in 1806 the Government was forced to set up a Commission of Enquiry. The Delicate Investigation, as it was called, cleared the Princess of being the mother of the child, William Austen, whom she had adopted, but although proof positive was lacking there could be little doubt of her adulterous behaviour. The result of this enquiry lost Caroline the King's favour – not only for the smear it cast upon her character, but because she, a woman, had allowed herself to meddle in politics. For the next eight years, until her departure for the Continent in 1814, Caroline continued her strange, rather desolate life, living mostly at Kensington Palace and being permitted to see her daughter once weekly. She had a knack, helped perhaps by her good humour and cheerfulness, and the impression of being hard-done-by, of commanding a wild devotion among the common people. The undoubtedly genuine, and volubly expressed, acclamation she received, infuriated her husband, whose own standing had sunk to unplumbed depths of execration.

One of the reasons why the Princess of Wales received the sympathy and plaudits of the Londoners was that they could not understand why her extra-marital affairs, which were conducted comparatively discreetly, should be the subject of an official enquiry and condemnation, whereas those of her husband, which were far more blatant, should be accepted, although possibly not approved. It was about the time of the Delicate Investigation that the Prince first became enamoured of Lady Hertford, whose husband, the second Marquess, was one of those whose advice on pictures and furniture George so greatly valued. She was already a grandmother, but that was seemingly to her advantage, for almost all the ladies who shared the Prince's bed were his senior by some years. The liaison was still flowering in 1811 when George III's doctors finally pronounced his malady as incurable, and the Prince of Wales was, in February of that year, sworn in as Regent, with full powers of sovereignty being granted him twelve months later.

The dignity and power that George had now achieved did little to alter his manner of living. He celebrated the event with a huge ball at Carlton House (to which his wife was not invited), and his boyish enthusiasm, energy and zest for life continued unabated, as did his unpopularity. He did not appear to realize (and might not have cared had he done so) that more was required of those placed in high authority than to take their ease on an island of luxury oblivious to the ocean of poverty that lapped around them.

The Regency opened in a blaze of glory with Wellington's victories in the Peninsula, and then Napoleon's overthrow, which was followed by the splendour of the allied sovereigns' visit to London. It was indeed a brilliant era, and the Regent himself did much to make it glorious, but while he enjoyed himself at Brighton, Ascot and Cowes, the first tremors of Parliamentary reform and industrial upheaval, which would shatter into fragments the structure of his world, were taking place. The Corn Law riots of 1815 were followed by mob violence throughout the country the next year, and in 1819 in St Peter's Field, Manchester, the Yeomanry were used to disperse some fifty thousand people who were listening, for the most part quite peacefully, to a radical orator preaching reform. Several innocent people died in what became known as the Peterloo massacre.

When King George III died in January 1820, England's new Queen Consort was in Italy, living with an Italian called Pergami, whom she had made her Chamberlain. She had gone abroad in 1814, it was hoped for good, and travelled widely and behaved wildly – for she was of course more than a little mad. And yet it is impossible not to feel some sympathy for her, because she had been treated abominably by her husband – and others. She was not even informed of the death of her daughter, Princess Charlotte, who, having married Prince Leopold of Saxe-Coburg, died in childbirth at Claremont in 1817. Nevertheless, when she learnt that she was Queen Consort she brushed aside those sent to try to buy her off, and landed in Dover on 5 June 1820, and quickly became the centre of a triumphal procession to London.

There followed a most distressing few months. While the King discreetly withdrew from London, the Queen – hailed and applauded by the mob – attended in person the debate in the House of Lords, which in the form of a Bill of Pains and Penalties amounted to the trial of the Queen for her conduct with Pergami. Had the affair not taken place abroad and with a foreigner, this could have been a trial for high treason. From July until November their lordships heard a mass of witnesses, and debated this sorry business; in the end the majority in favour of the bill was so small as to convince the Government that to send it to the Commons would never do. The matter was allowed to drop. The King had been anxiously seeking a divorce since 1817, and the worry over this was said to be partly the reason for his serious illness in 1820, but a divorce was not to be had. His ministers had thoroughly mishandled the whole affair, for action might have been successful if taken while Caroline was living abroad.

The King accepted defeat with as good a grace as possible, and by the summer of 1821 he judged that excitement had died down sufficiently for him to stage his coronation on what, as might be expected, was a scale greater than most. It must have been a source of some satisfaction to him that the Queen, who had been unsuccessful in her claim to be crowned, was refused admittance to the Abbey. Her popularity was now diminishing, and this sad, half-crazed woman died a few weeks later. The coronation banquet, the last of its kind to be held in Westminster Hall, was a gargantuan feast, and the King's Champion, in the person of young Henry Dymoke (for his father, as a parson, judged himself unfit to appear on horseback in full armour) threw down the gauntlet, also for the last time.

At the time of his coronation the King's popularity had begun to increase, and it was to gather momentum during the tours that he undertook soon afterwards. George had always loved important State functions and pageants, for which the Regency had been renowned. The climax was now to be reached in these visits, for after 1822 he was to live very much in retirement. When he learnt the news of the Queen's death, the King was in his yacht off Holyhead on the way to Dublin. This and the weather delayed matters somewhat, but after the funeral (which was the occasion of more rioting in London) the reviews, receptions and levees got under way. Everything went extremely well, and the King greatly enjoyed himself, the more so because part of the visit took place at Slane Castle, the home of the Marquess and Marchioness Conyngham – Elizabeth Conyngham had recently replaced Lady Hertford in the King's affections.

In September George set out for Hanover, on the way visiting the battlefields of Waterloo with the Duke of Wellington. His German subjects gave him a rapturous welcome, and this visit, too, was a tremendous success. The last of these grand tours was to Scotland in the summer of 1822, and once again he was fêted wherever he went. The pleasure that his visit gave the Scots was only slightly diminished by his appearance at the Holyrood House levee in full Highland dress with flesh-coloured pantaloons under his kilt. George IV was the first sovereign to visit Ireland since Richard II, and Scotland since Charles II, and his Hanoverian subjects had not seen their King since the days of George II.

By the time George became Regent his feeling for the Whigs, which never extended very much further than his hero worship of Fox, had undergone a change. They rather naturally expected an improvement in their fortunes, but their leadership was in disarray, and the Regent did not entirely trust them to prosecute the war so forcibly as the Tories. He worried over the problem to such an extent that he became suddenly and seriously ill – in much the same way as was to happen during the divorce trouble – but when he recovered he attempted a compromise and offered the Whigs some ministries, which their leaders Lords Grey and Grenville indignantly refused. Thereafter their party's relationship towards George became one of frustrated enmity. Spencer Perceval was confirmed in office as Prime Minister, and when he was shot in the House of Commons* he was succeeded by Lord Liverpool, who remained in power until suffering a paralytic stroke in 1827.

That George had other interests which he greatly preferred to politics did not mean that he refrained from interference or played no personal

---

* The Prime Minister was murdered on 11 May 1812 by John Bellingham, a man whose mind had become seriously deranged through his being ruined in the war.

part in the big issues of the day. On the abdication of Napoleon in 1814 it was he who successfully pressed for the return of the Bourbons, whereas the Czar and the Emperor of Austria had leanings towards Napoleon's son, the King of Rome; on such important matters as Catholic Emancipation and Parliamentary reform he held strong views; he exercised his prerogative of mercy wisely and widely; and on Canning's death in 1827 he virtually formed the Cabinet himself.

It was left to the King's brother to cope with Parliamentary reform, but George had to come to terms with Catholic Emancipation. When Liverpool died there was a grave problem about who should succeed him. There were three obvious candidates: Wellington, Peel and Canning. A few years back George could not bring himself to speak to Canning, who had championed the Queen, held decidedly liberal views and was for Emancipation; but the King had been forced to accept him into the Cabinet as Foreign Secretary, and was greatly pleased and impressed by his work there. In the end Canning was given the premiership, and the Tory party was immediately split (with Wellington in high dudgeon childishly resigning his command of the army), which left Canning little alternative to forming a government of a Whiggish complexion. The King quickly became enchanted with this great statesman, and before the question of Emancipation could ripple the peaceful waters, Canning died.

The next Prime Minister, Lord Goderich, was clearly not up to the task. The King liked him, for he allowed him to do very much as he pleased, but after only five months Goderich resigned. The King then had either to send for Wellington, or cut adrift from the Tories (whose treatment of Canning he had not forgiven), and accept a Whig administration. He chose the lesser of the two evils, and Wellington became Prime Minister. Here was a man who would not stand for the King's obstinacy and caprice; in April 1829, after much complaint, George gave his assent to the Roman Catholic Relief Act.

Some two years before he became King, George was introduced to a doctor called William Knighton. Knighton was a competent doctor, a capable financier and an ambitious man. He quickly made himself indispensable to George, who found in him a friend on whom he could count for help and counsel in private and State matters. From starting as the Regent's confidant in a more or less private capacity, he worked his way into becoming Keeper of the Privy Purse, and in all but name the King's Private Secretary. His influence was very great, and not nearly so bad as is sometimes represented; he was devoted to the King and served him unselfishly from 1818 until George's death.

The King's final years, spent very much in retirement at Royal Lodge, which he had had built in his own inimitable style, and

Windsor Castle, where Jeffry Wyatville's beautiful Waterloo Chamber and great Gothic designs had cost the nation not far short of a million pounds, were made much more pleasant by the attentions of Knighton and Lady Conyngham. The latter, a plump, kindly and rapidly fading beauty, was not clever, but very shrewd, and was probably closer to the King's mind than to his body. Even the Duke of Wellington (who disliked her vulgarity as much as he did the parties at Royal Lodge and the junketings on Virginia Water that he was obliged to undergo) often found it expedient to consult with her on matters of State before he approached the King.

George IV died at Windsor Castle on 26 June 1830. Although his final illness did not begin before the middle of April, he had grown unnaturally vast, with his legs and ankles swelling alarmingly, over the past two years. His last visit to Brighton was in 1827, and thereafter he had become something of a recluse, and seldom appeared in public, which was a pity, for the people had at last come to terms with him, and on the rare occasions that he did appear he met with something approaching approbation. He was never a particularly religious man, but towards the end he seemed to find the Bible that Knighton had given him a source of inspiration and encouragement, and the Sacrament, which he took in his room with Lady Conyngham, a real and meaningful comfort.

The people did not mourn the loss of their King; no one seemed particularly sorry or glad at his departure – the mood was mainly one of indifference. He certainly had not enhanced the prestige of the monarchy; on the contrary he left his successor the daunting task of trying to put it back on its pedestal. Nevertheless, there must have been a few who could overlook his faults, and remember him with kindness, for his ebullience, marvellous mimicry, personal charm and human qualities – even some of his weaknesses – must have made him an amusing companion, and at times an endearing one.

He was succeeded by Prince William Henry, the third son of George III, who had been born at Buckingham House on 21 August 1765. Unlike his eldest brother, whose attempts to join the army, or do something useful, had been constantly vetoed by his father, William was put to work in the navy at the age of thirteen. This entirely new venture for a royal prince proved at first to be a great success. The boy was given no choice in the matter. It was the King's solution for putting a bit of discipline into this unruly, tubby lad with a pineapple-shaped head surmounted by a crop of carrot-coloured hair. But William took to the life at once, and, over-coming the obvious difficulties of being a prince, was quickly popular with his shipmates. Moreover, his seamanship was to win golden opinions from such distinguished officers as Admiral Digby and Captain Nelson.

The Prince had joined the navy in the middle of the American War of Independence, and just at the time that the Spaniards and French decided to take advantage of Britain's involvement and declare war. There was, therefore, plenty of excitement for the young midshipman in the *Prince George*, for the ship was under Admiral Rodney's command, and among other actions was present at the battle of Cape St Vincent. No one could impugn William's courage, and he found himself something of a hero when the triumphant fleet returned to England. He even became, for a very brief period, the pampered favourite of his father and mother. But his boisterous behaviour on shore, his amatory escapades, and a serious difficulty that arose between the Prince and a senior officer detailed, on orders from the King, to supervise and discipline him, caused the King to beach his son for a while once peace had been declared.

The Prince spent the last two years of the war in American waters, returning home in 1783 in the *Barfleur* under the command of Lord Hood. There followed two years in Hanover, in every way unsatisfactory, before he was appointed lieutenant in 1785 and went to sea again in the *Hebe*. On being transferred to the *Pegasus*, and promoted to post-captain, he saw service in the West Indies. In command of a ship the Prince proved himself a stern disciplinarian, which was no bad trait had it not been accompanied at times by brutish behaviour. Undoubtedly his health suffered from the heat, which made his temper more uncertain, but this could not account for one particularly drawn-out and unfortunate affair with an officer under his command called Isaac Schomberg. Considerably older and more experienced than the Prince, Schomberg was tactless and overbearing, and no doubt gave his captain some cause for complaint. But the whole shabby business spotlighted William's inability at this time to work in harmony with his colleagues.

In April 1789 he was created Duke of Clarence, and his naval career was virtually at an end. Up to the rank of captain, although at times difficult to serve with, he was undoubtedly a competent officer, but now the Admiralty considered that neither by temperament nor experience could he be promoted to a command befitting a royal duke. As a royal duke William became eligible for a Parliamentary grant, and he received £18,000 a year. But this was not nearly enough to meet his requirements. It is difficult to know what these requirements were. He did not build palaces (indeed he was more inclined to give them away*),

* When the Houses of Parliament were destroyed by fire in 1834, William offered Buckingham House as their new home.

he had no interests in the arts, his drinking habits were moderate, and he was no gambler. Yet he was often heavily in debt. On leaving the navy the Prince settled first at Richmond, and then at Roehampton. During his naval career there had been one or two ladies he thought he could marry, but his father immediately took steps to prevent it. Now he startled the highly respectable inhabitants of Richmond by bringing to live with him a lady of very dubious reputation called Polly Finch. However, she was jettisoned after a comparatively short time when, in 1790, he fell in love with the well known actress, Dorothy Jordan.

William was now twenty-five years old, a likeable, rumbustious man, not over-endowed with intelligence, but honest, outspoken and without a trace of hypocrisy. He had been as wild and unpredictable as his brothers, with whom he had usually sided in their frequent disagreements with their father, but now he felt the urge for a more settled life. In Mrs Jordan he had found an ideal companion, for she was easily the best of all the royal mistresses. She already had children of her own, and in the course of their long association she was to give William five boys and five girls – young Fitzclarences, some of whom were to become a great trial to their father.

The couple lived in happy domesticity at Roehampton, and later at Bushey Park (where William had been made Ranger), for twenty years. Mrs Jordan pursued her career on the stage – with the absolute minimum breaks for child-bearing – and William, who much to his annoyance was not given employment during the French Revolutionary War, occupied himself with speech-making in the Lords, and exchanging scabrous jests with his cronies. The end came in 1811, when William, having carefully considered the advantages that marriage would offer, happened to meet Catherine Tylney-Long, a charming heiress who, he thought, would not only give him respectability, but settle his debts as well.

At the time, and subsequently, there were those who severely censured William for shamefully abandoning Mrs Jordan, and for leaving her to die in poverty and misery after she had supported him financially for many years. He did make her the best pension that he could afford, and she must have known that abandonment was an occupational hazard of mistresses (especially royal ones); nevertheless, much of the mud sticks. Nor did he have any success with Catherine, and with one or two other girls to whom he directed his heavy-handed courtship – young ladies, understandably, proved nervous of a middle-aged man regarded by many as something of a buffoon, heavily in debt and with ten bastards, even though he was a royal duke.

Matters became more urgent when, in 1817, Princess Charlotte died, and William, only two removes from the throne, knew himself to be a better risk than both his elder brothers. Eventually, after many humiliating rebuffs, he married Princess Adelaide of Saxe-Meiningen on 13 July 1818, in the Dutch House at Kew. The Duke of Kent married Princess Victoria of Saxe-Coburg in the same room at the same time. The Clarences lived for a year in Hanover, but then returned to Bushey, where it was quickly apparent that Adelaide would have a most beneficial effect upon William. She was a very virtuous lady with fixed ideas on what was best for her husband, and she seemed very ready to mend his ways – certainly his language became noticeably less lubricious. Lacking in humour, and with definite prejudices, which she stuck to obstinately and which were to be a handicap when she became Queen, Adelaide nevertheless in her quiet persistent way guided William's life into a more useful and sensible groove than that along which it had so far run. Sadly they had no children that survived, but she proved a loving and understanding stepmother to the unruly brood of Fitzclarences.

In 1827 Canning hit upon the idea of resuscitating the ancient office of Lord High Admiral that had been in abeyance for over a hundred years, and suggested that the Duke of Clarence should be appointed. The post was shorn of some of its former power, and the Duke was not to be a member of the Cabinet and could only act (except when at sea) through a Council. Many years earlier George III had written to Lord Hood saying, 'William was ever violent when controlled', and so it proved now and on other occasions. William had his own ideas about his duties, and would not tolerate control by a Council, some of whose members he accused, rightly, of obscurantism. In a little over a year he felt obliged to resign, for his somewhat high-handed behaviour caused too much disapproval. This was the navy's loss, because he had done much in the short time within the scope allowed him, and could have done more had he stayed.

George III's second son, the Duke of York, died in 1827, and from the time of his resignation as Lord High Admiral, William waited with ever-growing impatience (gargling against the germs that might yet deprive him of the prize), for the day when he would be King. It was to be 26 June 1830, when William was just short of sixty-five. The people soon found that they had a very different type of king to deal with, and one who was a great improvement on his predecessor. William abhorred the extravagance and flamboyance of his brother; great economies in the royal establishments were immediately put in hand, and ceremony was replaced with informality. The image that he desired to create, and which came to him naturally, was of a simple, unaffected, rather hearty man, who preferred to meet the people on foot rather than to be seen from a distance in a carriage. He even expressed a wish to dispense with his coronation; but in this he was overruled. Nevertheless it was to cost a mere £30,000 – some £200,000 less than the late King's.

This was a difficult and dangerous time to begin a new reign. There had been great unrest throughout the country during the past year or two; with the Industrial Revolution a totally different way of life, involving heavy machinery and new technologies, had come into being. There was a great shift from the country to the towns, where many had to live in squalor, hideously overworked and underpaid. The old order was changing – sometimes violently; a new middle class demanded better representation, and England's aristocrats looked upon this darkling scene with misgiving and misunderstanding. William was as much adrift as the others; he was not a clever man, but he had a lot of common sense. He realized that no government could withstand for long the emotive urge for reform; he did not like the unpopularity that was sometimes his lot, but he kept on course, doing what he considered was best for the country – for he was a great patriot. Above all, he was in almost everything prepared to allow his ministers to make the decisions, and he would stand by them so long as, in his opinion, they did not endanger the State. This perhaps entitles him to be called the first fully constitutional monarch.

The momentous events that led up to the passing of the Reform Bill in June 1832 can be only briefly outlined here. When William succeeded, the Tories under the Duke of Wellington were in power, but the Duke was soon to make it clear in a speech that he was in no mood for any kind of reform. It was a speech that also made it clear that his government must fall. After the election the King, with much apprehension, sent for Lord Grey – a somewhat austere man and a dedicated countryman, who accepted his political role out of a deep sense of duty – and agreed to back him, with certain reservations, in his attempt to pass the Reform Bill through Parliament.

The extreme measures introduced in the Commons by Lord John Russell may well have taken William by surprise – as they did the Tories, and even some Whigs – and it is much to his credit that he did not flinch from what he had been persuaded was in the best interests of the country. There were many – including Wellington and Queen Adelaide, whose Tory sympathies were a target for the mob – who genuinely feared that reform would lead to disaster and even revolution. William was not of this number, although he was extremely reluctant to meddle with the existing constitution, which he considered to be second to none.

The Bill was introduced in March 1831, and the Tories, having let it pass its first reading, failed by one vote to defeat it on its second. The Tory blundering eventually persuaded the King to dissolve Parliament, and an overwhelming Whig majority at the election ensured the safe passage of the Bill in the Lower House; but in the Lords it could not hope to fare well. The King at first would not countenance the creation of new Whig peers to swamp the Lords. All along he had hoped for a sensible compromise – he could never understand why neither party would agree to a coalition in the national interest.

When he did eventually give assurances to the Whigs, which seemed to give the Prime Minister carte blanche to create new peers, he was later to renege on finding that Grey himself showed signs of cold feet. The Whigs felt that they had been let down, and Grey resigned in April 1832. But in nine days he was back, for the Tories had no support and could not form a government. William had to agree to Grey's demands. He did, however, write to individual Tory peers suggesting that they should now withdraw their opposition, and as they realized that the battle was lost, they mostly absented themselves, allowing the Bill to go through. It received the royal assent on 7 June 1832.

These two years had been a severe test for any king who still exercised a personal role in the government of the country – no matter how limited – and William had come through them on the whole quite well. It was understandable that his popularity should suffer at the time of Grey's resignation, but in the general euphoria that marked the passing of the Bill it regained some of its former shine. Not that the King was given much time to sit back and enjoy any reflected glory there might be, for within a year he was plunged into another crisis, this time an Irish one.

The problem centred round two pieces of legislation: the Coercion Act – a measure to strengthen law and order – and the reform of the Irish Church. It was the latter that caused the King most concern, although in the end it was the troubles connected with the Coercion Act that decided Grey to resign in the summer of 1834. The reform of the Irish Church was almost a repeat performance of the Reform Bill, with the Tories in opposition, the King wavering (with the shadowy and malign figure of his ineffable brother, Cumberland, breathing Orange sympathies down his neck), and Grey urging him to create new peers. The end, too, was much the same, with the Tories eventually surrendering.

When Grey resigned, William reverted to his favourite theme of a coalition under Lord Melbourne, who had proved himself a most able and circumspect Home Secretary, and who had been recommended by Grey. Melbourne received his instructions at Brighton, and although he went through the motions of forming a coalition he knew very well that Wellington and the Tories would burke the idea – which they did. From the start the new Prime Minister had little chance of making a success of his first ministry, for the King was no longer happy with the Whigs – in particular two, Lords Brougham and John Russell – once the restraining hand of Grey had gone. The Government lasted just four months before the King dismissed them – the last British monarch to exercise this ancient prerogative. But he was not to be free of them for long. The Tory Prime Minister, Robert Peel, presided over a minority government, which was defeated in March 1835, and Peel resigned. The Whigs were back, less Brougham, whose factious conduct in Scotland during the last ministry, and his published abuse of the Queen at its fall, had made him obnoxious both to the King and Melbourne. This government, with its uneasy relationship with the King, was to remain in power for the rest of the reign.

While the principal problems of William's reign were centred round the demand for reform and innovation at home, there was much of concern to the country going on abroad, and Lord Palmerston at the Foreign Office became accustomed to the King's incursions into the field of foreign affairs. William was straightforward, honest and free from guile, which virtues could be a handicap to anyone caught up in the vortex of European power politics, and to make matters worse, he was inclined to be stubborn and dogmatic. He expressed his views very forcibly on such questions as the independence of Belgium – which he greatly favoured, not least because he had an abiding hatred of the French, who he feared might take the country over – the Turco-Greek troubles, the Portuguese Civil War and Russia's expanding sphere of influence in the Middle East. He was an amateur at the game and he made mistakes, but he had plenty of common sense, and his careful study of events meant that on occasions his opinions were of value to his government.

Apart from a very happy marriage, William's family life was stormy. His bastard children were grasping and ungrateful, and his heir, Princess Victoria, was kept away from the court as much as possible by her domineering and aggravating mother. The Duchess of Kent had been widowed since 1820, and although her thoroughly German temperament did not make it easy for her to enjoy life at her brother-in-law's court, she made very little effort to please; on the contrary, she went out of her way to be bloody-minded to the King and Queen. She refused to attend the coronation, or allow her daughter to, and she was constantly rude to the Queen.   .

The last straw came in August 1836 when William discovered that she had appropriated a large suite of rooms in Kensington Palace, some of which he had specifically ordered her not to use. He was determined to hold on to life until Victoria came of age, so that the Duchess would not be Regent. Shortly after the Kensington Palace affair, replying to the loyal toast at a banquet at Windsor at which the Duchess and Victoria were present, he made that point very forcibly, adding, 'I should then have the satisfaction of leaving the royal authority to the personal exercise of that young lady [pointing to Victoria], and not in the hands of a person now near me, who is surrounded by evil advisers, and who is herself incompetent to act with propriety in the station in which she would be placed.'

The King's wish was granted, for he died on 20 June 1837 – Princess Victoria had come of age on 24 May. The happy, boisterous, people's King had become in the last years an eccentric, disillusioned, rather sad old man; but he retained to the last his courage, honesty of purpose and ·loyalty – these are characteristics of a good man, which he was. He was not a good King, yet he was not a bad one. He had succeeded to a tottering throne; he steadied the wobble and left his successor with something of a chance.

George IV never did anything in a small way. His appetite was gargantuan, his capacity for liquor unbounded, and when he built or rebuilt a house, palace or castle, prodigious sums of money were made available for the finest craftsmen to create a building of awe-inspiring grandeur. He was, too, a talented and well-informed collector of pictures, tapestries, furniture and armour, and some of his magnificent collection can be enjoyed by the public today.

It is true that much of what George created was for his own pleasure – Carlton House in London and the Royal Pavilion at Brighton, for example – but at the same time it was his wish that the King of England should live, and be seen to live, in palaces worthy of his international importance, and his work at Buckingham Palace and Windsor Castle had this, as well as his own comfort, in mind. His was the inspiration behind the marvellous concept created by John Nash of the Regent's Park and the grand carriageways connecting the Park with the royal palaces; he wanted London to be a capital city distinguished by its beauty.

George IV's successor, the bluff, hail-fellow-well-met William IV had no taste for the arts and little appreciation of beauty. He seemed determined to show publicly how much he disapproved of his brother's extravagances; but at least it can be said that, although at times their fate hung in the balance, he did not in fact destroy what had been created.

Brighton
The Royal Pavilion. This gorgeous folly was built by George IV, when he was Prince Regent, in various styles and over a number of years. The Prince was first attracted to Brighton in 1783, when he installed Mrs Fitzherbert (whom he married illegally in 1785) in a modest house overlooking the Steine. In 1787 he commenced a much grander building under the guidance of Henry Holland, which was completed in 1802 and was a very pleasant, orthodox period house. However, the Prince soon tired of this, and, taking Humphry Repton's advice,

he ordered the rebuilding along Indian architectural lines; but the man who finally accomplished the rebuilding was John Nash, and by this time the unpredictable Prince was going through a Chinese phase. The result in 1821 was the exotic extravaganza that we can enjoy today – a curious amalgam of Moghul, Ming and Muscovy. Inside, the banqueting hall is delightfully vulgar, but almost all of the other rooms are exquisite, and beautifully furnished.

The Prince's horses were also to share this life of luxury, for at a cost of £70,000 a most magnificent stable block was built – over a period of six years – in Indian style with an iron and glass cupola eighty feet wide and sixty-five feet high. A building that once housed horses, which were the envy of the equine world, has now been converted into the superb Dome concert hall.

Claremont (Surrey), as it stands today was built by Clive of India (the huge bath, that can still be seen, must have been the envy of every nabob in the country!) who bought the property from the Duke of Newcastle in 1768, and decided to pull down the house that Vanbrugh had built for himself. But the royal history of this lovely Georgian house belongs to a later period, and is associated chiefly with George IV and Queen Victoria.

In June 1816 Claremont was given to George IV's only child, the Princess Charlotte, as a gift from the nation on the occasion of her marriage to Prince Leopold of Saxe-Coburg, and here she died in childbirth in November 1817. The Prince continued to live at Claremont for some years, and it was here that his niece, Princess Victoria, spent some of the happiest days of her childhood. Later when she became Queen, she and Prince Albert often used the house as a country retreat before they bought Osborne. Victoria gave the house to the exiled King Louis-Philippe of France in 1848, and he died there two years later. The last royal owners of Claremont were Queen Victoria's youngest son Leopold, Duke of Albany and his wife Princess Helen of Waldeck. Claremont is now a girls' school, but open to the public on certain Saturdays.

Edinburgh
The Palace of Holyrood House. (See also Chapters 9 and 11.) George IV's State visit to Scotland in 1822 was a great success – in spite of one or two sartorial slip-ups – and the throne that he used for the levee in the palace can still be seen in the Throne Room.

London
Chapel Royal, St James's Palace. (See also Chapter 8.) On the evening of 8 April 1795 the Prince of Wales (later to become King George IV) with all due reluctance married Princess Caroline of Brunswick in this chapel.

Stratfield Saye (Berks.), was the house that the Duke of Wellington eventually decided to buy with the £600,000 voted by Parliament in gratitude for the victory he had won at Waterloo. He had looked at many grander houses, and, indeed, his liking for Stratfield Saye seems to have been more for the position and the estate (at that time 5,000 acres) than the house. For the next six years or so he dreamed up designs in his head – and indeed on paper – for the building of a vast mansion in the north-east corner of the park. Fortunately there was insufficient money for the project, and so the Duke remained in this very lovely and comparatively compact house, most of which had been built in about 1630 by Sir William Pitt.

After his great military career the Duke did, of course, turn his attention to politics, and in 1828 became King George IV's Prime Minister. The house is full of interesting objects and furniture that were given to or collected by the Duke, including some superb china. In the stable block, the present Duke has laid out a fascinating exhibition of his famous ancestor's clothes and accoutrements, together with some items of historical interest. Stratfield Saye is about ten miles south of Reading off the A33 Basingstoke-Reading road.

Windsor Castle (Berks.). (See also Chapters 3–5, 11 and 13.) George IV and his architect Jeffry Wyatville, with the help of some five hundred workmen and more than a million pounds, wrought great changes during the mid-1820s to the castle. In particular, the private apartments were moved from the north to the south and east sides of the Upper Ward, and the existing buildings were altered to their present appearance, both inside and out. Wyatville also built the State Entrance and the Brunswick Tower; laid out the East Terrace Garden; raised the Round Tower thirty-three feet to keep it in proportion with the rooflines that he had also raised; he restored the medieval exterior of much of the castle, and extended the Long Walk to enter the Quadrangle by the gate that bears the name of his royal patron.

Another important alteration to the interior of the castle was carried out on the orders of George when he was Regent. Always a man who took a great pride in the martial glories of England, he commissioned Sir Thomas Lawrence after the victory at Waterloo to paint a series of portraits of the allied soldiers and statesmen who had contributed to the defeat of Napoleon. In order to house these splendid pictures, Wyatville put a floor across one of the two interior courtyards (the one known as Horn Court) that were in the centre of the north side of the Quadrangle, and a ceiling cleverly designed to provide light in what was a windowless room. The great room thus formed became known as the Waterloo Chamber, and in it, on 18 June each year, the sovereign holds a banquet.

York
The Railway Museum. Railways were in their infancy during the reigns of George IV and William IV (the first passenger-carrying train arrived in 1807), but by 1849, the year that William's Queen Adelaide died, they had become an important means of travel, and luxury coaches were being built for important personages. In the museum can be seen the coach made for Queen Adelaide, and also those used by Queen Victoria and Edward VII.

15

THE HOUSE OF HANOVER
Queen Victoria

On 24 May 1819 a daughter was born at Kensington Palace to the Duke and Duchess of Kent. The Duke was the fourth son of George III, and in the previous year he had married Victoria of Saxe-Coburg, the widow of the Prince of Leiningen. George III had not long to live; the Prince Regent's only child had died two years previously; the Duke of York was childless, and so the hopes for the Hanoverian succession rested principally with the Dukes of Clarence (later William IV) and Kent. But the Duke of Kent died eight months after the birth of his daughter, who thus became four removes from a very shaky throne. She was christened Alexandrina Victoria (and for the first eight years of her life was called Drina) in the Cupola Room of Kensington Palace. The circumstances were undignified because her godfather, the Prince Regent, objected to some of the names.

For her thirteenth birthday (by which time she was heir-presumptive) her mother gave her a diary, and from then onwards Victoria would faithfully record the days' events. Many years later she recalled in this journal that her childhood had been a sad one, and in some ways it certainly was. The loss of a father was partially offset by the attentions of her Uncle Leopold (her mother's brother who was still living at Claremont, where his wife, the Prince Regent's daughter, had died); and when he came to the throne George IV, 'Uncle King', did his best to be kind to her. But more serious was the lack of any suitable children of her own age to play with, for her mother's two Leiningen children were much older, and her closest companion, Victoire Conroy, was the daughter of her mother's comptroller, the man she came to hate, and who was largely responsible for the early estrangement between Victoria and her mother.

However, one event in her childhood was to have a long and beneficial effect. When Victoria was five years old, Baroness Louise

Lehzen, a German from Coburg, became her governess. She devoted herself whole-heartedly to the interests of her charge, and although the young Victoria went in awe of her, for she was strict and somewhat puritanical, Lehzen quickly became her constant companion, mentor and idol. The governess may have found her teaching duties, which were shared with other tutors, difficult, for Victoria was not fond of concentrated study, but it was Lehzen who was chiefly responsible for the future Queen's deep interest in history. Languages came easily to Victoria, and she soon acquired a working knowledge of Italian, French and German – the latter in spite of her mother's determination to bring her up entirely English. She came to love ballet and opera, and her drawing lessons were fruitful and enjoyable.

The years immediately prior to her accession were made more difficult for Victoria by the open dislike of her uncle, King William, for her mother, and the constant and unbearable presence of Sir John Conroy. William was fond of Victoria in his bluff way, and would like to have seen more of her at court, but the Duchess kept her away as much as possible, and, what annoyed the King more, encouraged Conroy in his organizing of semi-royal progresses round different parts of the country for the Princess – and her mother. Conroy was an unpleasant man and an ambitious one, who schemed for power; when Victoria was convalescing from a bout of typhoid fever he was insensitive enough to press his claim to become her private secretary. He seems to have hopelessly misjudged this outwardly easy-going girl, who concealed a strong character and a quick temper.

This hatred for Conroy brought her closer to her Uncle Leopold. Leopold, who had become King of the Belgians in 1830, showered her with advice in constant correspondence. He had a genuine affection for, and desire to help, his niece, but his attentiveness was not entirely disinterested. He saw himself as the *éminence grise* of the future Queen of England, and in thinking to strengthen the link he was instrumental in giving Victoria the greatest happiness of her life – his nephew, Albert of Saxe-Coburg-Gotha, as her husband. But although Victoria remained devoted to her uncle, first Lord Melbourne and then Prince Albert became the counsellors to whom she most looked for strength and guidance in the first part of her reign.

William IV died in the early hours of 20 June 1837, and by 5 am the Archbishop of Canterbury (William Howley) and Lord Conyingham, the Lord Chamberlain, were outside Kensington Palace. After some delay the Duchess of Kent led her daughter (a dressing-gown over her nightdress) down the stairs – closely followed by the faithful Lehzen – and at the door of the sitting room left her to enter alone and receive the homage of the gentlemen who had come to announce her accession.

Later, at 11.30 am, wearing a plain black dress,* she held her first Privy Council in the Red Saloon. She was just eighteen, a diminutive figure of only five feet two inches, but dignified and self-possessed. During the day she saw her Prime Minister, Lord Melbourne, on two occasions, and – what at the time may have meant more to her – she had her bed removed from her mother's bedroom to one of her own. For the first time she slept alone. That evening she recorded in her journal, 'I am very young and perhaps in many, though not in all things, inexperienced, but I am sure, that very few have more real good will and more real desire to do what is fit and right than I have.'

The Queen was crowned on 28 June. One or two minor hitches in the sequence of the service, through the ineptitude of some of the clergy, failed to detract from the splendour of the occasion, for which Parliament had voted £200,000; and that evening she wrote in her journal, 'I shall ever remember this day as the proudest of my life.' On 13 July she moved into Buckingham Palace; her mother, who now spent much of her time finding fault with her, moved there too, but the Queen took good care to see that they were separated by many doors.

Early influences on her were Lehzen, King Leopold through his letters and his confidant, Baron Stockmar, whom he had sent to England, and who was to become the devoted friend of both Queen Victoria and Prince Albert, and above all Lord Melbourne. Melbourne was an orthodox Whig. There was nothing radical about him – in fact he hated change and believed strongly in the predominance of a patrician society. He may have erred in concealing from the Queen that beneath the surface there was a strong current of discontent in the country, for he was a carefree man and a convinced optimist, who paid scant attention to the sufferings of the masses. But there can be no doubt that his devotion to the Queen was entirely beneficial, for with his sincere compliments, his patience, understanding and sympathy for her domestic difficulties (Conroy and her mother), and calm approach to the political problems of the day, he gave her the confidence that any young girl in her position badly needed.

The Queen became quite enslaved by the charm of her Prime Minister, considered herself a Whig, rejoiced at the Whig victory at the polls, and from early in 1839 it became obvious that the magic of Leopold was fading. It was now 'Lord M', as she referred to him in her journal, whom she consulted on everything from the political situation to the state of her health, which at this early age periodically gave her quite unnecessary concern. The very thought of his having to leave her

* This dress – now turned brown through age and bad storage in the war – can still be seen in the Museum of London.

could not be contemplated; but of course her ageing Prime Minister, and his none too robust party, could not endure for ever.

The sorry business of Lady Flora Hastings, who was one of the Duchess of Kent's ladies, might never have occurred had Sir John Conroy been removed from his post earlier, as the Queen had expressly wished, or had not the barrier between Victoria and her mother become by now impenetrable. Lady Flora returned from her Christmas holiday in Scotland in the same post-chaise as Sir John, and soon afterwards, in January 1839, complained of a pain in her stomach. Before long a small protuberance began to swell, and the rumour started that the girl was pregnant – it being darkly hinted that Conroy was responsible. The Queen's doctor, Sir James Clark, seemed to believe in her pregnancy, and there followed an unpleasant amount of palace intrigue, which chiefly concerned the Queen's ladies and Lehzen, but Victoria herself could not help being involved, and her involvement was the more unsatisfactory through her not being in communication with her mother. The unfortunate Lady Flora eventually submitted to an examination and was found to be a virgin. The Queen was deeply distressed at having wrongly suspected the girl. Even now the matter was not done with, for the whole affair was leaked to the press, and the Queen's popularity plummeted to zero. On 5 July Lady Flora died, and the post-mortem that she had insisted upon revealed a tumour on the liver.

While the Queen was being tormented by this miserable affair, an even worse calamity befell her. In May Lord Melbourne's Government was defeated, and he felt obliged to tender his resignation. What she had dreaded for the past two years had now come about; no more long talks, and cosy dinners; instead the awful Tories and their (at that time) much disliked leader, Sir Robert Peel. But Melbourne gave her some parting advice, among which was that she should not countenance a change in her household, save for the few holding political office. This advice was unfortunate, for it sparked off what became known as the Bedchamber Crisis. Peel wanted the Queen to dismiss the Mistress of the Robes and the Ladies of the Bedchamber, who were married to prominent Whig opponents of his proposed government. The Queen insisted that she must keep all of her ladies. An impasse resulted, and Peel felt himself unable to form a government. Lord Melbourne was back again – for a short time.* Lord Melbourne's government struggled on until June 1841, when the Tories won the election. This time there was no

* There was no precedent for this crisis, because in Queen Anne's day the position of the sovereign was different; after 1839 there was no further trouble, and in future the Queen was called upon to change only the Mistress of the Robes. There is now no rule that the Mistress of the Robes goes in and out with the ministry.

repetition of the Bedchamber Crisis, partly owing to Melbourne's wise briefing of Peel, and also to the tact and understanding of Prince Albert, whom the Queen had married on 10 February 1840.

Victoria had first met her Coburg cousins, Ernest and Albert, in May 1836 when the Duchess of Kent – prompted by King Leopold, and much to King William's annoyance – issued an invitation to her brother, Duke Ernest of Saxe-Coburg-Gotha, and his two sons, to visit England. The visit, as far as Victoria was concerned, was a great success. She found both brothers equally charming; however, the possibility of an engagement to either was not even discussed. But Leopold was patient and persistent. Despite Queen Victoria's ceaseless reiteration that she was not ready for marriage, he plucked Albert away from his beloved Rosenau Castle to journey to Windsor in October 1839. He came once more with his brother, Ernest, but it was Albert who had been groomed for the star role, and it was Albert who conquered. Lord Melbourne gave the Queen paternal encouragement, and on 15 October she, as etiquette demanded, asked the Prince to marry her, and was accepted. It was the beginning of twenty-two years of almost undiluted happiness for Queen Victoria.

Prince Albert was three months younger than his bride; he was tall and exceptionally handsome. He shared with Victoria a great love of music, and he was at his happiest leading the life of a country gentleman; he was a good shot and came to like hunting (which endeared him to English landowners); he had a good brain with a distinct scientific bent; he was conscientious, extremely hard-working, kind and loyal. He was in fact almost the paragon that Queen Victoria's journal made him out to be.

But it must not be thought that there was always complete harmony between them, for both partners were strong-willed, and Victoria's tantrums and temper were not always under control. Life was particularly difficult for Albert at the start. There was trouble over his household; the Queen seemed disinclined to allow him any major role, and Baroness Lehzen blocked his every attempt to carry out any of the badly needed domestic reforms in the Palace. But circumstances were not slow in coming to his aid. The assassination attempt of 1840 (which together with her marriage completely restored the Queen's popularity) placed him in the role of protector, the retirement of Melbourne drew him closer to his wife politically, and the very adroit way in which he managed to get Lehzen removed from the Palace and sent back to Germany in 1842 left him master in his own house. He may not have loved Victoria with the same overwhelming passion that she had for him, and although his devotion grew stronger each year, his sense of duty was always uppermost. He was to slave long hours, in his self-appointed capacity of private secretary, to supervise every detail of the Queen's private and public life.

The Queen and Prince Albert had nine children. The eldest, Princess Victoria, who was to become Empress of Germany and mother of the last Kaiser, was born in 1840, and Albert Edward, Prince of Wales, followed a year later. The youngest child, Princess Beatrice, was born in 1857. There were, of course, all the usual tribulations of rearing a large family – illness, delicate health, education and later on marriage arrangements – and in particular the Prince of Wales gave his parents considerable anxiety. This was chiefly because they failed to understand his inhibitions, which were largely of their making, and both Prince Albert and the Queen expected more from him than he was able to give. But by and large the Queen was immensely happy and lucky with her family, and they gave her the opportunity of enjoying – not of recapturing, for she had never had it – all the fun of children's games and hobbies. Furthermore, Prince Albert was instrumental in bringing the Duchess of Kent back into the family circle.

In order to obtain some privacy, and have somewhere in which to relax, the royal couple purchased Osborne in 1844, and some of the surrounding land. Two years later they pulled down the small house and built the present mansion in the form of an Italian villa. Having been enchanted by their visit to the Highlands, the Queen and the Prince rented Balmoral in 1848 – then a comparatively small building – and in 1852 they purchased the property. Here again the old building was virtually pulled down and a castle of more appropriate dimensions appeared in its place. It is difficult to know which of these two homes gave them the most pleasure. They did, of course, lend themselves to different modes of living. The Queen came to love her bathing, and the quiet walks and evenings with Albert at Osborne, while the Prince became an almost aggressive Scottish laird and sportsman when he was at Balmoral. Apart from these changes of scenery there were journeys abroad – a pilgrimage to Albert's birthplace, Rosenau, and visits to Louis Philippe (the first English sovereign to visit France since Henry VIII), and later to Napoleon III – although most of the Queen's visits to France and Germany were private ones towards the end of her life.

The Queen greeted the advent of Peel and the Tories in 1841 with considerable dismay and misgiving, and indeed for some little time afterwards she kept up a most unconstitutional correspondence with Melbourne on affairs of State. However, Prince Albert found Peel to be a man cast very much in his own mould. Both were serious and high principled; they got on very well, and gradually the Queen came to see that Peel was a Prime Minister who put country before party, and with whom she could work. By 1844 she was completely converted, and when a change of ministry came about in 1846 she was nearly as distraught at losing Peel as she had been when Melbourne left her. By now Melbourne no longer led the Whigs, and while their leader, Lord John Russell, was acceptable, their Foreign Secretary, Lord Palmerston, was very definitely not.

Palmerston had been Foreign Secretary in the previous Whig administration, but then Victoria's affection for Melbourne spun off on most of his team; now matters were different. Since her marriage the Queen had become more involved in Europe and more interested in foreign affairs; it is true she was not yet the grandmother of Europe, but the royal couple were related to most of the ruling houses, and foreign affairs had something of the flavour of a family business. In 1848 Europe was aflame with revolution; the Queen was appalled at these anarchic outbursts, whereas Palmerston had much sympathy for irredentism, although not for revolution. Moreover, he believed that a Foreign Secretary's first duty was to his Cabinet and Parliament, and he was inclined to withhold despatches from the Queen. The pith of it was that the Queen resented any attempt to take foreign affairs out of the hands of the Crown, and Lord John Russell had a most difficult time. In the end Palmerston overstepped the mark in giving unilateral recognition to Napoleon III in 1851, and he was forced to resign. However, he was soon instrumental in bringing down the ministry, and returned to the Cabinet in Lord Aberdeen's coalition – but as Home Secretary, in which post he was comparatively innocuous to the Queen.

Those years, 1848–51, were busy and important ones for the Queen and Prince Albert. While revolution blazed on the Continent, at home there was much discontent and trouble from the Chartist movement (so called from the six points made in the People's Charter), and in Ireland the great potato famine caused immense distress. Prince Albert had been responsible for filling a gap in the Queen's approach to her subjects that Lord Melbourne, through his own insouciance in the matter, had left open – he taught her to have sympathy and feeling for the sufferings of the poor. In 1849, just a month or two after a mad Irishman had made the fourth attempt on her life, the Queen paid a brief visit to that part of her kingdom. It was a success, but not a lasting one.

If Palmerston's departure from the Foreign Office in 1851 was something to rejoice in, the wonderful triumph of Prince Albert's Great Exhibition, which Queen Victoria opened on 1 May of that year, was very much more so. Inside the Crystal Palace was Britain's shop window at the beginning of her ever expanding industrial era. It was a triumph for the Prince and for Sir Joseph Paxton, who designed this huge temple of glass; it showed a good profit, and enabled the working classes – many of whom had the opportunity of visiting it – to appreciate the important part that they were playing in making Britain great. That venerable figure, the Duke of Wellington, who had been such a staunch support to the young Queen, was present at the opening, but he had only a year left to live. And with his death so many of the old guard had gone, for Melbourne had died in 1848, Queen Adelaide (William IV's wife) in 1849, Peel the next year and Lord Liverpool (a much valued family friend) in 1851.

The crowded decade of the 1850s contained for the Queen a mixture of anxiety, distress and much happiness. Shortly before the outbreak of the Crimean War in 1854, Prince Albert had become as unpopular in the country as Palmerston – still in Aberdeen's Cabinet – had become popular. The Prince was thought to be against Britain's participation in the war on account of his Russian relations, whereas Palmerston was the hero of a militant population. Any censure of the Prince the Queen took as a personal slight, and in the event when a war came no one worked harder than Albert to remedy the incompetent military administration. But perhaps for the Queen the greatest surprise of the war came when she found that she had misjudged Palmerston (who became Prime Minister in 1855), who later was to be commended in her journal as the one Prime Minister whom she and Albert were to find gave the least trouble 'and is most amenable to reason & most ready to adopt suggestions'.

However, Palmerston was still at the head of affairs at the time of the Indian Mutiny in 1857, and as the Queen's anguish and distress increased with the terrible news, she seems to have found him a little less receptive to her suggestions. But all was forgiven when he drew up plans to transfer India to the Crown at the end of the Mutiny, and when his government was defeated in 1858 there was another sorrowful farewell to be made, and the familiar apprehension towards the incoming Premier – this time Lord Derby. But 1857 and 1858 had their moments of great pleasure. In 1857, the older generation of the royal family now being mostly dead, there was no longer any awkwardness about precedence, and at last the Queen was able to give to her beloved Albert the title of Prince Consort, while the next year there was the sorrowful happiness of losing her eldest daughter in marriage to Prince Frederick of Prussia.

The Queen's mother died on 16 March 1861, and the greatest tragedy of her life was to befall her nine months later when the Prince Consort died in the Blue Room at Windsor Castle on 14 December. He had probably contracted typhoid some three weeks earlier, and the worry caused by an unfortunate, but understandable, amorous escapade of the Prince of Wales at the Curragh, his own refusal to give up his out-of-doors engagements, and the long, fruitful hours spent amending the draft concerning the *Trent* affair,* proved too much for a constitution already prematurely weakened by overwork and strain.

The Queen's grief was terrible. It totally disabled her, for she had lost the prop that supported life. Her immediate seclusion at Osborne, and her constant pilgrimage to kneel in prayer before the shrine at Frogmore could be understood by a deeply sympathetic public, and even the prolonged morbidity might have been forgiven the widow had she attended to her public duties. But these she consistently shunned, to the dismay of her ministers. Even on great family occasions, such as the marriage on 5 March 1863 of the Prince of Wales to the lovely and charming Princess Alexandra of Denmark, her neurotic behaviour cast a dark shadow over the proceedings. This absolute grief can be said to have lasted for five years; thereafter there was a slow awakening to the call of duty; nevertheless it was to be twenty years or so before she once again felt able to fulfil all the demands made upon her, and her continued seclusion was fertile ground for republican agitators, such as the radical MP, Sir Charles Dilke.

Two men of very different background and position did most to help her in these terrible years – John Brown and Benjamin Disraeli. Brown, a ghillie at Balmoral, was associated with the happy days when Albert was alive. He was excellent with horses, and now became the Queen's personal servant, bodyguard and companion on all her journeys at home and abroad. He was exceptionally loyal, and – except when dipping too deeply into the whisky bottle – most capable; his rough familiarity was something new and quite acceptable to the Queen. But with others he could be arrogant; the Prince of Wales and most of the household thoroughly disliked him, and his familiarity with the Queen was the cause of some public ridicule.

The Queen had known both Benjamin Disraeli and William Ewart Gladstone many years earlier when they were young Members of Parliament in the days of Peel. At the time she strongly disapproved of Disraeli's opposition to Peel, and she had nothing but contempt for Gladstone over his bigotry when called upon to support financial measures for papists. Now, in the late 1860s, they were both in the front rank of their respective parties. Lord Palmerston died in office in 1865, and Lord Russell failed to get full support from the party; this let Lord Derby in again with Disraeli as his Chancellor of the Exchequer. When Derby had to resign for health reasons in 1868, Disraeli became Prime Minister.

---

* Two Confederates, sailing in a British ship – the *Trent* – to plead their cause in England during the American Civil War, had been abducted when the ship was boarded by the Federalists. This at first proved too much for Palmerston's *Civis Romanus Sum* tenets.

Not since Peel had there been a Prime Minister whom the Queen really liked, but now all that would be changed. Disraeli proved a master at handling his Mistress; he flattered her outrageously, but Victoria had intuition enough to realize that beneath his golden phrases there lay a heart that was capable of absolute loyalty and genuine devotion. Gladstone, on the other hand, had not this knack of managing the Queen; he could be boring and prolix, and the man himself and his policies were a constant irritation to her. Unfortunately, Disraeli's first ministry lasted only ten months. The Conservatives (as the Tories were beginning to be called) had passed the second Reform Act in 1867, and this popular measure gave Disraeli and the Queen some hope for success at the polls in November 1868. But they were defeated, and Gladstone was at the head of a Liberal (Whig) Government.

Gladstone's first ministry, which lasted until 1874, was perhaps his greatest, and certainly the one that was most free from friction with his sovereign. His worst offence was his attempts to drag her from her retirement; she constantly pleaded illness. In 1871 she was indeed very ill, and in that same year she had the additional worry of nearly losing her eldest son, who was struck down by typhoid at Sandringham – a country estate he had recently bought. The Franco-Prussian War, as a result of which one empire disappeared and another came into being, found the Queen – rather naturally – Prussian biased; most of her countrymen resented Prussia's (really Bismarck's) aggression, and her attitude over this issue,* her continued seclusion and a recent rather unsavoury divorce case in which the Prince of Wales had been subpoenaed, all contributed to the unpopularity of the monarchy at this time.

But brighter days lay ahead, for with the return of Disraeli in 1874 there were to be six years in which she could work in harmony with a Prime Minister who valued her advice, and brought his Faerie Queene personal glory, and the country great renown. In 1876 the Prince of Wales had made a most successful tour of India, and happily his return coincided with Disraeli's success in getting the Titles Bill through a divided Parliament. On 1 May the Queen was proclaimed Queen-Empress and, in Delhi, Empress of India. It was a title that she had long desired; for most of her life she had been attracted by the mysticism of the East, and now she felt able to allow her love for the Orient full rein with a Durbar room at Osborne, Indian orderlies and Indian servants. A few months earlier Disraeli had made her another gift, so important to

---

* Later, in 1875, when Prussian aggression again threatened the peace of Europe, Queen Victoria made it very plain to everyone that Prussia must stop sabre rattling, and that another war could not be tolerated.

her Indian Empire, when he told her that she (one must admire his use of the personal pronoun) had just acquired a controlling interest in the Suez Canal shares. A great Empire, which for almost one hundred years was to give to its many peoples the strongest and most civilized polity in the world, had been born.

In March 1880, to the surprise of many, and the great chagrin of the Queen, Lord Beaconsfield (as Disraeli had become) and his Tory party were defeated at the polls. The Queen went to Germany, and from there did everything she could to get either Lord Hartington or Lord Granville to lead the new Government; but to no avail; it had to be the 'People's William' (an epithet the Queen abhorred), and she braced herself for what proved to be three or more terms of office before she was finally done with Gladstone.

Queen Victoria could never like Gladstone – they had such utterly different personalities – but she would admit occasionally to his nobility of character and devoted service, and she tried to be courteous and understanding. But on his return to office she relapsed into that earlier error of carrying on a confidential correspondence with her outgoing Premier. And when Beaconsfield died in 1881 and Lord Salisbury – whose humour, urbanity and culture she greatly admired – became leader of the Conservatives, she continued this practice to the point of acting most unconstitutionally, when in 1886 she passed him inside information in the hope that it would enable him to bring Gladstone down.

On almost every important political issue of the day – Afghanistan, Egypt, the first Boer War, Home Rule – the Queen and Gladstone were at variance, whereas with Lord Salisbury only Lord Randolph Churchill seemed to irritate her, and he irritated Salisbury as well. She did share with Gladstone a great horror at the incipient stirrings of 'Women's Lib', but they could find little else to agree upon, and when in 1885 he failed to rescue General Gordon from the clutches of the Mahdi in Khartoum the Queen was so furious that she sent him a minatory telegram *en clair*, which could be read by the post office clerks.

The closing years of the Queen's life were dominated by the two great Jubilees, which enabled her subjects from all over the world to demonstrate their love and respect. In a long and momentous reign there were times when the people had become disillusioned with the Crown – especially in those dark years when it seemed to many that the Queen wished to abdicate her responsibilities. But now all that was past; at the Golden Jubilee in 1887 and again at the Diamond Jubilee ten years later, a great feeling of pride and gratitude gave shape and substance to the emotive urge to cheer to the echo the little old lady who, for as long as most people could remember, had presided over their destinies.

The Queen's large family – she had twenty-nine grandchildren who survived infancy, and by the end of her life she had become the matriarch of almost all the royal houses of Europe – gave her much joy, but inevitably some anxiety. The behaviour of her sons – as might be expected from young men of spirit – did not always conform to her rigid code of conduct. The Prince of Wales had a knack of getting in and out of awkward situations; Leopold was very delicate, suffering from haemophilia,* which prevented him from leading the active life of his brothers. Probably Arthur, the youngest son, was her favourite; she was immensely proud of his distinguished service at Tel-el-Kebir with the Brigade of Guards in 1882. There was no shortage of eligible princes and princesses in Europe from whom to select brides and bridegrooms for her nine children. And although she did not always approve of the houses into which they married (all save Princess Louise, whose husband was Lord Lorne, married foreigners), she grew very fond of her sons and daughters-in-law.

As the years went by inevitably many relations and old friends began to drop away – and some sadly were not so old. Her second daughter, Princess Alice, had died on 14 December 1878, and in 1883 John Brown departed. His place as personal servant was taken by the Indian munshi, Abdul Karim, but in her affections Brown was irreplaceable. Prince Leopold – always delicate – died in 1884, and he was followed in 1888 by her much loved son-in-law, the Emperor Frederick. Saddest of all perhaps was the loss in 1892 of her grandson Eddy, Duke of Clarence, the elder son of the Prince of Wales. But even then her cup of woe was not drained; two more sons-in-law predeceased her, and in 1900, with her own health in decline, and worried by the long list of Boer War casualties, she received news from Coburg at the end of July that her son 'Affie', who had succeeded his uncle as Duke of Coburg, was dead.

By the end of 1900 that fire and spirit which had extorted so many wonderful exertions in the past was at last failing. So much had been accomplished in the past sixty-four years; enormous progress in communications, travel, hospitals, cure of disease, care of the poor, and the making of an Empire. Now, unable to sleep properly, and feeling tired and weak, she struggled on, still not quite defeated. On 18 December she left Windsor for the last time and headed for Osborne. Here her family gathered to say goodbye. The end came at 6.30 p.m. on 22 January

---

* Queen Victoria was a carrier of haemophilia, and through her children she passed it on to other royal houses – notably to the Romanovs, through Princess Alice, who was the grandmother of the Tsarevitch Alexis.

1901, and among those at her bedside stood Kaiser William II, her eldest, and still her favourite, grandchild, despite his foolish and oft expressed anti-British sentiments. On this occasion he behaved with a dignity and humility that won him universal respect. ·

For the Queen's last journey on 1 February the sun shone out of a cold sky. The coffin was taken to Gosport in the royal yacht *Alberta*, and from there by train to Victoria Station. As the solemn, but glittering, procession, with at its centre the gun carriage bearing the coffin draped with the Royal Standard, wound its way to Paddington, the large crowds stood in sorrowful silence. Some of them may have realized that they were witnessing the passing of an era that had been uncertain in its beginning, vigorous in maturity and glorious at its close.

Three days later her family buried her in the granite sarcophagus under the domes of the fine mausoleum at Frogmore alongside the husband for whom it had been built, and with whom she was now again united after the long wait of almost forty years.

Victoria's very long reign was distinguished more for scientific discoveries and progress, and for the fulfilment of empire, than for great artistic achievements. Victorian architecture is often condemned as solid and ungainly, although in fact much of it was very fine – especially ecclesiastical architecture. There was, however a tendency to imitate past styles, and a Gothic revival – led by Sir Gilbert Scott and Sir Charles Barry – became fashionable in many parts of the country.

Queen Victoria's early education included painting and drawing, and she became, with Prince Albert, an interested, although not particularly inspired, collector. Landseer found Queen Victoria an enthusiastic patron, while Prince Albert was influential in promoting Winterhalter's work. The Prince was deeply interested in any scientific advancement. There were many important innovations in this field during the reign, although most reached the greatest extent of their development after the Prince Consort's death. The telegraph system and the anaesthetic properties of chloroform, however, were the fruits of British brains in the first half of the nineteenth century. The telephone was first patented in the United States in 1876 by an American, but A.G. Bell was born in Edinburgh. The wonders of photography, X-rays and radium were a few of the other benefits of which people knew nothing when Queen Victoria came to the throne; and the revolution in transportation through steam, the internal combustion engine, and even the beginning of aeronautics, was to make travel more hazardous, but made the control of the great empire – which gave the Queen so much pride and joy – more practicable.

Bowhill (Selkirk). (See also Chapter 11.) Throughout the years the Scott family have been distinguished for their service to their Sovereign and to the State. The fifth Duke of Buccleuch held important offices of State under Queen Victoria and his wife, and later his daughter-in-law, were Mistresses of the Robes to the Queen. There can be seen in Bowhill a number of Queen Victoria's letters, and also a very delightful pen and ink drawing by the Queen of some children.

Claremont (Surrey), where Queen Victoria spent some of the happiest days of her childhood, is described in Chapter 14.

Frogmore, the Royal Mausoleum (Berks.) was the brainchild of Queen Victoria and Prince Albert. Hitherto it had been the custom to bury her predecessors in the royal vault in St George's Chapel at Windsor, excavated by George III. However, Queen Victoria was much impressed by the mausoleum erected for Duke Ernest of Saxe-Coburg by Prince Albert and his brother, and together she and the Prince planned one for themselves. In 1859 the Queen's mother, the Duchess of Kent, had a mausoleum built for her in the grounds of Frogmore House, where she was living, and two years later she occupied it. In the same year Prince Albert died and the Queen at once put into operation the plan they had formulated, selecting a site close to her mother's mausoleum. Work started at once on a design by Professor Gruner to be executed by A.J. Humbert. The tomb was designed by Carlo Marochitti, and Prince Albert's remains were placed in it in 1868.

The whole building, inside and out, is a magnificent example of Victoriana. The exterior is constructed of granite and Portland stone, and inside the walls and floor are of inlaid coloured marbles, while the walls and ceilings of the four chapels are decorated with paintings. The flawless Aberdeen granite sarcophagus and the recumbent marble effigies of the Queen and her husband (the Queen's effigy was made, but not erected, at the same time as the Prince's) occupy the centre of the Mausoleum, with the great dome stretching up some seventy feet above the tomb. In the chapels are monuments commemorating various members of Queen Victoria's family. Unfortunately, the mausoleum is only open to the public on three days in the year, and the huge crowds make it difficult to appreciate the peaceful beauty of this great funeral monument.

Hatfield House (Herts.), (see also Chapter 9), was the home of another of Queen Victoria's Prime Ministers, Lord Salisbury, who held high office three times, starting in 1885. The illustrious history of the house of Cecil, and the proximity of Hatfield to London, has resulted in close associations with royalty. Queen Victoria first visited the house nine years after her accession, and in the Long Gallery can be seen some of the gifts she made to the family, and other mementos.

Hughenden Manor (Bucks.), was bought by Benjamin Disraeli in 1847, twenty-one years before he first became Queen Victoria's favourite Prime Minister. He loved the place dearly, and moulded it in his own romantic fashion. He virtually rebuilt the house – although he preferred to say he restored it to its Civil War proportions – and made 'a garden of terraces in which cavaliers might roam and saunter with their lady loves'. At Hughenden, in 1881, he was buried beside his wife, and a few days later his Queen came to lay a wreath on his tomb. The house, which is situated just north of High Wycombe, contains many objects of interest connected with the Prime Minister, manuscripts of his novels, letters from the Queen, and some of the original furniture.

London
The Albert Memorial, Kensington Gore. This impressive piece of Victorian architecture was Queen Victoria's memorial to her consort, Prince Albert of Saxe-Coburg-Gotha. The Prince died in 1861, and the monument was sculpted and built between 1863 and 1867. Prince Albert is seated beneath a large and ornate Gothic canopy, holding a catalogue of the Great Exhibition for which he was largely responsible, and which took place nearby. The seated statue of the Prince rests on a very splendid marble-relieved pedestal. On the opposite side of the road is the Royal Albert Hall, designed by Francis Fowke and built between 1867 and 1871; behind the Hall stands another statue of the Prince Consort, which was erected as a memorial to the Imperial Exhibition.

Kensington Palace (see also Chapter 12), was Queen Victoria's principal childhood home. She was born and christened there in 1819 and, on the morning of 20 June 1837, she was awoken there to be told that she was Queen, and it was there that later that day she held her first Privy Council. Although certain exhibits connected with the Queen have been removed to the Museum of London, some of her toys and dolls can still be seen in the rooms she inhabited. Amid lovely pieces of furniture that enhance the beauty of the rooms are some large, and not so lovely, centrepieces and statuettes thought up by Prince Albert. Victoria left the Palace on her accession, but, thirty years later, Princess Mary of Teck, who was to become George V's Queen, was born in the same room as the Queen.

Osborne (Isle of Wight), was chosen by Queen Victoria and Prince Albert as 'a place of one's own, quiet and retired', where they could escape from the pomp and formality associated with their two large residences – Buckingham Palace and Windsor Castle – and the bizarre Royal Pavilion at Brighton, of which the Queen soon tired.

The house they found at Osborne was too small, so it was pulled down and in its place Prince Albert, with the help of Thomas Cubitt, designed a mansion in the Italian style, for he appreciated Italian art and architecture and felt that the land and seascape at Osborne, with its wooded hills and views across the Solent, had a certain affinity to Italy. The house was solidly built round an open courtyard, and for its time extremely modern. Ready for use in 1846, although not finished until 1851, Osborne House became, with Balmoral, the principal holiday home for the royal couple. After Prince Albert's death, Queen Victoria retired for a time to this house of many happy associations. Some ten years before her own death, which occurred at Osborne, the Queen had the Durbar Room laid out in Indian style by Indian craftsmen.

In the grounds there stands the Swiss Cottage, brought in sections from Switzerland in 1853, and erected for the use of the royal children. The furniture and fittings can be seen as they were in 1854, and in a nearby shed are the garden tools used by the children. Osborne is situated just a short distance south-east of East Cowes on the Isle of Wight.

Whippingham (Isle of Wight). This little village church, near to Osborne, was designed by Prince Albert, and in it his and Queen Victoria's youngest daughter, Princess Beatrice, was married to Prince Henry of Battenburg in July 1885. Ten years later, Prince Henry died of fever while serving in the Ashanti expedition, and in January 1896 was buried in this church; Princess Beatrice, who died in 1944, was buried alongside him in the chapel that she had prepared. Prince Henry's brother and sister-in-law (Prince Louis of Battenburg, later first Marquess of Milford Haven, and his wife, Princess Victoria of Hesse, who was Queen Victoria's granddaughter) were also buried in this church.

Windsor Castle, the Albert Memorial Chapel (Berks.). Queen Victoria gave this chapel its name, although she never intended it to house the remains of Prince Albert, whose wishes for a more rural setting were well known to her. The building stands on the site of a much older chapel, erected by Henry III, and used as the chapel of the Order of the Garter between 1350 and 1483. By 1547 the chapel had fallen into decay, and little was done – except to remove parts of the interior for other purposes – until Queen Victoria remodelled it, lining the walls with marble and crowning the roof with copper.

In the chapel can now be seen the tombs of the Duke of Albany, Queen Victoria's youngest son who died in 1884, and in the centre of the building Sir Alfred Gilbert's remarkable art nouveau memorial to the Duke of Clarence, the elder brother of George V, who was buried there in 1892. The recumbent figure of Prince Albert in white marble by Baron Triquetti completes this perfect piece of Victoriana. Below the chapel (but not open to the public) is the royal tomb house with the remains of many of the early Hanoverians.

16

THE INHERITORS

Queen Victoria's reign proved a watershed in the evolution of the British monarchy. As the prestige of the Crown progressively increased, so did its actual power decline. But the accession of King Edward VII did little to change the social scene. The Victorian age continued – varied in the higher echelons of society to suit the very different tastes of the new sovereign – until the domestic and foreign upheavals of George V's early years were followed by the cataclysm of the First World War.

Queen Victoria's long experience in foreign and domestic problems – stretching back beyond the memory of most of her later ministers – gave her a unique opportunity to offer wise counsel. This invaluable asset of continuity was denied Edward VII, because his mother had done her best to exclude him from any responsibility in – and to a great extent knowledge of – State affairs. He came to the throne late in life, but with an enthusiasm undimmed by the long years in which his mind and energy had been in shackles.

King Edward's great contribution to the monarchy is that he popularized it. Court life may have become more lax, and many of the King's intimates would not have been approved of by the old Queen, but he rigidly maintained the dignity of the throne, and his love of pageantry brought a welcome change from the past years. Before the end of his life, he had become immensely popular with the people.

His contribution to the well-being of the country lay principally in two fields – at home his work on army and navy reform, and abroad his princely diplomacy. King Edward always proceeded with caution, and was careful never to defy the constitution; his relations with his ministers (particularly Balfour) were forceful and often stormy, and although he never allowed his political beliefs to interfere with his duties, the King was very much a Conservative. He regarded Lloyd George and his radical policies (and to a lesser degree Winston Churchill) with considerable antipathy. But in the matter of army reform he worked closely and usefully with the Secretary of State for War (R.B. Haldane), and his friendship with Admiral Fisher made it much easier for the latter to carry out his important reforms, which inevitably aroused much opposition, but which had in the main the King's full support.

But perhaps King Edward's best work was done on the Continent of Europe. He was no statesman, and to say that he alone was responsible for the *entente cordiale* with France would not be true; but his good humour, his genuine love for France and the French people, his refusal to take offence, and his open hospitality won the hearts of the French, and made the work of his two great Foreign Secretaries – Lords Lansdowne and Grey – very much easier. It was the same in many other Continental countries, where his charm and obvious sincerity won from his fellow heads of State a respect and affection that extended through him to all his countrymen.

The rejection of Lloyd George's 1909 budget, with its stringent fiscal measures, by the Lords, and the subsequent Parliament Bill, sparked off a serious constitutional crisis, which was not resolved at Edward's death. King George V (like his son twenty-six years later) came to the throne in appallingly difficult circumstances. Lacking political experience (although much travelled and conversant with Dominion affairs) he found himself, after only a few months, having to promise to create, if needs be, five hundred new peers so as to avoid a dangerous political deadlock. Having escaped this embarrassment through the belated good sense of the opposition peers he was confronted, in the course of the next few years, with industrial unrest, resulting in an unprecedented number of serious strikes. In addition there were the demands of suffragettes; a Home Rule Bill for Ireland, which bid fair to manoeuvre him into an impossible constitutional position; and the outbreak of what was to prove the most savage war that the country had ever fought.

Nor, when the victory was won, was his path strewn with roses – far from it. The Irish problem, to which he made a most valuable contribution, erupted again; there was the first Labour government, the thought of which at first worried him, but whose ministers he treated with scrupulous fairness and soon came to like; a General Strike, which but for the remarkable tolerance of the British race might well have exploded into civil war; and the most serious financial crisis of the century, when his influence in persuading Ramsay Macdonald to form a National government was decisive. He brought to bear on each of these grave problems an unbiased, comprehensive judgement.

King George V was not a clever man, but he had the attributes of courage, common sense, dignity, devotion to duty, and an ability to understand and appreciate the needs of ordinary men and women. His respect for and adherence to the constitution, and his readiness to exercise, in a calm, competent manner, his prerogative 'to advise, encourage and warn' made him a King in the very first rank of history. It was the age of the wireless, and King George's deep, guttural voice speaking to plain men in plain language endeared him to millions, some of whom were able to show him at his Silver Jubilee how greatly he was loved. They looked upon him as the father of his people, who had guided them through their many tribulations.

Quite a different person was his eldest son, who succeeded him as Edward VIII in January 1936, and reigned for only ten months. He had seen his generation savagely mauled in the devastating slaughter of the war, and together with many of the survivors he felt a desire to break away from what these young men and women considered to be the outmoded conventions of a bygone age. His father could never understand him, and the Prince was not particularly concerned that he should. As Prince of Wales, Edward was dazzling and very accessible; he did an excellent job and was extremely popular. But would his ideas of a popular king presiding over a new-style monarchy have ever worked?

There were those – and some of them knew him well – who were convinced that he had the makings of a great King. But others felt – and they had as much, or more, to go on – that he was too mercurial, too impulsive and headstrong, perhaps even too flippant, to have ever settled down upon that immutable rock of probity, which supports the mystique of monarchy. The greatest service that he performed as King was to bow himself out with dignity when he realized that he could only follow the dictates of the heart by flouting the constitution. King Edward VIII might well have found it difficult over the years to reign constitutionally, but his regard for the monarchy was too great to allow it to become endangered in 1936 by a King's party.

When King Edward abdicated, the nation survived a dynastic tragedy through the self-sacrifice, courage and dauntless spirit of a younger brother, who without any training at all put on the mantle of monarchy and wore it with grace and distinction for sixteen turbulent years. The new King was a professional sailor, although his career in the navy had been cut short through delicate health. Not unnaturally he was appalled at the prospect of kingship thrust upon him so suddenly; State papers were unknown to him and public speaking a severe trial, for until the first year of his reign, when treatment immeasurably improved it, he suffered from a stammer. But after the initial shock he accepted his role without flinching, and saw as his first duty the need to re-establish the tarnished prestige of the monarchy. As a start his choice of the name George was inspired, for it created a father-image, and in fact he resembled his popular father in many ways.

The monarchy had by now become the symbol of family fidelity and rectitude, and unlike his predecessor King George was blessed with a wonderful wife, Elizabeth Bowes-Lyon, whose Scottish descent and dignified simplicity had already endeared her to the British people. He also had a young and happy family. His guide line was a determination always to do what he thought to be right, no matter what the cost to himself; he placed his duty to the country above all else.

The early years of European crises were testing enough, but it was in the war that King George's greatest contribution was made. He became a personal and very splendid example to the nation. Through his broadcasts, his constant visits to his troops at home and abroad, and the shared dangers of the blitz, the King – together with his great Prime Minister, Winston Churchill, whom at first he was not anxious to have – inspired the British people with an unshakeable confidence in ultimate victory. Nor was his contribution purely that of a courageous and imperturbable figurehead. In the early days he sent messages of encouragement to the leaders of oppressed nations, and throughout he was ever ready with advice; much of it may not have been taken, but we know that Churchill came to value his judgement.

The last six years of the King's life were less dangerous, but only a little less difficult. By now he was able, certainly in foreign affairs, to meet his ministers on level terms, for those in the post-war Socialist government started with little experience. To what extent it was the King's influence to give Ernest Bevin the Foreign Office instead of Hugh Dalton is uncertain – Attlee said it merely confirmed his own opinion – but it was a most fortunate appointment. In a rapidly changing world, and a difficult transitional period from Empire to Commonwealth, the King was particularly anxious that Britain's influence abroad should not suffer; his advice and encouragement at this time were invaluable, as also were his warnings of the dangers inherent in too much nationalization carried out too quickly.

Never strong, his health had been taxed beyond endurance by arduous years in a job that he had done superbly well. King George VI died in 1952 at the comparatively early age of fifty-six, leaving the throne very secure for a young daughter whom he had been at pains to prepare, in so far as time had allowed, for her stern task.

In the course of the fifteen hundred years, which is approximately the time span between the arrival of the men who worshipped Woden and Thor, and the third generation of the house of Windsor, the English and British monarchy has passed through some well-defined stages. The concluding pages of this book endeavour to summarize them.

The tribes who invaded England in the fifth century were led by chieftains, some of them little more than *primus inter pares*, but as the tribes – and indeed the races – began to merge, these chieftains found their power and their territory increasing. The Britons, whose resistance according to the Anglo-Saxon Chronicle was not properly broken until the third quarter of the sixth century, had kings, and no doubt their conquerors copied the idea of kings and kingdoms, because the Heptarchy had been established before the conquest was completed. Besides turning themselves into kings as their authority increased, these warriors were prepared to recognize a very shadowy overlordship by the strongest of their peers, for whom they coined the word Bretwalda. Bede tells us that the first Bretwalda was a South Saxon in the fifth century, but it was to be a further hundred years before all England could be said to comprise a loose confederation of kingdoms.

These early Saxon kings, who lived by the sword, were absolute rulers within their own kingdoms, but they took the advice (occasionally) of a small council, originally the *Comitatus*, consisting of members of their family and one or two trusted lieutenants. The *Comitatus* was the forebear of the *Witenagemot* (or Witan), which developed into the *Magnum Concilium* (Great Council) of later Norman times, until in the reign of Edward I it had evolved into a Parliament.

There was very little stability in the seven kingdoms, for religion was only skin deep and not a binding factor. If the king was strong he survived and his people prospered, if he was weak he and his people were prey to marauding neighbours and internal strife. Only two English kings – Offa and Athelstan – in the five hundred years between the first Saxon sovereigns and Canute had any influence outside Britain.

The Witan gradually came to play an increasing part in the role of the monarchy. Alfred, whose laws and administration were such an important step forward in the story of government, had his expanding kingdom regulated by a carefully ordained hierarchy. Directly under the king came the athelings (princes of the blood) and below them the ealdormen, who had viceregal powers in their districts, and these men together with the high dignitaries of the Church formed the Witan. When England at last became united, through the efforts of Kings Edward, Edmund, Athelstan and Edgar, the Witan was enlarged to include more bishops, ealdormen and thegns. It was this assembly that among its other functions had the duty of electing the king. Many of the Saxon kings died young, leaving boys not yet in their teens; the Witan would invariably pass these over in favour of a mature member of the ruling family, and this was often the cause of a disputed succession.

As the monarchy became more firmly established as the central authority throughout England, so also did the power of the ealdormen increase in the regions they controlled. Canute established the four great earldoms (the ealdormen had become known as earls by then) of Northumbria, Mercia, East Anglia and Wessex. This delegation of power worked satisfactorily – as did the feudal system that followed – so long as there was a strong king, but with a weak or absentee ruler the system was liable to collapse into anarchy. The advent of the Normans saw two important changes in the pattern of monarchy.

Feudal kingship, with certain modifications, prevailed in England for almost three hundred years. It was really an enlargement of the pyramid of power established by Alfred. The king, who in theory owned all the land, allowed his tenants-in-chief to enjoy rights and privileges over a part of that land in exchange for military service and certain other obligations, and they in turn made similar undertakings with their sub-tenants, and so on down the scale to the serfs. Feudalism, as a form of government, worked quite well for much of the time. It provided an orderly system in which everyone knew his place in the hierarchy, but it had its disadvantages. Even under a strong king there was too much decentralization of authority, and the common people were constantly subjected to the whims of petty tyrants; while with weak kings, such as Stephen, there was civil war, which was just what feudalism was intended to prevent.

The other important step forward – although it was not properly established until the time of the Angevins – was hereditary monarchy. The Witan had offered the Crown to Harold II, and although he had of course won it by conquest, it was the Witan that officially confirmed William I as king. And again it was the Witan (or Great Council), although not unanimous on this occasion, which elected Henry I. But by the time of Henry II, election had given place to the principle that still persists of succession by primogeniture. There are disadvantages to hereditary monarchy, but certainly since the introduction of ministerial responsibility these are eclipsed by the many advantages.

Henry II started, and his great-grandson, Edward I, completed, the abolition of feudal kingship. The lawless strife of Stephen's reign was not lost upon Henry, and he saw clearly the need for justice and security emanating from the centre. Through the destruction of many of the baronial castles, and a very considerable curbing of the powers of his tenants-in-chief, Henry dealt the feudal system a blow from which it never fully recovered. He became in fact an absolute monarch, although he tempered his authority by a very fair administration of law throughout the country. Moreover, this absolutism did not extend to the Church, as Henry found to his cost.

The power of the Church had steadily increased since the Conquest. By the time of Henry II the Church was immensely rich. Its majesty encompassed every detail of man's life on earth and hopes for heaven; it was the centre of all learning and teaching, and had become to a great extent independent of the Crown. This puissance originated chiefly from the claims of the eleventh-century Pope Hildebrand (Gregory VII) for universal supremacy over all Christians. In Saxon times priests and bishops were appointed by the Crown, who thus formed the link between the English Church and Rome, and Lanfranc, William I's great archbishop, although working cautiously for separate ecclesiastical courts, was content to leave the King's powers mainly unchanged. But the Vatican, flushed with victory over the Holy Roman Emperor at Canossa, insisted on having the sole power to consecrate bishops, and Henry I acceded to this demand on condition that homage was first done to the Crown for the stewardship of lands.

In Stephen's reign the Church's drive for complete freedom from secular control continued with some success. Clerical appeal to Rome was established, independent powers for papal legates, and the extension of the jurisdiction of the ecclesiastical courts to cover a wide range of lay matters were all achieved. Henry II set out to curb these powers of virtual self-government, and by the Constitutions of Clarendon succeeded to a great extent in doing so. But the martyrdom of Becket won back for the Church the right to appeal to Rome and the trial of criminous clerks. Thus was absolute monarchy restricted by the power of the Church. In the reigns of Henry II's son, John, and grandson, Henry III, the power of the barons also became an important factor. When absolute monarchy was tempered by the power of the Church and the barons, it marked the beginning of limited monarchy. And these limitations were extended in the reign of Edward I, through his own wise use of a composite Parliament.

The Model Parliament of 1295 was fully representative of those three concerns which amongst them controlled the country's wealth and power: the landed interest, represented by the peers and knights of the shire; the Church, represented by the bishops and mitred abbots; and commerce, represented by members sent from the boroughs. At the head of these three groups was the king, the symbol of national unity and, like his subjects, with duties and obligations that made him a part of the whole. Here then was a fully representative assembly of the three estates, with laws enacted by the king in Parliament, and although a further fifty years were to elapse before two chambers and a permanent Commons became established, this was the beginning of parliamentary monarchy, with Parliament's increasing control of the purse strings. It was also the end, or certainly the beginning of the end, of the feudal system, for besides this centralization of authority, Edward I towards the end of his reign was forced to make concessions in respect of military service abroad, which meant the raising of paid levies.

The wars of Edward I, and his grandson Edward III, have sometimes gained those monarchs the title of warrior-king, and certainly both of them spent much of their time in battle. But warrior-king is a loose term that cannot properly be applied to any single period of the monarchy. Up to the time of the Hanoverians the English Sovereigns were not only in nominal command of the army, but very often led it in person when it came to fighting, and many – Elizabeth I as much as any – deserved the epithet warrior.

For much of the fifteenth century the English monarchy, and therefore England herself, suffered a profound decline. This could always occur when a young, weak or uncertain king became controlled by factions. Sectional interests dominated national interests, and one king was exchanged for another, depending upon which faction triumphed. This monarchy through faction existed from the accession of the young King Richard II until the arrival of the Tudors brought a return to strong, almost absolute monarchy, scarcely troubled by Parliament, and latterly even less by the Church. But Henry VIII when, through his sales of confiscated monastic lands, he created a new aristocracy, sowed the seeds of a trouble that would eventually sweep the Stuarts, with their portentous belief in the God-given power of kings, from the board – for many of these new men were the Puritans and Whigs of the future.

The divine right of kings is a doctrine associated principally with the Stuart Sovereigns. This is largely because James I, in his *Basilikon Doron* and *The Trew Law of Free Monarchies*, brought up his son with the idea that he was an absolute monarch by divine right – 'a little god destined to sit on his throne and rule men'. And this son throughout his reign, and particularly at his trial, was steadfast in that creed. But the doctrine that kings received their title from God, and were accountable only to Him, stretched back far beyond the Stuarts, and had its origins in the need for independence from Rome.

Henry VII, on his succession, had to play it down together with the hereditary element, but when after the trials of the Interregnum the people – always monarchist at heart – recalled their rightful king, he ruled, in his own opinion and that of many others, by divine right. Furthermore Charles II ruled (the last King to do so) at the end of his reign as an absolute monarch without Parliament. But with the Bill of Rights in 1689, the doctrine ceased to have any practical meaning. Nevertheless, modern Sovereigns, while keeping strictly within the bounds of the constitution, still regard the monarchy, through the solemnity of their coronation service, as being 'sacramental, mystic and ordained'.

The Bill of Rights not only sounded the death knell of divine right, but it also shook the principle of hereditary succession – a principle upon which the Tory opposition was based. But the Whigs, having successfully achieved the Great Revolution, were not concerned with hereditary succession; far more important, they thought, was to end absolute monarchy, and to ensure that the Crown could no longer control Parliament. The Bill of Rights and the Act of Settlement of 1701 had these twin principles as their main purpose, and they were the foundation of constitutional – or parliamentary – monarchy. But in one respect the clock was put back almost to medieval days during the thirty years that followed the Revolution. The two-party system was in its infancy as a form of government, but it was at this time sufficiently partisan to create factions, and to ensure that who was king depended on which party was in power – in other words, parties or factions controlled the Crown instead of the other way round.

This unsettling state of affairs was not resolved until some while after the first Jacobite Rebellion, by which time the Hanoverians had become established. George I, rather than William III, was Britain's first constitutional Sovereign, and although the Hanoverian kings were in the main careful to adhere to the terms of the Act of Settlement, and work with Parliament, the Crown retained very considerable power during their reigns. Queen Anne (incidentally, the last Sovereign to exercise the veto) had attended debates in the House of Lords, but language difficulties made this impossible for George I, although he started by attending Cabinet meetings, and his two successors – especially George III – were always anxious lest the power of the Crown should be diminished. The choice of ministers remained one of the prerogatives of the Crown, and in the reign of George III a Prime Minister was expected to work within a framework approved, if not instigated, by the King. Both George III and William IV dismissed ministries, but William IV did at least allow his ministers to make independent decisions, and with Queen Victoria the monarchy became fully constitutional. .

The power of the Crown remained, however, legally undiminished. Queen Victoria could make treaties, cede territory, dismiss ministers, dissolve Parliament, create peers, and declare war, to name just some of the royal prerogatives. Nevertheless, it was in her reign that the Sovereign's power became progressively less. This was largely due to her first Prime Minister, who had given the Queen a good grounding in the Whig principle that the country was governed by the Queen in Parliament, and also to the fact that during the reign Cabinet responsibility developed as an important component of parliamentary monarchy.

The monarchy has never stood in such high favour with the people of Britain – and indeed with people beyond her shores – as it stands today.

This is due to the example of sincerity and self-dedication that has been set from the throne by the present Queen and her immediate forebears. There are those who would like to see a relaxation of court etiquette, a reduced privy purse, and a Queen who is socially more accessible; but such critics are in a small minority. More damaging perhaps in the long term is the excessive glorification of the Sovereign by some sections of the press and most of the people.

Millions will journey miles to spend hours in the rain, and even go nights without sleep, all for a brief glimpse of their Sovereign. Such efforts, often in the face of discomfort and hardship, display admirable loyalty. But the majority of these people would not cross the road to enter their church to worship their God. Has monarchy become a substitute for religion, and have we gone full circle to the days of the priest-king? Have we taken to heart too literally those parts of the ancient and impressive ritual of the coronation service (now witnessed by many millions through the wonders of television) that tend to emphasize the priest-king relationship? Those great anthems, the Sovereign clad in sacerdotal robes, and holding the Bible, being presented to the people and loudly acclaimed by the assembled lords, and the sacramental act of anointing, all proclaim him or her the servant of the Church and the Lord's anointed. Thus it has been for a thousand years – a great service of dedication, consecration and prostration, but not of deification.

The Crown now is much more than a symbol of national unity. It is the sole link that binds the millions of men and women of different races and religions that together form the British Commonwealth of Nations. It gives an invaluable measure of continuity to those who have to govern in the Sovereign's name, and yet being above party politics it is the inspiration and example that can heal divisions among men, and bring them together in a common purpose of mutual service.

Much of the popular enthusiasm for the monarchy may be based on sentiment rather than reason; nevertheless, the people of Britain and the Commonwealth can be grateful for the past and face the future with confidence, so long as they remain constant to that tradition of service and sovereignty that has evolved over many centuries of almost un-broken monarchical heritage.

King Edward VII took his pleasures in the shooting field, on the turf and in the culinary arts of his friends' and his own cooks. For the other arts he had little inclination, and he made no great collections. His two successors presided over a century that was wracked with wars and crises, which brought in their wake change, progression and retrogression at such bewildering speed that people have been left with little time, money or opportunity to do more than strive to safeguard what is left of Britain's rich and beautiful heritage. This has left us with very little that can be seen, which was – or is – directly concerned with the life or work of the Sovereign.

Belton House (Lincs.). The sixth Baron Brownlow of Belton was a close and loyal friend of H.R.H. the Duke of Windsor, and he it was who, at the request of the Duke (then King Edward VIII), accompanied Mrs Simpson to the South of France early in December 1936. The Duke was a frequent visitor to Belton, first as Prince of Wales, and then, a few months before his abdication, as King. There are many interesting exhibits of King Edward's brief reign to be seen in the house: the only known portrait, by Frank O. Salisbury, of Edward as King, which he sat for at Belton; the first pressing of the record of the abdication speech; and gifts from the King to his godson, the present Lord Brownlow. Belton House is about three miles north of Grantham, just to the east of the A607 Grantham to Lincoln road.

Broadlands (Hants.). The Tudor and Jacobean manor-house at Broadlands was 'transformed' in the 1760s into an elegant Palladian mansion by Capability Brown for Henry Temple, 2nd Viscount Palmerston. He also organized the landscaping of the gardens, while the interior decoration of the house was supervised by Robert Adam and Angelica Kauffmann. In the nineteenth century Broadlands was the home of the Prime Minister, 3rd Viscount Palmerston, and in 1939 it was inherited by Lord and Lady Louis Mountbatten. The house has had many royal connections: James I visited Broadlands three times, planting the mulberry trees that still stand in the walled garden; three hundred and fifty years later it became the honeymoon home of the present Queen and Prince Philip. In the rooms open to the public there are displays of mementoes from the years that Lord Mountbatten spent in India, Burma and the Far East.

Broadlands can be reached from the A31 Romsey by-pass.

Caernarvon Castle (Gwynedd). (See also Chapter 5.) In 1911 George V invested his eldest son, later Edward VIII, as Prince of Wales in this castle, and presented him to the people of Wales. This was in the tradition of Edward I, who created his son Prince of Wales when he was sixteen years old – not, as the legend has it, on the occasion of his birth – and who then came to the castle to receive homage. Although subsequently the eldest son of every Sovereign has had the title of Prince of Wales conferred upon him, no investiture took place at Caernarvon Castle until 1911. On that occasion Lloyd George was the Constable of the Castle and responsible for much of the organization for the ceremony. Fifty-eight years later, when Elizabeth II invested her eldest son with the insignia of Prince of Wales in the castle, the Earl of Snowdon was the Constable. On this occasion, after the Prince had paid homage to his mother, the Queen, he read his address to the people of Wales in Welsh.

Chartwell (Kent), was bought by Winston Churchill in 1922, and during the years that George VI's great war-time Prime Minister was in the political wilderness (in the late twenties and thirties) he spent many happy hours embellishing the property, building walls, repairing cottages, etc., with his own hands. Chartwell was to Churchill what Sandringham was to his Sovereign, a pleasant country home in which he could work, relax and entertain. Visitors can now see much of the house as it was in the thirties; the walls are hung with many of Churchill's own paintings, and his study has been left as he last used it. Chartwell is two miles south of Westerham.

Glamis Castle (Tayside Region, Scotland), which has been in the Lyon family for six hundred years, is steeped in Scottish history. It is associated now, in most people's minds, as being the childhood home of Queen Elizabeth, the Queen Mother, and the place where her younger daughter, Princess Margaret, was born. But there is much to see of great historical interest relating to earlier centuries including the sword, watch and tartan coat that belonged to the Old Pretender, who stayed at the castle in 1716.

Glamis Castle, for all its grandeur in the French château style and its great historical importance, is still very much a family home set amid the most lovely grounds; it stands some twelve miles north of Dundee, and is just off the A94 Perth to Stonehaven road.

Sandringham House (Norfolk), was found for Edward VII when he was Prince of Wales in February 1862, just two months after his father's death. His parents wanted him to have a country retreat, where the Prince could relax and enjoy country sports. Since that time, the house has served this very purpose for four Sovereigns; it has been a home and a place of happiness and relaxation. The Prince of Wales pulled down all of the house he bought, save the conservatory, which he preserved as a billiard room, and the present mansion dates from 1870. The principal rooms are light and well proportioned; portraits of the royal family adorn the walls in many of the rooms, but the dining room walls are hung with tapestries given to the Prince of Wales by King Alfonso XII of Spain. In the small drawing-room the seats of the wooden chairs are covered with tapestry embroidered by Queen Mary.

Windsor Castle, Queen Mary's Dolls' House (Berks.). Halfway along the North Terrace, near the main entrance to the State apartments of the castle, is a special room which houses Queen Mary's Dolls' House. This spectacular and quite beautiful dolls' house was given in 1923 to Queen Mary as a token of national appreciation and to help raise funds for charity. It was designed by Sir Edwin Lutyens and is a faithful replica of an early twentieth-century private house. It measures 8 ft 4 inches long and 5 ft 2 inches wide, and was made to a scale of twelve to one. Visitors can walk round it and see the various rooms, the most fascinating of which is probably the library with the beautifully bound books (specially written for the dolls' house by famous literary figures of the day) resting on Italian walnut bookshelves. Other rooms are delightful in showing articles of equipment, implements, and motor cars. In an adjoining room is a display of dolls in national costume from the collection of the present Queen.

Wolferton Station Museum (Norfolk). This was the station used until very recently by the royal family when visiting Sandringham, The bodies of George V and his son, George VI, started their last journey to Westminster Hall and St George's Chapel Windsor from this station. The buildings on the downside (arrival) have been bought privately and turned into a museum. The waiting-rooms and the lavatories have been preserved in their original state, and some pieces of furniture remain from the days when the rooms were used by Edward VII, Queen Alexandra and other members of the royal family. Wolferton is some eight miles north of King's Lynn off the A149 road.

INDEX

INDEX
Numbers in italics refer to entries in the gazetteers